Media Accountability and Freedom
of Publication

Media Accountability and Freedom of Publication

DENIS McQUAIL

OXFORD
UNIVERSITY PRESS

OXFORD
UNIVERSITY PRESS

Great Clarendon Street, Oxford OX2 6DP

Oxford University Press is a department of the University of Oxford.
It furthers the University's objective of excellence in research, scholarship,
and education by publishing worldwide in

Oxford New York

Auckland Bangkok Buenos Aires Cape Town Chennai
Dar es Salaam Delhi Hong Kong Istanbul Karachi Kolkata
Kuala Lumpur Madrid Melbourne Mexico City Mumbai Nairobi
São Paulo Shanghai Taipei Tokyo Toronto

Oxford is a registered trade mark of Oxford University Press
in the UK and in certain other countries

Published in the United States
by Oxford University Press Inc., New York

British Library Cataloguing in Publication Data

Data available

Library of Congress Cataloging in Publication Data

Data available

ISBN 0-19-874251-7

1 3 5 7 9 10 8 6 4 2

Typeset by Kolam Information Services Pvt. Ltd, Pondicherry
Printed in Great Britain on acid-free paper by
Biddles Ltd,
Guildford and King's Lynn

For
JAY BLUMLER

Preface

THE PROJECT UNDERLYING this book has its own history. It began
life as a course of lectures at the University of Amsterdam. It was later
transformed by the opportunity of study at the Shorenstein Center for
Press, Politics, and Policy at Harvard University's J. F. Kennedy School of
Government in 1996, thanks to the initiative of Pippa Norris. Although
the initial report of that work mysteriously lost its way in editorial mills,
I was encouraged by OUP to continue and to expand its scope. An
indispensable stimulus was the award of a residency at the Rockefeller
Foundation Bellagio Study and Conference Center in 2000, which drew
me back to the task and provided an ideal environment for reflection
and planning.

Inevitably a book of this kind has many contributory streams. A
specific forerunner was my own earlier enquiry into the standards by
which the performance of mass media might be objectively assessed
according to criteria of the public good (published as *Media Performance*
(Sage, 1992)). A principal difficulty of the project and one that has
slowed its completion was the ambition of writing a *general* account of
the issues of media accountability to society, with a wide application.
Each medium is distinctive and, despite globalization, mass media institutions (especially the press) are still essentially national in character,
rooted in the culture, traditions, and regulatory arrangements of their
own society. But there are also many shared features which make the
goal of generalization worth pursuing, especially within the range of
media systems that subscribe to western, liberal, or democratic principles (beyond which the book does not attempt to go).

The book was conceived in the Netherlands, whose media system is
characterized by a high and more or less equal degree of professionalism,
public spirit, decency, and diversity. It was finished in another, the UK,
where the media are certainly diverse and lively, but where the other
qualities mentioned are not always to be counted on. The third contextual influence was that of the United States, which produces a rich and
diverse harvest of ideas and evidence about the media and society, but
whose own media system seems, to an outside observer at least, to be
characterized by a one-dimensional version of professionalism, general

ossification, parochialism, and conformity, before even considering its extensive wasteland.

In the light of its real-world context, the enterprise of the book is bound to seem quixotic and impractical. Nevertheless, it is written with the conviction that the media, for all their failings, do make a vital contribution to a more just society and are getting better as well as getting worse. They are not unresponsive to the needs of society, nor do they resist all efforts, from within or without, towards 'improvement'. The ultimate purpose of this enquiry is to lend some support, however small and indirect, to these efforts.

The work could not have been accomplished without the encouragement and help of many people, both direct and indirect. I mention in particular my long-term collaborator and friend, Jay Blumler (to whom I dedicate the book). The purposes and quality of his work and the spirit driving it forward have for long been a source of inspiration. He has consistently advanced the cause of responsible media, as well as our understanding of their working. My motivation, while writing this book, has been sustained by collaboration on other projects with many colleagues (also friends). I have especially in mind my co-editors of the *European Journal of Communication* Els De Bens and Peter Golding; the 'soul brothers' Kaarle Nordenstreng, Cliff Christians, Ted Glasser, and Bob White; colleagues in the *Euromedia Research Group* too numerous to mention; colleagues in the Amsterdam School of Communication Research, especially Jan van Cuilenburg, Kees Brants, Jan Wieten, Holly Semetko, and Klaus Schoenbach; Yassen Zassoursky, Elena Vartanova, and others at the Faculty of Journalism of Moscow University; John Downing; and Karsten Renckstorf.

My work in progress on this book has benefited from the giving of seminars and lectures and the response received. There is always some helpful person behind invitations to contribute in this way. Space forbids naming names but the locations include the Universities of Amsterdam, Georgia (at Athens), Moscow, Oxford, Pennsylvania, Helsinki, Tartu, and Tampere; Doshisha University, Kyoto; and the Portuguese Catholic University, Lisbon. The University of Southampton has provided space and facilities when needed. At the Oxford University Press, Sophie Goldsworthy and Sarah Hyland have greatly encouraged me and Frances Whistler and Pat Lawrence have meticulously looked after the last stages of turning a defective manuscript into a book. I am very grateful to my wife Rosemary for all her unfailing encouragement and patience. To my brother Paul I owe thanks for drawing my attention to Mark Bauerlin's *TLS* essay on the protocols and unwritten rules for performing this 'thanking task'. More significant is the fact that as Secretary of the Royal Commission on the Press in 1975 he played a part in setting me out on this path of enquiry, although he is not, thereby, accountable for the consequences. Last but not least, I name my grandchildren who have helped me stay young enough to finish: Laurence, Alexander, William, Noah, Chaia, and Alice.

Denis McQuail,
Southampton, Hampshire
March 2003

Contents

PART I

The Context

1
Accountability for Publication in the Information Age

The concept 'information age' captures some widely agreed features of our times. In the wealthier parts of the world, at least, these features include large and rapidly growing knowledge industries based on information technology as well as a high level of dependence on information resources of all kinds. There is extensive computerization of all organized activities as well as an exponential growth in the production and flow of texts, images, and data by way of numerous overlapping and cross-cutting communication networks. More and more people are interconnected in this way, giving rise to the notion of a 'network society' (Castells, 1996; van Dijk, 1999).

These informatizing trends have several concomitants and consequences. One of them is the growing size, wealth, concentration, and global reach of private media corporations that control most contemporary mass media. These can now have revenues matching those of small countries and once established within states they exert influence on their own behalf (or that of their friends) and are not easy to control. Secondly, the push for new communication technology is endorsed by most governments and by industrial interests, with media consumption being viewed as an instrument for powering new economic development and encouraging investment. Thirdly, the spirit of free enterprise and the enhanced (or rediscovered) appeal of capitalism and liberalism have undermined or delegitimized earlier controls and regulations applied to the media and to communications more widely. Fourthly, digitization and the convergence of technology have undermined or made obsolete the sectorization of control and regulation of media, whereby different principles of freedom and accountability could be applied to different media (press, television, film, etc.). Finally, the new technology as well as the very scale and extent of global information flow make it more difficult to apply legal and regulatory control for specific purposes.

Not least important in the changing scene is the fact that the mass media have arguably become the main cultural institution and the principal means of public expression in contemporary society. In politics, the media have gradually shifted from the position of observer or messenger to that of mediator or participant, whether or not they choose that role. So important are they regarded as an influence on public opinion (see Iyengar, 1997) that even governments treat them with unwilling respect and adapt to their logic (Meyer, 2002). The media penetrate every corner of public and private life through the ideas, images, and information about events that they purvey. In certain respects the imagined and the real are not sharply distinguished. As a result, the content and significance of many events (and the status of actors in the public domain) have come to require certification by media attention. But it goes further than this. Whatever coherence and unity can be attributed to the perceived or imagined world we inhabit is for most of us largely dependent on the mass media. In brief, communication and information are more and more central to private as well as public life, to work, leisure, education, and consumption, and they intrude into virtually all aspects of experience.

The mass media, old and new, ranging from books to the Internet, are caught up in this informational revolution as a constituent part of the knowledge industry, as an institution that has to adapt to change and as itself an agent of influence in the further diffusion of new information technology innovations. The media are being transformed in their capacity, aims, and means and so too, inevitably, is their role in public life. This is the crux of the matter for present purposes and provides the starting-point and rationale for this book. Its broad aim is to investigate the consequences of the changes described for the ideas, principles, and means according to which the activities of the mass media are linked to the needs, expectations, and aspirations of the rest of society.

The term 'media' can variously identify an industrial sector, a set of technologies, a social institution, a set of firms and organizations with power in society, or an institution often referred to as 'the press'.[1] None of these meanings captures what is central to the theme of this book, although all are relevant. In order to get to the heart of the matter, our attention focuses on the core activity of the media since the earliest days of printing, which is to publish, to mediate between authors and original sources and an eventual audience or public, facilitating or realizing the act of publication. The term 'the media' collectively identifies all organizations, roles, means, and activities that contribute to publication. The latter means to bring expression into the open and to disseminate it further. Media accountability relates both to the purposes and also the consequences of publication. It refers to all ways in which public communication is 'accounted for', by its originators, its recipients, and those affected by it.

ON THE POWER OF MASS MEDIA

The public media of communication in their late twentieth-century forms were still identifiable by their 'mass' character (in forms of production, distribution, typical contents, and patterns of consumption) and reputation for influence in society. This applied to the media's capacity to communicate on their own account as well as to their uses for others, especially advertisers, political advocates, and propagandists. As to their own chosen objectives, most significant was their capacity to: capture and direct public attention; become a trusted source of information about current events; promote certain opinions; popularize certain fashions and lifestyles. As to the clients of media, faith in the power of the media has persisted and even grown unabated. New industries of advertising, public relations, news management, and public opinion research are based on a belief in the absolute necessity, not merely efficacy, of mass media as means of persuasion and control.

A rather simple notion of media power has survived the first century of mass media remarkably intact. Largely unsubstantiated assumptions about media effectiveness still underpin enormous expenditures of money on advertising and other forms of planned communication. It is true that media power is intrinsically hard to pin down or to prove in its effects. It is rarely generated by the media alone but derives from social forces that are channelled and harnessed, but never fully controlled, by the media. There is a self-fulfilling prophecy according to which once the media are defined as powerful everyone concerned treats them accordingly.

Rightly or wrongly, mass media are perceived to occupy a key position in the public life of most societies and have thereby attracted strong but divergent expectations and attitudes. Their influence may be feared or harnessed, but they are also expected to perform some essential tasks of public communication, especially in relation to democratic politics and the rule of law. They even receive incentives and rewards for doing so. They are frequently criticized by cultural élites but also adulated by the people, much as they love themselves. On the one hand there are calls for greater accountability and control because of their power, popularity, and potential for harming or benefiting society. On the other hand, their increased autonomy and importance to power holders takes them further outside the reach of traditional forms of accountability, especially law and the pressure of social and cultural élites. There are claims on the media to account for the use of their great and increasing power, but little clarity or agreement on the norms and rules that should apply or on the means of enforcing them under modern conditions.

THE NORMATIVE DIMENSION OF MEDIA ROLES

A number of pressing normative issues arise from the multiple and sometimes pivotal roles that media have come to play in society and from which they cannot escape even if they wish to. At the core of positive expectations facing the media is their contribution to democratic political processes. They are an essential intermediary (for both parties) between citizens and elected governments. The entire process of democratic election itself depends on several conditions that in turn depend on the media. These include the existence of an informed electorate, a well-formed and stable public opinion, and a readiness on the part of citizens to participate actively. Once elected, governments are supposed to be held continuously and publicly accountable for their actions and omissions. Public expectations concerning the role of the media in political life are shaped by norms of truth and fairness. The media may feel free to disregard such considerations, but cannot do so without consequences for their own functioning.

Somewhat similar remarks apply to the role of media in legal and judicial processes. These depend on there being open and accountable processes for making and hearing diverse claims and for implementing the law. A minimum of public trust is required for justice 'to be seen to be done', without which the law falls into disrepute. In practice again, the public media (and not only by way of 'news') are probably the main means for securing the necessary conditions of public information, trust, and transparency in matters to do with the law. They are accountable to the law and not vice versa, but nevertheless without their scrutiny of judicial process, the risk of injustice would be higher.

The great reach and efficiency of the mass media as a means of public communication have also attracted high expectations concerning their informative role in society. They are expected to provide a constant flow of factual information, analysis, and comment on essential matters. In so doing they serve commerce as well as other social institutions and ordinary citizens. For the latter they are a source of orientation and guidance on mundane matters and a source of warning about impending risks in matters of health, safety, and economics.

These remarks apply in varying degrees, but the general situation of public media in contemporary society is such that the requirements for conduct are nowhere entirely optional. In practice, most media have tacitly accepted a number of tasks in the public life of societies that have become customary obligations, with a normative component. In general, the fulfilment of public tasks is part of, and good for, media business, reflecting again the very mixed character of this institution. Should some media still not care to participate in this mutually beneficial enterprise, there is still little chance of entirely evading the influence of normative expectations. This stems from the power attributed to the media, however limited it may be in reality and however much they disclaim the notion. The media in almost all their forms are at permanent risk of being blamed for individual misfortune or collective malaise and of finding themselves in conflict with public opinion or even the law.

DISCOURSES OF ALARM

Blaming the media has been a popular pursuit since they first appeared in any form, with some constant topics, but also new ones emerging. Recently, the most prominent of such topics have been fourfold: the numerous alleged ethical failings of journalism and especially the popular or tabloid press; the distorting effect of media on politics; the perennial alarm at the harm media can do to children, but given new life by the accessibility of the Internet; and fourthly the numerous other potential harms to individuals and society associated with this new medium.

The alleged decline of journalism is usually exemplified by reference to even greater sensationalism, arrogance, aggressiveness, and a preoccupation with sex, celebrity crime, and scandal, to the neglect of balance, honesty, taste, decency, and reliable information. Egregious practices of the 'new journalism' include deception in gaining information, invasion of privacy and contempt for the dignity and feelings of those that come in their way, plus financial corruption. Failings once confined to the yellow or boulevard press are observed to spread to the once quality media, under intense competition. Professional and ethical standards of journalism seem to have declined rather than risen (see, *inter alia*, Belsey and Chadwick, 1992; Snoddy, 1992; Bogart, 1995; Fallows, 1996; Patterson, 1993).

The second area of concern identifies the media as a primary cause of a serious decline in political interest, knowledge, and active participation in democratic life. The media have been blamed for a lower sense of efficacy about the democratic system and greater cynicism about politicians. Political discourse and campaigning are also said to be in decline under the influence of 'media logic'. While the more pronounced symptoms of malaise have been observed, the incidence is much more widespread. The causes are typically located in the interaction between manipulative political propagandists and media whose values and interests increasingly lead them in search of conflict, bad news, personalization, scandal, sensation, infotainment, and conflict and away from the bread and butter of political information (see, *inter alia*, Entman, 1989; Blumler and Gurevitch, 1995; Blumler and Kavanaugh, 1999; Capella and Jamieson, 1997; Bennett and Entman, 2001; Norris, 2000).

The Internet has become the latest medium to provoke a 'moral panic' at the ease with which explicit sexual content can enter the home and be accessed even by children, as well as much other undesirable content, often without either legal prohibition or effective means of exclusion. To these worries have been added new concerns, not all strictly to do with published communication, but including: the unreliability of sources; the potential for contact with undesirable influences; defamation; fraud and other cybercrime; facilitating crime and terrorism; invasion of privacy; and destruction of copyright. At the heart of the new anxieties is the unregulated, non-institutionalized, unpredictable, and essentially unaccountable character of the medium itself, as well as its attraction and ubiquity.

ON PUBLICATION

As explained above, the media are, primarily and essentially, agents of publication. The key term in the preceding summary view of media obligations is the word 'public'. As a noun this refers primarily to the whole body of citizens or any subset of citizens consciously having some interest, identity, or situation in common. Being a citizen in itself implies having certain rights and duties and shared interests with fellow citizens. The word is also central to several other concepts, including: public opinion; the public sphere (or domain); the public interest; public accountability; public communication. Information can be made public by open expression and dissemination, otherwise it remains private in the personal life or as the confidential property of individuals or organizations. Despite the wide currency and common-sense meaning of many of these concepts, each one can be quite problematic and open to various definitions and interpretations. They are also quite closely interrelated.[2]

The wider range of potential responsibilities just referred to all stem in one way or another from the publication role. The process of publication refers literally to the 'making public' of information (also ideas, opinions, remarks, artistic works) in various ways, including printing, electronic transmission, performance, utterance in a public place, etc. Publication by mass media is, primarily, the act of an agent rather than of the original source or author of some 'message', although both are involved. The act of the author can be considered as expression, production, or creation, as in the act of speaking, writing, taking a photograph, or making a drawing.[3] The essential element of publication is something added to this, namely open dissemination, exposure, or performance. This means not only availability to all, but the clear identification of the speaker, source, or author.[4] Publication is distinguished in various ways from acts of private communication which we all engage in as individuals in private life or in non-public roles (for instance in work or in exclusive groups or associations).[5]

Published communication has no specific or restricted destination and its content after publication is held to be in the public domain, whether it is sold or given away. After publication it has no claim to protection on grounds of confidentiality or privacy. Content that has been published also acquires a special status in that it is presumed, *ceteris paribus*, to be in some sense verified by the act of publication. A certain claim to truth value or authenticity is made and usually accepted. This notion applies in particular to factual information.[6] The presumption is based on the customary understanding that established agencies of publication apply some checks and make an implicit claim of validity. Whether this is justifiable or not, published information is usually treated as reliable and higher in status compared with gossip, rumour, opinion, suspicion, etc. Publication cannot, in general, be revoked retroactively and it typically leaves behind some public record.

An important aspect of publication that also normally distinguishes it from private communication is the fact that it can have unanticipated and uncontrollable consequences for third parties and for recipients, as well as for originators.[7] This gives rise to the issue of responsibility for such consequences on the part of a publisher, especially where some harm is alleged to have been caused. A complicated equation can emerge involving claims about rights to publish, any harm caused, and the effect on public interest. Often the latter can be invoked in mitigation, or justification of the side effects of publication (for instance the need to criticize those with power). The fuller notion of accountability, as will be seen, has aspects that are similar to financial accounting when this kind of cost and benefit have to be weighed up. Such considerations do not arise in private communication, although there are also issues of accountability in the personal sphere (see below).

These features of publication, which, arguably at least, is the core activity of mass media, albeit in many different forms, entail a web of potential obligations and expectations, judgements of right or wrong, benefit or harm that lie at the root of accountability. Publication sets in train innumerable currents and reactions in the wider social context, demonstrable or alleged. These can extend far beyond the original intention and context of media publication and reception by its self-chosen audience.

WHAT IS NOW PROBLEMATIC ABOUT PUBLICATION?

Whether we consider the emerging media situation as problematic as well as new, uncertain, and challenging depends on our choice of perspective. It is possible to take a simple view of media as permanently in need of control, direction, and limitation in order to protect the interests of others, maintain the normative status quo, and advance some version of the public good. This would involve treating media in their organized forms as less entitled to the rights of a citizen to communicate freely and as having more obligations. Such a view rests on a high estimation of the power of media and of the dependence of other institutions on the quality of their performance. It tends also to treat media and communication as independent and isolatable sources of influence on events in the world and on cultural and social change. It leads to efforts to adapt and maintain pre-existing methods of control and regulation to emerging conditions, often focusing on technical or structural causes of new problems and thus on technical solutions (see Price, 1998; Lessig, 1999).

This perspective is challenged most strongly by those who interpret essentially the same trends (of media conduct and social change) as preceding the current 'communications revolution' and as liberating rather than threatening. Viewed like this, it is hard to see what is generally problematic about contemporary media developments, beyond the difficulty of managing rapid and even chaotic change, so as to optimize long-term benefits. However, even this is not such a small matter and many who see no general problem in the reduction of social control over communications do have some concerns about aspects of the increasing communication abundance which range from individual disorientation (addiction or overload) to greater structural inequality nationally and globally. It is clear, in any case, that the identification of problems of information and communication cannot be reduced to a simple clash between libertarians on the one hand and would be guardians of social norms and of the public interest on the other.

Leaving aside for the moment the specific issues of contemporary concern (as exemplified above), several general circumstances contribute to current public anxieties. One is the fact that change is being technologically driven, with innovation guided largely by what is possible with digital communication tools, rather than by any clear notion of what is needed or wanted. In any case, the result is now a plethora of competing technologies, from the mobile phone to the Internet, whose use, value, or benefit is unclear beyond the stimulation of economic activity and the filling of time for individuals. The wider implication is that there are virtually no rules, norms, or guidelines that indicate or express any ethical aspect of their use (see Hamelink, 2000). The spreading area of normlessness in relation to communication inevitably undermines or sidelines the many ideas of what is good or bad in human terms about public communication that have grown up slowly and with difficulty during a century or more of communication freedom and expansion. It is not at all certain that the seeming loss of normative territory, so to speak, will be permanent, but for the moment it is real.

The second circumstance is the yielding of communication development almost entirely to market forces and the withdrawal on a wide front from direct public intervention. Government has largely adopted the role of referee of market forces, with public interest defined largely in terms of well-functioning markets, with a few minimal guarantees of essential universal service and access (see Van Cuilenburg and McQuail, 2003). This means not only a lack of any purpose or vision from bodies that represent the public, but also the subordination of collective interests to what entrepreneurs perceive to have most immediate appeal to most potential consumers. This issue goes beyond the communication sector, but it identifies a specific problem of the new commercialism. This is the possibility that a small number of private (often transnational) corporations can control communication access, content, and infrastructure, with implications for personal freedom and democratic self-determination.

The third general circumstance is the increasing interconnection between previously separate channels and networks of communication. This applies to the physical infrastructures and means of distribution, to the organizational management, and to the types of traffic or content. The clearest example is the Internet as a carrier of mass communication (e.g. advertising, news, and entertainment for all), personal mail, individual expression plus intra- and inter-group communication, and much else. This has several unintended, but hard-to-avoid consequences including reduced privacy and confidentiality, greater uncertainty about the 'status' of any given communication and a general unsettling of virtually all the unwritten rules governing publication. In its most extreme outcome, it could expose everyone connected to a range of new risks and threats as well as to a greater degree of surveillance and actual intrusion by state or private power than has been known until now outside totalitarian societies.

As far as publication is concerned, several changes are under way. One is the increased dominance of publication decisions by financial and marketing considerations, reducing or confining the role of any 'author' and limiting the autonomy of communication professionals. By implication, creative, professional, and social responsibility criteria are subordinated to commercial ones. Another is the remoteness of such ultimate agents of publication from any audience, making a genuine relationship (even an imaginary one) impossible. Thirdly, there is increasing difficulty in identifying just who might be accountable for what aspect of publication.

Fourthly, the Internet itself is in some respects an entirely new channel and means of publication, although with characteristics that are not fully developed or clear. We can say at least that it offers virtually free access (in economic terms and without any gatekeeper or filter) to publication in a wide variety of media and genres and is receivable (in principle) by virtually everyone anywhere, with few attached rules or norms. The reality, as opposed to this potential, may be quite different. The changes under way are not all negative, but much is problematic.

ON COMMUNICATION RELATIONSHIPS AND ACCOUNTABILITY

Underlying the theme of this book is a broad view of communication as a social interaction between human agents, whether individual or collective. Communication is not simply an act of transmission of information or messages even if it can be reduced to this in terms of technology or some behavioural models. Equally, it is not just personal expression or display. It is about the sharing of meaning and the binding together of human societies, communities, and groups in common beliefs, understandings, and identities (see Carey, 1989). Communication in the fullest sense between individuals is interactive and reflexive with expectations of some response and opportunities for continuing exchange. All communication can be considered in principle as social behaviour in the Weberian sense of 'conduct that is intentional, subjectively meaningful and is oriented to the conduct of others' (Weber, 1964, 29).

The social character of communication derives not just from human agency and the social context (both relevant) but in the co-orientation to each other of those involved and in the attribution of meaning by participants to the event, the substance of the exchange, and its wider causes and consequences. The meaning that is conventionally assigned to the content of communication is derived both from the meaning given by the sender and the interpretation of the receiver. From this point of view, communication is always in some sense purposeful, even if it has no specific destination or overt goal.

The most important implication of these ideas for accountability is that communication always involves a real or putative relationship. It is this that has to provide the basis for terms of accountability between the parties involved, including any third parties affected or referred. It follows that in general we are dealing with different and overlapping networks of relationships between various agents, held together and kept alive by flows of communication. Questions of accountability (see below) concern not only the immediate interlocutors, but also others less closely connected. In this conceptualization, the term 'accountability' in its widest meaning encompasses all aspects of co-orientation in communicative relationships, including the claims and perceptions of others, and alternative meanings.

A further implication of adopting this perspective is that the weaker, more attenuated, and less visible the communication relationships are, the less likely it is that effective processes of accountability can operate. In the nature of social organization there are bound to be large variations in these terms. The closest communication relationships are likely to arise within families, close-knit small groups, and friendship circles and accountability is mostly immediate, continuous, instinctive, and relatively effective at least in maintaining appearances and attachments between individuals. In organizations, communication relations and accountability are largely formalized or routinized and have to be managed to achieve work or other goals. Most media-based communication lies at an opposite pole from either of these situations in the loose and voluntary context of free public association. There is little or no personal interaction. Senders and sources are usually remote in every sense from receivers and have no established ties or rules. Receivers are separate from each other, even if close in some ways. Emotional attachments to a source are rare and there are few obligations on either side. It is not even clear who is related to each other and the term 'relationship' itself is of doubtful application.[8]

Nevertheless, even with mass media there is an element of co-orientation and certain lines of connection can be established by behaviour and expectations on both sides. Communicators can address and even listen to an audience, real or imagined. Receivers make meaningful choices in attending to authors, sources, and content and often form vicarious attachments of affection, trust, and loyalties (as fans, admirers, etc.). Accountable relationships in a weak and non-binding form are common, but occasionally they are intense. These remarks apply mainly to 'traditional' mass media such as national press and television, but there are clearly many variants on either side of the modal type. For instance, local media and the party political or religious press usually involve stronger than average mutual ties between media and their own audiences. By contrast, there is a vast amount of individual media consumption that has little pattern, consistency, and no meaningful co-orientation at all.

The increasing hold of large global media corporations over news and entertainment is likely to attenuate further the sense of any relationship, since there is even less social basis for a shared outlook. Producers and distributors of media 'product' do not share any boundaries of community, outlook, identity, or experience with their actual or intended audiences. Contact is maintained by sales figures, ratings, and market research. At the same time, some properties of new media offer a potential antidote to these tendencies. We cannot simply assume that there is actually less accountability in general or that it is harder to achieve. On a wider view, it might be argued that accountability in some form or another is inescapable if communication is to take place at all.

PERSPECTIVES ON ACCOUNTABILITY

Accountability is not another word for control, nor is it the same as responsibility. Dictionary definitions do not take us very far, although they do focus mainly on the idea of being called to answer for (explain) some action (or omission) by someone else who has a right to expect this. This brings the meaning close to that of responsibility that has the same root in the word 'answer' (respond). Many definitions of accountability equate it with 'being answerable'. A somewhat wider view is provided by Giddens (1984). He writes, 'The idea of "accountability" in everyday English gives cogent expression to the intersection of interpretative schemes and norms. To be "accountable" for one's activities is both to explicate the reasons for them and supply normative grounds whereby they may be "justified"'(30). Normative components of interaction always centre upon the relations between the rights and obligations 'expected of the participants in a range of interactive contexts'.[9]

Against this background, we can view accountability as the entire process (within a communication relationship) of making claims based on expectations and appeals to norms, the response of the other party (rejecting claims or explaining actions), and any ensuing procedures for reconciling the two. Accounts offered in response to claims can be accepted or rejected by another participant either on the ground that there is no case to answer or on the ground that the claimant in the given case has no right to call for an account. The potentialities are both numerous and complex, especially when the recognition of obligations and the ability to make claims depends on the relative social power of the different participants.

These ideas are not easily applied to a typical mass media situation, because power is so imbalanced. Media publishers have the means and the power to publish at will, protected by legal rights and with no formal obligations beyond those to their shareholders, within the limits of the law. Other social actors affected by publication will hold varied expectations, but there is generally no shared framework of normative principles that is strong enough to justify claims against the media that go beyond some very basic legal rights. Claims also vary widely in their reference, some concerning individual matters where law may provide support, others refering to broad public issues that are not covered by law or regulation. In the latter case, most accountability claims can usually be rejected or ignored.

Several scenarios present themselves as capturing current trends. One is that accountability is evolving slowly in response to our experience of new modalities of communication, as part of a 'natural' institutionalizing process. In extension of this, it is arguable that a reasonable degree of accountability has been achieved in respect of the 'mature' twentieth-century media of press and broadcasting. In turn, this has now been challenged by 'new media' so as to require adaptation or extension of the relevant mechanisms. A second view is that accountability is just a more acceptable code word for control and that we are witnessing a liberating phase in the continuous struggle between forces of liberation of and through communication on the one hand and repressive or conservative forces on the other. The latter are resisting the supposed destabilizing effects of unaccountable and 'irresponsible' uses of communication. The liberation view largely equates accountability with restrictions on freedom of expression, especially where imposed by government.

Thirdly, there is much support in the literature on media ethics and normative theory for the view that public uses of communication are not just an expression or outcome of individual rights to free expression. Instead, they are a collective good that needs to be advanced, protected, and its benefits extended to all, with equal rights to receive as well as to send. By and large, this perspective involves a critical view of what has been achieved so far in making mass media more answerable to society. The aim should be to make all media more responsive to ethical considerations, human rights, and the needs and aspirations of citizens of a (global) society (see Pourciau, 1999; Hamelink, 2000).

ON THE CURRENT 'CRISIS OF ACCOUNTABILITY'

There have never been more than temporary truces in battles over publication and to speak of a new crisis is misleading. At root, there is a perennial and inescapable tension between freedom to speak out and any form of accountability, however justifiable. From this point of view, despite the distinction from control, all accountability efforts are liable to be perceived as continuations of the war against freedom under new guises. This is not necessarily paradoxical, since we can always be held liable by others for the consequences of many freely undertaken actions which are in themselves quite legitimate. The permanent uncertainty attaching to speech acts turns on issues of motive and demonstrable effect as well as on our view of the scope of freedom of expression.

Another aspect of the case is the existence of public as well as private benefits from free speech. As will be shown, the collective benefit to democratic politics from guarantees of free speech has to be weighed on a scale different from that for personal satisfaction or fulfilment that freedom of expression may provide (or costs that might be incurred). Public benefits may even entail harm to particular people and causes (for instance political opponents, powerful economic interests, or those deemed to be acting against the public interest). It is also important that free publication (uncensored and unlicensed) should not be chilled by threats, regulations, or sanctions after the event. There can never be certainty about what is in the public interest. If there were no bitter complaints and no debate following publication one would conclude that social life was either totally utopian in character, comatose, or dominated by total power.

Despite the continuity of the struggle between freedom and accountability, there are reasons for recognizing a new phase, one in which old precedents no longer serve. The greatest single cause of change is indeed technological, as it was when printing replaced handwritten texts. New media organizations based on new technologies have been able to bypass some of the rules governing more traditional media. Claims for conformity and responsibility to society cannot keep up with the pace of change. It took a long time for an acceptable framework of obligation and social control (formal and informal) to develop around the traditional media of press and broadcasting. Instances of sudden change in the context of operation can also be seen in the formerly Communist countries of east and central Europe, where the old rules and norms collapsed, leaving something of a vacuum. More widely, there are increasing areas of uncertainty about what can be expected or required in the way of media performance.

The capacity to police adequately publication activities on their current scale has fallen behind the pace of change despite the fact that electronic media forms bring new capacities for recording, searching, and identifying communication traffic and content. Some of the current challenges stem from the appearance of hybrid media for which no rules exist. The telecommunication network was originally developed for the telephone and was considered purely as a carrier medium, similar to the mail service. The content of a message was deemed to be private as between sender and receiver. Now the public telephone network carries all kinds of services that are neither essentially private nor akin to private correspondence. The telephone has become another public medium, for instance when used for supplying information, intimate services, or for selling and surveying. Numerous other networks are being developed, using cable for instance, to compete with the telephone system.

The line between private communication and open access has become quite uncertain. The Internet, for instance, has transformed private communication into public conversation. The right of privacy of communication is both called into question and at the same time may be more in need of assertion, against a background of enhanced possibility for tracking and identifying uses of the system. The uses made of old media—books, magazines, etc.—were private and never really knowable to an outsider, except in the most approximate and general way. It is not easy to see how this former degree of privacy can ever be restored or how obligations to respect privacy can be effectively enforced. The electronic media have gained significantly in their power, without yet having to answer for it, partly because there is no one there to answer.

The Net and Web are in much the same phase of development as radio was in the 1920s. There is a good deal of experimentation and very little control, regulation, or direction, except the urge to find ways of making the new media profitable. It is not even fully clear who owns what or is responsible for what and has power to make rules. It is likely that rules will have to be internationally agreed, but for that same reason much will depend on voluntary self-regulation and the pressure of market forces to establish clear ground rules.

IN CONCLUSION

Against this background, the main aim of this book is to examine the nature of accountability for publication in our time and to assess the means by which it may be advanced in the interests of better public communication. It is a basic assumption that the concept of media accountability, while inescapable, is still both problematic and insufficiently worked out. It is also used in a mistaken or too restricted way (for instance as meaning control or greater responsibility). The main aim will be to map out, characterize, compare, and evaluate the main meanings and forms of media accountability, as a contribution towards practical proposals and policies for handling claims and counter-claims about public uses of communication.

It is also an assumption that accountability has value in itself. Accountable communication exists where authors (originators, sources, or gatekeepers) take responsibility for the quality and consequences of the publication, orient themselves to audiences and others affected, and respond to their expectations and those of the wider society. This is not a definition of free communication, but neither is it incompatible with possible definitions of freedom. The potential obstacles to accountable mass media publication are numerous and varied, but not least amongst them are the unlikely bedfellows of commercial entanglement and libertarian dogma.

NOTES

1. 'Media' is a broader term than that of 'the press' which also features in discussion of the matters at hand. The press refers primarily to newspapers and periodicals and journalistic functions of broadcasting (see Lichtenberg, 1990b: 123). In most democracies, the press is identified by traditional and self-chosen tasks in relation to politics and also by attention to public figures and events. The press in this sense is often (loosely) organized as an institution, or treated as such in respect of rights and responsibilities.

2. For instance, in relation to the political role of mass media in particular, the following statements apply.

   i) The *public interest* requires that *public* entities and other organizations active in the *public domain* should be accountable *in public* (openly) to the *public* as a whole and to any relevant special publics or interest groups.

   ii) In turn, this depends on extensive and continuous *publication* of relevant information, ideas, and views in order to ensure the adequacy of the accountability process and to enable public opinion to form, change, and be expressed.

   iii) The mass media are widely regarded as the main instrument for achieving (ii) and as a result they are themselves publicly held to account for the performance of this task.

3. Authors can, of course, publish their own work by personal dissemination, exhibition, posting, or public performance, etc. The media have no monopoly of the act, although they have a very dominant position de facto and they do totally dominate

certain forms of publication, for instance broadcast television and cinema showing.

4. The *OED* gives two relevant definitions of publication. One is 'The action of making publicly known, public notification or announcement, promulgation'. The second is 'The issuing, or offering to the public, of a book, map, engraving, photograph, piece of music or other work of which copies are multiplied by writing, printing or any other process, also the business of producing and issuing copies of such works'.

5. There are grey areas, especially in the terrain of civil society, where discussion and debate take place between citizens and there is no clear separation between private opinion and its contribution to discussion in a larger circle.

6. In respect of fiction, publication does not certify reliability but it does serve to identify a source and make a claim of authorship, as well as guarantee the lack of corruption of the text as an accurate reproduction of some original copy.

7. Katz (1980) emphasizes the norm-enforcing role of publication. Many things may exist in 'common knowledge', without this being 'public knowledge'. Publication changes all this because it forces people to take account of the fact that the others know: 'Prior to publication, an actor may act as if only he knew—because he does not have to acknowledge that the others know as well...In other words the fact of publication of an act of norm violation forces the violator to face up to the demands of the norm upholders or to defy them openly.' These ideas help to explain why, in the eyes of authorities, publication itself may have to be punished as itself a deviant act. Publication that challenges authority cannot be tolerated as even very widespread discontent or nonconformity can. Much action taken against publication from earliest to present times is not even intended to prevent effectively the dissemination of unwanted ideas or expression. It has a symbolic character, a gesture of support for the authority and a demonstration of power.

8. This is close to the classic statement of the meaning of a 'mass' as developed by Blumer (1939).

9. This can be expanded (and translated) as follows:

   • Social life, in formal and informal contexts, is conducted (especially by way of communication) by participants who have their own (different) perceptions and interpretations of their actions and of what is going on.
   • Participants have ideas about their own rights and expectations about the obligations of others.
   • They often appeal to some presumably shared norms, ethics, or standards for support in their claims.
   • Because of different perspectives, such claims may themselves be contested, or the moral basis not accepted.

2

The Rise of the Media as Responsible Actor

TAKING THE HISTORICAL VIEW

It is impossible to establish any typical view of history, leaving aside the sheer amount and diversity of places, events, and circumstances. One can easily misread the past and find apparent precedents and equivalents for present-day concepts and situations, which actually had different meanings in contexts that have largely decayed and cannot be reconstructed. Equally, one can misread the present if one interprets a contemporary concept or practice in terms of past equivalents. Many of the contemporary forms and apparent functions of communication and central ideas in current debates about media freedom, authorship, publication, and influence do show up in times long past, but the line connecting them may be more linguistic than substantive. Nevertheless, even a summary version of the historical development of media publication can provide an angle of vision that helps us to understand the circumstances of our own time and place.

EARLY ORIGINS: BEFORE PRINTING

The notion of being (or being held) accountable for communication has deep historical roots. In the earliest known forms of human society, as reconstructed in a largely speculative way by sociologists and anthropologists, there was no distinct communicative role and no conscious processes of communication. Tribal societies were organic wholes, largely undifferentiated in spirit, stock of knowledge, and beliefs, although differentiated according to status, roles, gender, and age. Communication in the form of rituals and other symbolic forms contributed to solidarity and continuity. When more elaborated societies emerged, especially the ancient civilizations of the Near East, the technology of writing extended the uses of communication, without changing the primary function of communication as that of expressing the core myths of the society and maintaining its solidarity and also the hierarchy of power of its rulers. The work of communication was largely in the hands of a clerical or priestly caste close to the ruling élite. Much more complex forms of social organization required both more and also more diverse forms of communication, but all public communication was connected in some way with authority, whether in the form of inventories of goods, codes of law, taxation lists, myths and stories, or ceremonial procedures. The most important fact about any message was its source or origin. According to Harold Innis (1951), communication at this stage of social development was primarily about maintaining the structure of society over time. The sources of communication were unchallengeable and mediation (by priests or scribes) was largely an extension of the existing power structure. Any request for accounting, if that can be imagined, would simply take one to the source of authority, divine, royal, priestly, or tribal.

In Greek and Roman times, new kinds of public message made their appearance, new messengers and forms of mediation. Society was differentiated into separate spheres of activity (of politics, religion, trade, law, warfare, science, literature, etc.) and each sphere developed its own forms of communication. Private citizens as well as public figures, artists, and thinkers could and did express themselves publicly. The diversity and relative freedom of expression of classical times represents a shift from the unity and immobility of earlier forms of civilization. Institutionalized forms of mediated communication were emerging, with the writing of books in various textual forms and the performance of dramatic works in public.

In the Roman Empire, information of all kinds, private and public, became a vital commodity, flowing through channels of administration and carried by voices and letters of leading or active citizens. Communication served to maintain a far-flung empire in spatial terms by acting as a kind of nervous system of the body politic. Imperial postal services were developed to provide a communication infrastructure of roads, mounts, signal stations, ports, and ships. Public and political events were shaped by public opinion, especially the opinions of the population of Rome. To a very large extent, the development of communication was an urban phenomenon or connecting urban nodes. Innis (1951) characterized this later phase as the maintenance of society in spatial terms.

Most communication from the earliest times took place orally, even where written languages existed. Oratory, performance, and reading aloud, until comparatively recently, were the main forms of publication, more significant than the issuing of printed or other texts. The emphasis was on the fact of contact with an audience rather than the act of speech or writing in itself. A body of oral texts existed that provided a traditional stock of collective memories and ideas expressed in verse or song. The earliest known major examples were the *Odyssey* and *Iliad* of Homer, recounting the events of the Trojan wars, around 1200 BC, but not written down by Homer until about 800 BC.

While there is some doubt about the historical identity of Homer, it is from classical Greece and Rome that we have the first clear evidence of the idea and fact of authorship, in the sense of there being an individual responsible for originating ideas and stories, using language for some communicative purpose. In later classical times, many authored texts existed, their reproduction, storage, and circulation organized on quite a large scale and kept in libraries or personal collections. The composition and size of audiences and how texts were used and disseminated depended on the particular sphere of communication. Scholars and philosophers were more likely to consult written texts, while the wider audience for drama and stories would be either spectators to plays, listeners to speeches, or circles of listeners to works read out.

The development of the roles of author and listener/reader in the classical era also marks the point at which individuals can be held answerable for what they 'publish' or attend to. Accountability does not have to be imagined. It can be required of an author by public authority or by an audience. There is evidence of public conduct, there is a concept of influence on others with good or harmful consequences, and there is the possibility of rewarding or punishing an individual author. There are many examples from classical times, the most famous being that of Socrates who was charged with 'corrupting the youth', tried, and sentenced to death. The fate of Socrates reflects the general attitude to authorship in pre-modern times. It could bring both acclaim and risk in equal measure.

In Greece and Rome public authorities had a right and duty to control, or adjudicate on, all public expression touching on the larger public interest as defined by state or city. In Plato's *Republic*, another key role, that of censor, is explicated for the first time (Jansen, 1988). The primary task of the censor was to make sure that stories for children would not lead to any immorality. In Roman times there was an official post of censor as early as 434 BC, charged with suppressing the publication of whatever might subvert the state or offend the emperor. From ancient times, there have been laws against defamation, especially of figures in public authority (Foerstal, 1998). The underlying idea, then as now, is that publication is potentially dangerous to established order or morality and must be controlled or prevented.

By the end of the Roman Empire in the West in the fifth or sixth centuries A D, most of the key elements of contemporary practice and discourse relating to accountability for public communication were already in evidence. These included: a variety of means of expression (speeches, performances, written texts, music and song, etc.); diverse communication technologies (written languages, auditoria, musical instruments, papyrus, clay tablets, stone carving, etc.); different means of physical transportation of texts. A considerable variety of genres of communication in different media also existed, including plays and stories, poetry, history, scientific treatises, philosophy, types of painting and decoration, even daily news of events. The idea and actuality of public opinion, private and public morality, and ethics—essential elements of law and politics—all existed.

Most current 'communication roles' and occupations were already identified and well understood, including those of author, medium, audience member, scribe, actor or performer, artist, producers of materials for writing, carriers of messages, public criers, etc. Several of the activities were regulated under later Roman law. Certain subsidiary communication roles can also be found, including those of censor, archivist, collector of texts, librarian, reporter of events, and even that of sponsor, someone who commissioned or financially supported the work of authors and performers. Communication was also discussed and understood in terms of ideas of influence, cause, and effect, from both a positive and negative viewpoint. The theory and practice of rhetoric which was taught in schools was concerned with the effective use of communication to persuade others by employing devices of reason and emotional appeal in sophisticated ways. Aristotle's study of drama (in *The Poetics*) was similarly concerned with the devices by which artistic and dramatic works could achieve certain emotional and intellectual responses in an audience.

COMMUNICATION IN THE EARLY MEDIEVAL PERIOD

On the eve of the introduction of printing, in the mid-fifteenth century, the technology of production, reproduction, and transmission of communication had scarcely progressed since Roman times and, in respect of diversity and volume, still lagged behind, because of the dominance of religion in intellectual matters. Ideas concerning authorship, publication, and influence were scarcely more advanced. Public communication had been retribalized after the decay of Roman civilization in the West and it was mainly the influence of the Church that led to its eventual restoration. It was also the Church that preserved the remnants of written culture and the practices of scholarship and authorship, which it adapted to new religious purposes.

It is customary, if somewhat artificial, to distinguish between a monastic period lasting into the twelfth century from a more humanist period from the thirteenth century onwards, but both coexisted. The former is characterized by the concentration of written communication (in manuscript form) in religious hands and for religious purposes (prayer, ritual, promotion of belief and ecclesiastical authority, theology, training of clergy, meeting the practical needs of monasteries and church administration). After this period, there is much more origination of books and written texts in secular hands and for secular purposes. There is also more reproduction and circulation of texts by classical authors. There are new genres of entertainment, poetry, drama, and fiction. There is more writing and copying in the vernacular, as opposed to Latin. There are secular authors and audiences, especially connected to the various courts of kings and princes and in the towns which acquired rights as well as customs of citizenship.

An important key to the humanist 'renaissance' of the post twelfth century was the founding of universities across Europe. While still religious foundations, they taught secular subjects and drew extensively on the works of classical authors in both liberal arts and sciences. The organization of teaching in universities centred on the close study of authoritative texts. Typically a lecturer would give a series of lectures in the form of a commentary and explanation of the primary texts. Although the main medium of teaching was oral, the practice gave rise to a demand for copies of texts, both the original and the commentary.

This demand was met in major university centres such as Oxford, Paris, and Bologna by a well-organized trade in book production and selling, supervised by the university authorities. This involved extensive copying, illustration, and binding of manuscript books at controlled prices (see Febvre and Martin, 1984). This development meant that monasteries were no longer the only producers of books and the way was opened for book production and distribution to be a normal trade and business, increasingly outside the aegis of the Church. It led to the growth of a much extended market for a wider range of publications, recreational and practical as well as scholarly and devotional, with purchasers and collectors of books amongst the bourgeoisie and aristocracy. It also opened the way to a new market for popular works, despite limited literacy.

Important in the period is the development of the idea of 'publication' in itself. Until the new age, the universe of written texts in medieval societies, aside from legal documents, accounts, inventories, etc., and the most important texts of all, the Scriptures, consisted largely of works by established authorities, either classical (such as Aristotle, Plato, Virgil, Quintilian, etc.) for purposes of scholarship, science, and philosophy or written by Fathers of the Church (Jerome amongst others), along with devotional works, orders of service, music, etc. Virtually all was written in Hebrew, Greek, or Latin. While additions were made to the corpus of written texts they were not generally original or entirely new publications and the role of author was missing or uncertain[1]. There was much oral communication in many languages, songs and stories, but little in the early period that had an identifiable author, unless a prince or prominent figure acquired the attribution. The sources were usually traditional and communal.

By contrast, in the later medieval period, scholars, poets, and translators sought consciously to bring new works into the public domain and to claim authorship. The medieval idea of authorship, according to Minnis (1984), developed originally out of the idea of authority, the ultimate authority (as with the Scriptures) being the Divinity. Much thought about authorship originated in debate about the human role of the Evangelists as authors of the Gospels. Human authors, more mundanely, were still credited with a certain authority as well as carrying out the role of a writer. The Latin word *auctor* retained several connotations in addition to having some claim to being authoritative. One was that of originator or first cause. Others included the idea of truth or veracity, of authenticity and sagacity.

For a work to be authentic it had to be clearly established as the genuine work of a named and known author. During this humanist medieval period in Europe it seems that the idea of authorship emerged as an attribute of individuals and it gradually became customary for published written texts to carry the name of the author, along with a title and other means of identification and classification. This had practical significance for potential responsibility for the origin and effects of written texts. It both enlarges the potential rights of authors and potential obligations or consequences.

As briefly described, the emerging practices of authorship and publication seem largely to have been driven by circumstances and context, especially the needs of the educational and scholarly institutions, plus the emerging professions (of trade, administration, law, medicine) for which an education was being sought. Without any direct evidence of the motive of the increasing number of authors in the medieval world (aside from religious authors and the increasing number of religious dissidents) it is unclear to what extent authorship was a personal vocation or ambition, inspired by the impulse to express, influence, or acquire fame. Authorship as a conscious practice is embedded somewhere in the sequence of very pragmatic activities of production and distribution for use, although it is not easy to disentangle its meaning. The role of author was growing in the late scribal period and was not noticeably accelerated by printing. Even as late as the mid-sixteenth century the professional writer was still largely unknown (Hellinga and Tribe, 1998). In this period, it does not seem that authors could claim any rights or financial rewards for their work, although their copied work was sold and they might be paid by the producer.

From the late medieval and through a large part of the print era, the main way to make money from authorship was by way of patronage or following some other occupation. No personal contracts were made. New works were dedicated to, and presented to, prominent figures and a payment or reward was expected. This presentation was sometimes the effective publication, although in the later period printers would hope to recoup their costs by selling copies as well as by payment from authors. The reliance on patronage inevitably increased the likelihood of conformity of published work to reigning ideas and subservience to secular and religious authority.

In this period, freedom of publication was not an explicit issue. There was no notion of a right to freedom of expression, but nor was it generally threatened. Eisenstein (1978: 317) points out that printing was largely welcomed by the fifteenth-century church as a means of aiding the spread of the word of God. Censorship of printing was not imposed in the Holy Roman Empire until 1521 and somewhat later in England. The copying and issuing of manuscript texts was not controlled although little value or credence would have been attached to a text that was not in some way accredited. Some particular publications and authors (such as Wycliff in England) were identified as heretical or seditious by secular or church authorities, but authority was not challenged on any scale in the medieval period by publication and the coming of printing made no immediate change in this state of affairs. Nevertheless, the scale of publication, albeit in rudimentary forms, was growing and the circulation of written texts was quite extensive by the mid-fifteenth century, well in advance of the upheavals of the Reformation and the changing geo-politics of the Western world.

THE COMING OF THE BOOK

The heading above is taken from the seminal study by Febvre and Martin (1958/1984) of the effects of printing in Europe, especially France and the Holy Roman Empire. It preceded the better known work of McLuhan (1962) and Eisenstein (1978) both of which treated printing as having revolutionary consequences for the medieval world and subsequently for our whole way of understanding modernity. However deep and sweeping the changes in society that accompanied the increased application of printing and the spread of books and book culture, the immediate effects during the first generation or two do not appear to have been as remarkable as does the innovation itself, even to modern eyes.

Looking backwards in time, the gap between handwritten manuscripts and modern mass-produced and standardized texts seems almost unbridgeable. This is partly because it is not usually appreciated how little changed directly after the first printing in the 1440s. The workshops that produced manuscript books adopted a quite simple, but remarkably productive technology of moveable type and imprinting of paper that greatly increased speed of output and probably reduced costs. The craft and trade of the book incorporated the innovation, rapidly in the new centres of production in Germany and France, but not much else changed.

The demand for books and the sources of that demand did not change at once. Manuscript production did not cease. The appearance of printed books was modelled closely on that of manuscript. Books still had to be transported and sold by the same forms of organization. It took time for the larger clients of book production, especially ecclesiastical bodies, to appreciate the benefits of scale involved. There was no sudden change in the type of book to be produced, although the diversity of topics gradually increased and there was relatively more production in vernacular languages, especially German, French, Italian, Dutch, and English. Historical accounts of the impact of printing tend to emphasize the extent to which the whole book trade was organized on very commercial lines, often needing quite a lot of capital and having small-scale monopoly tendencies, responding to new opportunities in a very entrepreneurial way.

The developments of range and scale of print publication during the second half of the fifteenth century are in some ways remarkable, but they do not constitute a social or cultural revolution. They were not at first regarded as particularly challenging by civil authorities and they did not lead to a large-scale suppression of authorial talent. Church authorities, however, continued their policy of banning heretical and other forbidden works. The machinery of censorship gradually increased in severity and effectiveness until the eve of the Reformation, eighty years after the invention of printing. Most of what was printed was either existing manuscript writings or translations from Latin or foreign works. But the scale was impressive. Before 1500, Febvre and Martin estimate that 10,000 to 15,000 different texts had been printed. The printing success stories were mainly the result of printing editions of the Bible or other large orders of devotional books. Although historical scholarship seems to agree on the gradualness of change, there is no mistaking the implication of the sheer volume of new production. Eisenstein (1978: 45–6) quotes an estimate that more books were printed in the second half of the fifteenth century than had been produced by all the scribes of Europe since AD 330.

Gradually, printing in Europe found and stimulated other sources of profitable activity and many new specialized markets. The big successes were first in the area of popular imaginative literature, with stories of chivalry and existing popular sagas, such as the story of Troy, and secondly in the publication of the works of the Reformers, especially of Martin Luther on the continent. His translation of the Bible in German was published in 1522 and, according to Febvre and Martin, probably sold over a million copies in the first half of the sixteenth century and even more in the second half. The same authors tell us that in France and the Holy Roman Empire, the Reformation and its associated religious and polemical publications were so profitable to the printing and book trade that even apparently draconian legislation to regulate publication had little effect. The popular demand for the works of the Reformers in vernacular language was even more important than the general sympathy of the printing profession (for whatever reason) towards the new ideas.

In France and Germany, during the most stormy periods of the popular movements towards religious reform, the mid- to late sixteenth century, the book printing, selling, and importing trade kept up with demand for heretical and subversive literature, despite prohibitions and risks. The laws were largely ineffective, and the extreme punishment of execution was not applied to the leading figures in the trade (Febvre and Martin, 1984: 307) but to minor printers and tradespeople. Although authors were more likely to be punished than publishers, much of the banned literature was of foreign origin. In England during the same period, the control of printing was more centralized and effective, the direction depending on the shifting religious allegiance of the crown between Henry VIII and Elizabeth. Primary control of printing and distribution came increasingly to fall into the hands of the Stationers' Company, a trade cartel, incorporated in 1557, which regulated virtually all aspects of book printing, publishing, and selling (Johns, 1998).

During the long era of political struggle between royal establishment and Puritan dissidence that ended in the 1662 Restoration and a new order, book publishing in England was largely controlled by the authorities with the co-operation of the Stationers' Company, although an enormous amount of unregulated and fleeting publication of pamphlets, posters, and letters fed the battle of words and ideas. According to Johns (1998), the regulation of publishing was regarded as a positive benefit not only by the trade, but even by many categories of book user (e.g. scholars, lawyers, scientists) and of authors, because it provided accreditation and reliability.

Despite vicissitudes and many variations in the degree of freedom, the printing and publishing of books continually expanded and diversified during the seventeenth and eighteenth centuries in Europe and the New World, as demand and readership increased. Authorship developed into a more recognized profession, although with limited rewards and legal protection (although copyright was gradually established during the eighteenth century) and still very much beholden to influential sponsors and political or institutional support. The language of print material soon shifted from Latin to the vernacular and content became increasingly secular. The technology of printing improved in quality but the scale of production did not change very much between the sixteenth century and the eighteenth and even in the late fifteenth century print runs of several hundred had been common. A similar comment seems in order about the organization of the whole book business. The model of copying, binding, and selling in small workshops surrounding the medieval universities seems only to have been enlarged in scale and acquired more financial and political importance. The capacity of authorities to censor and ban print material certainly increased but was also increasingly contested or regarded as irksome by all involved in the book trade.

CONCEPTUAL DEVELOPMENTS LINKED TO PRINT

The coming of printing had several consequences for the notion of accountability, although change was not rapid, sudden, or directly attributable to print technology. Firstly the role of author was more clearly defined and recognized. As Kaufer and Carley note (1994: 136), before print, 'the role of the individual author did not become visible unless a text was found to be a transgression of church or government interest'. The identification of authors was prompted by a mixture of factors, including the legal efforts to make them and their publishers accountable. Aside from esteem in the emerging literary circles and aspirations to artistic or scientific achievement and recognition, there were increasing material and financial rewards potentially available to authors. Secondly, there was a recognition of a growing reading and buying public, as well as many specialized markets (audiences) for books.

Thirdly, although not new in itself, much more attention was paid to the text itself, with regard to its authenticity, reliability, and authority. According to Johns (1998) standardized printing did not eliminate problems of variation of manuscripts, but introduced new sources of error and uncertainty and increased problems of 'piracy' and plagiarism (although these notions are essentially linked to print). The status gradually acquired by the printed text was itself relatively new, aside from the works thought to be directly inspired by God (Scriptures and some holy writings). In earlier times, the written word was valued less than the spoken, regarded, according to Kaufer and Carley (1994: 169) as 'frozen speech'. It was not accessible to most people (lack of literacy) and lacked the presence and interaction of oral communication. Written texts were also lacking in evidence of their authenticity and authorship, except to scholars who studied them. In any case, new concepts of communication entered into experience with the rise of books and reading. New mediated relationships with authors were developed.

Gradually the text acquired something like its modern status as a fixed and reliable intervention in social discourse. It came to stand for, and even replace, the person of its author and to be regarded as a more reliable witness of intention than that which the author might subsequently claim or acknowledge. Eisenstein (1978: 113) comments on the role of print publication as tending to fix meaning and make it permanent. At the very least printed documents have a much greater chance of circulation and survival than handwritten ones.[2] The text also acquired an attributed power and influence as an independent agent, capable of good or harm. On these various counts it became even an object of surveillance and control by its various recipients or those affected by it. More recent theories, especially in the postmodernist vein, have undermined the validity and appropriateness of this view of the text (Kaufer and Carley, 1994), but it is still predominant in popular opinion and in the attitudes of regulators of communication.

Although the causes are much more fundamental than printing and publishing alone, there is no doubt that the rise of the book was closely connected with the gradual development of a much enlarged public sphere or domain in which opinions and ideas were aired, formulated, transmitted, and contested. The role of publication in the various manifestations of a new kind of public life of ideas, originating in the Reformation and humanist revolutions of the sixteenth century, was recognized by contemporaries as central and has been a defining feature of the very idea of the press ever since (see below). Perhaps the largest conceptual development of this age of the book was the new questioning of the legitimacy of the governmental control of ideas, for instance by John Milton in his *Aereopagitica* (1643) (see Chapter 8). The expression and dissemination by print of strongly held personal belief gradually became central to the idea of book publishing, although it coexisted with the older idea that pernicious, false, blasphemous, and harmful publication could justifiably be forbidden and punished.

THE NEWSPAPER

The essential idea of news must be as old as organized social life and even language itself. As a text genre news is datable to Roman times (the *Acta Diurna*) although the concept was largely reinvented and given new meanings in the modern era, exemplified in the newspaper and later in broadcast news. The origins of the modern newspaper are usually attributed to the newsletters that circulated in the latter sixteenth century, especially the Venetian *corantos* or accounts of current events. These mainly disseminated factual information about recent political and military events that were of relevance to trade and commerce. However, throughout the sixteenth century there is plenty of evidence of the circulation of accounts in a more or less public way by a variety of channels, primarily by word of mouth but also in printed and handwritten letters, newsbooks, and pamphlets, serving a variety of interests and meeting various needs.

Some of the material produced was intended as propaganda for official purposes, especially to rally support in conflicts with foreign powers. The embryonic printed newspaper produced in early seventeenth-century Amsterdam was characterized by its regular appearance, attention to current happenings, varied or miscellaneous contents and by having public, commercial, functions. Similar developments occurred elsewhere, especially in England and Germany (see e.g. Schroeder, 2001). Even so, the connection between news and printing is not absolute and, according to Atherton (1999: 40), for much of the seventeenth century in England, the handwritten newsletter was a more important form of written news, being regarded as more authoritative, up-to-date, accurate, and less censored. It was also more plentiful, since a regular printed newspaper did not appear in England until the end of the century.

Baran (2001: 4) concludes that print and manuscript news were about equally viable in seventeenth-century England and that 'there is no evidence that print carried more influence on the formation of public opinion than did manuscript'. Manuscript was less easy to control but it was also liable to punishment for offending the state. Although newsletters were generally written to one person of some higher rank, their contents were often widely circulated by word of mouth and read in public places throughout the country.

The various printed forms of news in the early period were often censored in the same way as books (although not in the Dutch Republic) and had various kinds of official sponsorship. On the Continent, this included support from municipal authorities. Towards the end of the seventeenth century almost every larger German city had its own newspaper, many issued more than once a week. Such newspapers furnished intelligence to political authorities as well as some potential for official influence. These newspapers were subject to routine censorship and they had no political agenda of their own (Schroeder, 2001: 147).

In England, it was forbidden to print domestic news during the first half of the seventeenth century, including accounts of debates in parliament (Levy, 1999). This in itself contributed to the popularity of manuscript news and reminds us of one of the limitations of print, in lending itself to more easily official control than does self-publication. This applies just as much in seventeenth-century England as under the Soviet censorship regime that encouraged *samizdat* publication. The general reputation of early printed news was not very high to judge from contemporary literary references, although it rated higher than mere 'rumour'.[3] The publication of print news tended to reflect the flow of foreign events or domestic crises and was neither regular nor in general a way of making money (although there are exceptions, including the printing of news in Amsterdam in English for export to London in the 1620s and the commercial newsletter that preceded the publication of an official Gazette in the 1660s).

Although there is plenty of evidence of great suspicion on the part of Church and state authorities towards the free circulation of news and of numerous forms and instances of repression, it is not certain that it ever served any generally subversive ends or had harmful effects for the state. According to Atherton (1999), much news was produced within a 'discourse of patronage', with credibility attaching to rank. Most news in the seventeenth century circulated amongst people of higher rank or income and was not intended for the masses.[4] Much had a patriotic or supportive slant and concerned domestically non-controversial foreign events and the only dangers from an official point of view lay in its being out of control especially where independently popular causes were expressed or fomented. Only later, especially during the eighteenth century in Britain and later on the continent, did the newspaper press acquire its overt partisan and polemic role.

Reviewing the newspaper as an important alternative print form to the book, certain key features can be underlined. First, a common idea of printed newspaper eventually emerges as a regularly appearing, non-governmental, source of current information intended for the general (reading) public and having several possible identities and aims, ranging from propaganda for state or party to more or less neutral facts of potential interest. This leads eventually to the idea of a publisher as an active agent in the selection and communication process as distinct from the notion of a combined printer and agent for authors that typified book publishing from the earliest (even pre-print) times. The publisher-editorial role of the newspaper adds a new kind of autonomous and therefore accountable actor to the existing trio of author, state, and public. Such a role was adopted in the nineteenth century by the radical, partisan, and, later, revolutionary press and more timidly by the liberal bourgeois press in many countries. The modern idea of a newspaper carries with it the connotation, often nurtured by the press itself, of being an active and significant participant in society. However, this is not necessarily inconsistent with the role of being an objective carrier of information. The titles of many early (and still current) newspapers express a variety of public roles.[5]

Secondly, there is a link between the relatively free or uncensored newspaper that appeared in some cities and countries and the emergence of a 'public sphere' as posited by Habermas (1962/1989). Whatever the strength of this particular version of the public sphere concept and its historical accuracy, there is no doubt that in the latter seventeenth and early eighteenth centuries something that is usefully described in this way did manifest itself.[6] In more free urban centres (such as London, Hamburg, and Amsterdam), wherever business or politics or law was practised, there were places where news was circulated, newsletters published, opinions on public matters aired and debated. This was even more widely true in later nineteenth-century Europe, where journalism played a vital role in reformist and national liberation movements. It is not absurd to consider a certain model of the (more recent) newspaper as itself a kind of public space or arena, where varied ideas and information are made public, compared, and debated.

The newspaper also came in the eighteenth century to be identified by authority as a more immediate, and therefore potentially greater, threat than the book and less easy to control by existing forms of pre-publication censorship, although vulnerable to other pressures the more it became institutionalized. The danger came from the immediacy and actuality of the news and opinion, its rapid diffusion at times of unrest, its orientation to, and availability to, a much larger public. Notable about the newspaper, compared to the book, is that it is not the work of an author, but an organization or institution, with diffused and uncertain responsibility for what is published, even if the matter can be formally dealt with in law.

In respect of reputation, authority, and credibility the newspaper from its early days lagged behind the book. Although efforts were made during the nineteenth century by way of an élite press to escape this lower esteem, the medium has not fully escaped the taint of sensationalism and untrustworthiness. In its subsequent manifestation in the twentieth century as a truly mass medium, the reputation of the press continued to be uneven although its reputed power to influence was much inflated. It has survived more or less unscathed into the twenty-first century still with a very ambivalent standing, no doubt reflecting its mixed record of nobility, villainy, and mediocrity.

A further innovation gradually cemented into place in the period under discussion was the emergence of civil law dealing with complaints against printers and publishers on grounds of defamation and thus a new line of accountability between publication and other citizens. The systems of licensing and censorship of printing of the sixteenth and seventeenth centuries were primarily directed at offences against Church and state, but they could also cover claims of defamation by individuals. However, there were large possibilities and an extensive practice of using printed materials to attack the reputation of others, though generally for some public cause. A category of print matter (in poster and leaflet form) in late sixteenth-century England was known as 'libells' (Atherton, 1999). In the eighteenth century it was common for newsletters and newspapers to engage in attacks on persons that would now be considered actionably defamatory. As the legitimacy of state control of the newspaper declined, so the recourse to civil law increased and the responsibilities of publishers (the newspaper being the most relevant actor) to other members of society were specified. These developments are reflected in the clauses inserted in constitutional protections of freedom of the press and the various declarations of the Rights of Man that recognized limitations on the freedom to publish.

MODERN MASS MEDIA

The story as told above takes us into the nineteenth century, since which time one might estimate that 90 per cent of the story of the mass media has occurred. Nevertheless, it will not be continued here, except to summarize the main implications for this book of the last hundred years or so of change. Most of the changes are familiar enough and can be expressed in a few key words, especially massification, diversification, industrialization, commercialization, institutionalization, and globalization. These refer to changes that have occurred more or less in that order. The extension of print media to an ever increasing and more literate audience during the nineteenth century was the result of technology and other social changes. Before then, the public media, with the exception of the Bible and some religious works, could not be regarded as truly intended for the 'general public' in a majoritarian sense.

Since 1900, communication has entered a phase of mass production and distribution far outpacing earlier forms, bringing with it complex organization, bureaucracy, and much employment and profit. Previous public communication had always been financially vulnerable and sensitive to audience demand, authorial supply, and political control or pressure. The conditions created by the mass press and subsequent innovations turned public communication into a very profitable business, with accompanying economic motivations, market discipline, and typical effects of concentration and increased scale, leading also to the globalization of many media commodities, especially news, films, and music.

The reference to the institutionalization of media underlines the fact that media have (mainly since the liberal and democratic revolutions of the nineteenth century) become recognized as social institutions that play an essential part in social economic and cultural life and in consequence are variously respected, feared, controlled, valued, and criticized. In unwritten return for social recognition and even protection, the mass media have become more conformist than critical. To some degree, this can also be viewed as a consequence of, if not a price paid for, the presumed fact of their widely greater power. It also reflects the constraints imposed by the market-place, in circumstances where conformity (in the widest sense) is usually more profitable or less financially risky.

The media have not completely shaken off their more raffish parentage, but in their mainstream variants they have by and large sought and acquired respectability and have become responsible as they have become professional. The radical, subversive, and scurrilous manifestations of earlier print media have not disappeared but they have either become institutionalized as tolerated variant forms (e.g. as sensational tabloids, pornography, propaganda, satire, political extremism, avant-gardism) in the spectrum of what is now a diversified media market; if not this, they have been marginalized, excluded, and pursued by authority, with varying degrees of legitimacy or public approval. Institutionalization has not meant total incorporation of public communication into the power complex, but the 'mainstream' media do show a tendency nearly everywhere to be respectful, if not supportive, of establishment or official positions and of the 'national interest' as so defined.

UPDATING KEY CONCEPTS

AUTHORSHIP

The effect of the rise of the mass media on the notion of authorship has been paradoxical. On the one hand, it has emerged more clearly as an individual role with clearly defined property rights and also personal legal obligations. In the book market, celebrity authors are generally the key to marketing strategies and publicity is personalized. On the other hand, the notion of author has also been diluted or even obscured in much media production. New kinds of author have emerged in audio-visual and musical communication (directors, producers, arrangers, photographers, and many other roles) and many such works are collective efforts of teams and production houses. The role of performers and stars (or media personalities) has also tended to overshadow the work of authors in many newer media forms, with a quite uncertain degree of responsibility for success, failure, or consequences.

It is harder to identify the first or efficient cause in the classic sense first outlined by Aristotle.[7] Aside from the decay of authorship in the sense described, important elements of media output are not apparently authored at all (e.g. much news and all advertising) and responsibility is usually attributed collectively to the media transmitting organization or firm. In respect of accountability, this shifts the focus away from individual authors towards generalized content (for instance, systematic bias) and media structure (for instance conditions of concentration, leading to uniformity).

PUBLICATION

The nature of publication has also changed along with the changes just mentioned, leaving aside the material facts of the great speed and scale of publication of the truly mass media. There is still a specific moment when the work of authors and the production organization becomes public by being offered for sale or openly transmitted, displayed, or performed, often preceded and followed by organized publicity. But the publisher role, that was obscured in the early print model of a chain of events from writing to distribution of copies of the work, is now more clearly identifiable as a kind of organizational gatekeeper deciding what is to enter into the chain of production and exit as distributed content at the other end.[8] At the same time, such publication decisions are fragmented and diverse. They can appear as the work of editors in chief or of owners or top managers of media firms. They can be in the hands of managers of distribution (rather than production) media, more often than not involving the *re*publication (or reissue) of works already in the public domain. In general, in line with changes in the concept of authorship noted above, publication in mass media is much less likely than in its archetypal manifestation to be an autonomous decision made by an author.

The latest mass medium—the Internet—has introduced new sources of uncertainty. On the one hand it does allow individual authorship and publication, almost at will, but with uncertain reach and effectiveness. On the other hand it has clouded the role of 'gatekeepers' such as Internet service providers and search engines, which have a interest in controlling the flow of content, but meet a potential danger when they are treated as publishers and held responsible for the content they disseminate. It suits them better for many purposes to be treated only as carriers. These uncertainties reflect the multiple functions of the Internet as a medium (for discussion of these points see Chapters 5, 14, and 15).

RESPONSIBILITY AND ACCOUNTABILITY

Only a few remarks arising from the historical view need be made at this point. It follows from what has been said about authorship and publication that a personal sense of responsibility for a work has both become harder to realize by possible authors and more difficult to perceive and pin down from outside. In general, a problem arises of identifying the location of any responsibility for accountability purposes, even if the law can always offer working solutions where it applies. Secondly, the line of potential responsibility towards an audience or society as perceived by an author (or even editor) has been obscured. The work of authors for mass media is usually completed in advance and independently of its transmission and reception. The response of, and influence on, audiences are even more remote. It is either difficult or not even necessary for a typical author, even when personally identified as the originator, to address a chosen and knowable audience, except in the most abstract terms. If a personal authorial sense of responsibility is present it is mediated and distanced through the organization of media production and distribution that imposes its own notions and criteria of responsibility, mostly having to do with success in the market and with avoiding troublesome side effects.

The modern forms of mass media organization also bring with them new consequences for answering the question 'responsibility *to whom*'? In media prehistory, this question did not have to be faced with any consistency or urgency (leaving aside the issue of forbidden content). Authors themselves decided the answer for the most part, although often with an eye to their chosen patron or personal reference group and significant others who might be pleased or offended. Early printers (as now) did not seem to have been much preoccupied with such a question, unless themselves allied to a political or religious cause. However, early printers did often have obligations to those who had invested in a particular publishing enterprise and looked to their potential sales. In contemporary media, the notion of the object of responsibility is usually well understood and overt, but limited to practical requirements. Media producers mainly see it in terms of audiences, often expressed as various consumer markets, shareholders, and clients such as advertisers. Beyond that it extends to certain institutionalized social or legal obligations (thus to society).

IN CONCLUSION

The idea of accountability for publication, in the sense of answerability, developed a good deal during the time span covered by this rapid survey. Change has mainly been in the form of a multiplication of meanings and situations where it might be offered, requested, or required. In crude terms, it seems to begin as an obligation owed to religious authority and to integrity in terms of scholarship and the stock of inherited (textual) wisdom. The personal vision and conscience of individuals extended this sense to encompass a wider notion of truth to which an author is committed, in art and science as well as in religion and philosophy. The involvement of printing with political and religious struggles from the sixteenth to the eighteenth century foregrounded accountability as being owed to state or Church, with extreme penalties as an ultimate sanction and a permanent state of control or harassment.

Coterminous with these conditions there was a growing trade in print matter of all kinds which introduced ideas of accountability to the reading public as well as to patrons and investors. Increasing freedom of publication removed the most severe threats from authority but were accompanied by new ideas of responsibility to 'society' and accountability for (harmful) effects. The age of modern mass media has transformed all these elements into new guises and added a new set of potential claimants on media, requesting or requiring accountability. These include governments acting on behalf of the public interest, political parties and movements, advertisers, lobbyists, and now 'spin doctors' and news managers.

NOTES

1. Eisenstein (1978: 121) quotes a passage from the writings of the 13th-cent. Franciscan St Bonaventure describing four ways of making (i.e. writing) books. One is to copy the work of another exactly (the work of a *scriptor*, or scribe). A second is to write the work of another author, plus additions from other works (the work of a *compilator*). The third is to write the work of others together with some own work in explanation (the work of a *commentator*). Lastly the writing of some original work, plus additions from other authors (this is described as the work of an *auctor*). No mention is made of a purely original piece of writing. Some of the uncertainty about authorship can be ascribed to disputes about the true 'authorship' of the Scriptures and other sacred texts.

2. As an example of the effect of publication in print, Eisenstein cites the example of the *Malleus Maleficarum*, an encyclopaedia of demonology compiled by two Dominican inquisitors which called for the extirpation of witchcraft in Germany. This was first published in 1486 and went through nine editions in six years, followed by diffusion in translation elsewhere, including England in the early sixteenth century.

3. Although this applies to England, a recent assessment based on content analysis of seventeenth-century German newspapers as well as historical records concluded that 'In principle, the first newspapers prove to be thoroughly trustworthy sources of information' (Schroeder, 2001: 147).

4. The seventeenth century German newspapers mentioned earlier had a print run of 200–40 in the 1640s (Schroeder, 2001).

5. The self-appointed role of the press in the life of societies is reflected in the titles adopted by early newspapers, many of them still current. There is great variety, but a relatively small number of recurring themes, within the family of European languages. The following is a preliminary view of press values and purposes as exemplified in titles:

   (1) Actuality and continuity (*The Times; Today; Journal;* 'Daily,' 'Morning,' or 'Evening' as prefix; *Courant; Almanac*);
   (2) bringer of information (*News; Intelligencer; Messenger; Chronicle; Courier; Informer; Advertizer; Reporter; Circular*);
   (3) identification with a place (name of city, region, or country, plus corresponding prefixes);
   (4) world coverage (*News of the World; Globe; Planet; Universe*);
   (5) speed (*Express; Mercury*);
   (6) wake-up call (*Clarion; Bugle; Drum*);
   (7) harbinger, forerunner of events (*Herald; Crier; Leader*);
   (8) being of the people (*People; Humanité; Labour; Citizen; Worker*);
   (9) being a 'voice' or spokesperson (*Voice; Echo; Tribune; Word*)
   (10) relation to the post service (*Mail; Post; Telegraph; Despatch; Messenger*);
   (11) guardianship (*Guardian; Argus; Sentinel*);
   (12) reliability (*Truth; Record; Ledger; Gazette; Tablet; Mirror; Trust*);
   (13) freedom ('Independent' and 'Free' in or as titles; *Libération*);
   (14) observation and scrutiny (*Examiner; Inquirer; Observer; Monitor; Eagle*);

(15) emblem and guide (*Flag; Standard; Leader*);
(16) source of Light (*Sun; Star; Spark*);
(17) guide to a topic (politics, finance, sport, etc.).

6. Raymond (1999) expresses doubts about the historical accuracy of Habermas's case study of the public sphere, set in London in 1694–5. He does not believe that the actual newspapers available could support the idea of their playing an active role in critical debate and opinion formation. Even so, the newspaper did generally promote political discussion through its publicness, periodicity, and the heterogeneity of its contents.

7. Minnis (1984) sets out the notion of an author (*auctor*) as explained by Aristotle in terms of four types of causation. The first, or efficient, cause is the author as the motivating agent of a text. The second relates to the material used, the material cause. Thirdly, there is a formal cause, referring to style and structure. Finally, there is a 'final cause' being the objective or end of a work.

8. There is a large literature on this theme in mass media theory and research, for instance reviewed by Shoemaker (1991). This tends to stress the process as one of a succession of decisions, funnelling and filtering the flow of communication according to various criteria of selection. These include organizational convenience, relevance or interest to an audience, cost, and profitability.

PART II

Normative Theory of Media

3

Publication and the Public Interest
The Sources of Media Responsibilities

INTRODUCTION

Considerations of obligation, duty, and responsibility have always been closely linked with authorship and publication, even where they do not account for much of the basic motivation. Since the early days of printing, publication has been driven by widely varying motives ranging from personal vanity to promoting religion and the interests of the state. There were also risks to authors and potential harm to others associated with publication. Against this background, a body of thought has gradually emerged, concerned with the rights and obligations of mass media in relation to society and with the values they are expected to respect. Some of these values relate to ethics and personal morality, others are of a public character. The emphasis here is on the latter. Even so, there is no sharp line between the two and the public role of the media institution (as distinct from individual authors) inevitably gives a public character to its conduct and performance in its central publishing role.

The various meanings of 'responsibility' as applied to publication are examined in detail later (Chapter 9), but a working definition at this point can be formulated as any expectation from society of public benefit (or injunction to avoid harm). This definition is deliberately open and refers to the relevant content of media responsibility (for instance, in respect of truthfulness, independence, fairness, decency, etc.), and to questions regarding the source and strength of any obligation, whether imposed or voluntarily accepted.[1] Notions of media obligation are often fragmentary and specific to a time, place, or set of circumstances. They are also often contradictory and ideologically motivated. Despite, or even because of, this there is value in trying to piece together as much as possible of the universe of expectations that can lead to the media being called to account.

The media institution that we have inherited from the continuing process of invention and application of communication technologies does not typically comprise any coherent system, even if it is often treated as a single entity. The media do not have any generally agreed or accepted 'social purpose'. They do carry out tasks that are important to society, but often incidentally to their primary task of earning a living, exercising various skills and professions, providing for others the means of public expression, and meeting needs of media 'consumers' and clients. We should, therefore, not expect to discover any definitive or unanimous specification of media rights and obligations from this exercise.

At the core of this exploration are questions about the nature of the 'public interest' (on the part of society) in what the media do. If the very existence of a public interest is contested along with the notion that media have some 'purpose', whether on pragmatic or principled grounds, then there is little point in going further either with the search for media 'responsibilities' or with questions of 'accountability'. This is not an easy matter to settle, and impossible without making some value choices and judgements.

THE MULTIPLE PRESSURES TOWARDS MEDIA OBLIGATION

The notion that media have obligations to society is a contested one, since it appears inconsistent with principles of freedom of expression. It is certainly rejected by libertarian theorists, except perhaps for the view that media should do all in their power to protect and exercise the right to freedom. This issue is addressed later in detail, but here we take the pragmatic view that, for whatever reasons, mass media are widely thought to have some obligations, behave as if this is the case, and actually fulfil a range of tasks that can be considered as contributing to the public good. This applies to private media as well as the not inconsiderable public sector that indubitably does have obligations to society. Some sources of obligation stem from external demands and pressures, carrots as well as sticks. Others are generated internally by the media's own essential dynamics.

Three main kinds of external stimuli prompt media to meet the needs of society. First, there is the 'public' as audience or potential audience and at the same time as a body of citizens. Their individual communication needs coalesce into a collective demand for a continuous supply of public knowledge and, as the bearers of public opinion, they exert pressure on larger issues. Secondly, there are numerous collective social actors whose aims and activities depend on the media providing essential communication services, whether commercial, political, or cultural. Thirdly, there are governmental and other authorities that have legitimate expectations of co-operation from the media (as from all citizens) on essential matters of public welfare and the national interest. It is hardly conceivable that an established mass medium (unless specifically motivated towards fundamental opposition) can resist the pressures indicated. Nor have they, under the normal conditions of a free society, much motivation to do so.

As to the internally generated impulses to 'serve society', there is no shortage of candidates. Three points should be made, even so. First, it is usually in the self-interest of a media organization to provide public benefits, for which they are rewarded either financially or by public esteem and influence. Historically, many media have identified themselves with a particular place, nation, region, city, or community. Secondly, the activities of media encompass the publication aspirations of many individuals and groups that set out to achieve some larger purpose, to change society for the better, or to bring into the public domain some original composition, for widely varying motives. Thirdly, in respect of journalism at least, there has been a gradual process of professionalization, leading to the adoption of norms and standards that include some recognition of a duty to serve the public interest.[2]

DEFINING THE PUBLIC INTEREST

The concept of a public interest is both simple and also very contested in social and political theory. As applied to the mass media, its simple meaning is that they carry out a number of important, even essential, informational and cultural tasks and it is in the general interest (or good of the majority) that these are carried out well and according to principles of efficiency, justice, fairness, and respect for current social and cultural values. At the minimum, we can say that it is in the public interest that the media should do no harm, but the notion entails many positive expectations as well as restrictions and forms of accountability.

This simple version does not take us very far in practice, since there are conflicting views about what is good for society as a whole and a widely held view (especially by the media) that it is not for the media to make this choice, but simply to follow where their owners, audiences, or clients lead. The difficulties of handling the public interest concept are inextricably connected with its potentially high significance. In this respect, Blumler (1997: 54–5) makes three key points. Firstly, just as in the case of government, there are questions of authority as well as of power: 'In communications, the media are similarly placed. The justification for their freedoms, their wide-ranging roles in society, politics and culture, and their place in regulatory orders depends ultimately on the public interests presumed to be served thereby'.

In short, the power of the media, like that of government, has to be used in a legitimate way, which is not far removed from the notion of responsibility. Secondly, Blumler argues that 'a certain transcendent quality attaches to the notion of the public interest. It is different from and, in policy terms, superior to particular interests. This entails a longer-term perspective, in which the claims of successor generations and the future of society are included as well as people's immediate needs'. Thirdly, 'notions of the public interest must work in an imperfect and impure world'. This means inevitable tension, compromise, and improvisation according to circumstances.

Two opposed versions of what constitutes the public interest and how its content might be established have been proposed by Held (1970). One is a majoritarian view, according to which the issue should be settled according to the overall popular vote. In the case of the media this would tend to equate the public interest with giving the public what it wants, pleasing the majority of consumers in the media market. This has the merit of providing an unambiguous way of determining the content of the public interest. The alternative view is called unitarian or absolutist, since the public interest would be decided by reference to some single dominant value or ideology. This would only work in a paternalist system in which decisions about what is good are decided by guardians or experts.

Neither the first (free market) version of the public interest nor the paternalistic model offers clear guidance concerning the dilemmas facing media actors, policy-makers, and even media theorists. As Smith (1989) points out, there has been a profound shift away from the idea that governments on their own can intervene effectively in matters of communication in order to secure the public interest, and towards a reliance on market forces to achieve what is most beneficial, especially when the public good is defined increasingly in economic terms. Smith also notes that, under conditions of globalization, the interests of the public may not coincide with the interests of a particular nation state. These observations have even more force at the present time and have already led to a weakening of public broadcasting and diluted public claims on private media. Nevertheless, the debate has been primarily about specific goals (for instance innovation and expansion) or effective means (market rather than state) and less about the core idea that society has a strong, even essential, interest in the quality of communication provision and services.

THEORETICAL FOUNDATIONS OF MEDIA OBLIGATION

There are several different sources of theoretical reflection on the role of media in society, ranging from general social and political theory to more media-specific normative theory. The amount and specificity of media-centred theory have increased along with the growing centrality of media in our time.[3] In the following description of theoretical source material a number of provisional headings are employed, even though identification and boundaries are often not agreed and not very distinct. The order of appearance is approximately chronological, although it will be appreciated that later 'theories' do not replace earlier versions, but often coexist or produce new adaptations.

THEORY OF SOCIETY

Much early sociological theory was explicitly or implicitly functionalist, interpreting what media do as having some necessary or positive contribution to the working of the social system. Hanno Hardt's (1979) collection of early (late nineteenth- to early twentieth-century) German sociological writing on the press explored such themes of the press as 'the nerves of society'; the 'conscience of society'; providing leadership; binding society together; satisfying needs for information; providing society with a mirror of itself; forming public opinion (in the work of Simmel and Max Weber). Early sociology emphasized the role of the press in promoting social order and continuity (e.g. Park, 1923, on the assimilation of immigrants or Janowitz, 1952, on urban communities) as well as in causing innovation and change (e.g. Tarde, in Clark, 1969). Lasswell (1948) and then Wright (1960) identified four main communication functions: one of 'surveillance of the environment', meaning collecting and publishing information about social reality; secondly, a 'correlation' function, relating to cohesion, interpretation, and main-taining order; thirdly, providing 'continuity' of the social order or 'cultural transmission' from one generation to the next; fourthly, enter-tainment, which diverts from problems and releases social tension as well as giving pleasure (see also Mendelsohn, 1966).

Other themes relating to the role of the media in society are to be found in a more scattered form in the work of twentieth-century soci-ologists. One such theme relates to the media as an 'engine of social change', through the diffusion of innovations, especially in the context of Third World development (Lerner, 1958; Rogers, 1962). Another allocated the media a role in the exercise of dominant power in capitalist society (by hegemony (Gramsci, 1971) or the 'engineering of consent' (Lipp-mann, 1922; Herman and Chomsky, 1988)). The media were also credited with holding totalitarian societies in place (by state censorship and propaganda). A modern version of functional theory credits television with the power to promote a sense of belonging (on a global as well as national scale) through sharing vicariously in symbolically significant public events (Dayan and Katz, 1992). The media have long been credited with playing a key part in the process of socialization, advancing social movements, and forging identities in political, national, ethnic, and local cultural terms. Contemporary theory emphasizes the degree to which most experience of 'reality' is now mediated through mass media (Thompson, 1995; Luhmann, 2000).[4] Despite the aspiration to objectiv-ity, sociological theory offers numerous pointers to the desirable, as well as the undesirable, roles that media can and do play in social life.

FREE PRESS THEORY

At first sight theory of press freedom does not seem a promising source of ideas about the possible obligations of the media to society. This is certainly true of what has been called the 'libertarian' theory of the press (see Siebert *et al.*, 1956). Nevertheless, media freedom is often justified in terms of social necessity and public interest. The origins of libertarian theory are usually traced to Milton's *Aereopagitica* (1644), which argued against control of the press on grounds of reason, freedom of conscience, and theology, as well as exposing the impracticality and undesirable consequences of the licensing and censorship system.[5] Later claims to freedom of the press (from censorship) that were included in various eighteenth-century formulations of the Rights of Man are hard to separate from general claims to freedom from autocratic government

(Keane, 1991). The right to free publication has since been viewed as an essential instrument for achieving democracy and a precondition of its adequate practice, especially as the means for holding those who have power accountable. Freedom of publication is necessary if critical and alternative voices are to be heard.

Support for freedom of publication has been derived not only from fundamental principle (the deontological view), but also from considerations of public benefit. This is especially true of utilitarian theory as expounded by Jeremy Bentham and John Stuart Mill. The realization of Bentham's principle of the 'greatest good for the greatest number' requires that government be guided by the wishes of all citizens, which have to be freely expressed. Mill (in *On Liberty*) argued that progress and welfare depended on the free circulation of ideas by means of which truth and utility would be maximized. In our own time, the suppression of free publication (as under communism and other despotisms) has been strongly associated with economic and cultural backwardness, lending support to the view that freedom is functional. However, this also opens the way to the view that where it is shown not to be (as where it leads to private censorship, monopoly, or interference in the democratic or legal process), it can be legitimately restricted.

Advocates of a free press (there are few open opponents) divide sharply on whether its essential meaning should be an absence of restraint (as in First Amendment law and theory) or, rather, a positive view in which freedom is measured by the extent to which real chances for access and publication are available in adequate degree and with a fair allocation of chances (this might be called the 'freedom for' position). This division of view is related to the 'deontological versus utilitarian' debate, just outlined, with advocates of a positive view of media freedom inclined to use public benefit as an argument for freedom and to attach obligations to rights. However, the fit is not exact, since some advocates of the pure libertarian position take the view that the public benefit will be greater, if freedom is absolute and no obligations or requirements are attached. The matter is also complicated by the overlap between the rights and chances to publish that exist and the ownership of the means of publication. These and other issues are explored further in Chapter 8.

DEMOCRATIC THEORY: THE PRESS AS THE FOURTH ESTATE

Contemporary political theory rarely gives much attention to the role of a free press (see e.g. Held, 1989), beyond recognizing its importance for democratic process, but there is little doubt of its absolute necessity.[6] The term 'Fourth Estate' (first coined by Thomas Carlyle in 1841 to refer to reporters in the British House of Commons) has often been used to characterize the position of the press in the process of government as a source of power equivalent with that of other branches, especially the judiciary and upper and lower houses of the legislature (parliament). The expression and idea were adopted in nineteenth-century Britain by the newly serious newspaper press, increasingly conscious of its influence.[7] Its essential elements were: autonomy from government and politicians; having a duty to speak the truth, whatever the consequences; and having primary obligations to the public and to readers. The power of the press was thought to lie mainly in its capacity to express and influence public opinion and to keep watch on government.

The political role of the newspaper press has changed and enlarged since the mid-nineteenth century but it is still hard to conceive the conduct of contemporary democratic politics without the extensive involvement of the mass media. Democratic theory as well as practice presupposes that citizens will be fully informed about events and circumstances and have access to argument, alternative points of view, and guidance.

Given the freedom of the press as described, the media have no obligation to meet these expectations. Even so, for a mixture of reasons, not least their own self-interest, media in working democracies do make some effort to live up to the Fourth Estate ideal. The Fourth Estate label has moved a long way from its origin as a mocking reference to the pretensions of journalism and tends now to sanctify its role.[8] From a critical point of view, the self-assigned Fourth Estate model overprivileges the powerful, established media in comparison with ordinary citizens, especially where they are more concentrated and have developed symbiotic links with political power.[9] It is also arguable that where the claim is made and taken seriously, it carries with it certain responsibilities, including an unwritten obligation to provide a dependable channel of communication from government to citizens and vice versa.

A PARTISAN ALTERNATIVE

There is an alternative to a Fourth Estate version of the political role of the press in democracy. This is a view of the press as politically segmented and polarized, with each political movement having its own medium. It is a press characterized by what is called 'external pluralism', in contrast to the 'internal' variety that offers all points of view and a balanced assessment of controversial issues within the same pages (or news bulletin). The partisan press has flourished at various times in different countries, with different variants. One is the vanguard, or elite revolutionary press, as exemplified in the revolutionary journal *Iskra* (spark) founded by Lenin in 1900. More usual is the partisan-press model in democracies, where newspapers support competing parties.

The partisan model largely disappeared in the United States during the nineteenth century and was found largely inconsistent with commercial needs, especially under conditions of concentration (one-paper cities) and also journalistic professionalism which favours 'objectivity' and balance (Hallin, 1996). Partisanship was also found inconsistent with broadcasting, for somewhat similar reasons (extensive government control, monopoly character, plus the needs of advertisers). Even so, an element of partisanship was introduced into some European broadcasting systems (especially in Italy, the Netherlands, and France) and support for politically committed journalism has not been entirely extinguished (see Patterson, 1998).

SOCIAL RESPONSIBILITY THEORY

Libertarian theory offered a solution to the dilemmas posed by the transition from a communal and hierarchic to a pluralistic and democratic form of society by promoting freedom of expression as an unconditional right of citizens. Democratic political theory (and practice) specified the requirements of the emerging democratic system and the press and the first generation of properly institutionalized media (newspapers) accepted some obligations to behave in order to serve the public interest (as they chose to define it). However, by the turn of the twentieth century, the growing 'massification', monopolization, and commercialization of the press combined to cast doubt on the working of the liberal model of press freedom left to its own devices. Socialists and radicals articulated the criticism and laid the blame at the door of monopoly capitalism, of which the established press was seen as a supporter (Seldes, 1938; Blanchard, 1977). Conservative critics were inclined to agree about a decline in standards and ethics and to blame this on the combined effect of unscrupulous press owners and the low cultural level of the new mass audience.

This reaction found an expression in the work of the American Commission on Freedom of the Press that was set up in the early 1940s as a private initiative to inquire into the failings of the press and into possible remedies. It was the first attempt to establish a basis of considered criticism and prescription concerning the social role of news media. The essential task was to ensure that the press would somehow earn its right to freedom by delivering on the unwritten contract made with the people to inform fully and freely. Its main outcome was what has come to be called 'social responsibility theory' (see Hutchins, 1947).

According to the Commission's report, press freedom is only a 'conditional right'. The press was asked to accept the task of performing a 'public service of a professional kind' and not just to meet the immediate demands of its own readers. In a later publication, Peterson (in Siebert *et al.*, 1956) set out the basic terms of the social responsibility theory of the press, which went some way beyond the requirements of the various ethical codes of journalism that were already current in the United States. Aside from the fulfilment of the informative role, the press was asked to contribute to the cohesion of society and the representation and expression of its diversity.[10]

Important features of the newly formulated theory included the view that freedom from restraint is not enough, there has to be freedom to pursue positive goals: 'to be real, freedom must be effective'; there must be the 'appropriate means of attaining those goals' (Peterson, 1956: 93). Social responsibility theory also held that 'government must not allow freedom it must actively promote it' (ibid. 95). The main author of the Commission Report, Hocking (1947) is quoted as writing that 'government remains the residuary legatee of responsibility for an adequate press performance'. This gave some theoretical legitimation to public intervention in the press, despite the claims of press freedom. It is relevant to note that social responsibility theory had a high-minded and anti-populist tone and tendency. This was (and remains) an obstacle to any enthusiastic adoption by much of the press.

The report was not well received by the American press itself at the time, partly because it feared losing some of its privileges, already under attack (Blanchard, 1977). Even so, the idea of social responsibility theory became an essential point of reference in the growing trend towards the professionalization and self-regulation of the press. It was also influential abroad at a time when press systems were being reformed or reconstructed after the Second World War. Across the Atlantic, in Britain, a government-appointed inquiry, the Royal Commission on the Press

(RCP, 1949), began its work in the year that the American Commission reported. Its terms of reference required it to assess standards of news accuracy and make recommendations about press structure. It was to lay the foundations for a General Council of the Press, designed to act as an instrument of accountability and self-improvement.[11]

Social responsibility theory in one form or another dominated thinking about the desirable relation between media and society and about the options for policy to improve the media for some decades after the Second World War and has not been completely dislodged by the deregulatory trends of the late twentieth century. In northern Europe, especially, it provided the justification for systems of press support and subsidy that recognized the importance of the press to social life and politics, particularly the need for independence and diversity (Smith, 1977; Picard, 1985; Humphreys, 1996).

PUBLIC SERVICE BROADCASTING THEORY

While public service broadcasting began as a practical (technical, administrative, and financial) solution to the problem of organizing coherent radio services in a number of European countries in the 1920s and 1930s, it has come to offer a distinctive philosophy of media provision that stands as an alternative to free market commercial media. It has been influential as a source of ideas about media responsibility to society precisely because it is founded on this very notion. Even in the heartland of free enterprise, the United States, the Federal Communications Commission over a number of years (following the 1934 Communications Act) developed principles of social responsibility and accountability for television and radio, without adopting the concept in name. Eventually, in 1967, a form of public supported broadcasting was introduced (see Hoffmann-Riem, 1996).

Public service broadcasting is certainly influenced by similar ideas to those found in 'social responsibility theory', but is much further developed because it can be implemented through law, regulation, and financial support without violating constitutional principles of freedom.[12] Its main principles are: universality and diversity of provision; democratic accountability to the public as a whole; responsibility for meeting general and special needs as decided by the public; a commitment to quality, not determined by profit or the market; and often some subordination to 'national' needs or priorities in cultural, economic, and political matters. Hoffmann-Riem (1996: 271 ff.) finds the main justification for extensive regulation of broadcasting, aside from the securing of interference-free transmission, to lie in the need to secure wide public access and to protect a variety of 'vulnerable values' as cherished in different societies (see Blumler, 1992).

DEVELOPMENT MEDIA THEORY

The situation of mass media in developing countries has always been characterized by circumstances that make liberal media theory less appropriate or even impossible to realize. Often, there is little or no freedom and media are obliged to follow the dictates of ruling élites or actual rulers. Several writers have identified a variant of 'development media theory' (e.g. Altschull, 1984; McQuail, 1983; Shelton and Gunaratne, 1998). This takes the requirement of a collective effort towards national economic and social development as being so pressing that media ought to accept development tasks in line with government policy. This implies active support for government informational and educational campaigns, the promotion of developments goals, and supporting national, regional, and local cultures. In news, media should aim for relevance to the condition of their society and connections with other developing countries in the same region. Media should be careful not to undermine the authority of government and its agents by 'irresponsible' criticism. While these ideas express a version of social responsibility, in practice they often serve to legitimize the surrender of independence and a subordination to whoever has power.

CRITICAL THEORY

Although social responsibility theory originally derived from criticism of the commercial press, it largely represented conventional and establishment views of the social obligations of the press. A 'responsible' press was not and still is not fundamentally threatening to a legitimate government, whatever its shortcomings. During the 1960s and 1970s, much more radical criticism, inspired by neo-Marxist and other radical ideas, was directed at mass media in general (see e.g. Mills, 1956; Marcuse, 1964; Schiller, 1969; Hall, 1977; Murdock and Golding, 1977; Herman and Chomsky, 1988). In its strongest forms, it rejected the whole set of media institutions, including public broadcasting, as simply serving as the informational and cultural arm of a capitalist–bureaucratic state apparatus, with little possibility of reform or democratization from within. It is not very relevant here to look closely at this body of theory for guidelines about media responsibilities, which it did not seek to provide. Even so, despite its destructive intention, research and criticism of media within this theoretical tradition does deploy certain standards of media quality and explicitly or implicitly presumes that media should be of service to society, albeit a different society purged of injustice and false consciousness.

Critical theory also has a cultural wing which has gone through different phases. In its earliest formulation, especially in the work of the Frankfurt School (Adorno and Horkheimer, 1972; Marcuse, 1964; Lowenthal, 1961), mass culture (the dominant culture of the media and of most people) was portrayed not only as abysmally poor in quality (aesthetic, ethical) but also effectively designed as an ideological tool used by capitalist media owners to captivate the masses, blunt any critical perspective, and divert them from the revolutionary tasks. It also misrepresented social reality, especially the true position of the working class, and promoted conservative ideology (see Hardt, 1991).

Latterly, critical cultural theory has been transformed by a revalidation of popular culture (cultural populism), largely rejecting Marxist analysis, and leading to a current situation, which might be identified with postmodernism in which a critical social analysis of media culture is hardly possible (see e.g. McGuigan, 1992). No agreed criteria of merit remain beyond personal taste, market success, professional skill, or artistic licence. This tendency undermines any notion of media obligation in cultural matters, although, in the real world, there continue to be expectations about quality and authenticity and media still face cultural criteria of performance from regulators and public opinion.

EMANCIPATORY MEDIA THEORY

A branch of critical theory came to espouse the promise of the first new media, especially because of the potential for small-scale, grass-roots communication in channels independent from dominant mass media. The counter-cultural ideas of the 1960s, anarchistic and individualistic rather than communistic, supported such a move and the then new technologies of interactive cable, CCTV, photocopying, pirate radio, recording, and replay, seemed to put the potential for communication liberation in the hands of the people and out of the hands of the publishing monopolies (Enzensberger, 1970).

The guiding principles uniting the loose coalition of ideas referred to here are participation, interaction, smallness of scale, locatedness, cultural autonomy and variety, emancipation, and self-help. The emphasis is often on the *process* of communicating rather than the content. According to one interpretation, this might eliminate the notion of any obligation to society altogether and with it any relevance for accountability. Both these concepts (responsibility and accountability) seem to belong to the past of typically massive media and homogeneous mass publics. In the future the relevant point of social reference and loyalty will be the voluntary community of interest, not any political entity.

These ideas about new and small-scale media are typically current in rich, media-abundant, and mature democratic societies. Much of the world is not like this. There is still room for theory that addresses the condition of struggle for basic rights. John Downing (2001) coins the term 'rebellious communication' to refer to media that pursue emancipatory and political ends in situations of oppression. Such media operate in a positive way in the critical tradition. They include those serving a political cause, ranging from female emancipation to the overthrow of oppressive or bourgeois regimes and include manifestations of alternative publication such as *samizdat* in the Soviet Union and grass-roots micro-media in developing countries or in situations of authoritarian rule or foreign occupation. According to Downing (2001: p. xi) they 'generally serve two overriding purposes: (a) to express opposition vertically from subordinate quarters directly at the power structure and its behavior; (b) to build support, solidarity and networking laterally against policies'. They are often stimulated by, and help to generate, 'new social movements' and in general have in common that 'they break someone's rules, although rarely all of them in every respect'. Much of the early theorizing surrounding the significance of the Internet has extended essentially the same line of emancipatory thinking (see Castells, 2001; Lessig, 1999).

The potential of the new technologies, as noted above, continues to excite speculation about new possibilities for freedom of publication, civic activism, and participant democracy (e.g. Jones, 1997; van Dijk and Hacker, 2000; Axford and Higgins, 2001). New media can unlock secrets and make much arcane information readily available to ordinary people very rapidly, with an empowering effect. In this version of theory, there are certain expectations of performance. Especially in demand will be ready access to the raw material of political debate and decision-making, direction connections with political leaders and candidates for office, and new means for expressing opinions and choices. The Internet can build bridges with developing countries as well as across national frontiers in pursuit of issues which are larger than those of local or national politics, including those of war and peace, the environment, globalization, and development.

In general, the new thinking about new media veers away from ideas of responsibility and also from measures for enforcing it. The editorial functions of new media are largely absent or unwanted, so their possible obligations are fewer.

COMMUNITARIAN THEORY AND THE MEDIA

Communitarianism re-emphasizes the social ties connecting people, in contrast to modern libertarian individualism (Taylor, 1989; Rorty, 1989; Sandel, 1982; MacIntyre, 1981). It stresses duties owed to society as well as rights to be claimed. In respect of media, relations with the audience take on a more mutual character, especially where they share a social identity and a place (an actual community). The ethical imperative of the media to engage in dialogue with the public it serves has been stressed (Christians, 1993). Communitarian ethics are derived from ideas of a universal moral imperative.

The commitment to a language of moral issues is difficult to reconcile with the norm of objective reporting. In some respects, the call is to return to a more organic social form in which the press plays an integrative, expressive, and articulating role. Not self-interest, but partnership is seen as the way forward.[13] The plea is for covenant, not contract. A press should promote democratic pluralism, by emphasizing the bonds which unite individuals to their own (minority) culture and to the larger society and general solidarity with humanity. We are offered an alternative to the 'mainstream contractarian version' of the role of the media in society (ibid. 105). Media should empower a 'common vision of an inclusive, cooperative society... communitarian ethics compels us... towards a rich concept of truthful narrative'. According to Nerone (1994: 70–1):

In the communitarian model, the goal of reporting is not intelligence but civic transformation. The press has bigger fish to fry than merely improving technology and streamlining performance... The question is its vocational norm.... In a communitarian world-view, the news media should seek to engender a like-minded philosophy among the public. A revitalized citizenship shaped by community norms becomes the press's aim. News would be an agent of community formation.

Communitarian theory of the press is in some respects quite radical. In some other respects it can be portrayed as anti-libertarian, although its spirit is voluntaristic. The impression of conservatism stems from its strong emphasis on an ethical imperative and community. It is certainly a theory which emphasizes active democracy and widely shared moral obligations of a social as well as personal nature.

PUBLIC JOURNALISM

Related in some way, but much more pragmatic and limited in its implications, is new thinking about civic or public journalism (Rosen, 1993; Schudson, 1998; Glasser, 1998) which originates within the practice of journalism itself. Its main thrust is a return to a more engaged form of journalism, to closer relationships between media and their audience, but also with the community. The (news) media are asked to do more to engage their audiences and be involved in their local communities in relevant ways. A basic premiss is that journalism has a purpose, which is to improve the quality of civic life by fostering participation and debate. Schudson (1998) describes it as based on a 'Trustee model' rather than a market or advocacy model: 'in the Trustee model, journalists should provide news according to what they as a professional group believe citizens should know' (136). Journalists themselves are 'professionals who hold citizenship in trust for us'. Glasser and Craft (1998) emphasize a different aspect of public journalism, referring to a shift from a 'journalism of information' to one of (public) 'conversation'.

Proponents of this new journalism have sometimes been guided by communitarian ideas but they are also reacting against the growing scale and distance of modern media from their social context, especially under the influence of conglomerization. Public journalism parts company with the tradition of neutrality and objective reporting, but it is not a return to an older tradition of partisanship and political advocacy. When expressed as a theory it has some affinities with versions of the public service broadcasting role, although in a more engaged and open-ended form. It certainly does not look to government, law, or regulation for support and has thus parted company from old-fashioned social responsibility theory. It is voluntaristic and compatible with the free market, although also potentially fragile and ineffective. On the whole, the movement has not travelled well from its origins in the United States, although the underlying ideas are widely understood.

MEDIA AND THE PUBLIC SPHERE

There is another orientation which offers an alternative to communitarianism and is more in keeping with the Enlightenment tradition. This is to be found in the notion of a 'public sphere', a term which has been rediscovered and given wide currency since the 1989 translation into English of Jurgen Habermas's (1962/1989) book entitled *The Structural Transformation of the Public Sphere* (see Calhoun, 1992). According to Dahlgren (1995: 7–8):

Habermas conceptualised the public sphere as that realm of social life where the exchange of information and news on questions of common concern can take place so that public opinion can be formed . . . since the scale of modern society does not allow more than relatively small numbers of citizens to be co-present, the mass media have become the chief institution of the public sphere.

The original public sphere described by Habermas referred to the notional 'space' (in terms of time, location, and conditions) where bourgeois intellectuals (from the eighteenth century onwards) discussed and developed ideas for political reform. The typical localities were coffee shops and the pages of newspapers, which were the contemporary equivalent of an imagined Athenian Agora or market-place. Physical access to such space is free and freedom of speech and association are assured. The more significant metaphorical space lies between the sphere of government and state action and the 'basis' of societies where the personal lives of citizens are conducted. This image also captures the role of the press in society. Necessary conditions for the operation of a public sphere include, then as now, besides the means of publication, a sufficiently educated, informed, or interested body of citizens and the potential for an informed and freely expressed public opinion.

Revived ideas of a public sphere also depend on the concept of civil society as a preferred form. A condition of civil society is one of openness and plurality without severe conflict, where there are many more or less autonomous and voluntary intermediate agencies and associations between the citizen and the state. These provide the focus for participation and identification and also insulate the individual from the oppressive power of a central state in the last instance or the pressures of a mass society. They help to maintain rights and freedoms.

The role assigned to media is to promote an effective public space (in the sense meant above) in which diverse voices can be heard, ideas exchanged and debated, issues of moment debated in a rational way, and public opinion formed. The ideas described seem to offer a suitable framework for embedding the contribution of new media such as the Internet which allow much more information and ideas to flow between citizens, experts, and politicians and between citizens themselves. The new media also facilitate new forms of (virtual) assembly and organization in support of causes.

The public sphere and civil society concepts provide a much less localistic vision than that offered by communitarianism, although no proper boundaries for the various social spaces which have a public character are indicated. The public sphere served by public communication is not exclusively a national space. It can be global or simply not defined in terms of legal administrative frontiers. Some writers (e.g. Keane, 1991) find the answer to reviving the public sphere to lie in a strengthened public service broadcasting. Others (e.g. Curran, 1996) prefer to look wider, for instance to the publications of voluntary and fringe organizations to the party press, where it still exists or to new types of 'civic media'. While there is no obvious solution to creating the media suitable for enlivening the public sphere, there is some agreement that it does need to include non-state and non-market media as well as commercial media.

LOOKING FOR A STRUCTURE IN PRESS THEORY

Not surprisingly, there is no single coherent message about what society has a right to expect from its media, arising from these varied theoretical sources. The views embodied in theory extend in time from the late eighteenth to the late twentieth century, during which dime there have been profound changes both in media and social contexts. Early ideas do not die, but each generation has to forge a new version of theory for its time. There are other limitations to the body of theory described. It applies almost exclusively to stable and developed Western-style democracies. It mainly concerns the political role of the media, with little to say about the much more extensive activities of the press in cultural and social matters, entertainment, and advertising. Even within its limited sphere of application, there are large variations of political culture, traditions, and ideology that give rise to different conceptions of the communication 'needs' of society and the appropriate means for meeting them.

There have been numerous, largely unsuccessful, attempts to provide a coherent account and classification of different theories of the press (see e.g. Siebert *et al.*, 1956; McQuail, 1983; Nerone, 1994; Nordenstreng, 1997) and there is little chance of achieving this goal on the basis of the foregoing summary. One large obstacle is the divergence of experience and thinking between the United States, Europe, and the rest of the world. Even so, we can discern the outlines of a structure of sorts in the materials presented. At the simplest level of analysis, there is a fundamental opposition between two traditions—one that emphasizes individual rights to freedom above all and another that gives priority, or equal weight, to public or collective welfare, including the requirements for an effective public sphere (see Fiss, 1997; Sunstein, 1993). In shorthand terms these could be called 'libertarian' and 'democratic' respectively, accepting the claims of protagonists.

At the same time, the two opposed camps are far from homogeneous in their occupants. Amongst the libertarians can be found radicals, anarchists, extreme conservatives, and free marketers of varying degrees of pragmatism. The other side includes professionals, social democrats, left-critical theorists, community activists, paternalistic conservatives, and moderate reformers. It is evident that other dimensions are involved besides the one outlined. The potential candidates include: left versus right leaning; public versus private sector advocates; essentialism versus utilitarianism; ideology versus pragmatism. There are too many possibilities for any simple or elegant solution to be found. However, for present purposes of examining questions of responsibility and accountability and related policy options it is useful to try to identify the main traditions of press theorizing that have figured in the development of Western media. These cannot, however, be broken down straightforwardly into coherent theories, exclusive alternatives, or descriptions of different national systems.

1. *Market liberalism* (*the 'free market-place of ideas'*). This holds that the free market is the best solution to the issues at hand as well as safeguarding individual rights. It is pragmatic about the need for some market and system regulation in the interests of efficient and fair operation but supports the rights of ownership and has no problem with 'big' media. In spirit it is generally utilitarian, claiming to achieve the greatest good for the greatest number by a minimum of intervention.

2. *Professionalism.* Questions of responsibility are handled by reference to the press institution and competent self-regulatory processes. Responsibility and accountability are accepted in principle, but must not impinge on professional autonomy. In general, this heading covers both Fourth Estate theory and Public Journalism. 'Social responsibility' notions are variably present.

3. *Democratic theory.* This variant encompasses a range of possibilities for identifying and meeting public interest requirements from mass media. The most interventionist variants support public service broadcasting and other non-market arrangements, such as subsidies for particular public goals. It welcomes partisan advocacy and favours support for access and diversity, limits on advertising, and other rules for broadcast media.

Other strands of theory are hard to accommodate under these three headings, but they can still offer clear guidance on questions of media responsibility and accountability. The main alternatives on offer are: communitarianism; radical libertarianism; paternalism or autocracy; radical left theory; alternative, small-scale media theory; development theory; communist theory. The relative relegation of there theories is not intended as a dismissal. It is simply a reflection of the predominant reality.

IN CONCLUSION

Despite their shortcomings, the materials presented in this chapter provide frames of reference and concepts for defining potential responsibilities of media to serve the public interest in different ways. We are also able to identify certain enduring values of public communication in the Western tradition that shape our notions of various potential responsibilities of media publication. Such 'publication values' are abstract in formulation, but they become concrete when they are taken up in debate and expressed (written down) in specific forms. These include: public policy statements and projects; laws and regulations; editorial manifestos; media professional codes of ethics and practice; tenets of public opinion; and regularities of audience tastes and preferences. The following chapter provides an outline and discussion of the main values that are relevant.

NOTES

1. A useful formal definition of social responsibility in connection with professional ethics has been formulated by Wueste (1994) as follows: 'When we speak of social responsibility we direct attention to or invoke norms that express legitimate and stable expectations respecting the conduct of persons in positions of public trust or power within a social practice or institution.'

2. For example, the code of the US Society of Professional Journalists (dating from 1926 and revised in 1973 and 1984) states under the heading of 'Responsibility' that 'The public's right to know of events of public importance and interest is the overriding mission of the mass media. The purpose ... is to serve the general welfare' (Nordenstreng and Topuz, 1989: 28). The Statement of Principle adopted by the Canadian Daily Newspaper Publishers (1973), under the same heading, states that 'the operation of a newspaper is no less a public trust, no less binding because it is not formally conferred, and its overriding responsibility is to the society which protects and provides its freedom' (Canada, 1981: 288). A practical version of the 'public interest' is deployed by the press in justification of some contested publication decisions. For instance, the UK newspaper *The Guardian* has an editorial code according to which the public interest includes: (1) detecting or exposing crime or misdemeanour; (2) protecting health and safety; and (3) preventing the public from being misled.

3. At one point, a seminal attempt was made by Siebert *et al.* (1956) to identify and describe four main 'theories of the press', on fairly common-sense grounds, labelled 'authoritarian', 'libertarian', 'soviet communist', and 'social responsibility'. The utility of this classification as well as the status of these four entities as 'theories' have since been called into question (see especially Nerone, 1995). However, no agreed alternative framework of theory has been constructed and the search continues (Nordenstreng, 1997).

4. In what is effectively a revival or social system theory, Luhmann (2000: 97) argues that the mass media mainly contribute to society's own construction of reality—they direct the self-observation of the social system. The media contribute to stability through promoting both consensus and dissensus.

5. Milton's pamphlet was written in protest at the passing of a law by the English (reformed) Parliament requiring the licensing of all printed works. Milton did not favour all authors or forms of publication and would retain punishments after the event especially for immoral and superstitious works, the latter in practice mainly Catholic (papist). According to Jansen (1988: 73) the right to free publication belonged to an elite, excluding women and the lower orders. Despite this, Milton's plea for freedom has appealed to later generations in their struggle against puritanical as well as political control of media. At one point in the *Aereopagitica* Milton wrote: 'If we think to regulate printing, thereby to rectify manners, we must regulate all recreations and pastimes, all that is delightful to man. No music must be heard, no song be set or sung, but what is grave and Dorick.'

6. The early American democrat, Thomas Jefferson, is often quoted as expressing a preference for 'Newspapers without Government' over 'Government without Newspapers'.

7. Schultz (1998: 24–5) cites a famous editorial written by Thomas Delane in the *The Times*, in 1852, in which he sets out the responsibilities of journalism in the political process. These are not the same as those of the government, sometimes even diametrically opposed due to a duty to speak the truth under all circumstances.

8. Schultz (1998) found that more that 70 per cent of her Australian journalist respondents strongly favoured a definition of their role as that of a Fourth Estate (defined in the question as acting as independent and critical watchdog of government).

9. In the view of Garry (1994), the Fourth Estate model 'accentuate[s] many of the faults of the existing mass media'. It strengthens an already too powerful press and 'accents the aloofness of the press from the people'. Its overemphasis on the adversarial and watchdog function may damage democracy by promoting cynicism and apathy. Many other critics voice similar views (see e.g. Bennett and Entman, 2001).

10. The main requirements of social responsibility theory (according to Hutchins, 1947) were that a responsible press should 'provide a full, truthful, comprehensive and intelligent account of the day's events in a context which gives them meaning'. Secondly, it should 'serve as a forum for the exchange of comment and criticism' and 'be a common carrier of the public expression'. Thirdly, the press should give a 'representative picture of the constituent groups in society' and 'clarify the goals and values of society'. In recent critical comments, Baker (1998) has criticized these goals as largely unrealizable (especially objectivity and representativeness) or meaningless (value clarification). In his view, social-responsibility theory presumes a consensual and ideology-free world. The alternative is a segmented and partisan set of media that will not cosy up to elites and centres of power (private or public).

11. Another Royal Commission on the Press (RCP, 1977a) took up a similar task of press reform in the UK thirty years later. Its report emphasized the connection between press freedom and the advancement of the public interest in a democracy by informing, scrutinizing those with power, and promoting both social cohesion and change.

12. For instance, Clause 10 of the European Convention on Human Rights (ECHR) while asserting rights of freedom of the press also specifically allows regulation of broadcasting. For purposes of protection from competition requirements, public broadcasting has also been recognised within the European Union if it fulfils the following requirements as spelt out in the 1994 Resolution of the Council of Ministers:

   - Provides a reference point for all and a force for social cohesion and integration. Provides a forum for public discussion. Gives impartial news, information, and comment.
   - Develops pluralistic and innovatory programming, without sacrifice to market forces.
   - Provides programmes for all as well as minorities.
   - Reflects different philosophical and religious ideas.
   - Contributes to diversity
   - Provides original programming
   - Extends choice by programmes not normally provided by commercial broadcasters. (See Porter, 1995.)

13. 'An ethical press anchored in such civic transformations presupposes human dignity and seeks interdependence. It admits natural prejudice but honours the possibility of peaceful change in a context of empathy and mutuality' (Christians, 1993: 103).

4

From Communication Values to Criteria of Performance

The theories outlined in Chapter 3 can be distilled into a set of values that are widely applied to publication issues. For the most part, the ideas discussed have been expressed in a positive way as obligations to society and to a lesser extent as aspects of professional responsibility. This is a somewhat one-sided and overt-theoretical approach to identifying the criteria of performance that are of primary relevance to processes of media accountability. It has to be supplemented by referring to another large body of concerns that arise from the practice of publication. These are mainly expressed in reactions (often critical) to what media do, reports of harm to individuals, groups, or society, and in fears of wider social consequences. The large and disparate universe of ideas that results is not easy to bring together under neat headings, but it forms an important part of the normative environment in which media operate.

The 'publication values' of the subheading above are introduced and, where appropriate, translated into criteria of performance that figure widely in accountability processes. The values are grouped under five headings: *truth; freedom; order and cohesion; solidarity and equality; right purpose and responsibility.*

TRUTH

Truth as a support for claims to freedom of publication and a standard applied to what is published predates all formulations of theory. The sources of truth in pre-modern times included: divine revelation; the authority of a church of religious belief; the authority of rulers; the personal wisdom, conscience, and reputation of authors, both ancient and new.[1] The Reformation and the humanistic and scientific renascence of the fifteenth to seventeenth centuries enlarged ideas of truth to encompass both the truth as determined by individual conscience and also scientific truth as established by observation and theoretical explanation.

The meaning of truth as verisimilitude and faithful reproduction of texts and content persisted and was reinforced by the requirements of science, law, government, and commerce. The organization, the business, and the regulation of printing played an important part in reinforcing and elevating this version of truth (Johns, 1998). It is arguable that early newspapers would never have established a key position in the seventeenth-century political and commercial world, without a strict attention to a notion of truth as verifiable facts (see e.g. Schroeder, in Dooley and Baran, 2001).

In the context of political struggles that gave rise to early principles of liberty of expression and publication, the idea of truth as an intrinsic value was undermined. Each party or faction had its own version of truth, based on self-interest or belief, with authority deriving mainly from naked power. In political contexts, the concept of ideology replaced that of truth and propagandists disregarded or abused truth at will (Gouldner, 1976; Jansen, 1988). Libertarian theories of the press supported the rights of individuals to express their views and perceptions of the world, with a more or less equal claim to truth, as long as the rights of others and the common good were not threatened. During the nineteenth century, rationalist and utilitarian philosophy identified truth more or less with the fruits of empirical observation and with the various reality-tests of competing ideas. Economic liberalism gave all versions of truth an equal right to enter the market-place of ideas, where truth would be determined according to experience, informed judgement, preference, or popular prejudice. Theology and science still struggled with each other for dominance in establishing truth.

In our own time, truth in publication has come to be primarily identified with reliable, verifiable data and with expert analysis and interpretation. The main criterion of truth has come to be utility, the test applied is the degree of conformity to reliably recorded 'reality', especially as represented by journalistic objectivity (see below). It is this version of truth that informs most social responsibility theory of the press and even critical theory makes an appeal to some notion of reality and seeks to expose bias and distortions of reality. Beyond the realm of news and information, truth is a value that supports more authentic forms of media fiction and culture. This refers, *inter alia*, to cultural integrity, authorial good faith, and the faithful representation of contemporary social and cultural experience. Claims to freedom of publication in democratic societies are stronger when they are based on an appeal to truth, whether religious, cultural, political, or scientific.[2]

Despite the secularization of the value of truth, there remains a significant core element of truth as either the voice of conscience or the speaking out of unpalatable truths about conditions or events in the society to which the truth-teller belongs, often with some risk attached. This may lead to suppression or marginalization by authorities. Or the discomfort may be widespread amongst a population that does not like to be faced with the reality of its own failings. This can apply to a range of matters, from racism to child abuse. Those who speak up may be admired for their integrity and fearlessness, but are not necessarily thanked or rewarded.

FREEDOM

The value of freedom in communication needs little explanation or justification beyond the connection with truth and what is obvious (but see Chapter 8). It is widely seen as the *conditio sine qua non* for realizing most other benefits of communication. It figures in virtually all theory, although with different degrees of emphasis. Even theories which are illiberal like to make a claim to genuine freedom, as when communist media claimed to be free from the chains of capitalist ownership. Most Western political and media theory, even in its critical versions, is agreed on the diverse benefits of freedom of publication, especially its indispensability in opposing state or other power; its contribution to truth and discovery; its link to social and cultural progress; its role in the formation of public opinion; its protection for critical voices; and its status as a fundamental right.

ORDER AND COHESION

Several distinct, but interrelated, values are covered by this heading. One is that of the unity and cohesion of a whole society, or some less extensive community. This value stands against internal dissension as well as individual isolation and social fragmentation. It supports ideas of a shared culture based on common experience, language, belief, and outlook. Secondly, communication in public is expected to respect and promote cultural values as well as to avoid offence to morals, religion, or public sensibilities. Its tendency is conservative more than radical, supporting consensus and tradition. Public communication is often expected to support as far as possible the influence of socializing agencies such as education, family, religion, etc. At the very least, it should avoid knowable harm to the vulnerable. Thirdly, there is a value of order in the narrow sense of absence of disorder in the form of crime, unrest, breakdown of law, and warfare. The desirable state of order in this respect is typically one defined or maintained by a legitimate political authority, especially one democratically chosen.

SOLIDARITY AND EQUALITY

The claim to equality can derive from a notional right to communicate as well as other human rights, or as an extension and derivative of principles of democracy. It is quite closely related as a value to that of freedom and also to the principle of justice (equality of all citizens before the law and of rights to the same benefits of citizenship of a given polity). What it means independently in relation to publication needs some explanation. On a purely abstract level we can say that all persons have an equal right to express themselves to others and to the society and to receive the expressions of all others. However, it is impossible to achieve or guarantee communication equality beyond the level of personal expression (speech, opinion and belief, religious practice, assembly and demonstration). Even equality of opportunity to communicate cannot be guaranteed in public communication and the predominant forms of mass communication are premised on the assumption that most public communication (where the few address the many) is not compatible with equal sharing of roles of sender and receiver.

This value cluster expresses a view more from below than from any legitimate authority above. It favours public communication arrangements, and forms and contents that are linked to groups and communities based on various criteria, including place, religion, class, ethnicity, gender, etc. It supports publication that strengthens the identity and cohesion of minorities and subgroups within the larger society and in so doing empowers them. Along with this version of solidarity-enhancing communication can be placed forms of publication that extend sympathy and empathy on behalf of the society to disadvantaged, victimized, or just unfortunate persons and groups. This extends to the attitude of caring for outsiders and unfortunates beyond the boundaries of the nation. In their study of investigative reporting, Ettema and

Glasser (1998) name solidarity as one of the three primary values supporting this form of reporting.[3]

The printing of sacred texts in the vernacular was supported by the principle of freedom of access, derived in turn mainly from the notion that all people are equal before God. Subsequently, claims to freedom of speech and print were political rather than theological in origin, based on the view that the powerless and oppressed have as much right to speak out as the powerful. Social responsibility theory and social democratic media theory in their various forms also enshrine the principle of equality, although mainly as the right of all to receive communication services of a sufficient quality to support a universal and informed participation in the public life of societies. In a wider view, the value of communication equality is closely connected with other democratic rights, including those of universal education, access to information, public libraries, and other information resources available to all.

RIGHT PURPOSE AND RESPONSIBILITY

With or without justification in theory or practical experience, public communication is likely to be judged according to a general notion of benevolence of purpose and acceptable conduct. This is less the case now than in the past, since the notion of what is good in this context has considerably fragmented. The content of this general value has been hollowed out, but there remains at least a core notion, widely subscribed to, that public communication should not knowingly cause harm (whether wittingly or not) to its recipients, third parties, or society and should accept appropriate responsibility for any potential harm caused. This value position is partly subsumed within the ideas of truth, order, and solidarity, but needs to be spelt out separately because ideas of causal responsibility are so central to accountability.

FROM COMMUNICATION VALUES TO MEDIA RESPONSIBILITIES

As remarked above, basic values are not necessarily mutually consistent and that applies to this particular set. The notion of truth can, for instance, be understood in a unitary way, logically excluding the possibility of multiple inconsistent truths. Where a particular single truth is backed by state power there is not much room for freedom or equality and the cohesion of society denies its diversity. In general the more that order is elevated to the highest plane, the less freedom of expression exists and truth is subordinated to other ends. Freedom and equality have often come into conflict, where freedom is understood as equal opportunity and lack of external constraint, rather than equality of outcome, while equality is understood in literal terms as a social ideal where most people share much the same provision and way of life. Egalitarian and solidaristic policies in communication as in other matters are likely to require limits on the freedom of some to own or use some of the means of communication. 'Responsible communication' is sometimes a euphemism for self-censorship.

The tensions within the body of communication values cannot be escaped or easily resolved, but they have to be accommodated within any coherent framework of proposed or accepted media responsibilities. In the Western liberal tradition, where policy-makers have attempted to establish a view of the public interest in media conduct, primacy has usually been given to the value of freedom which it is the duty of the media themselves to foster. Truth, order, and equality have then been viewed as standards in assessing how adequately or not the media are using their freedom. The most general underlying frame of thought thus treats freedom as a right and other values as responsibilities linked to this right. There is no complete agreement on this view. It is generally rejected by the media, but widely shared by the general public (see Chapter 6). Despite the wide currency of this view and the many empirical connections between the activities of media and essential processes in modern society (politics, economy, justice, etc.) we cannot speak of obligations on the media. Most of the connections arise from voluntary choice and the mutual self-interest of the parties involved.

THE TERMS OF ASSESSMENT OF MEDIA QUALITY

The media are held to account, if they are at all, according to a potentially wide range of criteria that express in more concrete and practical terms these basic publication values. The values outlined indicate how media *ought* to operate (in an ideal world) accordingly to widely held views that are expressed both in normative theory and in the continuous debate, criticism, and commentary that accompany the operation of mass media. None of this has any power or claim to constrain the media. Nevertheless, it represents the background against which any accountability process operates, in a given context. It provides the relevant terms of a critical discourse and is frequently drawn on in disputes and claims. In particular, it is this background discourse that channels and shapes expectations concerning the conduct of media in their many public roles and it also to some degree shapes the aims, commitments, and actions of mass media themselves. In the end there is always some constraint on the conduct of media and the line between theory of media performance and actual accountability in society is not easy to draw.

Judgements made in the context of accountability are also a form of quality assessment, although the notion of quality is always relative and its application depends on context, priorities, and perspectives as well as value preferences. In addition, the variety of media forms and divergence of purpose is great and it makes little sense to apply the same set of values and criteria to all media or even to a particular form such as 'the newspaper'.[4] Even as an exercise in criticism, there is little point, for instance, in berating sensational or tabloid newspapers for not being more like the political quality papers that they do not aspire to be, nor are wanted to be by their readers. Accountability usually only arises when a publication is charged with 'offences' that go beyond what freedom of the press allows or what society will tolerate.

In their framework for the assessment of media quality, Ishikawa and Muramatsu (1991) distinguish between levels of assessment and different perspectives, or vantage points. Mass media can be assessed at four main levels: structure, medium, channel, and content. The most relevant perspectives on quality are those of society and regulators, media professionals, and the audience. Different criteria may be relevant at the matrix points identified in this way. The levels of analysis can be explained as follows. Structure refers to all matters relating to the (usually national) media system, including infrastructure, distribution facilities, ownership, financing, and organization. The level of the medium involves a distinction between established branches or types of media (e.g. radio, press, television, music), usually with differing technologies, patterns of organization, public communication roles, distinctive content patterns, sometimes also regulatory regimes (see Chapter 5). While it is common enough to encounter general statements about the state of a medium (television, film, or the newspaper press, for instance) in public debate, it is scarcely possible to evaluate a whole medium or to hold a medium as such accountable for any failing or consequence.

At the channel level, the reference is to a specific publication organ (newspaper groups or titles, television organizations or channels, service providers, cable companies, etc.). At this level decisions are made and executed that have consequences for publication and both evaluation and accountability may be directed at specific organizations. Finally, and most clearly, the level of content identifies specific publications and presentations (articles, pictures, programmes, films, advertisements, websites) which may be the object of criticism or accountability claims.

The distinction according to perspective identifies different roles in relation to media, different goals and interests, and different competences in assessment. The interests of society, expressed in many ways, often by governments and agencies of civil society, can involve attention to all levels of analysis and involve political and economic questions equally with social and cultural matters. The media professional has expertise in relation to technical, managerial, and creative aspects of media operation that is also likely to be applied to channels and output. Finally the audience (although hard to separate from the 'public' of civil society) is mainly here conceived in the role of consumer, applying criteria of personal taste, utility, or satisfaction to channels and output. The basic publication values as outlined above are drawn on in different ways according to level and perspective. Here we are mainly concerned with conduct and content, but all three perspectives are relevant. The specific criteria for assessment derived from the basic values are outlined in the following sections.

TRUTH CRITERIA IN MEDIA PERFORMANCE

The development of mass communication has resulted in the emergence of new genres and subgenres of symbolic expression that make it impossible to apply a single set of truth criteria. The sources of change and uncertainty lie both in new technological forms (visual, aural, and interactive media especially) and also in the conventions of genres that indicate different ways of reading an apparent message in a given contemporary culture. Even so the basic marks of truth in communication have not been eliminated, since they are still upheld by non-media institutions (law, commerce, education, science, religion, family).

The most relevant indicators of truth in the context of performance evaluation are summarily presented in Fig. 4.1. The entries in this figure are divided according to those that relate to qualities of the content and those relating to the authors and their actions. The first set may be embodied in professional routines and procedures and are open to some

Qualities of content	Qualities of author
Accuracy	Integrity
Reliability	Authenticity
Verisimilitude	Personal truth
Balance	Courage
Demonstrability	Openness
Relevance	

FIG. 4.1. Criteria of truth in publication

form of measurement. The second set are more variable and less frequent in manifestation and more subjective in character. There is an implication here that only original authors and sources can answer for the truth.

Accuracy and *reliability* both refer to intrinsic qualities of a text, including correspondence with an original text or a stated source, having an authoritative origin, avoidance of transmission errors, observance of rules of language, and the factual form of presentation. All features of texts that contribute to its reliability can be referred to, including the potential for verification and the status of sources. Reliability is a matter of perception and experience, but it is usually related to objective characteristics of an informational text. Accurate and reliable texts normally also meet criteria of completeness and relevance. True accounts should offer sufficient relevant information to be correctly comprehended. In this context, the test of comprehensibility may also be applied to establish truth value. *Verisimilitude* captures the notion that a message claiming to be true should conform to an apparent reality that is observable to others. Different 'true' accounts should be mutually consistent and match the experience and observation of receivers, where possible.

The criterion of *balance* recognizes the subjectivity and uncertainty of all perception and interpretation and looks for an acknowledgement and representation in accounts of different perspectives and interpretations that are likely to be relevant to understanding.

Demonstrability refers to the potential for proving some fact, idea, or proposition to be true, by whatever means, including experiments, measurements, or later events. *Relevance* to the matter at hand or to the 'reader' is an aspect of truth, since without it texts are less useful, clear, complete, or reliable.

Integrity refers both to the good faith and conscientiousness of the source or sender and also to internal doctrinal, ideological, or philosophical consistency. Interpretations of events that cannot be tested by criteria of factual accuracy should be convincing in this respect. *Authenticity* is a related principle, referring primarily to cultural aspects of media texts. Texts of all kinds can be considered to be more or less true to the principles and practice of the culture of those who create, receive, or participate in media content or are represented in it.

Aside from ideologies and belief systems, individuals may have personal visions of what is right and true, their *personal truth*, which only they can validate. The recognition of such personal versions of truth and the importance of free expression in respect of them in whatever chosen form is an important element of Western culture and a component in the notion of human rights.

Courage is a publication virtue related mainly to integrity and conscience, displayed by those who expose truths that are uncomfortable for a society or its authorities, guided by conscience, professionalism, or social concern. It extends to accepting the risk of punishment or harm for telling the truth. *Openness* refers to a clear identification by an author of position, interest, or values, candidness, and transparency of purpose. Anonymous communications and hidden propaganda are the opposite end of the range.

This set of criteria can in principle be applied as appropriate to a wide range of media texts in whatever form. However, the truth of a message is never a property of the text itself, but is a construct that can only be arrived at jointly by original authors and sources, observers and reporters, the recipients of communication, and (where relevant) the participants in events reported. In practice, the conditions for attaining any complete truth in relation to ongoing human affairs are not attainable and some more or less agreed conventions of what to regard as truthful communication have to be developed, including a notion of the good faith of the communicator.

These remarks lead to a consideration of the various forms and characteristics of untruth in the media that are most relevant to accountability claims, leaving aside incompetence, malice, and fantasy. Two particular forms have been singled out as problematic. *Bias* describes a systematic (although not necessarily intended) failure to follow certain norms of truthfulness, especially in relation to news and information, by selective attention, selective omission, one-sided interpretation, or implicit negative judgement. In fiction it can apply to negative stereotyping according to criteria such as ethnicity, gender, religion, social class, etc. *Propaganda*, on the other hand, refers to conscious and systematic efforts to use the means of public communication to advance an ideological cause or the material interest of the sender or source, often by covert means and without regard for anyone else's truth or the true interests of the recipient.

Expectations about truthful practice on the part of the media are not confined to the sphere of information, but can apply to fiction and drama that draws only indirectly on the reality of human experience and where there are many different truths to be told. Perceived honesty of intention and integrity of subject-matter and treatment are the main guarantees of truth. Nevertheless, there are many ways in which media fiction can lie about reality. It can misrepresent, ignore, vilify people, situations, events, places, and ideas in systematic ways under the guise of telling stories.

The concept of objectivity is most often invoked and debated in respect of the truth value of news, information, and documentary where a truth claim is made by the genre itself. Most aspects of the information quality of media news and information can be formally assessed according to the conventional principles of news objectivity, although there is room for uncertainty about what standards are appropriate where divergent perspectives, opinions, and values enter into the case. The principal criteria of the objectivity idea can be found set out in Fig. 4.1, especially accuracy, reliability, relevance, and balance. A key element in the practice of objective journalism is also factuality—the provision of information in a form that is precise, verifiable, and not tainted by opinion. Facts make a strong truth claim (see McQuail, 1992: 197).

The criterion of balance recognizes the difficulty of eliminating value judgements from accounts of reality. News journalism can deal with this by seeking to report alternative perspectives on events, from relevant sources and standpoints. It can also try to avoid value-laden or sensational forms of presentation. As Westerstahl (1983) made clear, objective news reports always have an evaluative as well as a cognitive dimension. The very fact of selecting topics for notice in the news is guided by values. The criterion of relevance is especially important in this respect to journalistic objectivity. Relevance involves judgements of significance that can be made according to several criteria, including past journalistic selection, scale and intensity of events, external authority or expert opinion, public opinion, audience interest, or the estimate of the consequences of events for the audience.

Despite much criticism (see e.g. Hackett, 1984), objectivity as defined has widely acquired a definition as the modal form for 'truthful' reporting, even beyond the context of Western forms of society (secular, democratic, and capitalist for the most part). It provides practical guidelines that journalism can follow in situations of conflict and uncertainty. It provides some protection to journalists from the potential risks of reporting critically on the activities of powerful or dangerous protagonists, since media can distance themselves from the evaluations, opinions, and 'bad news' they report. This helps to protect press freedom. It means that a single medium can act as a channel for opposing factions and points of view and by the same token allows a medium to widen its potential audience beyond the circle of any one particular belief. This capacity to widen an audience also allows for the growth of global media and international audiences. In general the objective mode is popular with audiences as well as with most journalists, its rules are widely understood, and it contributes to the perceived trust and reliability of media as sources of information (see Lichtenberg, 1990a; Ryan, 2001).

FREEDOM IN PUBLICATION

Although freedom is a condition, rather than a criterion or attribute, of publication and we cannot objectively determine the degree of freedom of publication (except where constraint is obvious) it is possible to trace connections between the freedom obtaining and some outcome in publication. Where the freedom of media is justified on instrumental grounds rather than as an end in itself (see Chapter 8), benefits should be apparent. The main conditions for the exercise of freedom of publication can be summarized as the absence of licensing, of advance censorship, of any obligations to publish, or of restrictive laws punishing publication after the event; the availability of (and realistic access to) the means of publication (diversity of channels and absence of monopoly); and the absence of other hidden pressures or controls that inhibit publication.

The link between freedom as a structural condition and outcomes in publication is summarized in a simplified way in Fig. 4.2 (based on McQuail, 1992: 167). The key elements in a system of media publication characterized by freedom are independence and diversity. 'Access' refers to the conduct of channels towards sources and authors, leading to more or less diversity. Independence as a structural condition means freedom *from* certain legal restraints and also from unacceptable degrees of

FREEDOM PRINCIPLE

Conditions:

Independence of channels		Access to Channels		Diversity of content

Leading to:

Reliability of information	Originality	Critical stance	Choice	Change

FIG. 4.2. Freedom: from structure to performance

pressure from owners (despite their rights over property), governments and politicians, powerful sources and suppliers, large advertisers, and external pressure groups. The existence of such pressures is inevitable (and they are part of the process of accountability) but there is often uncertainty and dispute about how far they have to be resisted.

The expected benefits of freedom of publication can be considered as evaluative criteria that apply to media conduct and performance in content. These include, especially, the following:

- willingness to scrutinize and criticize those with political and economic power;
- the provision of information that enables readers to form sound opinions and a critical outlook;
- active participation in the political, social, and cultural life of the society by means of information, advocacy, and involvement;
- the promotion of cultural and social innovation by way of information and amplification;
- the provision of access channels for diverse voices and purposes; and
- investigations of failure, injustice, and wrongdoing of all kinds.

It is clear on several points that the potential benefits of freedom can be negated or denied where independence is not present or acted on. There is also no guarantee of such benefits since media are free to perform badly. The strategic interests of media owners may not be served by criticism of governments and powerful interest groups. Their financial interests may not benefit from too much originality, investigation, or diversity in content. Governments have generally more to lose than to gain from freedom used in the ways indicated. Advertisers generally prefer uncontroversial and predictable environments for their message. Even audiences can shy away en masse from the conflict, controversy, and challenges that characterize the forms of publication that most exhibit the marks of freedom in action. The pursuit of the theoretical fruits of freedom of publication can thus prove in tension with the requirements of media as a profitable industry. In practice, some of the tension is taken care of by a division of labour and role within media, informally arrived at, by which specialisms of channel and genre develop that are devoted to critical, investigative, and innovative publication. There are also informal settlements and understandings that police the frontier of control and freedom between media and the outside world.

No general agreements, formal or informal, can eliminate the conflicts associated with the practice of free publication. In the context of accountability it has to be considered as a double-edged problem. There are frequently heard complaints, on public interest grounds, that the media continually abuse their freedom, whether by harming individuals or social groups, undermining order or offending against morals, decency, or public opinion. On the other hand, there are also allegations that media fail to use their freedom well and submit, for base motives, to the various pressures described. They become lap dogs rather than public watchdogs, conformist and consensual. Since no significant constituency is clearly injured or much offended by the selective silence and inactivity of mass media, this rarely leads to any claim or challenge. In practice, therefore, most accountability processes do tend to add more to the limits on freedom than to promote it (see Chapter 8).

SOLIDARITY AND EQUALITY

The manner in which the media are expected to meet central requirements of the equality and solidarity value can be explained by differentiating between the levels of structure, content, and audience. Each of these has its own key criterion of quality, relating, respectively, to access, representation, and reception.

At the level of media structure the main issue of equality is the degree to which access to channels is available to individuals and groups. This may be settled according to either economic or social rules. In the first case, equality obtains where all have an equal right to own and operate means of communication (normally guaranteed where there is freedom of the press). At the same time, the resources required are nowhere equally distributed so, in practice, there is no equal access at this level.

Social rules may operate either in the form of licensing (as with much radio and television transmission) where considerations of equality between different interests may be applied as a condition or in the form of public service broadcasting, where such conditions are normal.

The question of equality in representation in communication content raises similar issues to that of access as sender, although the conditions are rather different. An individual, idea, group, etc., appearing as a referent of media content, does not necessarily want or seek access at all and could not normally claim any right to be represented, whether or not equally. However, the quantity and quality of representation is potentially problematic. Complete lack of representation in media (invisibility) for components of a society or culture is more often than not regarded as detrimental, although less detrimental than representation on unfavourable or unwanted terms. While the explanation for media blindspots (and even bias) is often circumstantial, there are grounds in fairness for claiming visibility and on acceptable terms.

Equality of audience reception (opportunity and achievement) calls for an adequate (extensive and universal) distribution system and efforts to engage audiences. For equality of audience reception to be meaningful as a communication right, given the wide range of possible communication tastes, interests, and needs, there has to be a diverse, abundant, and changing supply. Equality is therefore connected with diversity, itself a primary benefit of freedom and a widely valued principle of public communication in societies that make a virtue of their pluralism (thus most contemporary democracies). The more there is equal or fair access for individuals or groups (communities, beliefs, cultures) as owners, senders, or referents, the greater the likely overall diversity of media system and provision and the more likely individual receivers are to have a relevant range of choice. A pluralistic society is then likely to communicate better with itself, reducing tensions and strains. The value of diversity stands conveniently opposed to some more or less agreed evils, including monopoly, cultural élitism or populism, oppressive propaganda, conformism, cultural homogenization, and globalization. It is positively associated with tolerance, co-operation, multiculturalism, respect for human rights, and cultural autonomy.

There are alternative standards for assessing the desirable or achieved degree of diversity, with two main contenders. One is with reference to a reflective or representative form of diversity, meaning that the outcome (in access or representation) should correspond in its distribution with the relevant population or context. Essentially, this is a fairness principle, with media access proportional to the situation in the society as a whole. The main alternative is the equality or open access for all principle. The former has more chance of realization, but it does not promote change and in some circumstances the approach to equal access is desirable, for instance in giving rights to reply and channels for minorities to speak to the wider society and a chance for the audience to hear competing voices.

Most of the problematic issues that arise under the heading of diversity relate to the broad conditions of a media system and most particular media organizations can disclaim responsibility. There is no obligation or promise of equal or proportional access for different groups and interests, except possibly in respect of public service broadcasting. It is not easy to support an accountability claim against a particular channel for specific omissions or a denial of access, or for the general lack of diversity of the whole system.

In the course of their normal operation the media implicitly promote identity and a sense of belonging to any of several social units within the national society. They are mainly territorially based and address specific national, regional, and linguistically defined publics. Within this primary identification (and sometimes cutting across it) are other potential identifications based on social, cultural, and other circumstances (race, gender, religion, etc.). The internal identity of many such social and subgroups can be strengthened or weakened, depending on whether or not they have their own (minority) media of communication and on how such groups are treated in the majority media of the whole society. Less obviously and effectively, media can provide networks of interconnection or awareness between different sectors and interests of the same national society (based, for instance, on sphere of employment, income, region, age, disability, etc.).

Social solidarity is promoted at the level of the national society by the reporting of economic and cultural (or military) successes or of crisis and disaster. One very common manifestation is the promotion of patriotic symbols and the celebration of national achievements. There is no shortage of evidence that news reporting consistently reports external (world) events from the standpoint of national interest. A somewhat different notion of solidarity applies to attempts to be inclusive within the national boundary. This applies to positive treatment of minority groups and also to sympathetic reports concerning problems and hardships suffered by fellow citizens, in respect of health, poverty, or other misfortune (the 'social empathy function' of media that promotes understanding and help). This process may also be shaped by a subtext that distinguishes between the 'deserving' and the 'undeserving' of our sympathy. From an international point of view, media can also be seen as either undermining or promoting a more global notion of shared concerns.

ORDER AND COHESION

Expectations about media performance deriving from principles of social order and cohesion cut across most distinctions of genre, embracing all informative, cultural, and entertainment publications. The main sub-principles are those of law and order, political consensus, morality and decarcy, and national identity and patriotism. The expectations concerning media performance that there give rise to can be described as follows.

LAW AND ORDER

In respect of law and order, the media should provide privileged access to the legitimate authorities that deal with issues of crime and justice, security and defence, public order, and crisis and emergency. These channels should connect responsible authorities and the general public, allowing information, advice, warning, instruction on issues of security and order to flow downward, as it were, but also to convey information, reactions, and public opinion upwards. More generally, the predominant messages of the media in reporting and cultural content should discourage and symbolically punish crime and anti-social behaviour and reward pro-social attitudes and activities.

POLITICAL CONSENSUS

Support is expected for established political systems and procedures, in the form of relevant news and background information and a general servicing of the needs of the main institutions of government, politics, and law. Although rules are largely unwritten in these matters, privileged access will go to mainstream political figures and views, reports of parliament and other elected bodies. Political moderation will have preference over marginal or extremist sources. Limits will be set to terms of debate and conflicts will be dealt with in a judicious and balanced way. Rules of 'political correctness' will apply on contentious issues where public utterances are relayed.

PUBLIC DECENCY AND MORALITY

Most media operate according to unwritten as well as written rules of conduct in matters of potential offence to public mores, which are never precisely knowable. The general expectation is that media will support the reigning consensus about what is acceptable in the publication of potentially sensitive content dealing mainly with sex and violence, or both, and ranging beyond into topics of sickness, death, and the occult. Certain widely disliked behaviours, such as drinking, gluttony, swearing, and drug-taking, often enter into the problem content area. In some places, religion and blasphemy are still sensitive areas of publication.

NATIONAL IDENTITY AND PATRIOTISM

Media are typically tied to their place of origin and area of distribution by shared interests and outlook and processes of identification that largely work automatically. Such ties are often made visible in media content and in audience preferences. Since many mass media have a national location and identity, they tend to express and reinforce the values of their national society and are open to judgement accordingly for displaying too little or too much patriotism or ethnocentricity. Most of the time these attributes are found in differential patterns of selection and attention, but also in evaluative tendencies, usually where issues of national culture and interests are at stake. Similar expressions of identity and loyalty show up in relation to regions, cities, and localities, with media generally acting to strengthen attachment and preach home virtues and values.

RIGHT PURPOSE AND RESPONSIBILITY

Quite a number of the attributes of media conduct and performance in public could be listed under the general idea of what is right and proper, as indicated by locally applying norms and standards, as reflected in public opinion or indicated by formal or informal regulation. This applies especially to media activities that involve claims to truth or which have implications for law and order (crime, violence, decency, morality, etc.) or are seen as carrying some risk of harm to individuals and society at the receiving end. The general notion needs little further explanation in terms of criteria that apply under this heading. However, some matters have not been mentioned that have mainly to do with various ethical issues and forms of private (or personal) benefit or possible harms. In particular, the following desirable features of behaviour on the part of all involved in publication decisions and acts need to be mentioned:

- Being able to defend acts of publication according to predominantly good intentions, of whatever kind.
- Practising honesty in acquiring information for subsequent publication.
- Respecting the privacy and dignity of those involved in, or affected by, news events.
- Taking steps to avoid (unintended) harmful effects for third parties as a result of publication.
- Honestly (and thus without regard to commercial or career considerations) weighing public benefit against harm to individuals as a result of publication.
- Taking reasonable account of any (predictable) harmful consequences of publication on an audience.
- Following such codes of professional ethics and conduct that are applicable.
- Listening to responses (negative as well as positive) from an audience and those affected by publication.

IN CONCLUSION

This chapter has attempted to sketch the main outlines of the evaluative framework within which most judgements about the media from the point of view of society are made. The ground covered does not correspond directly with the more limited terrain of 'media accountability'. But it does help to show what values are relevant to the behaviour of the media and might be drawn on in shaping claims. The main difference between the larger question of expectations from the media and accountability in practice lies in the fact that the latter takes up specific and/or individual complaints and the processes involved, while the former is mainly concerned with broad issues of correct (or incorrect) practice and general, but unacceptable, issues of benefit or harm. There may be overlaps, but it is also possible for the media to operate quite legitimately and according to the reigning norms of acceptable conduct and still provoke claims on grounds of offence or harm caused to individuals or groups. The media may also transgress against some of the norms outlined and yet have no fear of being called to account because there is no claimant or accepted ground on which to act. If accountability were possible an entire branch or media system would be in the dock.

NOTES

1. Jansen (1988: 37–8) traces the value of truth in free expression to Plato and his defence of Socrates. In *The Apology*, Socrates is quoted as saying: 'If you propose to acquit me on condition that I abandon my search for truth, I will say: I thank you, O Athenians, but I will obey God, who, I believe, set me this task'. Plato goes on to assert that he will never refuse to say in public what he would say or think in private. As well as a strong claim for truth, it is also an affirmation of the 'sovereignty of conscience against arbitrary authority'.
2. In her examination of 195 US Supreme Court cases (between 1931 and 1995) in which issues of media responsibility arose, Hindman (1997) showed that 'the Court has valued the political and educational functions and defined press responsibility in terms of truth-telling and stewardship'.
3. Ettema and Glasser define the solidarity value as 'establishing an empathic link between those who have suffered in the situation and the rest of us' (1998: 189).
4. There are a great variety of forms ranging from the élite financial and political national daily newspaper to the sensational tabloid, with variants on several dimensions and standards and expectations to match.

PART III

Governance and Public Roles
of the Media

5

The Governance of the Media
Issues and Forms

CONTROLLING FREE MEDIA

The issue of accountability has to be addressed within some framework of governance in the widest sense. In contemporary usage, 'governance' describes systems and processes of control that are decentralized and multiple, involving networks of contacts, private as well as public agencies and activities, internal as well as external mechanisms, informal as well as formal pressures, incentives, and sanctions. It covers all means by which the mass media are limited, directed, encouraged, managed, or called to account, ranging from the most binding law to the most resistible of pressures and self-chosen disciplines. Governance has been described as 'government without politics', which is especially apt in this case, since political interventions in the media are more sensitive than in other areas of policy. Governance always involves some notion of a norm or standard, coupled with some procedures, of varying strictness, for enforcement. The use of force or arbitrary power to restrict or punish is also incompatible with the idea of governance.

The reasons for control and thus for media governance are not usually set out in any document and may even be hidden from view. They are often ambiguous and inconsistent. While they all derive in one way or another from the social, economic, and political value and power of the media, there are numerous potential beneficiaries and stakeholders. Five general reasons for control can be proposed. Firstly it is in order to protect the established order and provide government and other public authorities with means of influence. Secondly, control is needed to protect the many private and sectional rights and interests from potential harm or injustice and also to protect society from more general harm to morals, core values, etc. These two reasons usually imply some regulation of content. Thirdly, control may be seen as enlarging freedom of communication, when it opens up new channels, promotes equal access and universal provision, and encourages competition and diversity. Fourthly, it may be needed to advance or protect the values outlined in Chapter 4. Finally, control encourages change and technological innovation in directions that are thought to be of long-term economic benefit to the society.

ISSUES OF ACCOUNTABILITY

Both external control and also self-control are incomplete without some form of accountability, although control of media is not the same as media accountability and the two can be separately analysed and described. In exploring the values associated with publication and the expectations of society from the media, it is necessary to make two distinctions, one between public and private consequences and another between seeking benefit and avoiding harm. It is also helpful to display the various issues that arise in accountability processes according to these two dimensions, as indicated in Fig. 5.1.

Not all relevant issues fit neatly into any one exclusive category and the dimensions themselves are not clear cut or simple to apply. For instance a concern with law and order can be considered as both securing benefits and avoiding harm. Nevertheless, the classification is a reminder of underlying differences in the possible source and nature of claims that arise from publication. A summary description of issues is offered as follows, employing only the public/private distinction.

TYPE OF ISSUE

	Public	*Private*
Beneficial	Public sphere benefits	Quality of content or service

DIRECTION

	Harmful	Harm to society	Harm to persons or interests

FIG. 5.1. Classification frame for issues of accountability

ISSUES THAT ARE PRIMARILY PUBLIC
AND/OR COLLECTIVE

The protection of public order and security of the state   There are circumstances when publication has a potential for damaging security and
order. The issues of alleged danger or threat to the society relate mainly
to military and defence secrets; crime and criminals, with media having
a potential role in combating or stimulating crime; terrorist and insurgent activities, where publicity can be a weapon to counter or assist the
aims of terrorists; and civil disturbance and riots, where much the same
is thought to apply.

Respect for public mores   Most societies maintain broadly accepted
thresholds of taste and decency in relation to what is published,
especially in widely available forms, independently of issues of actual
harm. The matters involved usually have to do with the portrayal of sex
and nudity, language, graphic portrayals of violence, etc., which have a
potential for causing public offence. Offence to religious belief or sens-
ibility (blasphemy) belongs to the same category. Issues of taste and
respect also arise in relation to the representation of illness, death, bodily
functions, cruelty to animals, etc. Gratuitous disrespect for authority
and the degradation of national or patriotic symbols can be a matter for
control on grounds of public offence.

Securing public sphere benefits   Media publication can greatly assist or
hinder the normal work of politics, government, and the judicial system.
They are relied on for informational and other services, even if this is not
their primary purpose and it cannot be compelled or always legislated for.
In this context, public sphere benefits come in the form of extensive and
open flows of reliable, diverse, and relevant information. Critical and
politically or socially deviant publication has a contribution to make,
even if it is unlikely to be encouraged by any authority. Beyond a
minimum level of service from the media that the free market is likely
to deliver, there is much more that can be done to extend and enrich the
public sphere by way of information, access, and involvement. Media vary
in their willingness to serve other social institutions without any reward
or compulsion.

Cultural issues   Three main sub-issues can figure as a source of
claims against the media or as a basis for expectations of public
good. Firstly, there may be an appeal to the general quality of media
provision, according to reigning standards of art, education, and

culture. Secondly, there is the matter of support for the national language and culture, especially where this may be threatened by some form of foreign cultural invasion. Thirdly, there are issues of adequate provision for cultural minorities within a national society.

Human rights   The media are increasingly subject to requirements of respect for the human rights of social groups of various kinds, as they are represented in the media. Questions of prejudice, discrimination, access, and neglect are posed by those affected and by proponents of justice and solidarity.[1]

Harm to society   Fears are often expressed about the general and long-term effects on society as a result of unrestrained or irresponsible mass media publication, even where no harm is intended or envisaged. A wide range of issues is involved, including the social, educational, and moral problems of children and young people; the encouragement of crime, violence, anti-social behaviour, or aggression; a decline in moral standards; promiscuity and sexual deviance; and the encouragement of materialism and consumerism.

International obligations   National media often impinge on the territory of others and are potentially affected in some measure by the laws of other countries. Some systems of distribution (especially satellite, radio, and telecommunications) need international agreements to operate effectively. International institutions that deal with global issues of war, peace, justice, and social and economic development depend on some recognition or support from international media (see Hamelink, 1994). Although the principle of the 'free flow' of communication has generally trumped territorial sovereignty, there are still contentious issues (for instance, the different national laws relating to Internet website content).

ISSUES OF A MORE PRIVATE, INDIVIDUAL CHARACTER

The protection of individual rights   On a number of points, media actions are challenged on the grounds of the violation of rights of individuals that may take precedence over rights of freedom to publish. These issues relate mainly to possible defamation of character or actual physical harm (through incitement).

Offence to individuals   Aside from the large question of respect for reigning standards of taste and decency, there are many possibilities for publication to cause shock or offence to particular individuals, often unpredictably and without intention, sometimes as a result of accidental exposure to content intended for others. The nature of harm varies, but includes shock, alarm, fear, distress, and insult.

Individual harm   Numerous cases arise where a specific publication is suspected of causing a specific harm to an individual recipient, or of provoking a specifically harmful act. Most such harms relate to the imitation of, or stimulation to perform, an action of a criminal or violent nature, including suicide. Alleged corrupting effects on individuals from obscene or pornographic publications fall in the same category. Publication may also incite hatred or acts of physical harm to identified individuals or groups.

The protection of property rights in communication and information   The idea of intellectual property has been well established since at least the seventeenth century in Europe in respect of patents and printed works and has become even more salient as information becomes more central and more commercially valuable. The categories of information that can claim legal protection are multiplying, as reflected in the value placed on Internet domain names and the large sums spent on logos, images, etc. In principle, many rights in communication, whether public or private, also acquire some potential claim to legal protection.

OTHER MATTERS FOR REGULATION: STRUCTURE
AND ECONOMY

This description of accountability issues does not exhaust the potential list of reasons for systems of governance. There are a number of essentially structural or system issues to do with allocation of resources, economic regulation, and technical standards that also give rise to accountability. The Internet has widened the range of such issues, for instance in relation to encryption, cybercrime, and e-commerce. These are not central to the notion of accountability as defined in this book, since they are typically remote from actual issues of publication, where it is much easier for government to intervene.

The facilities for public communication depend on building and managing infrastructure of various kinds. They consume resources and often need to be allocated between competing operators in order to maximize the public interest. Questions of access to, and diversity of, the communication structures and many kinds of connectedness to communication networks are also central. Although these matters are also remote from the moment of publication they have long-term consequences for media conduct and performance.

Mass media have also become a significant area of economic activity and are regulated for the same reasons and in the same ways as other firms. In general, the unusual situation of mass media as a business affected by a public interest is often reflected in the politicization of certain decisions that would normally be left to market forces or to the normal market rules and regulatory agencies.

THE VARIED CHARACTER OF MEDIA GOVERNANCE

Control of the media may be inevitable but it often sits uneasily with aspirations to free expression and creativity. Its acceptability varies according to the type of medium concerned, the closeness of control to the point of publication, and the form taken by control. Even more so, perhaps, it varies according to the societal context, with different legal traditions and political cultures determining what is possible. On the first point, there has been a general acceptance, despite occasional protests, of the fact that broadcast (and similar) media may be extensively controlled for technical reasons, or on grounds of public policy. On the second point, control is more acceptable the more distant it is from actual content decisions. Rules about media ownership and conditions of access to channels (licensing) are accepted in principle. Pre-publication censorship by outside bodies or punishment after the event for (otherwise legal) expression are rejected. In between the two are many possibilities for control affecting content that may be accepted or not according to local conditions and circumstances. It is clear that freedom of publication does not protect all expression equally (see Chapter 8).

Much depends on the third element mentioned, the forms of control that are applied. These fall into five main categories: formal law and regulation; ethical and normative guidelines embodied in measures of self-government; the disciplines of the market; the media system's own technology and organization (its 'architecture'); and informal pressures of all kinds. For the most part, the restraining (or liberating) effects of the system and its architecture, as well as the working of the market, are accepted as more or less given and inevitable, although with occasional resistance. Specific legal rules and regulations affecting content are generally contested, but accepted as necessary in some cases where harm, offence, or trespass on the rights of others can be demonstrated. Ethical constraints are more ambiguously regarded and much depends on the degree of self-government involved and the lack of compulsion. There are fears, amongst journalists for instance, that ethical rules can 'creep' and acquire the status of regulation (Voakes, 2000; Drechsel, 1992).

This reflects a more general circumstance, that the various realms of control indicated are not strictly separated from each other and often overlap in their operation. The reference to informal pressure as means of control is in recognition of the fact that various agents of power seek to influence media content by various inducements or threats. Even legal and regulatory authorities often prefer to use informal means of control in place of formal powers, because of sensitivity about censorship, but also because they are sometimes more effective.[2] In general it can also be said of the means of control that threats and penalties are much less good at achieving improvements or benefits than at preventing some abuse.

Hoffmann-Riem (1996: 290) observes that strict and specific normative requirements by regulators are often counter-productive. In respect of the broadcasting sector, he distinguishes between an 'imperative' (or command and control) model and a 'structural' model. The former is mainly employed to control publication activities such as the advertising of drugs or alcohol or pornography, but it may have positive aims as in the former US Fairness doctrine, or as currently in Europe to safeguard minority and cultural programming and protect children. The 'structural' model seeks to influence outcomes by setting rules for the system as a whole and some guidelines for access, conduct, and service quality.

What follows is a typification of the ways in which relationships between the media and society are managed. In keeping with the definition of governance given above, there is really no system of control as such, only a set of loosely related processes occurring at different levels of operation and for specific purposes. The terrain can be divided according to two main dimensions, external versus internal and formal versus informal forms of governance, as sketched in Fig. 5.2. The labels describe the main types of governance, which are also guides to the main means of accountability, to be discussed in more detail later. In reality the distinctions are not easy to sustain. In particular, internal forms of governance (both formal and informal) are often prompted by external pressure.

FORMS OF GOVERNANCE

	FORMAL	INFORMAL
EXTERNAL	Law and regulation	Market forces and relations Pressures and lobbies Public opinion Review and criticism
INTERNAL	Management and financial control Self-regulation	Professionalism Organizational culture Norms and ethics

FIG. 5.2.   Typology of forms of governance

LEVELS OF ACTION AND ASSOCIATED ISSUES

Media governance projects operate at several levels, ranging from the international to the local. At the international level, the main issues that have arisen concern national sovereignty over communication space; technical and infrastructural matters requiring co-operation, such as the allocation of frequencies and satellite positions and now aspects of management of the Internet; copyright on cross-border publication, transmission, and reception; securing communication rights; propaganda and hostile communication; regional agreements between nations for common goals (as in Europe, North America, South-East Asia, the Arab sphere, etc.); the balance of international media flow; free trade in media products and services; development matters; and human rights. The main actors have generally been governments and representatives of major industries, with national publics playing little part.

Generally, industrial and economic policies and logics have dominated the scene. For such purposes international agencies such as the International Telegraph Union (ITU), the World Trade Organization (WTO), or World Administrative Radio Conference (WARC) have been effective because they promote the economic interests of major countries and media firms in a non-political way. Some media have their own international organizations that are concerned with protecting their interests against unwanted intervention. The Internet, of its nature, requires some form of international organization (see below). In the European region, the EU has managed to assemble elements of a system of transnational governance that has some scope for influence beyond the purely technical and administrative (e.g. in matters of freedom, diversity, advertising, content standards, and cultural integrity).

The fulcrum of media governance remains the national level, since the nation state is still the main political unit and because most mass media still operate predominantly within the boundaries of the nation state. Moreover, there are few genuinely international media, in the sense of publication and distribution organizations with significant global audiences, even though media products in the form of entertainment and information increasingly circulate in an international market and some operate under national flags of convenience (e.g. some transnational satellite broadcasters). In most countries a full range of policies and regulatory agencies for all media is to be found at national level and some typical features of this array are described separately below.

What counts as a region for administrative purposes varies a good deal from country to country (there are, for instance, significant differences between a US state, a German *land*, a UK province, and a Spanish autonomous community). A widely recognized ideal situation is one where there is both relevant local provision, and also local competition between media. Local voices and channels and locally resident minority communities also need recognition and access in national media. The more that regions (as opposed to localities) have some political and cultural autonomy (and especially a linguistic identity), the more likely they are to claim channels of their own on a par with national standards of provision. Countries with federal systems usually make provision for the devolution of some powers over the media. Germany is probably the leading example, with broadcasting and press laws existing for each of the sixteen *Lander*. In the United States (largely because of a general absence of media regulation), states and local authorities only have jurisdiction over some aspects of cable operations.

VARIATIONS IN THE *LOCUS* OF CONTROL

In addition to level in the administrative/territorial sense, the various issues outlined earlier can arise at different places in the media system or process of communication. This has direct implications for what mechanisms of governance might be both appropriate and effective and also for the precise point at which accountability takes place. The capacity of democratic societies to manage communication systems in an effective and legitimate way (thus for good reasons and without violating norms of media freedom) depends on making such distinctions. The simplest model is one that distinguishes between (and interrelates) media structure, conduct, and performance. This sequence corresponds approximately to stages in the process of publication and also to the relative distance from the act of publication and the product. For the most part, structure refers to the media system, conduct to what media organizations do, and performance to content and consequences.

GOVERNANCE AT THE LEVEL OF STRUCTURE

Structure refers to ownership (forms and actual arrangements), to legal conditions as well as the infrastructure for production and distribution. The term architecture of the communication system, referring to the arrangements of parts in relation to others in real or notional space, is also apposite (Lessig, 1999). Different media offer different possibilities for regulation. This is a large terrain governed by a wide range of instruments of control, including government policy, laws, financial measures, and technical and other regulations, all varying according to the nature of the particular media branch, as indicated below. Control of structure in itself does not necessarily have any direct implications for actual content published or disseminated, thus allowing a wider scope for intervention by society in structure without trespassing on media freedom. The main structural matters that attract some form of governance on grounds of public interest are as follows.

- The relationship between the state and the media.
- Conditions for owning or operating mass media in the national territory.
- Concentration of ownership and competition.
- Public ownership of media and accompanying regulation.
- Diversity, access, and universal service.
- Infrastructural questions, with especial reference to transmission facilities for electronic media.

Typically, all of these topics belong within the public domain and are subject to political debate or policy proposal. They are all likely to be dealt with, if at all, by forms of governance that are formal and external (laws and regulations), although informal pressures play some part. On the whole they are distinct from the set of accountability issues outlined earlier in this chapter. They do not normally provide a basis for claims against the media since they relate to the general condition of a notional media system or institution that does not exist as a legal entity and cannot be called to account.

GOVERNANCE AT THE LEVEL OF CONDUCT

The area of conduct refers to what media organizations do internally and in relation to their environment and mainly falls under the scope of self-government. Even so, certain issues of conduct do enter over into the public domain. Amongst these are the following:

- Editorial independence and the internal freedom of editors, journalists, and other creative personnel within media organizations.[3]
- Ties to sources and issues of equity, transparency, and probity in gaining information and giving access.
- Questions relating to privacy and confidentiality are both aspects of conduct as well as of content and of ethics.
- Ethical matters. Many aspects of the selection, treatment, and presentation of content and professional self-government.

GOVERNANCE AT THE LEVEL OF PERFORMANCE

The performance of the media relates primarily to matters of content, quality, and effects, and the public interest issues arising have largely been dealt with already. It is in this area that detailed claims are made by individuals and on behalf of groups or society as a whole. They relate to quality (variously defined), to potential harmful effects, and to benefits claimed or looked for from the media in terms of order, public sphere expectations, and cultural provision. By definition, free media control what they publish and in principle external control can only be applied after the fact of publication. Most content issues are settled by media managements according to their internal policy and market conditions. Even so, there is some scope for external control and accountability. Issues of content are more likely (than those of structure or content conduct) to be a matter of general public awareness and deep feeling, especially where norms of public decency, patriotism, ethics, and lawful conduct are invoked. The media are more susceptible to pressure on such specific points, where their actual rights to publish are not challenged (only particular actions) and where their own commercial interests are not necessarily at stake.

FORMS OF GOVERNANCE: FORMAL AND EXTERNAL
AGENCIES AND MEANS

The state, or its executive arm, always has ultimate power to control the media, by suppression, taking over control, and banning certain publications if need be through supra-legal, though not necessarily illegal, actions. In democracies, this can only be justified by considerations of 'real and present danger' to the public or state, to cite the US doctrine on this matter.[4] More often, the state and its security agencies prefer to use more informal means: threats, pressures, favours and news management, or private appeals to media on grounds of public interest. The terrain of state intervention and influence cannot be fully mapped and it varies considerably from one country to another, depending on the political culture. Freedom of publication notwithstanding, there are numerous grounds for interference.[5] But the main forms and means include the following:

- Constitutional provisions guaranteeing freedom, but often indicating some limitations with respect to the rights of others.[6]
- The justice system and general law (including international agreements) play an important role in relation to the media, freedom notwithstanding, allowing claims against the media to be pursued by individuals and outside interests, including government. There are numerous legal requirements relevant to public communication but not necessarily specific to the mass media. These cover such matters as libel, privacy rights, freedom of speech, intellectual property rights, freedom or control of information, contempt of court, election and political campaign conditions, opinion polling, official secrets legislation, respect for national symbols or high office holders, respect for human rights, public order, obscenity and blasphemy, and more.
- There is also a body of media law that applies specifically to mass media in many countries. Apart from early press censorship laws, this generally began in the form of legal provisions for particular media, beginning with telegraphy, wireless (point to point) radio, and telephony, and continuing with laws for radio and television broadcasting and on through the range of new media and new forms of distribution (cable, satellite, etc.). Much of this kind of law can be generally regarded as enabling as well as restricting. Specific aspects of the newspaper press have been legislated for in

some countries, usually with a view to protecting them from concentration or closure.[7]

In the many countries in which there is a public broadcasting system, there is always at least one branch of media law with an extensive reach over structure, conduct, and broad lines of performance (see Barendt, 1993; Hoffmann-Rien, 1996; Crauford-Smith, 1997). Media laws vary according to local circumstances, traditions, and political culture.[8] In Europe and elsewhere (Japan, Australia, Israel, India, etc.) the single most dominant agency of media governance has been (and often still is) a public broadcasting organization instituted and financed (directly or indirectly) by government and usually answerable to the national parliament. In some cases they were overtly used as instruments for government and political party influence.

- An accelerating trend has also been the establishment of national centralized media regulatory agencies with wide responsibilities over different media (see Robillard, 1995). Examples include the Conseil Superieur de L' Audivisual (CSA) in France, the new OfCom in the United Kingdom, the High Authority for the Media (AAM) in Portugal, the Media Council in the Netherlands. The main impetus has been the convergence of different media plus the wish to have a more coherent and consistent regulatory regime.[9] These bodies have a multiple function as agencies of government media policy, a mechanism of accountability, a forum for settling disputes, and a channel for public reactions and complaints.

GOVERNANCE: INFORMAL AND EXTERNAL FORMS

Media structure, conduct, and the performance of the media are open to outside influence from various sources by a range of other more informal means, some permanent and general, many occasional and issue specific. The principal manifestations are as follows:

- The media market is the most influential source of outside pressure, even though it is not usually thought of as a form of control, since it is itself largely undirected, having no 'purpose' or 'policy'. Even so, the disciplines of competition and the demands of clients and audiences are very constraining in a consistent and predictable way and have a bearing on a range of publication issues.

- Governments have other means for bringing pressure to bear on media, aside from legislation or direct regulation. One ubiquitous means of influence is the political control of some appointments to otherwise independent agencies of regulation or co-regulation. A device used in the post-war period (1945–75) was to appoint a Commission or Committee of Inquiry to examine aspects of media structure and performance, on behalf of the public interest or even ostensibly on behalf of the media themselves. These bodies typically had a quasi-governmental character, but qualify as informal because of their occasional character and very limited powers, especially where the press was concerned.[10] The direct results of such inquiries in terms of more effective control or improved standards have generally been judged as meagre. But, equally, little or no evidence of any harm to press freedom has been found and their activities had the general effect of stimulating debate, collecting evidence, and reminding the press of their potential responsibilities to society.

- There are numerous other possibilities for pressure on the media from outside bodies or organized public opinion. Many interest and pressure groups target the media on their own behalf, especially in search either of attention to their cause or of more favourable (or less negative) representation (see Montgomery, 1989). Some agencies are set up specifically to monitor media coverage on particular issues and use findings and publicity as a point of leverage.[11] In many countries there are voluntary consumer organizations acting on behalf of the audience that aim to reform the media, especially on matters to do with morals, decency, ethics, young people, and family values.

- Aside from such organized pressure groups, there is a permanent influence from public opinion that reaches the media by way of the media's own audience research as well as from general public opinion surveys. Topics typically relate to current issues, especially relating to sex and violence, but also to political bias and media coverage of big issues (war, disaster, scandal).

- Review and criticism of the media in other media has been a growing element of informal influence, as the range and diversity of media systems have grown and the 'media' themselves have become a major topic of coverage.

- Education and research carried out by independent non-profit bodies (including universities) have a potential for the surveillance of media performance. Book and specialist journal publications as well as teaching can make an input into public debate and ultimately into professional conduct and even government policy.

GOVERNANCE: FORMAL AND INTERNAL CONTROL

There are three main types of formal internal control (that can be relevant for public accountability), although the line between what counts as internal rather than external is not at all clear. These are ownership; management; and professional self-regulation. The first two can be dealt with together.

OWNERSHIP AND MANAGEMENT

Most media are private property that can be used for whatever publication purposes their owners choose. This inevitably involves owners in the wider governance process. Most relevant in this context are three matters: the degree to which they choose a politically influential role in society or are regarded by political actors as so doing; secondly, the degree to which the pursuit of purely commercial objectives interferes with the (chosen or not) political or social role of the media; and, thirdly, the use of actual powers of ownership in relation to publication decisions. In contemporary democratic societies there are some normative expectations in all three areas, although the reality is often different from the norm and also hard to establish. Firstly, if media owners choose a political role they can no longer claim to be simply running a business. Secondly, publication cannot only by guided by profit motives, without surrendering some claims to professionalism and status. In practice, most of the time, the wishes of owners are adequately served by voluntary (and thus informal) anticipation of their wishes, without any need for censorship.

It is obvious that day-to-day management of the media and all that lies behind it in terms of organizational structures, routines, and practice are at the core of the governance process as defined earlier. Much of what enters the scope of public accountability consists of actions that have been chosen or approved by media managers (decision-makers). It is reasonable to conclude that privately owned media are to a large extent governed by their owners and managers. This means that the power of media is indeed concentrated in a relatively small set of hands in most countries and also across countries.

Of particular significance are the numerous trade associations that exist nationally and internationally in almost all branches of the media. Their aims are to protect the self-interest of member organizations and they can often form powerful lobbies in respect of government policy and regulation.

MEDIA SELF-REGULATION

Straddling the boundary between external and internal control (because they are often the result of external pressure and serve to manage relations with the outside) are numerous forms of media self-regulation. Goldberg *et al.* (1998: 313) stress the continuity between formal regulation and self-regulation, what is sometimes called co-regulation. They characterize it as a 'technique of regulation rather than an alternative to regulation'. Dennis (1995: 697), while stressing the lack of formal accountability in the United States, observes that 'public criticism of the news media has . . . inevitably led to a de facto system of accountability'. The same applies to other democratic systems. Unlike management control, self-regulation follows certain set procedures and normally has a public face. It mainly deals with issues of conduct and content, where freedom of action is claimed by the media, but where normative limitations are also recognized. The application of self-regulation is sometimes required by agencies of government as an alternative to direct regulation, for instance in the case of classification of films or of videos for hire or where licensing conditions require some form of monitoring, codes, or complaint procedures.[12]

Bertrand (2000) has elaborated on the concept of 'media accountability systems' which include the terrain under discussion, but also on forms of external response. He defines a 'media accountability system' as 'any non-state means of making media responsible to the public'. The main general means he identifies are training; evaluation (criticism of performance); monitoring; and feedback (to and from the public). The thirty-seven different accountability systems that he identifies are classified as either internal (including surveys, ombudsmen, and ethical codes); external (including media education, journalism reviews, monitoring watchdogs, consumer organizations, and regulatory agencies); or co-operative (letters to editor, press councils, public access). The first and last categories at least qualify as self-regulation.

Aside from the wish to escape external control, self-regulation is adopted for two main and divergent reasons, one being to present a favourable public image, the other a wish to raise professional standards. The earliest examples of self-regulation are to be found in the publication of codes of journalistic practice or ethics, dating back to the 1920s. These codes typically express general ideals and minimum rules of conduct designed to protect the public and also the objects of reporting and their sources (see Nordenstreng and Topuz, 1989; Laitila, 1995; and Chapter 13). Press councils were widely instituted to administer self-regulation and later the institution of the ombudsman or audience representative in disputes. In television, production codes were instituted (sometimes also for film), typically applied by management with more rigour and designed to reassure the public and regulators and to limit potential harm. Advertising often has its own codes of standards and industry mechanisms for dealing with complaints which contribute to improving the generally rather negative image of advertising.

Even where the collective media will is present to police their own actions, the means of enforcement are rarely available, outside the broadcasting sector. Both the strength of self-regulation and its compatibility with media freedom are usually thought to reside in its voluntarism. The enforcement of judgments, except in the minimal form of corrections or apologies, is usually regarded by the press itself as a danger to freedom as well as contrary to the spirit of self-regulation. Nevertheless, the current trends of media expansion and deregulation increasingly rely on self-regulation to meet the demands of public opinion for quality and accountability (see Chapter 13).

Defenders of media freedom do not necessarily welcome this tendency, especially where news journalism is concerned. There is some force in the view (see Kepplinger and Koecher, 1990) that effective self-regulation would be incompatible with some essential aspects of the journalistic role (especially as social critic and catalyst or watchdog on those with power). It has also been remarked that the professionalization of journalism brings with it greater possibilities for control and the likelihood of conformity rather than increasing independence.[13]

GOVERNANCE: INFORMAL AND INTERNAL CONTROL

It is typical of organizations that have creative, normative, or ideological tasks that internal participants play an active part in setting and realizing goals, without following fixed rules. This topic is difficult to deal with systematically as an aspect of governance, but also impossible to leave out of account. Media professionals and authors are always making choices and taking decisions on their own account, for which they are willing to accept responsibility, and also trying to influence other individuals and also the activities of the organization. Because of their semi-public character, media actors also from time to time step out of their internal role and seek to exert wider influence.

In addition, there are innumerable pathways of informal influence inside the larger institution and across its border. Norms of conduct and working practice are set informally within the workplace and learned through informal socialization and example (see Breed, 1956). Some of the more visible features of internal, informal control are to be found in various activities connected with the notion of professionalism. These include professional education and in-house training; a wide range of more or less internal (but open) publications (such as journalism reviews); plus competitions, festivals, and prize-giving events that are conducted by and for a wide range of media. These activities highlight matters of skill, performance, and success and develop internal standards of good performance. There is no way to measure the influence of all this, but it is likely that peer judgement is more influential than most external forms of accountability and it extends across the boundaries of any single media organization.

INTER-MEDIA DIFFERENCES RELEVANT TO GOVERNANCE

The scope of control and regulation varies considerably between different kinds of media, with a basic distinction to be observed between three main media types with corresponding regulatory models (see Pool, 1983). The *print* media model is the oldest and it involves the least degree of regulation, mainly because print has benefited most directly from democratic and libertarian trends and long-established principles of free expression.[14] In addition, they can be regarded as 'consultation' media (Bordewijk and van Kaam, 1986) in the sense that the initiative in their use is generally taken by the 'reader', who is thus an active, voluntary, and responsible partner in their use. The audience, consequently, does not need to be protected from unwanted influence.

As far as technology of production and distribution are concerned the film medium and to a certain extent that of recorded music belong within the same category as printing. Both are essentially consultation media, with items of published content selected and paid for by audience members. Certain principles of artistic and cultural freedom of expression also apply to film and music. Nevertheless, neither (especially not film or popular music) has enjoyed the same degree of freedom from regulation as enjoyed by print media. The social control of film originally stemmed from the regulation of public performance (in relation to health, safety, timing of public showings, etc.). However, much more stems from an early and widespread anxiety about the potential impact of film, especially on the impressionable young, leading to a fear of harmful effects (see Foerstal, 1998; Sutter, 2000). Regulation of film and music has origins in the public control of theatrical shows and reflects their identification mainly as entertainment or art, rather than as political media.

The second model (in chronological terms) is that of so-called *common-carrier* media. These are forms of communication designed for individual point-to-point, often interactive, communication processes. The earliest example is that of mail, followed by the electric telegraph, then the telephone and personal wireless telephony. Currently the category of relevant media is much enlarged to include mobile phones and the numerous different uses of the Internet (although where this belongs is still not settled). From the beginning such media, whether used for personal or business purposes, were regarded as public facilities, but for private use.

The contents carried are regarded as private and intended only for the person at the point of reception. This principle of mail, telephone, and e-mail privacy (and thus freedom from content regulation) is widely agreed, although it is subject to some other considerations of public interest (e.g. in relation to crime and security of the state) and also criteria of misuse and deliberate harm to others (leading to prohibitions on sending certain items). Common-carrier media constitute networks connecting everyone to everyone. They have gradually become internationalized, so that we are potentially connected to a global network, limiting the effectiveness of any national-level controls and regulations and extending international control across frontiers.[15]

The third model, that of *broadcasting*, originated in the 1920s, when the uses of radio were extended in many countries to become the means of public communication from 'one to many' (or mass dissemination in some cases). The model is usually characterized in terms of its original means of transmission: powerful ground transmitters covering a delimited geographical range and with limited channel capacity. An essential feature of such transmission was the fact that available and usable radio frequencies (spectrum) were limited in number. The allocation of this transmission space to competing applicants became the basis for close supervision, quasi-monopoly systems, and extensive regulations for content and purpose.

Much the same considerations applied to television up to the introduction of satellite transmission in the 1980s. In addition to the issue of spectrum scarcity, the control of broadcasting was justified by a belief in its potential impact in and on society that far exceeded that of film. This helps to explain why there has been no great reduction of regulation as scarcity has diminished, nor much prospect of it disappearing soon. The mainly territorial character of broadcasting has made it both easier and more acceptable for broadcast media to be asked to conform to the norms and values of the area they cover (locality, region, or nation state). Rights to free expression in broadcasting have gained more recognition but they have also continued to be contested, partly on grounds of fairness (justice), diversity, and equality in matters of access as well as on grounds of impact. The separate identity of these three models has been reduced by the development of cable and satellite distribution systems from the 1970s onwards. These were much less constrained by capacity, but they were still regulated for other reasons, although in differing ways and degrees in different countries. They still generally lag behind terrestrial distribution as a means of delivery. The fact of lower regulation does not seem in itself to have been a major factor in their diffusion.

Aside from the question of different regulatory regimes, different media offer different practicalities for the where and when of any legitimate intervention, thus varying according to the particular architecture of each medium. The physical arrangements of book and newspaper production make them vulnerable to intervention, even though they are formally most protected. Their output is also easy to monitor. Broadcast or cabled radio and television are usually controlled at the point of entry and vulnerable to interference at the point of transmission. On the other hand, the volume of continuous output defies close monitoring at the point of transmission.

THE HYBRID REGULATORY STATUS OF INTERNET (WEB)-BASED MEDIA

The Internet is still relatively free from (and proof against) routine control of access and content, but it too operates under a variety of constraints and it is dependent on a technological infrastructure that is outside the control of any publisher but within the control of largely unaccountable business firms and service providers. There are also signs that entry barriers are rising (Goldberg et al., 1998: 297). Along with its freedom it lacks any guarantee against arbitrary (even secret) intervention by authorities of one kind or another. According to Lessig (1999), its potential 'regulability' stems largely and paradoxically from its own intrinsic architecture, especially its dependence on 'code'. Its electronic form makes it particularly vulnerable to automatic surveillance programmes.

Its uses are also particularly susceptible to arbitrary private censorship by Internet service providers (ISPs) and other 'gatekeepers', and it is especially under threat from private claims or government legal pressures. According to Kim (1999: 80), 'First Amendment rights on the Internet have a snowball's chance in hell'. A few years later this seems just as applicable. The possibilities for direct control of the Internet are, however, quite limited in scope and effectiveness. They include existing law; new laws to be developed; blocking, filtering and labelling mechanisms; parental control; and self-regulation by the industry and/or the Internet community (see Greenberg, 1999; Verhulst, 2002).

It is still unclear where the new media based on the Internet really belong in relation to the three models outlined, to the extent that they are still valid, since they combine elements of common-carrier and broadcast media and even fulfil print media functions (for instance in electronic newspapers and making much information openly available for consultation). The original three models exist mainly in the sphere of national-level regulation, while the new media are argued to be primarily international in character. This, along with the internal diversity of functions, makes it very difficult to find any agreed regulatory principles or procedures (Akdeniz et al., 2000). The Internet is not usually specifically regulated at national level and is treated as a generalized facility or form of use of the telecommunications network.[16] It is not, however, immune from the many legal provisions that affect all public communication (Gringras, 1997; Edwards, 1997; Drucker and Gumpert, 1999; Sutter, 2000; Langford, 2000; Biegel, 2001).

Nevertheless, its commercial potential depends on its being run in an orderly and efficient way, which is an invitation to enlarge the scope of (self-)regulation. Its effective working as a global network has required a fair amount of organization by various more or less voluntary, open, and democratic international bodies and the scope of their activities is widening (Marsden, 2000). One main body (the Internet Society) has dealt with technical standards, education, and policy issues. Another, the World Wide Web Consortium (W3C) tries to regulate the World Wide Web, while a third major agency, the International Consortium for Assigned Names and Numbers (ICANN), has responsibility for Internet co-ordination and for allocating and settling disputes over ownership of domain names (Slevin, 2000; Charlesworth, 2000; Castells, 2001).

Not insignificant are the very many industry-related bodies that set technical standards, norms, and protocols, largely beyond the scope of public policy or debate, but sometimes with far-reaching consequences.

In addition, there are other organizations emerging that pay more attention to issues of undesirable content, freedom, and censorship, a prominent example being the British-based Internet Watch Foundation (IWF), which is the main self-regulatory body of the Internet service providers (see Slevin, 2000). The range of issues on which the Internet might be held accountable differs somewhat from those applying to other media. The main concerns, according to Greenberg (1999), are privacy, fraud, surveillance, integrity, and overload. Wall (2000) distinguishes between 'harmful' and 'criminal' aspects, and identifies a somewhat different set of key issues: obscenity, trespass, theft, and violence—this referring to psychological hurt and alarm. At the national level there are different stages and kinds of what Wall calls 'policing' of the Internet. He distinguishes first between three types of agency in the governance process: interest groups promoting a general value or policy standpoint; bodies that seek to make rules, such as policy makers and legislators; and organizations that enforce rules. Amongst the latter are three further types: Internet user groups enforcing norms on their own participants by pressure; Internet service providers with potential liabilities for harm (a more direct form of self-regulation); and the police or other authorities mainly dealing with actual illegal actions.

In practice also, the United States and the European Union are effectively home to a very large part of the Internet at the moment and have some capacity to form and implement policies, although they have been slow to do so. For the most part, the Internet is subject in principle to laws in countries where traffic originates or is received (without clarification on this point). It is difficult to control directly and benefits from the current situation by having a relatively high degree of freedom, but suffers because of abuse, uncertainty about its legal and other responsibiliites, and its vulnerability to arbitrary censorship, from which it may not with any certainty claim protection or immunity.[17] While the Internet has been celebrated for its freedom, Branscomb (1995) questions whether, as it becomes more influential, it will be able to escape the fate of broadcasting, for that reason alone.[18]

CONVERGENCE AND THE FUTURE OF MEDIA GOVERNANCE

The existence of separate regimes for different media has been increasily challenged by the fact of convergence that has largely removed or undermined the technological basis for the distinctions and also, in practice, many social-cultural distinctions between types of media. The technological justifications for certain parts of regulatory regimes have ceased to carry weight, especially the argument from spectrum scarcity. There is a general abundance of transmission capacity, reducing the dependence of audiences on monopolistic suppliers. In practice, all media are becoming potential consultation media, with active user interaction.

Convergence has been heralded for a long time and it has still not had the effect of unifying regulatory regimes. Goldberg *et al.* (1998) express doubts that convergence of regulation will ever arrive and about its desirability. There will always be arguments for regulating different services differently and even some virtue, on grounds of diversity, access, and counterbalancing interests, in maintaining part of the media in public control. Law and regulation are likely to develop new forms such as the setting up of regulatory agencies with a wide cross-media remit, which end up making their own law (Goldberg *et al.*, 1998: 311).

The main implication of these remarks about the new and more complex landscape of public concern and potential regulation is that the particular medium of delivery has indeed become a much less determining factor in the system of governance. There is no intrinsic basis for arguing that television and film should be strictly controlled and newspapers, books, and magazines should be free from regulation. The historic residues of control of all media in varying degrees remain, but attention has shifted more to specific forms of publication that may have particular consequences for certain audiences. Attention is less likely to be translated into control of the medium as such, in effect controlling the gates for *all* traffic, and more likely to be expressed in a variety of forms of accounting and accountability, varying in strength and the procedures involved.

Many commentators have remarked on a watershed in regulatory tendencies that has accompanied the rise of new media. The general tendency has been away from the 'imperative' model (see above, p. 97) as indicated by Hoffmann-Riem (1996) and towards much more self-regulation or co-regulation. To quite a large extent the shift is accomplished by relinquishing many decisions to market forces, within a broadly controlled media system environment. Feintuck (1999: 209) refers to a larger trend affecting many areas of public policy according to which 'public bodies have moved away from "rowing" (meaning the actual provision of services) to "steering" (meaning control over the direction such services will take'. This applies primarily to the deregulatory trends affecting broadcasting, but it also implies a reluctance to regulate the Internet as such (i.e. as a separate medium).

There are several implications for accountability. One is that there is less direct and formal accountability by agencies established to represent the interests of society or those affected by publication. Secondly, there is a shift of the onus of accountability for many issues of public concern on to the relation between media and their audiences (in their capacity as consumers of services) and to audiences themselves. Audience members are expected to look after their own interests in respect of offence or harm by selectivity, family editing, or active response, by being more responsible consumers. The demassification of media is supposed to make this a more realistic expectation as well as more inevitable, but in fact the imbalance of power between increasingly large media operators and the public has not really changed.

IN CONCLUSION

It is not surprising that regulation and control, albeit in changed forms, have not gone away, despite the trend to free communication from controls, driven by very mixed motives. There are equally mixed forces working on behalf of the continued control of communication, including the police and security services, parents concerned about their small children, and media businesses wanting an orderly and secure environ-

ment for e-commerce and making profits from property and performance rights. Those who want to maintain control of the media are not
much concerned about the elegance of logic or arrangements as long as
the goals are achieved. What this means in practice is that older controls
tend to be maintained albeit in weaker forms and are extended to new
media, wherever there is a regulatory vacuum.

NOTES

1. What is called 'political correctness' may also effectively put certain extreme public
   utterances beyond the pale in some circumstances. Holocaust denial, Nazi revival-
   ism, racism, and prejudice of various kinds may for instance be effectively inter-
   dicted even where there is no legal restraint. It should be noted that the phrase
   'political correctness' is always pejorative, implying some distaste for such rules.
2. Hoffmann-Riem (1992: 194), writes with reference to the strongly regulated electronic media sector that 'Supervisory bodies usually prefer to resolve conflicts by
   informal means rather than have recourse to their formal powers. The tools they
   employ may extend from "raising eyebrows" to informing the public and
   threatening to use official sanctions. They try to avoid friction and to prevent
   the differences from ending up in court'.
3. In several European countries, the freedom of expression of journalists has been
   secured by agreement, though not law, by way of so-called 'editorial statutes' (as in
   Germany, the Netherlands, and Norway) or a conscience clause as in France. In
   Norway, a newspaper editor has the sole right to decide what is published (see
   Humphreys, 1996).
4. The doctrine was formulated in a Supreme Court judgment of 1919, relating to the
   conviction of a socialist for mailing leaflets encouraging draft resistance during
   wartime. The words of Justice Holmes were 'The question in every case is whether
   the words are used in such circumstances and are of such a nature as to create a
   clear and present danger that they will bring about substantive evils that Congress
   has a right to prevent' (Smolla, 1992: 98).
5. Boyle (1988) lists more than twenty reasons that apply in different (democratic)
   countries for limiting publication. They include public order, morality, health,
   violence, obscenity, racism, blasphemy, privacy, war, election situations, and so on.
   Even the United States, often portrayed as the bastion of free publication, has a
   long history of intolerance towards some forms of dissenting publication, especially where foreign notions or 'anti-Americanism' is perceived (Demac, 1988;
   Powe, 1991; Smolla, 1992; Garry, 1994; Bracken, 1994; Foerstal, 1998).
6. More detail about freedom laws and limitations is to be found in Chapter 8. The
   earliest legal guarantee of the freedom of the press was added to the Swedish
   constitution in 1766 and is the forerunner of most contemporary guarantees of
   freedom (Picard, 1988: 43). The similar Norwegian legal text dating from 1814 is
   quoted by Picard and gives an idea of typical limitations: 'No person must be
   punished for any writing, whatever its contents may be, which he has caused to be
   printed or published, unless he wilfully and manifestly has either himself shown or

incited others to disobedience to the laws, contempt of religion or morality or the constitutional powers...or has advanced false and defamatory accusations against any other person.'

7. For instance by establishing conditions under which subsidies or other forms of public support may be given. But Press Laws can also contain restrictive provisions. The 1881 French Press Law ended censorship and proclaimed freedom of the press, but also retained some restrictions on reporting, restricted rights to French citizens, and imposed an obligation of legal responsibility on newspaper publishers. After the 1944 Liberation, legal provisions were added to restrict concentration (see Barbrook, 1995). The most extensive support system for the press is still found in the Nordic countries (see Picard, 1988).

8. For instance, in the UK a Broadcasting Act regulates most aspects of commercial television and radio, while public broadcasting is regulated similarly by License and Royal Charter. In Germany, each of 21 *Lander* has its own broadcasting law, with a potential reference to a Federal Constitutional Court. The Netherlands has brought all media-relevant legislation together in a single Media Law. Broadcasting in France is regulated by a single State Agency, the Conseil Superieur de l'Audiovisuel (CSA) and the newspaper press falls under a Press Law, dating from 1881.

   In his study of broadcasting legislation in six countries (including the United States), Hoffmann-Riem (1996) inventorized the main fields of supervisory action, with the key areas as follows: 1. Pluralism, diversity, fairness, and impartiality; 2. Political broadcasting; 3. News accuracy; 4. Quality of programming; 5. Strengthening national and regional production; 6. Protecting juveniles; 7. Standards in matters of violence, sex, taste, and decency; 8. Advertising; 9. Consumer protection.

   The United States presents an exception to the pattern of national media legislation, mainly as a result of the constitutional principle ruling out law-making for the press. Even so, there are regulatory bodies, especially the Federal Communications Commission (FCC), which was established by the 1934 Communications Act. More recent legislation includes the 1992 Cable Act, the Telecommunications Act of 1996, and the 1990 Children's Television Act. There is also no shortage of rules, all subject to review by the courts (see Napoli, 2001: 227–50). In respect of broadcasting, the main 'public interest' obligations that have been placed on commercial broadcasting by regulators relate to responsiveness to community needs; provision of educational and informative programmes; indecency and obscenity; TV advertising; access for political candidates; and fairness (see Napoli, 92).

9. Paradoxically, the underregulated United States provided the chief original model for these bodies, in the form of the Federal Communications Commission. According to Robillard (1995, *passim*) their main tasks are as follows:

   - dealing with disputes at the highest level of principle that touch on questions of media freedom and independence from government;
   - adjudicating complaints from the public about media publication actions;
   - dealing with general moral and other ethical issues as they are seen to relate to media;
   - policing advertising standards and dealing with complaints;

- representing the interests of viewers and listeners as consumers;
- advising government on media and communication policy;
- classification of content (film and video) according to type and suitability;
- allocation of press subsidies.

10. The (non-governmental) US 1947 Commission on Freedom of the Press provided an influential model, despite its lack of effectiveness. It was followed by the UK Royal Commission on the Press (1947–9), mainly concerned with lack of diversity (in effect political bias) and with alleged low standards of reporting. Two other Royal Commissions on the Press (in 1962 and 1977) reported on the state of newspapers in the UK. Other examples are to be found in Sweden, Germany, Canada, and the Netherlands. The Swedish Press Commissions of 1971 and 1976 provided the research support and political argumentation for subsidy systems designed to protect political diversity and competition. In Germany a Press Commission in the early 1970s considered problems of concentration and related matters, leading to pressure for a Press Law that would protect the rights of journalists to freedom of expression (editorial statutes or 'conscience clause'). These efforts were successfully resisted by publishers, although in 1976 the anti-cartel law was strengthened in its application to the press (Kleinsteuber, 1997). In the Netherlands, a government-commissioned inquiry into all media paved the way for a Media Law (1984) that provided for an integrated framework of regulation within which the new media of cable and satellite could be located, without significantly affecting broadcasting or the press. The Canadian Press Commission of 1981 mainly addressed the issue of newspaper ownership concentration, but led to no substantial change (Canada, 1981). In the United States, the 1947 example was never repeated and the role of government was much less than elsewhere. Even so, several high-level public inquiries were launched into the role of the media in some issues of public concern, especially related to crime and violence (see Chapter 7 n. 12).

11. Foerstal (1998) provides an inventory of 32 such advocacy/monitoring organizations in the United States alone.

12. The main forms of self-regulation as defined here are formal complaints procedures; codes of ethics and press councils; content classification systems; disciplinary committees of journalists; advisory editorial boards; and the application of production codes.

13. Olen (1988) argues that journalism *should not* become a profession since it involves the exercise of a right to freedom of expression that cannot be monopolized by an institution (that of journalism). The critical role of the press may also oblige it to act in risky and even irresponsible ways (as defined by authorities). In the view of Soloski (1989), professionalization is a double-edged sword, leading to increased support for the existing order. This view echoes some of the criticism of social responsibility theory and public journalism.

14. There are numerous explications of press freedom (see also Chapter 8). One succinct definition by the UK Royal Commission on the Press reads: 'We define freedom of the press as that degree of freedom from restraint that is necessary to enable proprietors, editors and journalists to advance the public interest by publishing the facts and opinions without which a democratic electorate cannot

make responsible judgements' (RCP, 1977a: 8–9). This definition would not be in accord with US First Amendment traditions. A libertarian view is provided by Krattenmaker and Powe (1994) in the form of four principles, as follows: (1) 'Editorial control over what is said and how it is said should be lodged in private, not governmental hands'. (2) 'As a matter of policy, governments should foster access by speakers to the media'. (3) 'Government polices should foster diversity in the media market place'. (4) 'Government is not permitted to sacrifice any of the three foregoing to further goals associated with either or both of the others'.

15. The internationalization of the regulation of common-carrier media dates back to 17th-cent. postal treaties and more recently to the International Telegraph Union of 1865 and the Bern Postal Congress of 1874 (see Cate, 1997).

16. Some early victories for freedom of the Internet may be claimed, against a background of increasing restriction. For instance, the US government failed in its attempt to apply the 1996 Communications Decency Act to the Internet. However, there is much creeping control by way of classificatory systems voluntarily applied by service providers (Foerstal, 1998) and by the actions of security and police services as well as much caution in the face of potential legal claims.

17. With reference to the influence of foreign legal decisions about content dissemination (e.g. in Germany and France), Foerstal (1998) comments that 'The borderless quality of the Internet appears to be an international liability, not the great benefit that has been claimed'. This view has been strongly vindicated by the judgement (in Dec. 2002) of the Australian Supreme Court that an Australian plaintiff can sue the American firm Dow Jones in the Victoria (Australia) courts for defamation in on-line material distributed world wide via a financial information service website (Barrons), despite the relatively few subscribers to the service in question in Australia.

18. In this connection, there is evidence of public support for regulation to a degree not much less than that for broadcasting. In the United States, a Reuters 1997 poll found 50 per cent agreeing that the government should restrict the kind of material that can be transmitted on the Internet (Greenberg, 1999). In the UK, a 1998 Consumer Association survey found 58 per cent agreeing that the 'Internet undermines the morality of the nation' and a similar percentage favoured the regulation of pornography on the Net in particular (Svennevig and Towler, 2000).

6

The Responsibilities of the Media
Alternative Perspectives

A FRAME OF REFERENCE

The various theories about the social obligations of mass media (as described in Chapter 3) all turn on two assumptions. The first of these is that media, beyond their immediate goals of satisfying audiences and making money, have a number of roles that are important for society, especially in relation to democracy, social order, and social change. For the most part these secondary objectives are not separate from, or incompatible with, their primary goals. They are reconciled by the fact that any role performed for society has to be fulfilled by first satisfying the needs of citizens, social groups, and institutions, which is in any case the business of the media. The second assumption is that the media are (and should be) free to choose their own role, express their own views, and publish the views of others, without external pressure or subsequent penalty. This is widely regarded as a necessary condition for achieving both primary and secondary objectives, even though it excludes the notion of obligation.

The consensus on these points can, however, be elaborated and interpreted in quite different ways, according to opinion and belief and depending on where one stands in relation to the media system. Not surprisingly, there are certain media roles and obligations that are not always or fully agreed (especially those that relate to participation, advocacy, and criticism) and some are not even mutually consistent. For the purpose of analysing accountability we need to consider the main alternative standpoints on media responsibilities, without necessarily having to reconcile them or weigh them against each other.

The main vantage points from which the media responsibilities might be viewed and their performance judged have already been identified as those of state, society, media, and audience (or public) (see Chapter 4). We can also take into account certain actors, agencies, and interests with

State (government)   Capital (the market)

MEDIA

Civil society (the public)

FIG. 6.1. The media in a triangle of societal influence

whom the media have continuous relations and dealings. It is helpful to stand even further back and look at the media complex, as suggested by Nordenstreng (2000, drawing on Galtung, 1999), as occupying a key position in the space of a triangle whose three main points are capital (or the market), state (or government), and civil society (the public).

As shown in Fig. 6.1, this scheme provides a wider, non media-centric framework for considering media responsibilities. State and government are actually and conceptually separate, but for the most part the interests of the state have to be expressed or defended by a government in office and the two can be treated together as far as the role of media is viewed. Civil society stands for the many non-governmental associations and institutions (including public opinion-forming agencies and the public itself) that occupy and give life to the public sphere, setting limits to the power of both capital and state. All of these rely on the media to carry out their different roles. The media in this view are essentially free, but secondary to other (political and economic) institutions and have no clearly specified role in society (a corollary of their freedom). Their main activity is best conceived as mediating relationships (by way of communication flows) between and within the other elements in society.

The media are usually more intimately connected with the market than the scheme suggests. Their independence from it is consequently more limited. On the one hand, the position of the media is in many respects the same as any other branch of business, thus primarily concerned with profitability (although there are not-for-profit media). On the other hand, the media enable markets to operate effectively and they help to legitimate the system of production and consumption. Even so, the media are not simply an agent of the market system and give voice to varied understandings of their own role in society. The outcome of this is to identify four main perspectives points from which to view the media, namely those of state and government; actors and agencies seeking access and other benefits; the public in various roles; and the media themselves, or different interest constituencies within media.

THE PERSPECTIVE OF THE STATE AND GOVERNMENT

Unlike a government, the state does not, of course speak, but a voice of the state can notionally be heard by way of constitutions, symbols, ceremonies, legal texts, and court rulings. The state is also heard through government policies and the claims and requirements of government departments. In these forms, the voice of a democratic state is presumed not to be speaking on its own behalf, but on behalf of the whole society, in which capacity it executes the wishes of the public.[1] The power of the state is used to enact and enforce certain basic requirements concerning the media, such as were agreed to be for the general good. It is the power of the state that guarantees, through law, the freedom of media from censorship or arbitrary control, including interventions by governments. In doing so, it also certifies that this freedom is necessary for the good of society. In the circumstances of guaranteed media freedom, the modern state cannot legitimately allocate obligations to the media, beyond normal compliance with law.

The main social obligations of the media, as seen by government, relate to upholding the law and meeting certain essential requirements of other social institutions.[2] In times of war and crisis and in pursuit of serious crime, media freedom is likely to be subordinated to 'higher purposes' (Smith, 1999).[3] Most mainstream mass media *choose* to serve the interests of the state in such matters, usually acting in line with public opinion. This does not mean that media have to accept a civic or patriotic duty as proposed by governments. They have other, primary, obligations relating to information and inquiry that prevent them from accepting at face value any demand for support for a national (and thus state) interest, interpreted as it usually is by particular officials or a particular government administration. In principle, media must also reserve the right to oppose government, short of advocating violence.

In circumstances of war the state, via government, may claim a suspension of normal rules of free expression and a duty of loyalty on the part of the media.[4] They have also made wide use of their de facto power to limit access to the site of events, effectively controlling reporting. In some recent cases of limited warfare (including the Falklands, Gulf War, Kosovo, Israel, and Afghanistan), governments have shown an inclination to press their claims to media support, generally backed by public opinion. In modern times of (even very limited) war, the media's relation to the state has become more rather than less sensitive because of the enhanced role of information and publicity in war and international relations (especially with regard to its potential effects on public opinion), coupled with the globalization of information. It is important to the state to have maximum control of the information environment of its activities, yet also more difficult to achieve this in practice or claim it as legitimate.[5]

The availability of media channels to governmental leaders for communicating with the general public at least some of the time on terms decided by government itself can be argued as a right and necessity both for effective government and for democracy (see Seymour-Ure, 1974).[6] The reporting of parliaments and similar governmental deliberations was originally regarded as a right to be fought for by the press and broadcasting, but has subsequently come to be seen as a media duty that is not always welcomed and increasingly neglected. Regulations for public broadcasting often state some requirements in respect of access for different forms of political communication.[7]

The media can be a useful source of intelligence about events in society, the state of public opinion, a government's own standing, etc. The 'informational role' of the media is thus seen somewhat differently 'from above', even if it is no less important.[8] The coverage by the media of election campaigns in democracies is the main area where a case has been made for a media obligation to give full and fair access and coverage (Baker, 1989, 2001). There are many examples of laws in democracies limiting certain kinds of publication that might have an adverse effect on the conduct of elections, as well as rules governing campaign finance.[9]

The media are always subject to the law and can be forbidden from acting (by way of publicity) in ways that are thought to subvert the work of the judicial system and/or pervert the course of justice. Governments also wish to maintain control of information they regard as essential to their operation. In practice this usually goes much further in the direction of secretiveness than can be justified and the media are seen as a permanent threat. The battle between government and media for control of information is a continuous one, with new fronts being opened up as the Internet develops. Information management in and out of elections, but especially at times of crisis, is now a salient feature of public communication involving much propaganda, manipulation of news agendas, and the extensive deployment of spin doctors (see e.g. Swanson and Mancini, 1996; Blumler and Kavanagh, 1999).

These and other strands merge into a definite, albeit ill-defined, concept of a public duty, as perceived by government, that attaches to the media institution, one that goes beyond the duty of an individual citizen. This is one reason for suspicion of the concept of social responsibility. The perceived public responsibilities of the media are often endorsed by public opinion, sometimes more strongly than the government or the state could legitimately claim. The media themselves often accept some of the attributed obligations, even when emphasizing their autonomy and adversarial stance.

THE PERSPECTIVE OF THE MEDIA THEMSELVES

Each media sector (and within it each organization or channel) determines its own limited goals and responsibilities in terms of content and quality. The most general key to appreciating the media's view of their own obligations is their need to attract and keep an audience (of their own choice), through whose eyes they set goals and judge their own performance. It is what Tunstall (1971) called the 'coalition goal' of media organizations, uniting different internal outlooks (e.g. of management, editorial, or technical personnel). Secondly, as we have noted, private media firmly resist or reject the notion of any obligation or responsibility that is imposed from outside even if they often comply for their own reasons. In practice, this reflects a third general principle governing how most media judge their obligations: the value or cost that attaches to them. Public broadcasting aside, most media have an ultimate profit objective and responsibilities are accepted and fulfilled in some relation to their cost or benefit for their owners. For instance, meeting the generally accepted journalistic responsibility to uncover truth will be influenced by the relative cost of the work and the relative interest for audiences (Murphy, 1976; McManus, 1994). Media perspectives vary according to their role and position in the hierarchy of an organization (Cantor, 1971; Engwall, 1978), each group having its own view of its primary purpose. The views of editorial and creative personnel are most likely to include ideas concerning obligations to the wider society, whether or not expressed in terms of satisfying an audience (Tunstall, 1971).

MEDIA OWNERS

Systematic inquiry into the ultimate owners or controllers of media organizations is scarce, but some generalizations are possible about the strategic conduct of large media firms. Early proprietors of major newspapers and television channels were sometimes (even typically) inclined to have personal projects and to equate the wider goals of their media with their own personal agendas, especially on political and social issues. At least this is the way that the history of the media has typically been written. Contemporary owners are more likely to view the responsibilities of the media as generally limited to providing a service to their clients and audiences according to high technical and professional standards. This is not a denial of social responsibility but a claim to autonomy in fulfilling it. One of the rights of ownership is still to put a medium (in practice it is usually a newspaper) at the service of a chosen social or political goal.[10] It is also common, despite globalizing trends, for a medium such as a newspaper or broadcasting station to serve a particular community or region (its chosen market) and to adopt its interests and welfare as its own. This has been shown to apply at local level (Gieber and Johnson, 1960), but there is good reason to expect it to happen at the national level also.

EDITORS AND JOURNALISTS

The most relevant intermediate category in the hierarchy of media organizations is that of editor in newspapers or executive producer or controller in television. Editors tend to be torn in two (or more) directions, especially in having an obligation to carry out the wishes of the proprietors that employ them and also having a commitment to professional goals and an allegiance to the staff that do the main part of creative and journalistic work. As such they have dual, often conflicting, responsibilities. Aside from pleasing proprietors as a (management career) goal, the options are likely to lie between having some influence on society outside, maximizing the quality of the product according to professional goals, or pleasing the audience (and increasing sales/ income) (see Tunstall, 1971).

Editors are likely to come into most direct touch with divergent internal and external claims and assertions of the responsibility of the media. The very fragmentary evidence that exists about the views of editors in general seems to show little difference on ethical questions between them and journalists (see Meyer, 1987; Anderson and Leigh, 1992), although editors are more sensitive to business needs and outside pressures. In most commercial news organizations, editors do not have much scope for determining the responsibilities of their news organizations and are hemmed in by business and professional criteria. Nevertheless, they typically do see themselves as needing and having some degree of autonomy in publication decisions. There is also evidence that editors see some threat to their autonomy from the (concentrated) power of owners.[11]

From a series of inquiries, now increasingly international and comparative in scope, there is a good deal of evidence on how journalists perceive their own role in society. There is also much variation between countries and between respondents (Weaver, 1998; Patterson, 1998). Nevertheless, two broad dimensions can be discerned along which the interpretation of press responsibility can be gauged. One of these is an *active–passive* dimension, reflecting a varying view of how involved and participant journalists should be in political and social life (see Cohen, 1963; Janowitz, 1975; Weaver and Wilhoit, 1986; Donsbach, 1983; Weaver and Wilhoit, 1996). Passive here does not mean doing nothing but playing the part of observer and transmitter of information first and foremost. Activity means taking the initiative to search, investigate, and, if need be, expose.

A second dimension differentiates between the *neutral* and the *advocacy* role, the latter involving taking sides in conflicts and campaigning for certain goals according to some consistent set of beliefs (Johnstone *et al.*, 1976; Köcher, 1986; Patterson, 1998). It is hard to be both a neutral observer and a committed advocate at the same time. Even so both positions have a place in the broad view of press responsibility offered by the ASNE (American Society of Newspaper Editors) statement of principle. Press responsibility can be considered as involving a spectrum of roles that can be carried out by different persons, organs, and sectors of the media.[12]

Weaver and Wilhoit (1986, 1996) also distinguished three main roles according to the self-recognition of (US) journalists. The most frequently occurring role is that of interpretation and investigation. This implies an objective or neutral stance in relation to the reality, but it also recognizes a certain normative task in the social and political system. It includes the role of watchdog on, and critic of, those with economic and political power, to be exercised on behalf of the public (see Gleason, 1994).[13] It gains its legitimacy mainly from ideas about democratic political accountability. In practice, it is not always even-handed and there is no reason why the essential purpose of the 'watchdog' practice (investigating and exposing) cannot be carried out just as well in a partisan mode.

The second main role identified by Weaver and Wilhoit is that of the effective disseminator of accurate and relevant information. This is expressed in the notion of 'getting information quickly to the public'. Most journalism in practice is devoted to this. The third role that appears in the American situation is that of adversary of government (see Rivers and Nyhan, 1973) but it occupies a very minor position. Certain other services to society are recognized in varying degrees by journalists, including the provision of a forum, platform, or meeting place for the public expression of diverse views; the forging of a local or national consensus (Fjaestad and Holmlov, 1976); the interconnection and interrelation of different sectors in a society; and the support for cultural identities.

International comparisons (e.g. Patterson, 1998; Hallin and Mancini, 1984) underline the varying degree to which national media systems are partisan and ideological in character, for historical reasons. The United States seems to have the least partisan media system, connected perhaps with the degree to which it has become concentrated (in local markets) and also more fully professionalized (i.e. neutralized) than elsewhere. Journalistic role conceptions centre on various informational tasks, including analysis and interpretation, but declining a strong opinion-forming or social interventionist role (Weaver and Wilhoit, 1996).

Where the media are more openly politicized, as in several European countries, the role of journalism cannot be sharply separated from the role of political activists and objectivity is not a supreme virtue. In post-communist Russia, for instance, there is evidence (e.g. Wu *et al.*, 1998) that journalists still tended to opt for a more politically and culturally active role than in the West, while stepping back from the watchdog role. This reflects both continental European norms and also perhaps a residue of journalistic education according to Soviet theory. The case in other former communist countries seems to be different. Oledzki (1998), for instance, found Polish journalists to be very close in role conceptions to their US counterparts.

In the exceptional case of public broadcasting, responsibilities to society, decided according to national priorities, are openly stated as the goals of the broadcasting system (see Hoffmann-Riem, 1996: Barendt, 1993; Blumler, 1992; Atkinson and Raboy, 1997). These goals do not differ much in broad outline from the acknowledged range of purposes of mainstream commercial media but the fact that they are formally ac-knowledged makes a big difference to the question of accountability and they do include aims that are unlikely to be profitable for commercial media.[14] For obvious reasons, public broadcasting is prohibited from active partisanship, although some degree of politicization can occur.

Although news media often adopt an autonomous role in some controversial and politically sensitive matters, the established media or mainstream media, whether press or broadcasting, generally take up a position of bystander in relation to critical events (in keeping with their role as observer). The notion of press as a Fourth Estate or power in society is misleading in this respect, because the power of the press is not usually exercised in a consistent and intentional way. The media serve too many different masters (including shareholders, advertisers, lobby and pressure groups, all powerful sources, not to mention diverse audiences) to be able to live up fully to professional ideals that are not even fully shared within the media.

The press does at times operate according to social ideals, communitarian purpose, or social conscience, in keeping with the mixed character of the media institution, being both principled and commercial. Brodasson (1994) wrote of the 'sacerdotal' strand in the journalistic tradition that impels some publications and journalists to altruistic purposes, sometimes at great cost (Waisbord, 2000). The dominant model of profit-making and subordination to power is not all pervasive. There are many radical and alternative media outlets, even if on a small scale and with minority audiences (Downing, 2000). There are also remnants of a politically engaged press sector that puts its unpredictable weight behind the forces of revolution or change (or even reaction). The public journalism movement (see Chapter 3), although working within the mainstream and having no political agenda, also represents a disinterested commitment to some desirable social objectives, especially the promotion of a participative citizenship (Glasser, 1998).

CODES OF JOURNALISTIC ETHICS AND TELEVISION PRODUCTION CODES

Many questions of media responsibility are addressed in codes of professional media ethics and practice, voluntarily adopted by journalists or in the form of production codes that are widely, and less voluntarily, applied in television broadcasting. Many of these codes do implicitly or explicitly accept certain wide responsibilities to society, along with potential causal responsibility, but they rarely involve any firm obligations of a proactive kind. They have often been introduced under some pressure to protect the media from outside control, and they cannot be interpreted as reflecting the actual views of those within the media, or actual conduct. Laitila (1995) compared the journalistic codes of thirty-one European countries and concluded that they all more or less agreed on the main ethical principles. These were truthfulness; the defence of freedom of expression; equality and non-discrimination; fairness in gathering information; respect for sources and referents (including privacy issues); and independence and integrity (e.g. refusing bribery).[15]

A typical feature of codes is that they express potential responsibilities to a number of different claimants (Evers, 2000). They are also designed to protect the status and professional integrity of the journalistic profession as well as to make promises to society. Not all codes promise very much to society. The Code of Practice first adopted by UK newspapers in 1991 and administered by the Press Complaints Commission, aside from a reference to the public's 'right to know', largely confines itself to promise to avoid various forms of misconduct ranging from inaccuracy to harassment (PCC, 1999). In general, it would be a mistake to draw hard conclusions about public service, or much comfort, from the contents of ethical codes.

Production codes in television place more emphasis on avoiding potentially undesirable and unintended consequences and offence to the public, especially in the matter of violence (individual or collective), swearing, representation of sex, vulnerable groups (including children), offence to taste, morals, and protecting certain minorities (ethnic or otherwise). They also pay attention to the possible role of broadcasting in amplifying unrest and protest or unintentionally promoting civil disorder and being manipulated by insurgent terrorists (Schmid and de Graaf, 1982).[16]

CONTROL OF THE MEDIA GATES: THE PERSPECTIVE OF ACCESS-SEEKERS

The role of the media in society has often been conceived as that of a 'gatekeeper' (Shoemaker, 1991), selecting who and what should be given access to channels of publicity or made visible in the public arena. The forms and criteria of access are extremely diverse and there are many different media gates and gatekeepers. Self-chosen media roles often include those of expressing public opinion or reflecting the reality of society, or providing a platform for different voices. Some media formats are specifically designed for such purposes, including letters to the editor, invited articles, reports of political campaigns, radio and television debates, talk-shows, phone-ins, and other participation programmes. Apart from this, much space is sold for advertising of diverse kinds or as sponsored features and information. Less visible, but just as important, is the access given without payment to press releases and publicity from interested parties. These varied forms of access are governed by largely unwritten conventions and norms. But it is relevant to consider how the media look from the point of view of those outside trying to get in, whether novelists seeking publication, would-be film-makers, or advertisers and PR firms.

No agreed view exists of what the responsibility of media gatekeepers might be since there is no general right of access to the media.[17] But there is an approximate hierarchy of expectation about legitimate claims to access, as well as certain approximate norms about fairness, as viewed from outside. Three main kinds of issue arise. One concerns cultural production and the giving or withholding of access to would-be writers, artists, performers, film-makers, etc. Secondly, there is the more specific question of access as a source to channels of news and publicity, especially where the allocation and exercise of power and influence are involved. Another relates to the representation of society in media fact or fiction, especially considered in terms of component social groups.

In none of these matters can the media be said to have any binding responsibility, but there are often secure grounds for expectations about media conduct as gatekeepers. Because they collectively monopolize the means of publication a claim (albeit a weak one) of responsibility can be laid against this power. They are not themselves censored and should not apply the equivalent of censorship (see Foerstal, 1998). Nor, it might reasonably be held, should they behave in a discriminatory, unfair, or unethical way in the allocation of public space. In the case of broadcasting, this is often made clear in licensing conditions.

In respect of access to media channels more generally, claims are usually based on one of four criteria that are in varying degrees regarded as legitimate: relevance (interest) to the audience; money; an appeal to an agreed and fundamental social or cultural norm; some form of social power. These are widely discrepant and do not in equal degree support any claim for access. The first of these criteria (audience relevance) is an across-the-board rule of thumb derived from a model of free media, in which the latter are presumed to exist to meet the needs of their chosen audiences and take publication decisions accordingly (Westley and MacLean, 1957). Money, directly or indirectly, rightly or wrongly, is probably the main determinant of access but, on its own, not enough to back a claim for access. The selling of access, except openly and under conventional forms, undermines the credibility and standing of media organizations.

Social and cultural norms support access to the media in varied and often indirect ways that do not need to be explained in detail. The point at which normative pressure from outside (e.g. an appeal to certain values, rights, or the public interest) shades into the exercise of social power is bound to be uncertain. However, in giving way to pressure, the media can usually appeal to intrinsic news values and they can also refuse, if they are willing to accept the consequences.

The correlate, if not consequence, of access being allocated on the grounds of any of the four criteria named is a systematic bias against voices, causes, and groups that are not obviously interesting to the audience, unable to supply suitable content, have no money or social power, and are not supported by social norms. Leaving ordinary citizens aside, this identifies quite a large sector of society, especially the poor, deviant, old, sick, immigrants, marginal, and oppositional groups (see Paletz and Entman, 1981). These are likely to deserve media treatment only in the context of some problem for the rest of society, leading only to negative attention (even if sympathetically treated).

THE VIEW FROM THE (MEDIA) PUBLIC

The quality of media performance is a perennial topic of public opinion in many countries. Surveys show that the general public does have stable attitudes towards the media as an institution as well as expectations and opinions about the quality of content and service. Even so, it is not easy to be sure what the public really thinks about what the media *ought* to be doing, aside from opinions about what they actually do. Audience ideas of media responsibilities often diverge both from the media's self-view and also from the tenets of normative media theory. This may reflect an element of naïvety on the part of the public, but it also reflects basic differences of interest as between public and media as well as different ideas about responsibility. It is not surprising that the formal position of the media in society in terms of its rights and responsibilities is not well understood by many citizens.

There is a risk of exaggerating the extent to which the public as audience are deeply dissatisfied with their own media. Most of the time, where the market system operates effectively, there is little reason to doubt that the audience gets what it most wants, or at least it likes what it is given. Aside from this question, there is plenty of evidence that the audience does have a fairly well-articulated view of the wider contribution of mass media in personal and social life (see McQuail, 1997). The range of media functions attributed by the audience include the provision of: relevant and useful information, including warnings of risks and danger; interpretation, guidance, and advice; entertainment and diversion; a basis for social contact with others; insight, enlarged experience, emotional release, and models for identification. Compared with these personal and public satisfactions that are sought and for the most part found, public complaints against media may seem peripheral.

A central issue on which views diverge concerns the degree of freedom that media should enjoy, especially from government control or legal action. There is a good deal of evidence, going back some time, that the public believe the media to have too much freedom. McMasters (2000) reports survey evidence showing that large numbers of Americans favour restrictions on public speech and even changes in the First Amendment to allow restrictions on a variety of speech acts, especially relating to campaign contributions, desecrating the flag, racially offensive speech, or sexually explicit material (see also Wilson, 1975; Hentoff, 2000; Sanford, 1999). Golding and van Snippenberg (1995) report Euro-barometer evidence showing that significant minorities in Western Europe in the mid-1980s (in Britain a majority) still regarded book censorship as legitimate in some cases. Other survey evidence from the same period showed a majority in several European countries disagreeing with the freedom of newspapers to publish confidential government defence papers. It is still early to assess public attitudes to the freedom enjoyed by the Internet, but indications are that the public is more alarmed at the threats it poses than concerned about its freedom. A 1997 Reuters poll in the United States found 50 per cent agreeing that government should restrict the kind of material that can be transmitted on the Internet (Greenberg, 1999: 94–5).

Although the media system of the United States offers less opportunity for government intervention than in Europe, the general drift of public opinion there has for long favoured intervention when required in the national interest (e.g. in circumstances of war or disorder) or to maintain certain essential social and moral values. There is a surprising degree of intolerance of the expression of deviant or unpopular views in the media and of tolerance for censorship and control. Wyatt (1991) reported a range of findings endorsing limits on free expression. Substantial minorities of Americans would not support any protection for editorializing in newspapers during an election campaign (28 per cent), for journalists criticizing the military (23 per cent); for criticizing political leaders (22 per cent); for siding with foreign governments (36 per cent); for reporting national security issues without government approval (45 per cent); and for projecting winners of elections during voting (55 per cent).

In general the support for full protection was on all issues less than support for no protection at all. On matters of sexual deviance, blasphemy, pornography, and 'improper speech', illiberal and restrictive attitudes to free speech and publication were even more marked. The report concluded (Wyatt, 1991: 32), 'Our assessment of the willingness of Americans to support free expression [is] gloomy indeed'. Some explanation of this situation may be found in the finding of another study (Andsager and Miller, 1994) showing that a large minority (about 30 per cent) do not believe that freedom of expression belongs to the media at all (as distinct from individuals).

According to Immerwahr and Doble (1982), the American public strongly supported the public role of the media in political life to the extent of favouring laws that would require newspapers as well as television to give equal time to major party candidates. Opponents of controversial policies should be given as much coverage as those in favour of them. The public rejects censorship but does approve of 'fairness-enhancing' laws. In explanation, the authors invoke what they called a 'listeners' perspective' on media rights and duties on the part of the public, as opposed to a 'producers' perspective', that is characteristic of journalists. This is reflected in support for measures to ensure a balanced treatment of politics and access for all main points of view on disputed issues. As Gleason (1994) argues, there is also evidence of significant support in public opinion for the watchdog role of the press.

The audience assesses its own informational needs, without much regard for (or understanding of) the rights of media (especially newspapers) to free expression. On more routine matters of journalistic ethics, however, survey evidence seems to show that the normative expectations of the public largely correspond with the media's own proclaimed standards as contained in codes of ethics and practice (Braman, 1988; Lind, 1999; Bergen et al., 2000). This conclusion reflects the fact that codes of journalism have generally been drafted so as to reflect public opinion. The reference is mainly to aspects of objectivity, fairness, and independence from government and special interests. In an over-view of American attitudes to their media (Whitney, 1986), the authors conclude (24), 'Without doubt, media credibility and confidence is on the public mind. More fundamental issues such as freedom of the press and the autonomy of media from various pressure groups... rarely gets sustained public attention.' In one sense, the apparent ignorance of the (American) public about the First Amendment may not matter, but when it is expressed in the finding that 'a solid majority of Americans ... are convinced that "the press has too much freedom"' (Hentoff, 2000, and confirmed by McMasters, 2000), it indicates a definite atti-tude to the media and a climate of constraint that goes beyond lack of awareness of legal niceties.

Similar conclusions as those relating to journalism apply to public views on issues of sex, morality, and decency. Production codes and classificatory schemes for film and video generally conform to the expectations of public opinion, sometimes leading, sometimes lagging behind (see Gunter and Winstone, 1993). Continuous survey evidence in the UK shows a very constant and quite high level of support for the current degree of public regulation of television (around 55 per cent found it 'about right' and 25 per cent even 'too little' according to Svennevig and Towler, 2000). There are, inevitably, large variations of satisfaction within the general public and evidence that some minorities are entirely dissatisfied. Such views are partly based on (moral) principle and personal offence, partly on considerations of potential harm or offence to vulnerable groups, such as children. Some minority dissatis-faction also reflects distaste for the low quality of much popular media fare. A distinction is made by the public between the undesirable exposure to unwanted content and the voluntary selective attention to dubious or adult fare. In this matter the media are expected to match content to the appropriate audience effectively.

An important aspect of public expectations from the media concerns the related issues of trust and credibility. Three main factors are in-volved. One is that of objectivity: there has to be confidence that infor-mation is accurate, complete, and reliable. Secondly, there is the matter of reliability: the public wants unbiased information and analysis that does not have a hidden agenda or serve special interests. Thirdly, the public (as audience) appreciates it when they believe that journalists are looking out for and representing their interests (those of the public) (see Gaziano and McGrath, 1986, 1987). This kind of trust is most likely to be generated by local news media or sources that are very familiar. The general issue of trust is a large one and should be of concern for all media, with a relationship to accountability (of media to their audience). By various accounts the media have been losing trust and once lost it is hard to regain, just as it has proved difficult for new media (e.g. on-line news) to gain trust (Johnson and Kaye, 1998; Althaus and Tewkesbury, 2000; Schweiger, 2000).

The media audience makes consistent and generally plausible distinctions in their expectations between different kinds of media, especially television and newspapers, and between different channels and newspapers. The differences generally reflect institutionalized variations (e.g. a newspaper press that is both less regulated and more political than broadcasting) as well as the self-positioning of various types of media channels within the spectrum). Television is consistently named in many countries as the main source of news and also the most credible and trusted source.[18] Fitzsimon and McGill (1995) show, however, that when asked about the daily newspaper or television news service the respondent was personally most familiar with, favourability was very high (around 80 per cent). The relatively favoured position of television reflects its enforced neutrality, the patchy record of the press, and its simple popularity as a news source.

Confidence in the press as an institution is low in the United States and has declined fairly steadily in the last quarter of the twentieth century (Fitzsimon and McGill, 1995: from 24 per cent in 1976 to 10 per cent in 1994). The press as an institution still seems to be more highly regarded than journalism is as a profession, a finding not confined to the United States. Only 17 per cent of respondents attributed either high or very high standards in honesty and ethics to newspaper journalists in 1994, compared to 30 per cent in 1981, with TV reporters scoring somewhat better (ibid. 99). There are quite large variations between countries, but in general the public standing of the media seems to be higher in Europe than in the United States. Within the European Union, the highest public levels of trust were in the broadcast media (television and radio).

IN CONCLUSION

The differing perspectives on media obligations and perspectives as outlined reflect a complex and changing rather than an essentially puzzling situation. There are many basic differences of interest and perception that defy reconciliation. Despite the great variety of media and situations there are some general keys to exploring this terrain, leaving aside the many national variations. Firstly, although governments generally keep their distance, they are impelled towards various degrees and forms of involvement with media by their own needs and their obligations to respond to various constituencies in society. This leads sometimes to rhetoric and exhortation directed at the media, sometimes to regulation, more often to varied kinds of informal pressure and inducement.

Public attitudes towards the media can best be understood in terms of several inconsistent requirements. We appreciate the need for media freedom but also want respect for proper order and decency of conduct and content. The pleasures and entertainment of media are hard to separate from their excesses and failings. We want trustworthy sources of information but are more likely to reward sensationalism and triviality.

The media themselves are ambivalent about their own role and in fact have multiple models to choose from. These include models based on social responsibility; commercialism; partisanship, critique, and advocacy; sensation and gossip. There are often mixed models and tendencies towards globalization and concentration are heading in this direction. The result is much inconsistency, with uncertain outcomes.

NOTES

1. This exposes an ambiguity in the identification of different vantage points, since the state and public are not independent of each other. The media may also claim with some justification to speak 'on behalf of' the public. Here, however, we are concerned with the state as an advocate of its own essential powers, rights, and necessities.

2. Hindman's (1997) study of US Supreme Court decisions relating to the mass media concludes that, despite the high level of freedom, they (the Court) 'acknowledge the media as only one of many institutions operating in society, institutions that cannot have complete freedom if society is to function ... no institution ... can do whatever it wants' (149).

3. In practice, all democratic states restrict the rights of free publication under exceptional circumstances. In US jurisprudence, the doctrine of 'clear and present danger' permits intervention by presidential order to suppress publication of sensitive information. In fact, historical accounts suggest that a great deal of suppression, short of formal censorship, is more typical than exceptional in wartime. Smith (1999) concludes that 'censorship in some form has occurred in every major war the U.S. has fought' (27). In the Second World War, Roosevelt created an Office of Censorship and later an Office of War Information, both

charged with voluntary censorship and propaganda activities (Foerstal, 1998). In several countries, including the UK, broadcasting legislation allows government to take control of radio and television transmission under emergency conditions. In the UK the Official Secrets Act can also be used or threatened to protect what government decides to be secret, and an informal censorship system (known as 'D Notices') is available at all times to request silence from the press on particularly sensitive matters.

4. During the Gulf War (1991), the Allies effectively imposed restrictions on news reporting of the armed conflict. A survey reported by Dennis *et al.* (1991) found that 57 per cent of the US public agreed that the 'military should be given more control over how news was reported'. In the wake of the destruction of the New York World Trade Center on September 11, 2001, newspapers were asked by government to suppress certain information and leaders of the film industry were summoned together to discuss ways in which they could support the War against Terrorism. To a lesser extent, other modern conflicts have witnessed some aggressive outbursts against the media by governments of participating states for not being sufficiently supportive (see Morrison and Tumber, 1988; *EJC* (2000)).

5. The claim that media have a patriotic duty is sometimes more widely interpreted as requiring them to be respectful about foreign national leaders and symbols and not to bring a country into international disrepute or to cause diplomatic difficulties (especially where large business deals are involved). From time to time political leaders complain about the negative image of their own country being disseminated abroad, usually overestimating the extent to which their own national media are noticed in other countries. The laws that exist in some countries to limit foreign ownership of media are indicative of a presumed national interest.

6. Some early forms of newspaper were officially sponsored by national or local governments for purposes of communication to the public. Governmental action to support the political role of the press is sometimes by way of a financial subsidy. One major reason for the public financing of broadcasting (in Europe especially) is the expectation of an active and co-operative role in political communication. There are also direct or indirect subsidies in several countries in return for certain forms of political access, especially for broadcasting of parliamentary proceedings, for broadcasting abroad, and during election campaigns. In the United States, large sums of public money are used to subsidize presidential election campaigning, in addition to private finance.

7. Public broadcasting regulations also generally require a diversity of expression of political views, coupled with overall balance (Barendt, 1993; Hoffmann-Riem, 1996). Early FCC requirements in the United States upheld a fairness doctrine obliging radio and television to give adequate opportunity for alternative views on controversial issues. Although abandoned as a rule, broadcasting practice still tends to practise fairness in these terms, on its own account.

8. There is little systematic evidence on the point, as distinct from many anecdotal accounts, but it is interesting that in one US survey (Abrams and Hawkins, 1984) of the views of 'state lawmakers' concerning the functions of the press, the two leading functions selected were 'surveillance' and 'keeping in touch with the community'.

9. In some countries (e.g. Germany and Spain) political advertising in the press is forbidden except during election campaigns. Other countries impose restrictions only during campaigns (e.g. France and the UK) (see Article 19, 1993). See also McChesney (2000b).

10. However, the use of proprietorial influence to advance a personal cause or help a friend is generally frowned on by editors and journalists and not usually openly admitted by owners (see Meyer, 1987).

11. Garry (1994) found that most editors, whether independent or belonging to chains, thought concentration of ownership threatened freedom of the press. The UK Royal Commission on the Press (1977b) survey of editors reported that 26 per cent viewed the influence of proprietors as a threat to the freedom of the press. Australian journalists interviewed by Schultz (1998) overwhelmingly rejected the right of media companies to exclude news on the grounds of their own commercial interests. However, almost a third thought that pressure from owners was an obstacle to the media playing a watchdog role (p. 258).

12. The complete list of roles deemed 'extremely important' by the respondents to the Weaver and Wilhoit (1996) survey was as follows:

- Investigate claims and statements made by government (67 per cent).
- Get information to the public quickly (69 per cent).
- Discuss national policy while still being developed (39 per cent).
- Avoid stories where facts are not verifiable (49 per cent).
- Give ordinary people a chance to express their views (48 per cent).
- Develop the intellectual and cultural interests of the public (18 per cent).
- Concentrate on news of interest to the widest audience (20 per cent).
- Provide entertainment and relaxation (14 per cent).
- Be an adversary of public officials by being always sceptical (14 per cent).
- Set the public agenda (5 per cent).

13. For instance Meyer (1987: 225), found that 85 per cent of media respondents—publishers, editors, and staffers—agreed that an adversarial relationship between the government and newspapers is 'healthy for the country' in the long run. In her survey of Australian journalists, Schultz (1998) recorded overwhelming support for a critical, watchdog, role for the press in relation to government. There was a striking gap between the preferences of journalists for the Fourth Estate (watchdog) role and their estimation of the reality of the Australian media: 66 per cent agreed strongly with the Fourth Estate idea, but only 10 per cent thought it reflected the actual situation in Australia. The main obstacles to the watchdog role were perceived to be legal, state secrecy, and commercial considerations. According to Gleason's (1994) analysis the adoption of a 'watchdog role' is problematic for the US press because it implies some restriction on their freedom (for instance not to be watchdog).

14. For instance, the Agreement between the State and the Swedish Public Broadcasting Organization (SR) requires the latter to provide an all round supply of programmes in the Swedish language that, *inter alia*, convey news, information, and comment; stimulate debate and the formation of opinion on social and

cultural issues; scrutinize authorities and private enterprises; promote artistic and cultural innovation; cater for a variety of interests; cater for linguistic and ethnic minorities; and pay attention to the needs of the handicapped.

15. The structure of the codes (Laitila, 1995) showed a division between the two principles of external accountability to society and, internally, the protection of journalism itself. The full scheme is as follows:

    To show accountability to the public:

    - Truthfulness of information.
    - Clarity of information.
    - Defence of public rights.
    - Responsibilities as creators of public opinion.

    To show accountability to sources and referents:

    - Gathering and presenting information.
    - Integrity of sources.

    To protect the professional integrity of journalists:

    - General rights and prohibitions.
    - Protection from public powers.
    - Protection from employers and advertisers.

    To protect the status and unity of the journalistic profession:

    - Protection of the status of journalism.
    - Protection of solidarity within the profession.

    To show accountability to the employer:

    - Loyalty to the employer.

    To show accountability to the state:

    - Respect for state institutions.

16. Television codes place more emphasis on possible effects, are more detailed, and also and more likely to be applied by management than are press codes. This reflects the greater power of government to regulate as well as the pressure of public opinion.

17. As Lichtenberg (1990*b*: 119), puts it, 'There is no "right to be published".'

18. The Eurobarometer survey for 1999 for fifteen EU countries reported an overall average of 67 per cent saying they tended to trust television, compared to 49 per cent for the press, with much higher ratings for both in some countries. Both levels seem a good deal higher than those found in the United States and are higher than figures recorded in 1997. The UK had the lowest score in Europe for trust in the press, at 24 per cent.

7
On the Media as Cause

The allegedly harmful effects of mass media have been a perennial topic of debate and object of research. Despite this, several obstacles continue to stand in the way of definite conclusions, whether the issue is approached from a political, legal, normative, or social-scientific perspective. First, there is little agreement on what constitutes harm, because of different value positions. Secondly, there are always other factors at work besides the media, often more potent in their effects. Thirdly, although there are many individual cases where media have been, prima facie, a proximate cause of harm, and there is little doubt that harm is sometimes caused, it remains very difficult to establish conclusive proof. Finally, all efforts to 'blame the media' run up against resistance on the grounds of claims to free expression.

There is a larger issue that concerns the appropriate attitude of media communicators and publishers to the consequences of their activities. How far ought they to feel responsible for the effects of publication? In many other contexts (e.g. law, health care, commerce, public administration), the purposes of action are usually transparent and subject to public judgement as to their effectiveness. Those involved are accountable for failings of commission or omission. Despite what has already been said about the responsibilities that are *perceived* as attaching to the media, public communicators cannot be classified in the same way, and not only because of the freedom to communicate. It is also because purposes are often multiple and divergent, unclear (even to the communicators) or not agreed; because effects are not certain before or after the event and have alternative valuations; because the wind of truth 'bloweth where it listeth'; and because creativity cannot be bounded. Perhaps most important is that a no-risk policy would be completely incompatible with open communication and would destroy the benefits of communication along with possible harm. At the same time, the media cannot claim any blanket immunity from being held to account for the consequences of their actions, especially since they often take credit for many positive effects and are rarely accused of deliberately causing harm. But there is also an extensive grey area of potentially harmful effect from publication where the media may or may not intend harm by their publication, acknowledge responsibility for harmful effects, or be called to account for them.

COMMUNICATION AS INTENTIONAL INFLUENCE: HISTORICAL ROOTS

In the prehistory of media, as sketched in Chapter 2, publication (expression/emission in public) and authorship were both closely connected with the idea of influence, for the most part understood in terms of an intention to have some (positive) effect on an audience. The main strand of the Western tradition concerning communication in public has been to presume intentionality either as intrinsic to the act or as an inevitable consequence of doctrines of personal moral responsibility for actions.[1] In the classical era, oral communication (oratory) was systematically studied under the heading of 'rhetoric', which was concerned with the use of language to achieve persuasive effects on listeners. Aristotle's *Poetics* was similarly concerned with the achievement of (mainly emotional) effects on audiences by way of drama. Public authorities in Greece and Rome paid attention to potential harm that might be caused by written or oral public expression, hence the office of *censor*. After the decline of the Western Empire, and later in early medieval times, the central task of communication in public was either the propagation of the Gospels and Christian religion or the dissemination and exercise of the secular power.

Alongside the purposes of instruction in religion, some sources and texts were identified (by others) as *wilfully* heretical and as likely to undermine true belief. Publications regarded as subversive of authority were treated in a similar way and attempts were made to suppress them. In early medieval scholarship and science, both oral and written communication were centred on the transmission of truth or of authoritative accounts. The main aims were instructional (educational), inspirational, or philosophical. It seems only later and gradually, accompanying the proliferation of printed material of varied kinds and the extension of readership beyond the literati that the idea of unintended influence took root, especially in respect of harm (although unintentional harm was also understood as a possible result of imperfect copies of texts or deviant translations of Scripture, especially into the vernacular).

The typical forms of harm that were envisaged in late medieval and early modern times could be classified as religious error, civil disaffection, or personal moral corruption. The dangers of unintended harm from publication were usually associated with the uncontrolled spread of publications to the ignorant, unlettered, and supposedly more vulnerable common people. For the most part, publications in Latin were regarded as safer than those in a vernacular language. The first English statute on the topic (2 Henry IV 1401), entitled *De heretico comburendo*, mentions the writing and making of books apt to corrupt their readers (Trapp, 1998: 36). Later statutes, e.g. of Henry VIII in 1543, forbade the reading of the English Bible to women, apprentices, serving men, husbandmen, and labourers (Trapp, 1998: 38), presumably on the ground that they might be led into error. Men of higher rank might read the Bible aloud to others, but women of similar rank could only read in private. Printing increased the risks of harm from publication because of the scale of production and dissemination. Everywhere licensing was imposed. In the Ottoman Empire, printing itself was banned until the early eighteenth century for fear of heresy (Briggs and Burke, 2002: 16).

In the early decades of printing after its invention in the mid-fifteenth century, the writing and making of books was inevitably a calculated affair, given the costs and time involved. Books were produced for particular markets and types of user. They were also expensive and acquired primarily for their use value, in professions (especially law), in scholarship, in education, and religion. This reinforced the connection between a given publication and a specific purpose. From the late fifteenth century, printing was being used (at least in England and France) by the state as an instrument of propaganda, especially in international conflicts. The association between printing and propaganda was intensified during the Wars of Religion and dynastic conflicts of the sixteenth and seventeenth centuries and there is no more purposeful form of communication than propaganda.

The gradual secularization of publication as printing gathered pace enlarged the range of texts available and required some revision of the then contemporary notion of influence. The most relevant new genres of publication in this respect were fictional, or quasi-fictional (myths and legends). Initially, literary (imaginative) publication was largely confined to circles around the court and the nobility and largely escaped censure from Church or state. There is some indication of a differential tendency in the early print era (the late fifteenth century) for literary texts such as poetry and romances (in different languages) to figure in the reading of gentlewomen, alongside more devotional works (Meale and Boffey, 1998). However, such material in popular and widely circulated forms was likely to be viewed as harmful, potentially leading to vanity, idleness, lust, and other sins (see Lowenthal, 1961). The Protestant reformers were more likely to be censorious than their Catholic precursors, although the sixteenth-century Counter-Reformation also reinforced suspicion of popular literature and entertainment. The distinction between intentional and unintentional influence was not generally made in respect of fiction (as it might be in the case of suspect religious works) and what mattered was the feared harmful effect on the morals of the reader.

MEDIA POWER AS A BELIEF SYSTEM

Against this background, it is not surprising that questions about publication and its influence (and therefore accountability for effects) have traditionally been framed on the assumption that publication does generally have knowable effects, and that these effects can be considered either as intended or not intended (although this may not affect responsibility). In the same tradition, judgment of intrinsic merit and of good or bad intention is presumed to be possible on the basis of evidence of manifest content as provided by an informed, unbiased, and presumably well-intentioned observer, or according to some clear moral or ethical code. This way of framing acts of public communication does not properly take account of the gradual transformation of communication practices from their religious and didactic origins to their secular expressive and instrumental forms as entertainment and information.

Even so, the frame has persisted into the modern era at least in public debate about the influence of mass media. There is still a tendency to take the manifest message (as sent) for the intention and even for the deed (of influence) itself. Early research into media content and effects struggled, without entire success, against the assumption that effect could largely be read from content alone (see Berelson, 1952; Holsti, 1969). Even today, regulatory action is still routinely taken against content on grounds of 'inscribed' effects waiting to occur (as in matters of libel or obscene publication).

The situation as outlined lies at the root of much of the confusion and misdirection of effort that has characterized both the search for effects of mass media and approaches to media accountability for effects. Old ideas have not been adequately adapted to what is known about mass communication. The framing of ideas about media power has (unsurprisingly) not been left to philosophers or social scientists. It has largely taken place in the arena of public debate, expressed in public opinion and popular belief and often under the influence of self-interested publicists and others with a stake in the presumed effects of the media, positive or negative, including the media themselves.

The media's self-perception (and proclamation) of their own power has played a significant role. The media are still committed (by their roles as public informer, advertiser, and entertainer) to promoting a belief in their own power, despite occasional disclaimers of responsibility when it is politic to do so. Public communicators (propagandists and advertisers) continue to behave as if the media have a calculable power to influence, and public opinion still seems as ready as ever to endorse the idea. It is not surprising that society in its collective actions and stance in relation to media power has generally chosen to follow the dominant belief system, despite its quasi-mythical foundations.

CONCEPTS OF POWER AND INFLUENCE

Several meanings of the power ascribed to the mass media are embedded in the belief system just described. First of all we need to keep in mind that we are talking about *communicative* power, as distinct from physical force, about words and images, not actions or material interventions. While there is much dispute about the meaning of power in social theory, a good starting-point is Max Weber's summary definition of the concept as 'the chance of a man or a number of men to realize their own will in a communal action even against the resistance of others who are participating in the action' (Weber, 1964: 152).

Communicative power lacks the element of coercion or material reward which makes for full power in this sense and for effective control of another. What remains is the dominance of one party in a (communicative) relationship, but one based on factors of reputation, trust, attraction, conviction, expertise, and symbolic or psychic rewards and penalties, not forgetting communicative skills and resources. Communication can also deploy an appeal to moral and normative commitments and political or ideological commitments that are the basis for much human action. These are considerable assets, but not easy to calculate, predict, or manipulate with any certainty. Nor is their amount and effectiveness (actual or potential) easy to measure.

The original belief system presumed a defining case of media power as one where sides are taken, ideas propagated or attacked, and a systematic process of information, persuasion, or education engaged in. The process was also, as noted above, typically perceived as purposeful, in pursuit of some end designated by the source or communicator. In fact, this ideal type is quite inappropriate to most situations of mass communication, where influence in this sense is not usually sought by sender or receiver. Despite this, it has proved difficult to remove the twin notions of purpose and coercion (even if symbolic or psychological) from the media effect discourse.

The version of the power of the media outlined is not entirely misleading when the media are considered as exerting strong general (environmental) constraints on the actions of others. The condition of public opinion (itself partly formed and made known by the media) ultimately sets limits to what political actors can do on many matters, and perceptions of the strength and direction of opinion can exert a strong influence.[2] Thus the expected consequences, intended or not, of publication enter into the reality of contexts for actions and such effects cannot be easily reversed or displaced, even by physical or financial power.

In the systematic analysis of media effects, the concept of *power* has not usually been regarded as very appropriate and preference has been given to other terms, especially persuasion; influence; behavioural stimulus; information process; and affective response.

PERSUASION

Persuasion refers exclusively to the deliberate use of communication to achieve some aim in terms of the belief, attitude, opinion, or action of a person. Purposeful communication of this kind appears in a wide variety of media forms ranging from propaganda on behalf of some political party or other belief (e.g. religion) or some collective social goal (e.g. a national war effort) to diverse specific goals (in relation to health, safety, civic conduct, etc.). The main differentiating variables in processes of public persuasion may be considered to be the degree of psychological coercion or of collective social pressure that is involved. Persuasion is always strongly controlled by the sender.

INFLUENCE

Influence is the main alternative concept to that of power in respect of communication. Parsons (1967) treated influence as an intentional form of social interaction and described it as a means of causing a 'decision on *alter*'s part to act in a certain way because it is felt to be a good thing for *him*...not because of the obligations he would violate through non-compliance'. It is thus generally non-coercive and often has a moral basis (an appeal to shared norms), involving a mutual orientation of sender and receiver. A process of influence is not necessarily deliberate and can be initiated by the receiver as well as by the 'sender'. It overlaps with the situation of unintended or unforeseen effects from communication. The term influence is mainly applied to cognitive processes such as opinion forming and to action that may follow on, such as voting, purchasing, etc.

Where effects on imagination, impressions, images, pleasure, or identity are concerned, the term influence may itself be inappropriate here because of the baggage it carries, for instance the connotation of one-directional transmission of flow and the association with cognition. In such cases, outcomes depend very much on the receiver and also involve emotions and feelings.

BEHAVIOURAL STIMULUS

There is a fairly clear category of media effect that embraces a range of individual acts, considered as direct reactions to some specific media stimulus. The scientific attitude of mind initially adopted some form of Pavlovian stimulus–response model from early psychology to deal with some of these matters, although more especially behavioural reaction (see Skinner, 1959; McQuail and Windahl, 1993). According to this model a media message (sound, word, image, text) is a stimulus that becomes associated with some other object of desire, admiration, or motive. This model, although much criticized, remains a popular frame for explaining how the media cause behaviour in those exposed (their audiences), whether intentionally (as with advertising and consumption) or not (as with entertainment).

It is the unintended behavioural effects, so conceived, that have received most attention, especially in the context of undesirable or anti-social actions (see also n. 9 below). These include violence (including suicide and the imitation of violent acts), crime, drug abuse, sexual promiscuity or deviance, and the abuse of children and women. In such cases the media are said to stimulate, teach, or trigger certain forms of behaviour, especially those who are vulnerable or predisposed through youth, gender, or other circumstances (see e.g. Comstock *et al.*, 1978; DeFleur and Ball-Rokeach, 1989; Gunter, 1994; Harris, 1994; Bryant and Zillmann, 1994; Perse, 2001).

INFORMATION PROCESS

The information process refers to the transmission or learning of cognitions (knowledge, opinion), as distinct from the stimulation or encouragement of feelings, emotions, beliefs. In the present context, the main reference is to a wide range of intended and unintended consequences (including the acquiring, remembering, and understanding of the information itself) of media use. Although certain informational genres or formats (news, analysis, documentaries, etc.) usually come first to mind, it is quite possible to learn about reality from fiction and to develop structures of cognition that are subjectively constructed. Numerous media formats including fiction, advertising, and news especially draw on facts, images, and ideas concerning the real world that for many or most people are the only source of their knowledge of the world, beyond limited formal education and personal experience.[3]

Information processes vary in terms of intentionality on the part of both sender and receiver. They are also usually interactive in producing results, that is to say, that learning generally requires involvement, co-operation, or suitable motivation on the part of the receiver. The term informative power may be used of a medium to refer to its potential capacity for transmitting information (irrespective of its value or accuracy), but it has to mean more than just the reach and overt content of the medium and must take account of audience attitudes, selectivity, and typical uses. It also implies a reference to the the information value, readability, and attractiveness of media texts.

AFFECTIVE RESPONSE

The category of affective response refers primarily to effects that are manifested in palpable emotions and feelings experienced during or after media experience. These include liking, aversion, fear, hate, shock, happiness, distaste, etc. The more forceful the impact and the more apparent the manifestation, the more appropriate would be the term reaction rather than response. Most affective response is positive and intended (as an effect). However, in our context, the main relevance is to questions of offence or disturbance caused by media exposure and possible harm to young or vulnerable persons exposed (often unwittingly) to the type of content in question (often violent and dramatic, also sexual in nature).

THE BASES OF MEDIA POWER

To go further in the prediction or explanation of possible effects from the media we have to look more closely at the various bases of communicative power. Since the early days of research into purposeful mass communication (e.g. Hovland *et al.*, 1951; Klapper, 1960; Trenaman, 1967; McGuire, 1973), different elements and factors in the communication process have been identified as relevant to successful communication. The variables in the situation have to do with: the source; the channel; the content; the presentation form; the audience; and the contextual conditions. Without going into detail, we can say that a message is more likely to be effective when it comes from an attractive and/or authoritative source by way of a major and reputed channel, when the message is prominent and has relevant content characteristics,[4] and when the audience is attentive and disposed to be influenced. Many different conditions of reception can contribute to, or detract from, actual media communication processes, but especially those that have to do with a personal 'need to know', positive disposition, and with the presence of support in the immediate group or social environment for the direction of the message. These points underline the fact that medium and message alone are not usually in themselves powerful, except as they activate, or are in line with, other social communicative processes.

Phrases such as the 'power of the media' or the 'power of the press' are not empty of meaning, but media as such have no real power beyond that of attracting attention (the power of publicity). However, the attribution of power to the media can in itself make an independent and significant contribution to the capacity to exert influence. It invites attempts to use media purposefully and enhances their status. It may well increase trust and esteem for the source on the part of an audience. This has implications for media responsibility and possible liability for consequences. The more authoritative or popular a source or communicator is, the more probable is some effect, especially when the message is carried by a large-scale and popular medium. While the extent of an effect cannot be predicted from these two factors (of source status and scale of dissemination or impact) alone, they are the most visible factors in situations of alleged effect. However, the causes of any effect are never entirely under the control of the communicator, but lie with unpredictable variables of context and audience (see Comstock *et al.*, 1978).

DIMENSIONS OF THE PUBLICATION ROLE

Public debate about the effects of mass media as well as media research itself has often been based on the presumption of a linear sequential model of intentional communication or that of stimulus response, as described above. This model lends itself best to legalistic thinking about the accountability (for the effects) of communication, in which perpetrators and victims need to be identified and causes established. However, it is a misleading view of most communication processes and not even very appropriate for dealing with the mediated character of influence by way of the mass media. Alternative models or types of publication role need to be considered and are introduced below. Before doing so, some distinctions are in order, according to four main dimensions, namely authorship; intentionality; authority; and self-determination. The distinctions involved help to classify the publication roles.

AUTHORSHIP

The same (independent) mass medium (such as a newspaper or TV channel) originates and commissions content as well as relaying much from outside. It expresses its own opinions as well as giving or selling space for other opinions to be publicized. It collects and publishes information according to its own agenda while also passing on much from other sources and news agencies. Media vary according to the degree in which they are identifiable as an author but most media most of the time do not offer clarity on this point. Where accountability is involved, the question of authorship has, nevertheless, to be answered.[5]

INTENTIONALITY

In general, the more purposeful a publication (that is, one more likely to have a clearly envisaged and stated goal), the more appropriate it is to identify it as a potential cause. However, intentionality in its fullest sense is largely confined to situations where the media are acting in a primary role as author, advocate, informant, or publicist. More often than not the content they carry embodies the purposes of others and the media's own purpose is only to attract and serve an audience. The degree to which media can actually distance themselves from the purposes to which they provide facilities or access can be disputed, although by the long-established convention of the freedom of the press, they can legitimately do so, subject to some risks.[6]

AUTHORITY

The dimension of authority is linked to potential effect. In fact it is not a single dimension, since there are different kinds of authority in media communication. One kind stems from closeness to real political or economic power; another from certified expertise and information value; another from the fame and esteem of the source or communicator; another from personal attractiveness to an audience. Even so, the potential for influence depends on a general factor of acknowledged authority, source appeal, and/or credibility. The more authority in any sense is involved, the more likely is some effect, and the more justification for attributing causal responsibility.

AUTONOMY OF SUPPLY OR RESPONSE TO DEMAND

The linear model of influence, as sketched, generally involves a view of an audience as passive, dependent, malleable, and susceptible to influence, which reinforces the attribution to the media of causal responsibility. In reality, much of what the media transmit is either at the behest of audiences and tailored to their wants or very much within their capacity to select or respond to in variable ways. The more this applies, the less the potential responsibility of the media or their liability for consequences. This observation exposes the inverse relation between media claims to influence and their disclaimers of responsibility: the two are not very easy to reconcile.

ALTERNATIVE MODELS OF MASS MEDIATION (PUBLICATION ROLES)

These considerations allow us to construct alternative models of the relationship between the various actors in the media communication process, from origination at source to reception by an audience. The origination of content takes place in a variety of ways and between origination and ultimate reception by an audience the media have different mediating roles: they collect or select; they process internally to make content suitable for transmission; they publish and retransmit according to their monitoring of audience interests. In carrying out these actions as part of a general publisher role, the media establish relations both with external 'originators' and also with audiences. These mediating roles are variants of their role as publisher. Although there are various possibilities,[7] for present purposes the main alternatives can be described as follows.

MEDIA AS SOURCE OR AUTHOR

In this version, the media are not mediating at all but originating a range of content. This case fits those media of news and comment that choose an opinion-forming or campaigning role. In-house editorial commentary, investigative reporting, and watchdog or critical reporting, as well as interpretation of events, are to be found. Influence is usually intended and causal responsibility not denied. The case also applies to many audio-visual media that produce or commission original cultural productions and entertainments (film, video, TV shows, etc.).

THE AGENT OF AUTHOR MODEL

Media provide (independently) the organizational and technical means of production and distribution for an individual author (of various kinds) to reach an audience, but without having any share in the authorship and correspondingly less responsibility for the content of the message. Authorial intention may not be specified by, or even known to, the transmitting medium. Causal responsibility of the carrying media for (typically unknown and unpredictable) effects is typically low.

AGENT OF SOURCE MODEL (ADVOCACY, PROPAGANDA)

This role relates to the case of media being in the service of (or controlled by) would-be agents of influence. These are usually institutional or collective sources, with propaganda goals (political, ideological, religious, commercial). The media act as their mouthpiece and amplifier, or simply as a channel. By convention, independent or neutral media can disclaim any association with such content. Nevertheless, the clear awareness of goals and potential effects opens the way for some association with sources and attribution of responsibility.

THE GATEKEEPER/DISSEMINATOR (AMPLIFICATION) MODEL

Media provide the organizational and technical means for information about events, plus voices/messages, to circulate in society, with content and intention determined by senders/sources and selection mainly influenced by perceived audience interest. The main example is that of news. The central feature of the media role in this model is the process of selection and editing. This role overlaps with what have been termed functions of 'platform', 'bulletin board', or 'forum' for access and debate. Similar remarks concerning responsibility for consequences apply here as to the preceding type.

AGENT OF AUDIENCE MODEL

Some media (and forms of media) seek only or primarily to provide what their chosen audience might want, with no other selection criteria or communicative purpose of their own or on behalf of others. The implications for responsibility are unclear, although it seems reasonable to regard the audience as at least sharing the responsibility for any effects. The media make their own choices for transmission, but, if the media audience market is working properly, the ultimate responsibility lies with audiences that freely choose to attend or not and any consequences may be held to lie at their own door. The main problem with the notion of audience 'self-culpability' lies in the inevitable inefficiency of both editorial selection and audience attention. The delivery of much media content is not very finely tuned to the tastes and preferences of audiences and there is much unintended and unwanted exposure.

These different models of media roles are not mutually incompatible and often coexist in the ongoing activities of any large scale media organization engaged in publication. The arrival of the Internet in the spectrum of media further complicates this picture. The primary media role (of gatekeeping or editing) has largely disappeared in this medium except as represented by service providers or search engines whose editorial and selecting role is limited and, because often invisible, not very accountable, although this latter role seems to be growing in significance as the medium is more commercially organized and regulatory agencies press for order. In principle all Internet sources are still their own publisher and responsible for their own content. The Internet is simply a carrier except where determined otherwise (see Chapter 5).

TYPES AND PROCESSES OF MEDIA EFFECT[8]

Aside from the question of intentionality, the effects of the media can be distinguished according to whether they are short term or long term. The former are mainly those which can be directly manifested in the immediate behaviour of individuals as when they buy advertised goods, vote in a certain way, or show other kinds of reactions (e.g. shock or horror). It is in this area that much attention to the media as a cause has been concentrated, partly because a causal connection is more direct and observable. By definition, long-term effects are less easy to connect with any specific antecedent event and other factors must play a part. Thirdly, there is a distinction to be made between positive and negative effects, although issues of accountability generally arise only in where harm is alleged. Beyond this, there are several different mechanisms of effect to be noted, with varying implications for the responsibility of a source or of the media, including learning, triggering, imitation, identification, etc. (see also n. 9 below).

These distinctions have obvious implications for attributing causal responsibility, but they are also difficult to apply empirically The media may deny any causal role in responses that are unintended, unpredictable, and random in their incidence, even when a statistical probability exists of some undesirable occurrence within some time frame (as in other areas such as traffic accidents). Important distinctions exist within the category of content suspected of having harmful direct effects on individuals. It is quite common for content with positive or blameless intentions (such as news or literary classics) to have unintended negative effects, for which responsibility may reasonably be denied.

Within the category of long-term effects, especially, the distinctions are even more numerous, finer, and harder to establish. Many effects are collective rather than individual, including voting patterns; lifestyle, health, and consumption patterns; non-participation or social isolation; the distribution of public knowledge; cultural tastes; and many other phenomena. It is already clear that the consideration of long-term effects is quite far removed from any precise moment of contact between media and audience. It is also unlikely, on the face of it, that we can clearly allocate causal (or even moral) responsibility, separate media from other potential causes, or produce adequate proof of effects. The remoteness of provable effects from particular publication decisions does not absolve media decision-makers from responsibility, but a different frame of reference and effect discourse is called for.

The type and availability of audiences also enter into assessments of media responsibility, even if only by convention. Thus certain media and forms of publication can be approximately restricted to certain categories of audience. An important distinction is usually made between voluntary and involuntary exposure. Certain media contents such as street poster advertising and peak time television on main channels have a large probability of being seen by nearly everyone (or anyone), with little chance of selection, avoidance, or filtering out. Some audience members are likely to be confronted with unwanted or inappropriate content. Other content is only available at minority times (e.g. the early hours of the morning) or on minority channels, where it can match the expectations and standards of particular audiences.

A perennial topic of debate, and a divider amongst schools of thought about media effects, has been the choice of a basic model of effect processes. It is clear from what has been said that different models are appropriate for different purposes. Even so, for purposes of accountability for real life events, rather than theorizing, there is a tendency to favour the earlier 'transmission' model of direct effect. Much attention has been given to the possibility of a direct causal link between media exposure and physical harm being done to others by the persons exposed.[9] This hypothesis applies to events such as the Columbine school massacre (Heins, 2000) or the similar case in Erfurt, Germany, in 2002 which led Chancellor Schroeder to call for scrutiny of the role of the media. There have been numerous court actions in the United States over the years relating to individual cases. In a review of US court decisions in fifteen such cases, Dee (1987) found that liability was thought to depend mainly on the presence or absence of negligence, which in turn depends on whether there is an 'unreasonable' degree of risk of harm being caused by the conduct of the media in the specific instance. In none of the cases studied was there a successful action, mainly because of the claim to First Amendment protection. Even so, Dee concluded that the concept of negligence (and foreseeability) is relevant to the accountability of the media, especially where young people are involved.

Calvert (1997) has proposed an alternative and for some purposes more appropriate 'ritual' model, first outlined by Carey (1975). The application proposed is for cases of hate speech, where victims are minority groups rather than individuals. Calvert describes the transmission model as directing the attention of courts to 'direct immediate and overt behavioural changes, physical responses, and mental anguish suffered by the targets of hate speech'. By contrast, the 'ritual model...points to a different harm. It is a long-term cumulative harm that accrues with repeated use of racial epithets directed at targeted minorities... [that] promotes disparate treatment'. This offers a useful alternative way of thinking with wider applications, such as in respect of pornography. The ritual model is not suitable for determining liability for a specific case of hate speech, but illuminates the problem for courts and legislatures. The example of sexual harassment in the workplace is offered for comparison. Some risks to freedom of speech are recognized (see also Heins, 2000).

THIRD-PARTY EFFECTS

Publication can have harmful consequences not only for their immediate audiences but also for others. At one end of the spectrum of possibilities are instances of personal defamation where the harm is done to specific individuals who are the subject or referent of communication rather than the recipient.[10] Many unintended harmful effects are quite minor, relating to inaccuracy and misquotation, but the incidence of such failings is surprisingly high (Pritchard, 2000). Publicity in one medium can lead to the invasion of the privacy of an individual by other media. There may well be other side effects of exposure to unwanted publicity.

Further along the spectrum are instances of social groups or minorities being misrepresented, ignored, or treated negatively on the basis of media reports. The immediate effects are on the cognitive and affective outlook of the actual audience, but others are affected in turn through personal contact. As long as media operate within the limits of the law they are free to do quite a lot of harm to third parties, without these seeking, or even having much chance of, redress. Many such victims of the media are powerless and unable to respond. Depending on time and place, they include such groups as the mentally ill, criminals, addicts, immigrants, gypsies, and other deviant or marginal groups. At the end of the spectrum are allegations of collective harm to culture, morals, or a whole society. In general the more identifiable the alleged victim(s), and the nearer in time the alleged offence (publicity), the stronger is an appeal to causal accountability.

STANDARDS OF PROOF OF MEDIA EFFECT

Many of the issues that are considered under the heading of account-ability have been framed on the assumption that evidence of media effect *can* be secured, notwithstanding the complexities of the causal process. This assumption goes beyond what is usually required for implementing law and regulation, where actual proof of causation is rarely required, even where it might be attainable. Evidence of the act of publication and its content (as in defamation cases), plus a convincing argument on reasonable presuppositions, is normally sufficient. There are different approaches to the question of evidence of effect in different legal systems.[11] There is a long history of social scientific inquiry into media effects and its findings often figure as evidence in public inquiries and debates about the influence of the media (especially in relation to violence and social disorder). The official consensus is now that media violence does have effects on violent behaviour, but there is still uncer-tainty about how much and under what conditions.[12] The extent to which the media have caused or encouraged civil disorder is still un-determined, despite inquiries into violent episodes.[13]

A related area of research has been into the effects of sexually explicit material. Here assessments tend to divide according to the standpoint of the researcher. Even so, Perse (2001) concludes in her review of research that such material does encourage the acceptance of violence against women and desensitizes those exposed to it. She observes that 'exposure to pornography seems to be associated with harmful consequences' (229). Despite this simple statement, there is a long and continuing history of debate on the causal link between media 'pronography' (of which there is no agreed definition, beyond the public display of explicit sexual matters) and harmful or illegal behaviour. Einsiedel (1988) reviewed the work of public commissions in three countries (Britain, Canada, and the USA) and reached three relevant conclusions. One is that social-scientific evidence has been unable to settle the issue (see also Paletz, 1988). Secondly, preconceived attitudes shape the outcomes of deliberations (she identifies in particular liberal, feminist, and conserva-tive positions). Thirdly, the interpretation of evidence is subordinated to political and ideological considerations.

Against this background, what more can be said in general about the possibility of proving media effects according to conventional standards of causal reasoning, bearing in mind that 'words are not deeds'? We can ask, first of all, whether the media do achieve their *intended* communicative effects, according to the logic of causal reasoning. If this is not the case, then proving unintended effects is likely to be even more difficult. The transmission of news, for instance, has been shown in a variety or experiments and surveys to be followed by some increased public knowledge of events reported in the news (e.g. Robinson and Levy, 1986). The general structure of public knowledge in people's minds also corresponds quite closely with the structure of information as it has been presented.[14] However, learning from news has also been shown to be very inefficient and incomplete.

Despite claims and beliefs, the evidence for the effectiveness of advertising is similarly patchy and uncertain (e.g. Stewart and Ward, 1994). Although the general conditions for influence on public opinion in political communication are known, the precise amount of effect in given cases has always been unpredictable in advance and uncertain after the event. All in all, there is a great variability and uncertainty about the effects of intentional mass communication. Not surprisingly, this applies even more so to the situation of unintended effects. The multiplicity and complexity of factors that contribute to any plausibly expected media effect is too great to be handled conceptually or operationalized by current or foreseeable research methods and models.[15]

The proof of direct cause is always going to be elusive and much evidence from media effects research, even in the areas named, is counter-intuitive to popular belief. There is much more evidence of 'non-effect' or unintended effect than of intended effect. A good deal of what does receive much media attention and publicity does not seem to leave any trace at all. There is great variability in the effectiveness of all intentional communication, with little capacity to predict the degree of success in any given case.

In practice this means that the attribution of responsibility and the exercise of accountability can never depend substantially on 'hard evidence' of causation. The apparatus of testing for effects does not lend itself to the circumstances or timescale of most accountability claims. Any empirical inquiry will have to follow a complaint and the outcomes can only be applied by argument to particular cases. This differentiates most situations of media liability claims from other actions for harm caused, as in courts of law, or medical or financial. Inquiries in such areas can reconstruct specific sequences of events preceding the event at issue. This is rarely possible in the case of alleged media harm. However, the main point of weakness concerns the nature of the connection between publication on the one hand and reception and response on the other. This connection is largely indeterminate because of the fundamental reflexivity of human perception and conduct. It is also interactive, with the receiver playing an active part.

SOME LESSONS FOR MEDIA ACCOUNTABILITY

In assessing the implications of the preceding material, we need again to make a simple distinction between media responsibility and accountability. The first refers to any obligation, whether voluntary or not, on the part of the media to consider the consequences of their publications, the second, in this context, refers to measures taken after the event to require media to answer for the consequences of their activities. This leads in turn to redefining the potential causal responsibility of the media (see Chapter 9).

Secondly, we need to consider fairly carefully what purposes are served by trying to establish the responsibility of the media for effects. Several non-exclusive possibilities can be indicated. One purpose is to protect the public in a general way from various (consensually agreed) harms that have been attributed to the media, especially those relating to violence, crime, and disorder. Here precautionary reasoning, based on evidence of risk, plays a part. Secondly, there is a somewhat different issue of achieving conformity on the part of the media to reigning standards of taste, decency, or morality. This may be considered as a (cultural) environment-protection goal or as recognition of community rights over public display. Thirdly, there is a wish to protect particularly vulnerable groups, especially children, from exploitation and harm, given their limited powers of choice or resistance. Fourthly, there is the question of the causation of specific harm to particular individuals, in which case we should attend both to questions of probability beforehand and to evidence of intention or negligence after the event. Fifthly (although not lastly), from a libertarian or even cultural perspective, the issue of media effect has to be very critically regarded so as to minimize the cost to freedom of any conclusions drawn. With these points in mind we need to look at the following matters.

- There has to be confidence that the alleged potential stimulus is actually present in the media and is reaching audiences to such a degree as to make any claim or judgement plausible. The actual audience reached, its size, and appropriateness for the content come into any assessment. Since this is the easiest part of any evidence-collecting procedure (although not easy), the standards of evidence should be high. Intended effects on intended audiences (in terms of size and characteristics) are generally covered by the media's self-defined responsibilities to its audience.

- This leads to the issue of motivation and degree of culpability on the part of the publisher, which has to play a part in any judgement. On the one hand, publication with potential (but unintended) harmful effects calls for an account to be given in justification. The kind of effect and degree of negligence are at issue. On the other hand, where publication is deliberate, there may be positive intentions and alleged harmful or offensive content may be justified on grounds of truth or the public interest, or on aesthetic grounds.

- In considering intention, the position of the media (a medium) in the publication process has to be taken into account, including its degree of control, motivation, and awareness. The more media act as conduits rather than original sources, the more responsibility is lessened or shared. In the case of news, for instance, media are constrained by unwritten rules and expectations to report material whose content is determined elsewhere.

- The degree of intentionality is intrinsically uncertain and hard to determine by others, especially where secondary or hidden meanings are involved as they often are. There is no simple rule that responsibility increases with intentionality, although that is sometimes the case. Responsibility for alleged effects, especially the more distant social evils, may even be rejected by the media not only on the grounds that they are not intended, but also that they are unpredictable in their occurrence, and that they almost certainly have other causes.

- Media also differ according to their standing in society (related to their authority and esteem) and their openly chosen role (e.g. ranging from business information to soft pornography). Such matters define their self-chosen responsibility and to some extent their degree of influence.

- The effect of communication depends on factors other than the mass media, such as personal communication and supportive contexts and normative frameworks. In many cases, the media are much more limited, time bound, and peripheral than other forces at work. It is important to make as accurate an estimate as possible of the likelihood of any effect under given circumstances.
- In so far as members of an audience, with sufficient prior information, choose their media and contents (and even sustain certain kinds of provision by their demand), they can be considered responsible themselves for any effects that occur (at least those that they experience directly, but with less certainty for third-party effects).
- Last, but certainly not least, is the necessity of clearly formulating the approach adopted to questions of effect. The alternatives are quite numerous, but four basic approaches offer themselves. One involves following a moralistic or ideological logic, guided by judgement of content and ideas of what is good and bad in publication, rather than being influenenced by precise evidence of effects. Secondly, there is an approach that focuses on the short-term harmful impact on individuals, with implications for punishment or compensation. Thirdly, there is a long-term or environmentalist logic, which looks to the indirect, cumulative consequences for the society and its members of certain systematic patterns of publication. Finally, there is the libertarian view which takes a sceptical look, not so much at allegations of harm, but at the cost to freedom entailed and even the possible harm caused by suppression.

IN CONCLUSION

Given the extreme difficulty of establishing proof of cause at all, it is doubtful if the question of effect should play as large a part as it does in the discourse concerning media responsibility. The more that proof of effects (especially harm) is regarded as a necessary condition for requiring accountability, the less easy it is to justify any claim or action against the media. On the whole, the media have benefited from the tendency to define issues in terms of measurable effects and have hidden behind the near impossibility of achieving anything better than statements of general probability about any past or future effects of publication.

A more fruitful alternative is to hold the media responsible for their own actions as publishers and disseminators, not for the consequences of those actions (bearing in mind the varying nature of media responsibility as outlined earlier) but for publication actions themselves. This means proceeding on the basis of informed criticism, argument, explicated values, and standards as well as systematic evidence concerning the nature of the content published. In effect, this involves at least a partial revival of the moralistic approach. Concepts of harm and value are intrinsic to the dialogue, but should be treated as perceptions, preferences, beliefs, judgements, and definitions that individuals, communities, and societies are entitled to make and act upon in consistent and transparent ways. As a counterbalance to the inevitable bias of such an approach, we should turn not to the scientific, evidence-based model, but to the larger implications for liberty of any accountability measures proposed or implemented.

Such an approach involves a revaluation of cultural, moral, ethical, and aesthetic considerations as opposed to behavioural ones. It is also able to do more justice to the complexities and ambiguities of communication, to the great variety of contexts of reception and potential interpretation as well as to the continual changes in standards. This more normative approach carries some risks. In particular, it seems to lend support to the idea that we can protect the audience by classificatory and filtering devices and other forms of quasi-censorship. However, many problematic features of contemporary public concern about the media turn on issues of quality (good as well as bad) as much as on questions of harm.

NOTES

1. This emphasis on intentionality has persisted into modern communication theory. There have been numerous definitions of communication and Dance (1970: 201–10) identified 15 types of definition, each one emphasizing a particular feature. One of these was intentionality or purposefulness as a necessary condition if we are to speak of acts of communication. It is clear, even so, that there are many possible degrees of purposefulness and much apparent communication has little or no conscious purpose. In the case of mass communication, communicative purpose in the sense of intending and/or envisaging an effect is often completely absent (see Westley and MacLean, 1957).

2. A type of media effect (known as the 'spiral of silence') has been posited that involves the formation of opinion according to perceptions of what is the dominant view of the moment. Individuals are predicted to seek security by publicly

expressing or admitting to what they believe to be the most acceptable, widely current, and thus consensual opinions. Their main source of knowing what these might be are said to be the mass media (see Noelle-Neumann, 1984). There are mixed outcomes from tests of this hypothesis, but it remains plausible in certain circumstances and is consistent with other social psychological theory (Katz, 1980).

3. A tradition of research under the name 'cultivation theory' has for some time investigated the development of ideas about social reality in line with the predominant patterns of representation of the same features of reality in the content of the media (especially television) (see Gerbner *et al.*, 1984). The outcomes of research are typically somewhat unclear, but there is no doubt that on some topics and under some circumstances, something like a cultivation effect does occur, for instance in perceptions of the physical geography of the world (see Rosengren, 2000).

4. Different characteristics matter for different effects, whether intended or not, good or bad. In respect of media effects on violence or aggression, Roberts (1998) concludes that nine content factors are linked to the probability of effects. These are the nature or qualities of perpetrator and victim; the reasons for violence; the presence of a weapon; the extent and graphicness of the violence; the degree of realism; whether rewarded or punished; the consequences; whether humour is involved or not.

5. Typically, there are legal procedures for determining authorship, for instance by requiring a named person to be held accountable for what is published (e.g. an editor or publisher).

6. This claim is likely to be disputed where the message carried is offensive to authority or in situations of oppression or emergency. In most countries the media may be held liable for any allegedly harmful content they carry, even when done in good faith.

7. It is helpful to consider the media as having evolved a set of distinctive secondary or mediatory communication roles of their own that match originating or primary roles, in the following terms.

COMMUNICATION ROLES

Primary	Secondary (mediating)
Author	Publisher
Advocate	Forum/podium
Informant	News conduit
Entertainer	Stage
Publicist/Propagandist	Billboard

8. There are numerous overviews of research on this topic, but the most recent and comprehensive is Perse (2001).

9. A case was brought against a death-metal-music band, Slayer, for aiding and abetting in the murder of a Californian teenager by fans of the band (*The Guardian*, 24 Jan. 2001).

10. Instances in Britain of attacks on suspected paedophiles named in the press provide fairly conclusive evidence of actual physical harm. In the wake of the events of 11 September, there were many reports of attacks on Muslims in western countries, attributed, although without much evidence, to the influence of media in stirring up anti-Muslim hatred and associating terorrism with Islam (even if unintentionally).

11. Most countries have laws forbidding certain kinds of pornographic or obscene publications. However, the definition of the material varies and so does the grounds for objection, sometimes having to do with offence to public morality, sometimes the aim of erotic arousal, sometimes danger or actual harm caused (see Feinberg, 1987). Legislation in the UK (the Obscene Publication Act, 1959) defines as obscene material that 'tend[s] to deprave and corrupt persons' (exposed to it). In the United States the definition of obscenity for purposes of withholding First Amendment protection is determined by three rules (from a 1973 Supreme Court Ruling, Miller v. California): that an average person finds that the material 'appeals to prurient interests'; that the work 'depicts in a patently offensive way, sexual conduct defined by the applicable state law'; that the work 'lacks any serious, literary, artistic, or scientific value' (summarized from Perse, 2001: 225). US law also differentiates between indecent speech (permitted) and obscene speech which cannot be transmitted. In no country does it seem that actual evidence of harm *caused* is necessary for banning or punishing certain contents.

12. The conclusion of the American Psychological Association evaluation of research was that 'violence on television does lead to aggressive behavior by children and teenagers who watch the programs' (quoted in Perse, 2001: 202; see also Roberts, 1998; Wartella *et al.*, 1998).

13. For instance, the civil unrest and violence experienced in the United States during the 1960s led President Johnson to appoint a National Commission on the Causes and Prevention of Violence. Its report (Kerner Commission, 1968) reached no clear conclusion about the contribution of the media to the problem. A report on behalf of the Surgeon-General (1972) into the relation between television and violence cautiously concluded that viewing violence on television might tend to increase aggressive behaviour. Another commission (the President's Commission, 1970) examined evidence for the link between obscenity and pornography and crime and expressed doubts that a link existed (Easton, 2001). In the UK, an inquiry into the causes of rioting that shook Britain in 1981 included a study of the role of the media (Tumber, 1982). The context of such inquiries is one where scientific detachment in drawing conclusions is hardly possible and usually one where much more fundamental causes are at work.

14. One of the most secure hypotheses of media effect research (the so-called 'agenda-setting' process) posits that the publicly perceived importance of issues, events, or policies is determined by the relative salience of relevant news media reports over a relevant time period (see e.g. Dearing and Rogers, 1996). Although there is evidence to support this view, the role of the media as the primary causal agent has not been conclusively proved and it may never be possible to do so, since the news media tend to act as an agent of other sources.

15. This rather destructive comment on the prospects for research into media effects need not be read as dismissive of past efforts or future possibilities for worthwhile

research. Rather it embodies the view that quantitative empirical research cannot cope with the unpredictability, irregularity, and chaotic character of specific communicative events involving many different individuals and an enormous number of potential stimuli and variables. What research can and has done is to explicate certain logical processes that help to explain what is going on and here there is much more to be done.

8

Freedom and Accountability

In the Anglo-American and French republican tradition, freedom of the press was firmly established by the end of the eighteenth century as an ideal, a necessary condition for a democratic (self-governing) and just society and a practical objective of legal and political reform. Since then it has been a shorthand term for the right to own the means of publication and to publish without needing a licence, suffering advance censorship by agencies of the state, or facing arbitrary or unreasonable punishment for the act of publication after the event. It is a companion to other liberties, all named in the 1789 French Revolutionary Declaration of the Rights of Man and the 1791 First Amendment to the Constitution of the United States, namely freedom of religion, of speech, of assembly, and of the right to petition government.[1]

This is still the core of the matter in political and legal terms as it is incorporated in most democratic constitutions or common law. Largely because of the circumstances of its origin (in struggles against despotic or autocratic governments) advocates of freedom of the press have identified the state or its agencies as its principal enemy and have required the state to deny itself rights of control, interference, and sanction, subject to the rule of law and the wishes of the people. In this basic version, freedom of the press is an essentially negative concept, without filling in any notion of purpose or preference as to the use of the right, although it is also an idea that is still infused with a primary concern for open and diverse political and religious expression. Even so, the arguments that originally supported the claim to freedom of the press claimed certain benefits for society as well as for individuals and government has not been seen as the only enemy.

History is written not only by the victors, but also by the writers. At the start of the twentieth century, the main victor could be identified as the free market. The main writers were the free market mass media or their owners and apologists, whose view of press freedom was inevitably coloured by self-interest. In another sense, the main victor in our time has been the United States, whose concept of press freedom is enshrined in the sacred text, much embellished, of the First Amendment to the Constitution (1791), which clearly identifies government as the enemy.[2] The dominant text gains authority not only from the early history of democracy, but also from much twentieth-century experience of state dictatorships in many other countries not far from home. However, this has led to some distortion, or selectivity, in the press freedom narrative, which needs to be corrected. The eighteenth-century European theorists that influenced the US Constitution were not only antagonistic to the state but also to abuses of private power, for which the public power could provide some remedy (Holmes, 1990).

As the press become more industrialized, commercialized, and monopolized at the end of the nineteenth century and well into the twentieth century, critical voices have focused more on the distorting effects of the market system and increasing media concentration on freedom of publication (see e.g. Baker, 1994; Entman, 1989; Herman and Chomsky, 1988; McManus, 1994; Murdock and Golding, 1977; Sunstein, 1993; and many others). Critics have called for more not less government action to limit private monopoly power and to make the media more accountable as well as accessible. As Barendt (1998) observes, 'The agenda of political and social debate is not determined exclusively, as the Orwellian perspective holds, by the government but by newspaper barons and media conglomerates' (31). At the very least, no account of press freedom can ignore its dual character and the fact that both government and the free market can have both negative and positive implications for effective freedom of publication. The main alternative (but intertwined) strands can be best summarized as a distinction between a 'libertarian and a democratic theory of speech' (Fiss, 1997: 2). There is an underlying conflict of values between liberty and equality that cannot be readily resolved either in theory or practice.

DISTINCTIONS AND DEFINITIONS

Press freedom is a special case of the wider claim to freedom of expression, especially in speech. It is differentiated from this by two main features: it always involves public expression; and it involves material forms of production and distribution and the possession or use of property. The first point is important because of the greater potential consequences and the often larger purposes served and also because it represents a crossing of a line between thought and action. Moreover, publication cannot be denied or undone. The second point matters because it enlarges the scope and scale of the act of publication, gives it a specific location, and renders it more open to control. It also connects the right to publish with the right to own property. There are differences in practice in the degree of opportunity to speak or to publish, the former unlimited, the latter always scarce. Finally, there are differences in the degree and kind of accountability that attaches to personal expression in speech or other symbolic form, compared to publication, although neither is *ipso facto* unaccountable.

In a certain light and because of the necessity of material means of production, the right to publish is simply the right to use one's own property as one chooses and this has been alternatively regarded either as strengthening or weakening the case for immunity from control, depending on how positively or negatively the ownership of property is viewed (see Lichtenberg, 1990*b*). If private property is regarded as sacred and inalienable, intervention by government can only be justified in extreme cases and certainly not for determining the uses to which property should be put. If private ownership is viewed as a limitation on the rights of others and conditional on good behaviour, the way is open for outside direction or accountability. This conflict of interpretation can be avoided if we recognize freedom of publication as a quite separate right with its own independent justifications.

The separation of publication rights from property rights is also important, because it corresponds to the distinction between the contents of communication and the material means of production and distribution. This allows modern media regulation to be directed towards the (infra)structure and ownership of the press without directly affecting media content. It also recognizes the possibility of free expression by means not privately owned (as with public broadcasting systems).

The distinction between free speech and publication by way of a free press gives rise to another set of issues. The established (free market) press typically bases its claim to autonomy and relative immunity from accountability on the right to free expression. However, as Lichtenberg (1990*b*: 105) points out, 'it does not follow that whatever supports freedom of speech also supports freedom of the press'. She cites two reasons for this, one being that 'considerations internal to the theory of free speech itself may provide reasons for limiting freedom of the press', as when the media suppress information or limit access to channels of publication. Secondly, she points out that 'the modern press consists largely of vast and complex institutions that differ in essential respects from individuals and from the early press'. It certainly appears that public opinion makes a clear distinction of this kind and gives much less support for the freedom of the media (see Chapter 6).

This is a reminder of more complex distinctions that give rise to uncertainty about the degree of freedom of publication that can be claimed and about where it is located (who owns it) and what it means. It may be necessary to distinguish not only between individuals and the press (in the original form or its modern equivalent); a new category may be needed for contemporary large-scale media firms and conglomerates. The different forms of expression are not free in the same sense or degree, with varying requirements for controls and accountability. Most problematic and most important to deal with is the third category, since, as Barendt (1998: 30) points out, 'at the end of the twentieth century, virtually all significant speech is mass speech'.

Making these and other distinctions (for instance between press, broadcasting, and the Internet) does not necessarily work to the detriment of claims to freedom by the press or mass media. It also opens the way to giving them certain rights and protection, beyond those possessed by ordinary citizens, in order to aid them in fulfilling certain public interest tasks, including those of investigation, criticism, and standing up to pressure.

As befits a fundamental principle, the central idea of press freedom has remained quite static over time, despite many ambiguities and problems in application under varying circumstances. The latest phase of media development, that of the Internet, has revived much earlier concern about the distinction between what is private and what public where issues of accountability are involved.

The main tenets of the press freedom idea can be summarized as the rights of individuals or organizations (media firms, governments, associations of civil society) to:

- own the means of publication (production and distribution);
- produce, publish, and distribute information, ideas, or other content in print or other medium without a licence, without advance censorship, or threat of later penalties, subject only to other laws that apply;

- collect and exchange information, including attending and reporting on meetings open to the public;
- refuse to publish any particular matter.

This summary is not restricted to the case of the newspaper press, although the latter does still have a central part to play in the complex of public communication activities, both as original source and as carrier of the content of others. It does not apply to other media to the same degree, especially not to television and radio broadcasting in their capacity as systems of public communication.[3]

POSING THE PROBLEM

The central question addressed in this chapter can be expressed in words written some time ago by Doris Graber, when addressing a similar general issue: 'How to hold the press accountable for irresponsible behavior that endangers public and private welfare without destroying the independence of the press has remained a problem without a solution' (1986: 274). The concept of accountability remains to be fully explored (Chapter 9), but for present purposes it can be defined as any process by which communicators answer (voluntarily or not) for the purposes, contents, or consequences of their acts of publication.

At first sight it looks as if the concepts of accountability and control are not only related to each other in a definitional sense, but also inversely and progressively, such that greater freedom means less accountability and the latter must inevitably diminish the degree of real freedom. This is certainly the position most often taken by the press itself in liberal–capitalist press systems and by libertarian theorists (Merrill, 1989). However, the concepts are not necessarily incompatible and have considerable potential to vary independently. There are forms of accountability and ways of achieving it that are not inimical to press freedom, depending on how that is defined. In particular, freedom of expression need not be conceived only in negative terms, with no restraint or limitation, but also positively, where the benefits of freedom are identified and actively promoted, even by governments. Where an affirmative view of press freedom is chosen, accountability can be seen as one means of extending access, promoting higher standards, and monitoring performance in the public interest.

Most statements that formally recognize freedom of expression and of the press couple it with references to limitations and obligations. The eighteenth-century English jurist, Blackstone, writing in 1759, commented on the legal position of the publisher as follows: 'Every freeman has an undoubted right to lay what sentiments he pleases before the public; to forbid this is to destroy the freedom of the press; but if he publishes what is improper, mischievous or illegal he must take the consequences of his own temerity.' Article 11 of the 1789 Declaration of the Rights of Man states free expression is 'subject only to an accounting for abuse of that freedom as determined by law'. Contemporary texts all have similar clauses.

The Constitution of the United States, in its First Amendment, is unusual in making no exceptions to its absolute requirement that 'Congress shall make no law...abridging freedom of the press...', but, as many commentators have pointed out, freedom to publish is not unlimited by law or other means in the United States.[4] The United Kingdom has no written constitution, but legal practice both upholds the freedom of the press and also sets certain limits, as is the case in all democracies (see Article 19, 1993). Both the Universal Declaration of Human Rights of the United Nations (Article 19) and Article 10 of the European Convention on Human Rights specify some of the limitations on claims of freedom of expression.[5]

Leaving aside the many countries where promises of free expression are simply not respected, it is clear that the exercise of free expression, by whatever means, is hedged in by many restrictions and by potential demands for accountability, especially where others are affected to any significant degree by a public utterance. This applies with especial force to what has become by some criteria the main means of public communication, namely radio and television broadcasting.

Aside from untangling the relationship between freedom and accountability, there are a number of other questions that need to be addressed. One concerns the essence of *media* freedom and the arguments and values that support it. As noted earlier, it is not identical with the personal human right of free expression and the distinction needs to be further explored, with particular reference to the difference between arguments from absolute principle and those from expediency or practical objectives. There are also problems over precisely where the right to free expression is located and to whom it belongs in the complex institutional set up of modern media. These need to be resolved if we are to answer the question about just who (in the media) can be held accountable to whom (outside the media), on what type of issue, and on what grounds of complaint (if complaint it is).

FREEDOM FOR THE PRESS AS AN INSTITUTION

The press as an institution has no clear definition or boundaries despite frequent and sometimes specific reference (in such phrases as 'press gallery', 'representatives of the press', 'press conference', 'press rights or privileges', 'press ethics', the Fourth Estate, etc.). However, the wider press institution (usually of a single country) identified in this way is often collectively credited with having freedoms of speech and publication, given responsibilities, and held to account in public debate and by public opinion for its failings, despite having no status in law. The lack of definition and clear boundaries are an intrinsic feature of the press, consistent with the claim to freedom which lies at the heart of its activities. Whatever the essence of the press consists of, it cannot be to control the right to freedom of expression, since that would imply an institutional monopoly of a right enjoyed by all.

For the most part, the core activity of the press is the collection and regular (weekly or more frequent) publication of news and opinions about recent events of potential general interest. The predominant tradition of the press so defined has involved the roles of discoverer, assembler, and carrier of accounts and observations from various sources rather than that of a self-originator and disseminator of views (although there are other traditions and versions, e.g. the party press). The principle of press freedom does not distinguish between origination and dissemination or between types of publication. Any organ of the press can act freely as a legal person and can also be held to account. Where there is freedom of the press, any person can constitute themselves as a publisher, subject to some local rules.[6]

The press institution often has more customary rights and even privileges than are mentioned in formal statements of press freedoms. Such rights vary from country to country but include such matters as privileged access to information and locations where events are occurring (e.g. courts, crime scenes, war zones); some legal privileges, such as concealment of sources or rights to silence; special access to communication facilities and subsidized distribution; tax or financial benefits; various advantages given to professional journalists; other forms of public support. These and other features of the press institution reflect an extended notion of press freedom. They stem from an implicit identification of the press with the public, either as its representative, surrogate servant, or guardian of its interests. They also imply a positive notion of press freedom that is absent in constitutional statements. In doing so, they also connect freedom with various notions of responsibility, as described above, although not necessarily with accountability in any direct or specific form. It needs to be pointed out that the press has more 'privileges' than special rights and these more often than not work to the advantage of authorities and news sources rather than the public by helping them to manage information, as in the 'news pool' arrangements during the 1991 Gulf War.

ALTERNATIVE BASES FOR CLAIMS TO PRESS FREEDOM

The story often told to explain press freedom paints it as a fundamental right hard won by courageous democrats and publishers in the struggle against illegitimate royal and state power. However, this leaves a good deal open to interpretation, especially the question What then? Is press freedom to be prized and valued for its own sake or is it for the practical benefits it delivers? If treated exclusively in terms of the former, it supports an absolutist case against any government constraint or intervention. This is essentially the negative version of press freedom. The alternative interpretation constitutes a functionalist or consequentialist theory of the press. In this view, freedom is necessary if the press is to fulfil its expected role in a democratic society. This requires the press to be extensive, open, responsive, and critical. It is these attributes that lie at the heart of a positive or affirmative theory of the press and each of them has libertarian connotations.[7]

Glasser (1986) argues that neither version is superior in its protection of individual liberty: 'Rather, the essential distinction between the two focuses on whether the state should involve itself in bringing about the equal application of basic liberties. From the perspective of a negative conception of freedom, the press is under no obligation to extend its liberty or to accommodate the liberty of others... the essence of libertarianism is the denial of responsibility' (92–3). By contrast, an affirmative concept of press freedom recognizes that 'the tyranny of private transaction poses as much of a threat to individual liberty as the tyranny of government regulation'. The press should consequently have an obligation to enlarge the opportunity for expression and broaden its range. In general it 'embodies an expectation that the press will serve not just itself but the larger community'.

The first version (freedom for its own sake) involves an essentialist or 'deontological' view, according to which actions are judged to be inherently right or wrong. According to Schauer (1986: 771): 'Much of free speech theory can be located within this philosophical division. If speaking freely is a "natural right" then the liberty of speaking ought to be protected by a properly constituted state regardless of whether it is in the public interest to do so.' Schauer goes on: 'Usually these theories are couched in terms of self-expression, self-realization or self-fulfilment, but the core idea is the same—speaking is part of what it is to be a person, and restrictions on that expression of personhood by the state are simply wrong'.[8]

There is a considerable tension between the two basic approaches to justifying press freedom, turning essentially on the degree of reference to popular will or majoritarian power. The utilitarian/consequentialist view gives precedence to judgements about the relative value to the public of different types of utterance and possible limitations on speech, judgements that must be made by the public or its representatives, albeit by democratic means. It subordinates rights to considerations of public interest, according to which some forms of accountability may be required.

On the other hand the essentialist approach offers no clear way of distinguishing between one expression and another (all may be personally self-fulfilling), or of penalizing a speaker for harmful consequences. Effectively it divorces 'a theory of free speech from a theory of the public interest' (Schauer, 1986: 774). This has corresponding implications for accountability. In the essentialist perspective, there are no real grounds for expecting anything other than personal or moral responsibility. Although ultimately as well as logically opposed, these two different approaches are not necessarily mutually exclusive. But the choice needs to be recognized.

Emerson (1970) emphasized that the essentialist position does not deny responsibilities to others in the society. It also rests on a 'fundamental distinction between belief, opinion and communication of ideas on the one hand and different forms of conduct on the other' (1970: 60). This is a distinction between expression and action that recognizes the right of the state to exercise control over actions. A basic ingredient of the theory is the marking off of the special area of expression from other kinds of human conduct. According to Emerson, expression 'is normally conceived as doing less injury to other social goals than action. It generally has less immediate consequences, is less irremediable in its impact.' These are important arguments for protecting freedom of speech, but it is not certain that they are equally valid for publication in the mass media when speech actions may have much greater power to affect others materially and directly.

Close to the essentialist position is the view that relates freedom of expression to the discovery of truth. However, truth can be valued on consequentialist as well as essentialist grounds. It is said to emerge from the clash of opposed views and doctrines, whether or not these may be judged erroneous. The modern version is generally referred to as the 'theory of the market place of ideas' (see Chapter 11), which holds that the maximum flow of, and competition between, diverse kinds of information and opinions will also maximize the chances of truth being recognized.[9]

The link between freedom of expression and property rights has, as noted already, been invoked as a powerful defence against regulation or government restriction, especially in the United States. Lichtenberg (1990b: 120) argues that the appeal to property rights is based on an absolutist notion of the latter and ignores the fact that non-media businesses are not immune from regulation. She concludes that the 'typical claim of editorial autonomy by publishers and editors is a disguised property claim—it is the assertion of a property right in the guise of a free speech right'. By implication, there is a sleight of hand seeking to benefit from liberal principles.

The main counter-argument to private media owners' freedom claims based on market sovereignty is that the right to freedom of publication is ultimately justifiable according to the rights of the public to receive good quality and diverse information and other communications. If so, this should override the privileges of owners. The view that freedom of speech is as much for the listener as for the speaker was invoked in the United States as a basis for FCC regulation of some aspects of broadcasting content. In Europe and elsewhere extensive regulation of broadcast content derives from a similar claim on behalf of the public, with concomitant procedures for accountability. According to Scanlon (1990: 43) if property requires law to protect it, it is not surprising that the press should also 'require affirmative state action aimed at securing the preconditions for effective freedom of expression'.

VARIABLE PROTECTION AND CLAIMS TO FREE EXPRESSION

Despite the strength of essentialist arguments and the insistence of true libertarians that only absolute abstention by government will serve, there are considerable variations in practice in the kinds of content (and means of communication) that can claim full rights to free expression. As Loveland (1998: 11) points out: 'Not all speech is protected by the First Amendment' and, additionally, 'governmental bodies may legitimately impose time, manner and place constraints'. In examining the arguments for confining regulation to structures and means of communication, Scanlon observes that 'It is impossible to argue sensibly about freedom of expression without recognising the fact that some forms of expression are of higher value than others' (1990: 350). Certain communications are forbidden in advance on grounds of their intrinsic content, even where no censorship exists. There are many examples of words, spoken or printed, which could be interpreted as tending towards some illegal or harmful act and forbidden and punished after the event. Exceptions to free speech protection can be and are made to combat terrorism or protect defence secrets.

There are a number of general guidelines with respect to the claim for protection of speech or for disregarding it, under the First Amendment (Smolla, 1992). Most relevant is the *harms* principle that does allow speech to be penalized where it causes harm.[10] Smolla calls attention to the rule that causation has to be established in a rigorous way, connecting the speech with the actual or feared harm. Under the heading of harm, there is a general hierarchy of justification for prohibition or punishment. Two main factors are involved. One is a distinction between harm to persons and to property. The former takes precedence, as for instance in cases of incitement to kill or injure or where a speaker may receive a violent reaction.

The second dimension distinguishes between physical harm, relational harm, and reactive harm. In the case of persons, relational harm arises in the case of damage to reputation and reactive harm where emotional distress is caused or privacy invaded. The heading also covers offence caused to groups as in racist or sexist speech, or pornography. In accordance with the same hierarchy we can see that alleged socially harmful effects, as for instance through the portrayal of violence, come lower down in the scale and are less likely to justify restrictions on publication. They are less direct, immediate, precise, and harder to prove.

From the media point of view, this hierarchy is also a relevant frame for classifying its potential obligations or in responding to claims made against it. The media are more likely to be held legally to account for the kind of harm that heads the list. Since the cases of physical harm to individuals from publication are uncommon, attention concentrates on relational and reactive harm. The latter gains strength from the greater number of people likely to be involved. However, physical harm can result from publicity (see Chapter 7). Unpopular or deviant individuals, such as suspected terrorists and paedophiles, can be identified and persecuted. Racial or religious minorities are sometimes victimized after negative media publicity. People have been driven to suicide following some public accusation or revelation in the media.

Van Alstyne (1992) has made a formal analysis in a similar vein of the general structure of application of First Amendment protection. Firstly, he notes that 'freedom of speech' in the constitutional sense does not actually apply to all speech—it has a bounded scope, excluding a number of categories (aside from incitement), including perjury, obscenity, and defamation. Secondly, with reference to the possible causation of harm, two principles come into play. One is the probability of harm being caused as a result of speech (or publication), the other is the gravity of evil implied in the harm. This has already been discussed. In general, the higher the probability of an effect and the greater the evil, the less protection can be claimed. One should probably add to this, even if it does not figure in Van Alstyne's analysis, that the scale of harm and the number of those reached by a given publication always plays a part in assessing the justification for suppression or punishment.

The history of the press freedom idea strongly associates it with the need to protect certain kinds of expression and publication, especially those to do with politics and religion, even if this is not specifically written into constitutions and legal clauses. There are good reasons for this, since matters of belief and opinion can be expressed under many guises and there is no certain basis for making content distinctions. The neutrality principle mentioned above should also cover this situation, although the fact of variable protection according to content casts some doubt on the possibility of genuine neutrality. Figure 8.1, based on Van Allstyne (1992: 171), expresses one possible view of how different kinds of content rank according to being protected.

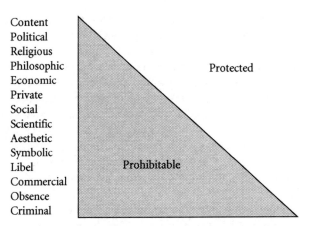

Content
Political
Religious
Philosophic
Economic
Private
Social
Scientific
Aesthetic
Symbolic
Libel
Commercial
Obsence
Criminal

Protected

Prohibitable

FIG. 8.1. Degree of First Amendment protection (Van Allastyne, 1992: 171)

The content items and their rank order are likely to vary from country to country, since they depend on the reigning norms, traditions, and political culture. There are different views on what can be considered harmful and on what the threshold of offence might be. In some countries insulting speech about national leaders or symbols (President, royalty, the flag, etc.) is tolerated while in others it is not. Blasphemy and pornography are treated quite differently in different countries in terms of freedom to indulge in them publicly. In the United States, obscenity (as defined in Chapter 7 n. 11) is not permitted while displays of extreme violence and 'hate speech' directed at race or religion are not forbidden (Heins, 2000). In most European countries incitement to racial hatred is illegal, while in some cases obscenity is not sanctioned at all. Despite differing legal provisions, this hierarchy has a general validity. Nowhere do defenders of free speech campaign as vigorously, or if they do with as much success, for the rights of pornographers, blasphemers, or racists as they do for political activists or oppressed minorities.

VARIABLE CONTENT AND FORMATS, VARIABLE FREEDOM

As indicated in Fig. 8.1 there is a stronger claim to freedom in relation to politics, religion, science, and aesthetic matters. These are closely related to identity, self-fulfilment, participation in society, and the search for truth. Some other structuring principles can be deduced. For instance, publication of factual information (or opinions about current issues) as opposed to fiction of all kinds, humour, and entertainment tends to have greater privilege. The news media generally face less regulation than entertainment media. The truth value of information is more demonstrable and thus a fundamental communication value is activated (see Chapter 4). The publication of information can also be more easily supported according to the utilitarian (functional) arguments for freedom. Information in general has a higher potential use value and it is necessary for participating effectively in democratic political processes.

What is less apparent, although possible to account for according to the same principles, is that certain formats for information enjoy more protection in practice than others. Direct expressions of political opinion are protected, while some forms of propaganda may not be, for instance documentaries sponsored by governments, political movements, or commercial vested interests. There is an increasing number of intermediate and unclear formats, especially on television, where doubt exists about the degree of their reliability, truth, or information value. This relates especially to so-called 'infotainment' and 'docudrama' and also to reality programming that is open to hidden manipulation. Even more problems of this kind affect the Internet, where the source is not easy to validate.

These format variations are related to the question of authorship and the variable publication role of media as outlined in Chapter 7. Where content has a clear authorship and an identified person or organization behind it, it has stronger claims to freedom as well as being more accountable (perhaps because the right to free expression of an individual is involved as well as media freedom). The media themselves can be a primary author in this sense. The apparent readiness with which Internet service providers bow to pressure to remove controversial websites may stem from the application of this principle and also illustrates the difference between a medium as author/publisher and a medium as carrier. If the argument of this paragraph is valid, the seeming paradox presents itself of freedom and accountability being positively rather than negatively correlated in the libertarian belief system.

In the order of values under review, a disputed place is occupied by commercial communication, especially advertising (as indicated in Fig. 8.1). In general it has been and often still is regulated and controlled in ways which effectively deny its equal claim to free expression, even if it is not subject to censorship and can be freely published in most media. The failure of advertisers to gain complete freedom is not easy to reconcile with the principle of freedom of publication. The reasons are to be found in residual negative social attitudes and in the potential for harm to some of those exposed, especially vulnerable or sensitive groups. Unwanted exposure to advertising can itself be a source of public offence.[11]

Variations in the application of freedom of expression rights are related to the accompanying responsibility and accountability. A higher claim to freedom attaches to expressions (or publication) for which the speaker accepts full personal responsibility and is regarded as having honesty and integrity of purpose with respect to the intended audience or the public and society at large. The attribution of integrity has to be earned and willingness to be accountable is one way of earning it. In itself, this serves to connect freedom with responsibility. Established reputation matters and certain forms of expression (as noted) are more likely than others to carry guarantees of integrity.[12]

At the other end of the scale (with lower status in terms of attribution of rights of expression), the main examples (excluding the criminal and the pornographic) come in the form of commercial communication (as discussed), various kinds of propaganda, and some popular entertainment (e.g. gossip, scandal, sensationalized news). In the absence of voluntary or credible communicator responsibility (although an exception may be claimed for advertising), there is stronger pressure for external accountability, especially of enforceable kinds in the form of law and regulation. In these circumstances, accountability (on behalf of the receiver) is activated when responsibility (on behalf of the communicator) is missing or weak.

Another aspect of the case concerns the variable balance of power in the public communication relationship. In general, there is a case for greater power (especially in terms of ownership and control of the means of communication) to be accompanied by greater accountability. The greatest potential benefit of freedom of expression should not go to the powerful, but to the relatively powerless or should be exercised on their behalf. This was certainly the view of those who struggled for freedom and it is firmly embedded in majority opinion and conventional wisdom, whatever the reality.

From this point of view, accountability can be considered as the means by which the communications of the relatively few powerful are restrained, checked, and balanced on behalf of the many receivers and also of the disempowered would-be senders. This in turn implies the need for standards and adjudicators that are independent of the powerful. An implication of these remarks is that effective accountability applied to communicative power needs to have some means of affecting the situation. This means limiting the freedom of the powerful to communicate, for instance by limiting the size of cross-media ownership or share of the audience reach or by offering alternative channels and access to others.

WHOSE FREEDOM IN THE MEDIA?

The main candidates for claiming the right to press freedom, aside from any individual author, are media owners plus outside sources and voices. It can also be argued that freedom of expression belongs primarily to the public, constituted in some collective entity and for whose ultimate benefit it is often said to be exercised.[13] It is extremely difficult to say who amongst these candidates (if not all of them equally) can actually claim to exercise the freedom of the press, except by assertion. For instance the Canadian Royal Commission on Newspapers (Canada, 1981) opens with the words: 'Freedom of the press is not a property right of owners. It is a right of the people'.

Legally, the right of ownership allows a proprietor to include or exclude any message. In practice, publishers are rarely personally involved in the business of publication and most decisions are made by someone in an editorial role, including the decision to admit or exclude an external source or would-be communicator who has no right as such to publish in any given medium. Ruggles (1994: 149) concludes that according to the predominant legal interpretation of free speech (and media) rights, editors only enjoy proxy rights. Any privileges they enjoy stem from their actions as agents of media firms and their owners who actually own the rights of selection, etc. In practice, journalists and media production staff also work according to editorial assignment with only limited autonomy (see Chapter 6).[14]

There are recurring (sometimes endemic) conflicts where editors and journalists feel under pressure to act against their own conscience in some publication decision or where the editorial staff find themselves in conflict with management. The issue of internal media freedom is not easily settled or disposed of. It is kept alive not only by the continuing globalization and conglomeration of media firms, but also by the striving of the journalists (and others in the media) towards the degree of autonomy that is usually regarded as the mark of a profession. Being a professional means having wider responsibility for actions and having the freedom to live up to claims and expectations. Baker (1989: 253) finds the idea of identifying press freedom with freedom for press professionals inherently plausible in the US context and also consistent with popular understanding of press freedom, although its acceptance would require legal rules protecting their freedom from abridgement by owners. The practical obstacles to instituting such rules are, however, formidable.

The situation of uncertainty about the location of freedom rights does not in itself relieve essentially facilitative media personnel (in the case of the news media) of moral responsibility for what is published by the organization they work for, but it does diminish their probable sense of personal responsibility for any given published item and thus their potential accountability. The general division of labour, the extent of routine, and the large scale of media organizations all reinforce this tendency. One consequence of this in increasingly large-scale media enterprises is for a diminution of any real accountability. Responsibility can often be plausibly passed up the chain of command where a chief executive or owner can then plausibly claim to have clean hands. In the case of film, television, music, and book publication, and some other similar media, publication freedom rights are more clearly exercised by individual authors, artists, and performers. They are less likely than is the case with news media personnel either to accept responsibility or to have responsibility attributed to them.

AN ASSESSMENT: THE RELATIONSHIP OF FREEDOM TO ACCOUNTABILITY

There is no doubt that freedom of publication, even in established democracies, is constrained at every turn and in ways that will not be overcome by any liberating or deregulatory act on the part of any authority, and probably not by any simple expansion of opportunities for public communication. The freedom of speech available to a media organization is of a different kind from that of the individual speaker. As well as speech it has a high component of action—the deployment of material resources—and the two are hard to separate. The action of publication cannot ever be completely without constraint or consequences. It may often only be free in the sense of being legally permitted.

Amongst the constraints on publication, the main types of formal accountability (laws, regulations, and self-regulation) probably do not even rank very high on the list of obstacles to freedom.[15] On the whole the media do not seem to need any accountability mechanism to ensure their conformity.[16] We cannot conclude that forms of accountability are simply the same as any other constraint, nor that freedom and accountability are inversely related, as if simply opposite poles of a single dimension. Less accountability does not mean more freedom in any wider sense of the term.

The fact that there is a great deal of control built into processes of mass communication that serves as a form of anticipatory accountability is not in itself reassuring. This kind of accountability is usually impossible to separate in its effects from commercial or other pressures and constraints. In large-scale media operations there is little scope for individual freedom of expression by individuals, employed or not, who seek to communicate creatively or informatively. In practice the exercise of the right to free expression has 'migrated' to management and ownership. The theoretical proposition that accountancy and freedom are compatible and may even reinforce each other has a hollow ring in these rather typical circumstances.

Publication freedom and accountability are interrelated in varied ways, sometimes as opposites but not necessarily or exclusively so. Often, accountability is a price paid, often voluntarily, for freedom or regarded as an essential accompaniment. There are other threats to freedom than those posed by most current forms or proposals for greater media accountability. This applies especially to the effects of inequality of wealth and power that largely determine who shall have, or not have, access to the means of publication. In this respect the right kind of accountability would have to work towards redressing the imbalance and requiring access for other voices.

There is a good deal of independence both conceptually and empirically between the two principles of freedom and accountability. Freedom of publication is not a fixed or zero-sum quantity, such that any limitation can reduce the availability of the whole. It is not even quantifiable. Even if one thinks of accountability as reducing opportunities to communicate one is faced with an ever-expanding capacity and new forms of communication (media) that generally outpace any attempts to impose accountability in restrictive ways. Not only are there more channels, there are more people or voices in a position to speak, and more topics to speak about in an expanding social and cultural environment.

Accountability much of the time only operates to give shape and visibility to existing unwritten rules of public communication, which not only constrain in some degree but also facilitate. In some of its forms, rules of accountability, as noted, increase freedom by requiring balance and access for different voices and protecting certain minorities. The independence of the media and their public esteem can both be served by more accountability. Where responsibilities are self-chosen and adhered to, threats of intervention are less likely to succeed. Where media try to set and meet high standards of quality and service to an audience they are rewarded by attachment and loyalty. While such situations are threatened in practice by the rapidly changing media market and technology, the underlying principles are likely to survive. Accountability is itself much more than constraint and in some forms it is intrinsic to a full sense of free human communication, whether in a personal or a wider social context. Without accountability, communication is simply one-way transmission, limited in purpose, lacking response, guidance, or even known effect.

IN CONCLUSION

The general conclusion is that the two principles are interrelated but ultimately independent of each other. Accountability can threaten freedom if it is enforced by censorship and repressive measures applied by the state, but in some manifestations it has positive effects. It is even possible to conceive accountability as the alternative, if not the reverse, of censorship and other forms of repression. In any case it is different and the aim should be to reconcile the two principles and try to identify forms of accountability and their implementation that do not restrict and may even promote freedom.

NOTES

1. The text of the 1789 Declaration of the Rights of Man is reproduced in translation by Barbrook (1995: 10): 'The unrestrained communication of thoughts and opinions being one of the most precious rights of man, every citizen may speak, write and publish freely, provided he is responsible for the abuse of this liberty in cases determined by law'. According to Barbrook this clause was strengthened by Robespierre in a 1793 version of the Declaration so as to exclude any justification for political censorship. Article 7 reads: 'The right to express his thought or

opinions, either by means of the press, or any other manner...cannot be forbidden'.

2. Although the First Amendment has been increasingly invoked on behalf of freedom of speech, it does not seem to have much of a historical pedigree in this respect. Ruggles (1994: 61) reports that the first US Supreme Court decision involving an appeal to the First Amendment did not take place until 1897, when the Court upheld a Massachussetts Supreme Court decision that the Boston municipality were justified in forbidding a black clergyman from preaching his anti-racist message in a Boston public park, contrary to by-laws. The ground of the decision was property rights. Ironically, the original Massachussetts judgment was written by Oliver Wendell Holmes, later champion of the 'free market place of ideas'.

3. Justification for restricting the freedom of broadcasting has been summarized by Hoffmann-Riem (1996) under five main headings: interference-free communication; access to the media; performance quality and viability; financial conditions of operation; and unification of the European broadcasting market. In the United States the main support for the constitutionality of broadcast regulation has been on grounds of scarcity. Bollinger (1991: 67) cites Judge Frankfurter's (1943) authoritative ruling on this topic, which argued that because 'radio is inherently not available to all, some who wish to use it must be denied'. Giving licences to some users was judged not to be a denial of free speech, since the right to free speech does not include the right of access to broadcasting. Later Supreme Court judgments, especially in the *Red Lion* case (1959), according to Bollinger embraced affirmative regulation of broadcasting enthusiastically, treating the press, not regulation, as the main threat to First Amendment principles, because of monopoly and private censorship (1991: 72–3). In the United States, a supreme court ruling in 1915 removed First Amendment protection from the cinema, although this was over turned in 1957 (Foerstal, 1998).

4. See Hindman (1997); Bollinger (1991). Civil actions on various grounds can be taken against the media, despite press privileges. For most of its history, the First Amendment was almost a dead letter, involving no ruling on the press until 1931 (Blanchard, 1977). In the mid- to later twentieth century its application supported press freedom on some key matters, especially by increasing the possibility of criticizing public officials and figures (the *Sullivan* case, 1960) and rejecting the claim that the media have to give open access to all (the *Tornillo* case, 1974). Where national security issues become involved, the press has less protection (see Foerstal, 1998; Patterson, 1993; Herman and Chomsky, 1988; Smith, 1999).

5. The ECHR adds the following to its promise of freedom: 'The exercise of these freedoms [to free expression], since it carries with it duties and responsibilities, may be subject to such formalities, conditions, restrictions or penalties as are prescribed by law and are necessary in a democratic society in the interests of national security, territorial integrity or public safety, for the prevention of disorder or crime, for the protection of health or morals, for the protection of the reputation or rights of others, for preventing the disclosure of information received in confidence, or maintaining the authority and impartiality of the judiciary.'

6. In some countries, the press law requires registration as a publisher (as in France), and sometimes requires a certain scale of distribution (in Russia a registration requirement exists beyond a circulation of 1,000).

7. The distinction between 'positive' and 'negative' concepts of press freedom is attributed by Nerone (1995: 84) to Isaiah Berlin (1958), who argued that negative and positive liberty figure in two parallel streams of democratic political philosophy and both can be reconciled. The main differences between the two concepts of freedom can be summed up in the following table of oppositions.

Two concepts of press freedom compared

Negative	Positive
Individualist	Collective
Freedom	Responsibility
Equal opportunity	Equal outcome
Natural rights	Moral duties
No restraint	Limitations of freedom
Absolute value	Value relative to ends

8. An author closely associated with arguing for the intrinsic value of free speech on grounds of self-expression refers not only to the right to self-fulfilment and human dignity, but also to 'basic Western notions of the role of the individual in his capacity as a member of society' (Emerson, 1970: 71). He points out that the purpose of society, in this view, is to promote the welfare of the individual, not vice versa. Thirdly, he links the issue to the principle of equality, especially the right of each to share in common decisions. From this flow rights to access to knowledge, to form views, communicate needs and preferences to others, and participate in the society. To put obstacles in this path is to elevate society and state to a despotic position.

9. There have been a good many caveats to the theory based on observation of how media markets actually work. Schauer (1986: 777) queries the theory on more fundamental grounds. There is really no evidence or compelling reason to think that 'truth has some inherent power to prevail in the marketplace of ideas, or that the distinction between truth and falsity has much explanatory power in telling us which ideas are likely to be accepted by the public and which are likely to be rejected'.

10. Other principles include that of neutrality: speech cannot be punished just because it is deemed undesirable or false according to one particular perspective. Secondly, there is the emotion principle, which gives equal protection (compared to information and argument) in principle to expression that is rude, rough, shocking, emotional, and in itself offensive to some. Thirdly, the symbolism principle holds that symbolic forms of communication like demonstrations, expressive behaviour, flag-burning, etc., are equally protected. In practice symbolic communication of these kinds may be considered as actions and also more easily linked to actual or potential harm.

11. More generally, 'commercial communication' is still not well founded according to the main justifications for freedom of communication mentioned above. It cannot be regarded as the self-fulfilling personal expression for any individual or organization, it is not necessary for the human dignity of the advertiser, it is not

fully dedicated to truth (according to the common opinion), it makes no necessary contribution to the political process or civic culture (except political advertising). Despite its importance for a market economy it is not even certain that unrestricted advertising is essential for an economic system. Ruggles (1994: 15) formulates an argument against protection of 'commercial speech' on the grounds that it is not freely interactive communication and, therefore, not truly free speech. Audiences have no right or opportunity to reply and the goals of the communication event are oriented entirely towards the interest of the source (typical of all propanda).

12. The objective news account described earlier is an example of a format that owes its status in part to the fact that it is backed by evidence or sources that the media are able and willing to cite if called upon. Generally, the media acknowledge failings of accuracy when challenged on factual grounds. This is a minimal, but still important, form of accountability practice.

13. Baker (1989) examined the relative claims of the public, press personnel, or media owners to own freedom of the press and finds a claim on behalf of the public a weak one, largely because it is unclear what it means and therefore difficult to translate into any practical arrangements, with the possible exception of public broadcasting. He comments: 'Although "freedom for the public" sounds good, it has little clear content. The public may benefit most by protecting some narrower group's freedom—for example the freedom of owners or the press professionals' (252).

14. An international comparison of the views of journalists (Weaver, 1998) shows that perceptions of autonomy vary according to job satisfaction and the reality of the political and economic environment. In North America perceived autonomy was at a very high level. In Europe it was lower and more variable. It looks as if satisfaction with autonomy also relates to the prevailing political culture. Where journalists aspire to a watchdog or critical role (as in Britain and Australia) they are dissatisfied with the freedom permitted.

15. The main sources of constraint are familiar or obvious, including the working of the free market, which can have a chilling effect on controversy and novelty for three reasons: compliance with proprietorial interests or prejudices; fear of offending any sizeable sector of the audience; and fear of offending or losing advertisers. A second explanation lays the main blame at the door of the routinization of media production that systematically reduces creativity and originality or unpredictable acts of publication. The third enemy of freedom is the old one, the government or public power, although the ongoing evidence for this is usually sporadic, given the symbiosis typical of media and political systems.

16. There is also plenty of evidence of a strong general media tendency to support the prevailing order and ignore or delegitimize alternative points of view or sources of information lacking political or economic resources.

9

Responsibility and Accountability
Conceptual Distinctions

PROBLEMATIC ISSUES

Although both terms under review have already been liberally used, with short definitions and in their common-sense meanings, they repay closer attention. For one thing, they are often used more or less interchangeably and sometimes as if synonymous. According to philosopher J. R. Lucas (1993), responsibility equals either answerability or accountability. In his view the core of the matter is being asked the question 'why did you do it?' about motivation for any act or omission. This definition of accountability presumes that the question is legitimately asked and that there is some well-founded reason that it will be answered (even if no compulsion). This caveat also opens up another large issue, since, for an answer to be expected, there must first be a clear and agreed definition of the situation in which the parties to the exchange are interrelated.

The words in question share a similar etymology in English as well as in other languages in being related to the verb 'to answer'. The common link is forged by the general notion of answerability, although this term is itself unclear. However, the confusion is not simply semantic, but stems from similarities and differences in the situation where the issue arises. These, in turn, depend on the rules that apply in a particular social concept and a given situation. These rules can be very diverse and can apply with varying degrees of compulsion. In the case of the mass media, there is no single set of rules and many degrees of freedom. Moreover, as we have seen, the media generally reject external attempts to impose responsibilities and they resist being subjected to accountability procedures for their acts of publication. Nevertheless, as argued earlier, the media do in varying degree accept certain obligations, duties, or tasks and some procedures do exist for gaining compliance.

The key idea here is succinctly put by Hodges (1986: 14):

The issue of responsibility is the following: to what social needs should we expect journalists to respond? The issue of accountability is as follows: how might society call on journalists to account for their performance of the responsibility given to them. Responsibility has to do with defining proper conduct; account-ability with compelling it.

However, the statement also begs several questions, firstly by assuming that journalists *should* respond to social needs. Secondly, it presumes that the responsibilities in this matter are known and have been given in some way. Thirdly, accountability is associated here with compulsion. If we are to avoid getting mired immediately in arguments about the rights of, and limits to, media freedom we need to take a step back from these assumptions. In turn, this requires us to explore further the meanings of both terms both in the specific context of media publication and also as more widely used.

THE WIDER CONTEXT

Examples from other contexts are helpful. In politics, government, and bureaucratic organizations, the notion of responsibility can be readily understood as a set of tasks or duties that derive from the specific functions and fields of competence pertaining to particular offices and roles. A given office-holder will, in principle, have the authority as well as the means to carry out the tasks assigned. There is also a hierarchical chain of command that identifies who will be answerable at what level for the performance of the given tasks, which takes care of the question of accountability. In this context it is clear that accountability is related to power and authority. Feintuck (1999: 121) distinguishes two aspects of public accountability: 'The first means a requirement to give an account of one's actions to the public.' The second means 'to be accountable in the sense of being liable to sanctions if found to have acted in breach of some requirement or expectation attaching to the exercise of power'.

In law, whether criminal or civil, responsibility is also defined, not by position or office, but by a set of rules that apply to all individuals and legal actors. Most such responsibilities are negative in character, since, in liberal societies, the positive duties of citizens are kept to a minimum, but there is still a sizeable number of actions that we are required to take and that constitute our legal responsibilities, ranging from caring for our own children to paying taxes. In this context the distinction made above between responsibility and accountability is quite clear, since the latter involves a consequential checking on the former, and both are defined by the same legal texts.

Responsibility carries a special meaning in the context of the professions. A member of a profession is trained to practise a core skill, requiring autonomous judgement as well as expertise. Professionals have an inviolable duty to serve the interest of their clients and often some wider social and public responsibility is attributed and accepted. The work of professionals is governed by a set of appropriate ethics as well as being based on knowledge and skill. Standards are maintained and monitored and membership of the profession accredited or withheld by an independent professional body. While strictly speaking, according to this version, there may be no media professions (Singletary, 1982), the several types of media work (and journalism in particular) can claim some elements of professionalism, especially on the basis of dedication to high quality, possessing skills and knowledge, and following an ethical code (see Oledzki, 1998), but also on the basis of accepting wider responsibilities to clients and society.

In business, responsibility has mainly been defined in terms of obligations accepted by employers in relation to their employees and suppliers to customers or clients. In both cases there is often a basis in law, but many responsibilities are customary or subject to negotiation according to the interests and balance of power of the parties involved. The acceptance and fulfilment of responsibilities by business actors is mainly determined by considerations of long-term self-interest and maintaining good customer relations, although ethical principles may also play a part and moral responsibilities exist alongside legal obligations (Brummer, 1991).

It is also relevant to consider the case of personal social interaction (interpersonal relations), since this accounts for most human communication and is also the source of many of our ideas about social obligation and responsibility. Interpersonal communication is characterized by its essential *reflexivity*. We are enmeshed in complex webs of expectation of and from others (in the carrying out of their roles rather than as known individuals) and we are tied to others in complementary and similar ways. We develop shared understandings about mutual responsibilities and respond continuously to each other accordingly in speech and behaviour. As described by Semin and Mansfield (1983) various forms of personal accounting play a key role in reflexive social action.[1] Most interpersonal accounting is routine and unproblematic, following familiar interpretative frames or schemata. Only when rules are broken or normality is disturbed are individuals asked to give an account of their actions or to defend themselves from accusations. This mainly comes in the form of an explanation, justification, or apology.

It is apparent from these comments that the terms under review do vary in meaning from one context to another and the case of the media cannot be dealt with according to a standard model. The media situation is unusually mixed, on several dimensions. The activities involved have a public character and are for the most part carried out in public view. They vary in their substance and significance, morally and socially, being both 'sacred' and 'profane'. They involve individual communicators as well as formal organizations. They are characterized to an uncertain and limited degree by professionalism and autonomy.

Some key elements of meaning are, nevertheless, common to the different contexts described, including that of media work. One is the existence of a constructed or taken-for-granted normality according to which actors (individuals, office-holders, organizations) are expected to behave in a certain way, perform certain tasks, meet certain role requirements. Another is the existence of an appropriate set of rules, whether formal or informal, which identify and define breaches of normality. Thirdly, some actions are required to repair the situation and restore normality when rules are broken. The case of media responsibility (for the effects of publication) poses particular difficulties, because of the contestable character of any rules (arising from the condition of freedom) and the multiplicity of media 'normalities'.

MEANINGS OF MEDIA RESPONSIBILITY

A large literature has grown around the idea of responsibility, especially in the fields of religion, law, ethics and morals, and other branches of philosophy. In the case of the media, the question of responsibility has been discussed mainly with reference to both the professional and social responsibilities of the media (see Chapter 3) and with reference to legal and ethical dilemmas that face publishers in their daily work (see, for instance, the earlier discussion of media roles, in Ch. 6). Most of this media-related discussion has been very pragmatic—concerning what to publish or not, specific cases of conduct or performance, whether or not the media should carry out some task in the public interest. Responsibility as a concept in itself has not been much examined, beyond the dual issue of what media ought to do and why they should have to do it.

The wider literature on responsibility indicates a range of meanings that it is helpful to consider and to apply to the media case (see especially Downie, 1964; Blizek, 1971; Haydon, 1978; Smiley, 1992). The principal 'meanings' of responsibility described below have been derived, for the present purpose, from various sources. The list is eclectic in character, but not exhaustive. Much of the relevant literature on responsibility, true to its origin in ethics and legal philosophy, deals with the situation of actions that have undesirable or problematic consequences, leading to blame and some form of sanction or punishment. A central issue is often the degree of liability that attaches to the main actor in the case. This bias has to be resisted and corrected in key respects, since the responsibilities attributed to the media are often positive, not relating to harm and often of an informal kind (rather than laws or clear rules).

With this in mind, the following aspects (or types) of media responsibility can be distinguished and described.

- Any voluntary *promises* made by an actor to others entails responsibility. This includes contracts or agreements freely entered into that may become legally binding. These are mainly to be found in editorial mission statements or implicitly in the composition or content of a given media channel, publication, or service. An audience is given to expect a certain type and quality of content and service. General claims to serve broad social purposes are sometimes made by leading media figures. Hodges (1986) writes of an 'implied contract between media and society'. In reality certain pressures on mainstream media are not resistible (e.g. giving access to government communications or support to proper authority). Voluntary codes of ethics often promise fulfilment of some public role.

- *Competence* to act with awareness of potential consequences and with sufficient freedom and means to carry out actions is a general condition of being held responsible in other senses and contexts. In law a person can only be held liable for actions if judged to be competent in these terms. We are thus speaking of a competent person or agency that can be said to have a responsibility for the consequences of their actions or for failing to act. In general, an established media organization would be considered competent in this sense, but individuals using the media or some marginal senders might not.

- The normal expectations concerning *tasks and functions* that attach to social roles, work positions, and status can be seen as responsibilities. As noted above, specific professions have a core skill for the exercise of which members are held to account. In occupying a role we accept responsibility for carrying out certain tasks and applying relevant skills competently.

- *Duties or obligations* that are imposed on individuals or organizations by some legitimate external agency, such as the law or a regulatory body, constitute another type of responsibility. They can have either a positive or a negative character. In principle, the media are as much subject to the law as other citizens and other legal entities, but their role also gives them some privileges. Public service broadcasting is a special case, always entailing obligations to society.

- Responsibility in the sense of having (allegedly) caused something is described as causal responsibility and is central to legal procedure and the establishment of guilt or innocence. Depending on the case, various degrees of causation can be involved (Semin and Mansfield, 1983).[2] This variability also applies to possible media effects (see Chapter 7).[3] The issue also arises as to whether acts of publication (expressive and symbolic actions) should be treated in the same way as physical acts, in respect of causation.

- Responsibility can be directly linked to the idea of eventual liability, in a way not fully covered by the notion of causal responsibility. Essentially this refers to the attribution or acceptance (or not) of any blame or sanction (independent of any evidence of causal responsibility) as a result of alleged failings.[4]

- The notion of *moral responsibility* involves a differentiation from both causal and (legal) liability notions. The reference is to some sense of being indirectly blameworthy for sometimes remote ills such as Third World poverty or world pollution, where the source of responsibility lies in personal conviction or conscience.[5] The media may be considered to be morally responsible for much harm, even if little of the world's ills can be directly or conclusively laid at their door. This opens up a line of argument and analysis which is quite different from the legal or scientific mode that has been deployed to this point. It also involves questions about the scope (or lack of it) for ethical conduct in modern media organizations.[6]

- The idea of *conscientiousness* is a version of responsibility not fully covered in the preceding account. It describes a condition of an active and inwardly driven pursuit of positive goals, duties, and obligations. It applies typically to individual authors, but it can also describe the approach of an organization. Some media are also committed to ideal or ethical goals, alongside or instead of a profit motive.

While all these meanings are to some degree relevant, a more economical set of basic types, in a form more useful for our present purposes, may be seen in Fig. 9.1. Their underlying meaning has been explained.

Several of the types of responsibility overlap and interconnect and the set as a whole is cross-cut by a number of dimensions and distinctions of kind and degree. Three distinctions in particular should be emphasized. One is the degree of voluntarism that is involved, with much room for choice in relation to promise-making and moral responsibility. Secondly, there is an external–internal dimension. Some aspects of responsibility are of a public kind and subject to outside pressure and claims, especially in relation to causal responsibility and duties and obligations. Others are more likely to arise and be handled within the organization or media institution. Thirdly, the responsibilities differ in terms of a moral–calculative or material dimension. This separates especially moral from contractual responsibility.

The term media responsibility conceals not only widely varying expressions and types of obligation, but also differences of location of a given responsibility within the whole institutional complex. As a result, we can speak of responsibility being located at different levels, although these levels are not necessarily in a hierarchical relation. The main locations are at the level of the media institution as a whole; the ownership; the organization and its management; the professional employee; and the individual author or performer. Although some types of

Contractual or promise-keeping
Fulfilling the task of a role or occupation
Fulfilling duties and obligations
Causal responsibility
Moral responsibility

FIG. 9.1. Main types of media responsibility

responsibility are more likely than others to find expression at a given level, there is no general or necessary correspondence between types and levels.

Finally, it should be kept in mind that responsibility is always owed *to* someone, even if that someone is the society as a whole. There is no need to elaborate on this point, although reference can be made to Fig. 10.1, which sets out the main partners with whom the media do have relations of accountability. Much the same applies here.

MEANINGS OF ACCOUNTABILITY

Apart from what has already been said about accountability being to do with gaining compliance with obligations, formal definitions do not help greatly, because of the diversity of contexts and the near synonymity with responsibility. However, some definitions do take us further. Christians (1989: 40), in arguing that to move to an enforceable code of ethics for media we need a conceptually adequate notion of accountability, defines it as 'a reckoning properly requested and given, a statement explaining conduct to legitimately designated partners'. With reference to the social responsibilities of business corporations, Brummer (1991: 14) writes that '"being accountable" refers to the capacity, willingness, need or requirement to render an account of one's actions or inactions'. Moreover, it must be made *to* someone; *for* something; on the basis of certain *criteria*; and with varying degrees of strictness. Brummer also mentions the main alternative partners in any accountability relationship (see Chapter 10), where responsibility is attributed. These include those to whom a promise is made; those to whom one has a legal duty; those who are affected by one's actions and those who have the power to affect oneself in return (the so-called 'reverse-impact' model); colleagues and employees (sometimes called 'stakeholders'); and owners and shareholders. The categories all have some relevance for the media.

We can add to this that accountability always involves a relationship between those concerned, since at the very least an account has to be requested or addressed by someone from someone. An exception may seem to arise in the case of personal moral responsibility, where an actor is held accountable to conscience, although often on the basis of presumed harm to real but unknown others.

MAIN TYPES OF MEDIA ACCOUNTABILITY

While the variation between a range of contexts is high, there is a limited repertoire of types and meanings of accountability that applies quite widely, and certainly to the mass media in one way or another. The main variants can be summarily explained as they arise in relation to media in the following terms.

- The giving of an *explanation* for contested actions can include both the strictly factual account as well as an explanation of motivation and even the giving of justifications. It is unusual, even so, for the media to explain or justify their publication decisions, unless under pressure from some agreed complaints procedure or when obliged to in legal actions against them. There is a *confessional* variant in which the account comes in the form of a spontaneous admission of guilt, apology, remorse, etc., in respect of contested publications.
- Routine and regular *information provision* and reporting about activities and performance is a common form of continuous public accountability. The degree of informational accounting and reporting varies according to the status of the media organization concerned. Public or quasi-public media are obliged to report regularly, especially on matters to do with content, editorial policy, audiences reached, and financial matters. Private media firms tend only to publish financial data as part of their routine flow of information (e.g. to shareholders). But they are obliged to provide information about audiences reached in order to gain advertising, and such information is in practice in the public domain. Information of a kind is also provided for reasons of publicity.
- *Financial accounting*, especially relating to profit or loss, can be considered a special case of information provision, characterized by the fact that the financial 'account' is not a 'story' or narrative but an unambiguous mathematical procedure, with set rules. For commercial media, this may be the most important form of accountability, compared to which, most other forms are peripheral, lacking a cutting edge, and not leading to any improvement.
- Media are also routinely *evaluated* by some form of *rating* that measures audience reach, approval, or relative popularity. Quality of content and service may also be evaluated. Aside from what

the media initiate themselves, much criticism (also praise) reaches the media directly in the form of letters, phone calls, etc. We might even suggest that this 'audience accountability' is a type almost unique to the media domain.[7]

- Regular public adjudication of *media conduct and performance* by an external agency to check on the maintenance of standards is mainly confined to audio-visual media where goals and standards are laid down by regulation or where self-regulation is formally applied.[8] Broader reviews of media performance are, however, undertaken periodically either for general public or sectional purposes (media-monitoring). They typically involve systematic research and the collection of evidence by official or self-appointed watchdogs.

- Where formal complaints procedures exist or where liability for consequences is alleged, formal processes of *claim and adjudication* are set in train. An account is demanded for some specific action where harm or failure is alleged and assessed by formal third-party procedures as in lawsuits. The *paying of a penalty* may be considered as a form of accountability in itself.

- The media are the object of much public *review and criticism* from a wide variety of sources, including political parties, pressure groups, self-appointed media watchdogs, writers and researchers, as well as from other media, not forgetting public opinion. As a contribution to public accountability, the main value is to promote debate, even if the media are rarely very self-critical and avoid criticizing each other, for a variety of reasons, except by way of factual news reports.[9]

More variants of accountability could probably be found as well as other ways of classifying the various types, although it does not help to multiply categories and one can deal more easily with a more restricted set. The most relevant types, each one involving a distinct meaning and pointing towards a certain procedure, are set out in Fig. 9.2.

As in the case of responsibility, there are alternative ways of interrelating what seems a rather disparate set of ideas and processes. There is a general differentiation between processes of accountability of a public, external, and open character and others of a more internal, specific, and quasi-private or technical character. Secondly, there is a distinction between accountability that is promised, based on voluntarily accepted responsibilities, and accountability that is required by an outside actor

- Verbal: explanation; information; justification
- Financial
- Performance rating
- Complaint and adjudication
- Public debate
- Liability for consequences

FIG. 9.2. Main types of media accountability

or agency. In this case it is usually followed by some adjudication process.

Related to this is a third differentiation between types of accountability according to whether they are formal and binding, with material penalties, or verbal and symbolic in character. The more strict and formal type usually applies where four conditions are present: firstly, some measurable harm is alleged (e.g. to reputation or by incitement); secondly, a direct, causal connection (see 'causal responsibility' above) is posited; thirdly, accountability is required from outside on the basis of some claim or complaint; fourthly, there is a violation or law or regulation. In these circumstances, accountability tends to be equated with liability and the compulsory payment of material penalties after formal adjudication.

As against this are types of accountability which are not only voluntary but typically involve purely verbal forms of account (e.g. explanation, information, apology, justification).[10] We can consequently identify two main models of accountability, one being best described as 'liability', the other as an 'answerability' model (see Fig. 9.5). The general rationale for accountability is to achieve some repair, improvement, or return to normality, although in practice this is sometimes lost sight of. Accountability tends rather to focus on the allocation of blame and punishment rather than on encouraging, or contributing to, better performance.

VARYING FORMS OF ACCOUNTABILITY

In the light of this discussion, and bearing in mind especially the relational character of accountability, three main variants of media accountability (for publication) can be distinguished. These are shown in Fig. 9.3.

A. Unilateral/autonomous forms
  - Reference to conscience
  - Reference to an imagined other
  - Professionalism
B. Bilateral forms
  - Reference to a non-binding contract or promise
  - Producer–consumer relations
  - Reference to a normative goal (e.g. a social cause, faith, movement, group)
C. Trilateral forms
  - Formal complaint procedures
  - Legally binding contracts and commitments
  - Other legal and regulatory obligations
  - Cases where the 'society' is the claimant

FIG. 9.3. Main variant forms of media accountability

The entry for unilateral forms of accountability relates firstly to all expressions of individual and personal responsibility where values and beliefs are a stimulus to action. Personal moral obligations shade over into professional ethical standards that are more widely shared. Media organizations can also autonomously accept responsibility for some aspects of conduct and submit to accountability procedures. However, the generally low degree of professionalization of the media means that such feelings of obligation often remain personal and only serve to connect particular communicators with their real or imagined audience. Alternatively, accountability is confined within a circle of colleagues. Accountability is not confined to matters of morals, ethics, or professional quality, but also arises out of the wish of media communicators to please their audiences and to establish some kind of stable relation with a desired target audience. In pursuit of such vicarious relationships, mass media communicators are known to imagine or construct the kind of audience they want to address and appeal to, in the absence of face-to-face contact with, or direct knowledge of, the actual audience.[11]

In the case of bilateral forms of accountability, there is always a defined and real other party to the communication transaction established at the level of the media organization or the professional group. There is a promise of certain standards and levels of service, in terms of content type and technical quality. There may be a published code of ethics or conduct, although compliance is usually non-binding and self-adjudicated. But the media do often give rise to expectations that become constraining and even inescapable in practice. A newspaper, for instance, that is established to serve a particular community or section of the audience defined in some way cannot easily transform itself into something else in terms of aims and public expectations. Where media exist to serve some particular cause (political, social, or religious), the bilateral nature of the relation is typically formalized as well as transparent. In these circumstances there is likely to be a direct and interactive connection between the medium and its chosen public.

The trilateral type of accountability relation always involves a third party, in addition to the media on the one hand and, on the other, some party affected (the claimant). Four main subcategories are indicated in Fig. 9.3. The first three are largely self-explanatory. The fourth type of trilateral forms refers mainly to those alleged media effects where there is no specific victim or claimant but where the consequences for society or some vulnerable group (e.g. children or minorities) are alleged. The complaint is not usually made by someone affected directly but in the name of the society or the public good on behalf of the victim. The three parties to the situation are thus media; audience in a passive role; society as embodied in public opinion or some advocate of the public interest, eventually a political body. Accountability here is usually accomplished, if it is at all, in what is sometimes referred to as the 'court of public opinion'.

ALTERNATIVE MODELS OF MEDIA ACCOUNTABILITY

The distinction that has been made between the media's own promises and external claims is not usually a simple dichotomous one. There are many grey areas where the degree of obligation of media is not fixed or not clear. Media obligations are also of widely varying kinds ranging from avoiding specific harm to achieving some long-term good and with varying degrees of obligation or compulsion. Accountability processes vary accordingly. Christians (1989: 36) distinguishes between three main 'levels of accountability': liability; moral sanctions; and answerability. The first term relates to conditions where formal and defined obligations exist along with a threat of penalties for failing to keep them. Moral sanctions have been discussed in relation to moral responsibility and arise where personal conscience or professional or organizational ethics indicate appropriate forms of conduct. The third term, answerability, is discussed further below, but essentially relates to circumstances where questions are raised about performance that call for public explanation and debate, even if no clear rules have been broken or accusations of harm made.

In a similar vein, Blizek (1971) distinguished between legal, moral, and social responsibility, each involving a different adjudicator, procedure, and rules of evidence. The three terms approximate to the three levels of accountability just mentioned. In the case of legal responsibility, an issue is handled with reference to agencies of state power. In the second case, the personal responsibility of the individual actor to conscience is at issue, with appeals to moral principles. In the third cases, the reference is external—to the views of others in the society. Blizek emphasizes the distinction between legal and social responsibility. The first denotes the simple notion of an agent, an action, and an effect which can be demonstrated to follow (or not to follow) from the action. The second is more complex and involves adjudication by a third party: 'Social responsibility is not a relationship between cause and effect, but a relationship between an agent and some consequence, as prescribed by an adjudicator... The adjudicator is at liberty to impute responsibility in situations which are not causal' (Blizek, 1971: 110).

In this threefold distinction of types of media accountability process, there is an implicit gradation of constraint on the media. Liability implies the existence of responsibilities that are not optional and are usually enshrined in law and regulation. An appeal to moral responsibility can also be backed up by considerable pressure, for instance by way of public opinion or efforts to strengthen laws. Answerability operates in an area where an exchange of information and ideas takes the place of threats on freedom to publish. In such processes, responsibilities may be attributed to the media, but this is quite different from any requirement or demand, backed by sanctions.

Another set of distinctions that applies to the responsibilities rather than the processes has been suggested by Hodges (1986), in terms of their being assigned, contracted, or self-imposed. In the first case, there is a clear link with liability and the obligations concerned are not self-chosen or voluntary. They are specified in laws, regulations, licensing agreements, and charters of public broadcasting bodies, etc. The second category applies to obligations which may or may not be chosen by the media concerned but are agreed and have to be delivered, under much weaker penalties. Hodges suggests that these kinds of obligations arise because of an 'implied covenant' between press and society. This might describe, for instance, the expectation, reinforced by long custom and mutual agreement, that a given national press will give continuous and adequate cover to the sayings and doings of government and report on the political process. Similar implied covenants can arise between a medium and its own regular audience concerning what to expect. The third category relates to desirable aspects of media service, responsibilities which are openly aspired to and may carry some moral obligation to fulfil (e.g. by reference to a professional code of ethics). But they are not enforceable or actionable, except by means of criticism and debate (the realm of 'answerability').

These various distinctions are clearly related to each other and provide the basis for distinguishing the two main models of media accountability as already foreshadowed. One of these couples assigned and formally contracted responsibilities with the liability for carrying them out. A second model relates to obligations that are either customary and implicit in past and present performance or that have some basis in claims and promises of moral responsibility. This can be summarized in a general scheme, as shown in Fig. 9.4.

Free media do have the right to be irresponsible or simply to deny responsibility as long as they do not break the law in so doing and some would argue that they even have some obligation to use this right to the limit, certainly under circumstances where their freedom is being threatened or where there are compelling political, social, or moral issues at stake. The expression 'publish and be damned' need not be only a cynical expression of press irresponsibility, but a serious exemplification

FREE MEDIA
have
RESPONSIBILITIES
in the form of obligations
which can be either
ASSIGNED or **CONTRACTED** or **SELF-CHOSEN**
for which they are held
ACCOUNTABLE
to individuals, organizations, or society
(legally, socially, or morally)
either in the sense of
LIABILITY or **ANSWERABILITY**
for harm caused   for quality of performance.

FIG. 9.4. The relations between media freedom, responsibility, and accountability

of the virtue of courage that is included amongst basic publication values (see Chapter 4). There are many instances where pressure is put on the media in the name of responsibility or the public interest to avoid publication of certain content. There is no easy way of distinguishing between legitimate and illegitimate forms or actual instances of such pressure to be responsible. Nor can breaches of social responsibility rules by the media be easily classified as justified or not. In these circumstances a general claim by the media to freedom to deny that they have responsibilities beyond the letter of the law has some validity.

TWO ACCOUNTABILITY MODELS COMPARED

The concept of answerability, suggested by Christians (1989), provides a suitable label for the main alternative to the liability model (see also Blatz, 1972). It implies responsiveness to the views of all with a legitimate interest in what is published, whether as individuals affected or on behalf of the society. It includes a willingness to explain, defend, and justify actions (and general tendencies) of publication or omission. The outcomes of answerability may or may not lead to improvements, concessions, or apologies, but they do express and reaffirm various norms relevant to the wider responsibilities of the media in society. The emphasis is on the quality of performance rather than on specific harm caused.

The liability model of accountability is mainly invoked in cases where the media are believed to be capable of causing real harm to individuals, certain categories of people, or society as a whole. The idea of causal responsibility, as discussed above, is central to this model, and thus to the identification of identifiable agents (and media organizations) that can be held accountable for publication acts). As Fig. 9.5 shows, the model applies to adversarial situations where parties are in conflict with each other, employing advocacy and counter-advocacy. There is an emphasis on winning or losing and penalties take a material form. Accountability in this form is not a search for truth or reasoned explanation or a negotiation leading to settlement. The parties to the dispute are distant from each other and the process is not designed to bring them together or produce reconciliation. This applies whether claims are laid against the media by injured individuals or by public authority on behalf of society. The media typically resist and make no concessions beyond the minimum required.

ANSWERABILITY		LIABILITY
Moral/social basis	v.	Legal basis
Voluntary	v.	Imposed
Verbal forms	v.	Formal adjudication
Co-operative	v.	Adversarial
Non-material penalty	v.	Material penalty
Reference to quality	v.	Reference to harm

FIG. 9.5. Two accountability models compared

There is a range of possibilities between the extremity of trying to enforce liability on the media that claim freedom to publish and the much softer, discursive accountability forms that belong to the answerability mode. There is no general rule for deciding what model or intermediate variant to follow in a given case. However, there are difficulties and drawbacks about the liability model in relation to public communication that argue in favour of applying and developing answerability models of media accountability to deal with a wider range of disputed matters. The arguments for this view can be summarized as follows.

- The liability mode is more threatening to freedom of publication, since it can involve specific restriction on publication and heavy material penalties. Such penalties have a 'chilling effect' even when not actually applied.
- The liability model offers more advantages to wealthy claimants against the media or wealthy media against small media, because of the legal costs involved.
- The liability model relies on being able to prove cause and effect in circumstances where it has proved notoriously difficult to establish causal connections (or intentionality) in communication (see Chapter 7). The liability model presumes that 'publishers' can be called to account for the consequences of publication. Leaving aside the threat to freedom of expression, there is a general question mark about whether speech acts can be properly treated in the same category as other actions where harm is alleged (Bracken, 1994).
- The answerability model allows a reasoned and principled defence of publication on libertarian grounds and is more likely to lead to positive developments in the voluntary acceptance of more responsibility by the media.

- There is always a need to balance the wider public interest in open communication against the private material interests that may be affected. Engaging in critical publication, for instance (the watchdog role), is bound to cause harm or offence to its objects. It is extremely difficult to strike this balance and the procedures of litigation and contestation are not necessarily very sensitive to these matters.

Although a stronger case can be made on libertarian and ethical grounds for answerability as a mode of approach to communicative disputes, modern conditions of global media and heightened commercialism are not conducive to its potential applicability. The mass media are increasingly likely to be owned by international corporations that are not inclined to make voluntary commitments to society or to embrace higher ethical standards on principle. For one thing, they often have no clear link to any national society and relations between media and audience or general public are typically weak and distant, governed only by the market-place. Apart from this there is an increasing tendency to use litigation to enforce responsibilities and settle disputes in several spheres of public life (e.g. the quality of health and education provision). Individuals increasingly assign blame and seek (financial) redress from organizations and institutions. The viability of the answerability model depends on the presence of certain conditions, including the willingness of the media in principle to accept some responsibility for what they do and be responsive to external claims concerning moral responsibility.

IN CONCLUSION

The relationship between responsibility and accountability is not as simple as it has sometimes been made out (for instance, even in this chapter on page 190 by defining accountancy as the means by which media can be brought to fulfil their responsibilities) or by treating responsibility as an internal phenomenon and accountability as external. As Dorman (1991: 165) suggests, responsibility may be a more acceptable term to the media themselves because it has a connotation of voluntariness rather than an imposed obligation. Plaisance (2000) is correct to emphasize the significance of the interactional element of 'being accountable'. He also concludes that 'the concept will continually take different forms based on the philosophical approach used to determine the nature of that responsibility'. He contrasts, in particular, the consequences of holding a libertarian view of responsibility with a social responsibility view. The difference is largely one of degree. But there are also variations of type of both concepts, as this chapter has tried to show. Plaisance is also correct to conclude that the 'shape-shifting nature of the concept [of accountability] contributes to the volatility of debate surrounding the conflicting nature of freedom and responsibility'. The meanings of accountability will depend on the values that are invoked in relation to publication, whether as speaker, audience, publisher, or other interested party.

NOTES

1. The relevance of this for fulfilling the wider professional task can be illustrated by reference to the following statement by an experienced journalist (Walker, 2000: 240): 'True accountability relies on self-knowledge, and cognition in turn rests on a principle of difference: to tell a convincing tale about yourself to an external interlocutor is to start to give an account.' Walker attributes the idea to Day and Klein (1987: 5). He also writes: 'If Day and Klein are right, that accountability presupposes agreement about the language of justification to be used by actors in defending their conduct, then the accountability of those whose business is the daily use and reshaping of the language itself becomes critical.' He adds: 'Yet self-exculpation by journalists is rare.'

2. Semin and Mansfield (1983) identify five levels (or variants) of the case. One is simple association, where an actor or action is circumstantially or temporally linked to some harmful consequences (as, for instance, being a member of a religion that practices intolerance). A second is impersonal causation, where actions may have real, but unforeseen, indirect, and long-term harmful consequences. This raises questions concerning moral responsibility. Thirdly, there is a variant where the consequences could be foreseen, strengthening the case for attributing causal responsibility. Fourthly, there is the case of direct personal causation where the link between cause and effect is not in doubt. Finally there is the question of justifiability, where there is both intention and effect, but the actor claims the right to act according to other imperatives (as with collateral damage in warfare). Although these remarks apply to interpersonal relations, all of these conditions are relevant to the issue of media responsibility for harm caused.

3. The responsibilities of the media are often commonly debated within a framework of causal responsibility, despite the relative paucity of conclusive evidence of direct and harmful effects on individuals or society as a result of the activities of the institutionalized media (see Ch. 7). It is rare for the media to be the sole or even main potential causal factor. There is also little evidence (and rarely even an accusation) of intentional causation of harm by the media, even though there may be a widespread absence of scruple about possible effects. Where intentional

acts of publication are believed to have caused harm, they also usually fall under the heading of unforeseeability or justifiability. For instance, news reports can have negative consequences for some, but the responsibility to report overrides unpredictable consequences.

4. In general, the media do not accept liability for the consequences of publication, for practical reasons, but also because to do so would mean surrendering some degree of freedom of expression.

5. According to Smiley (1992), moral responsibility is 'essentially the Christian concept of sin minus the authority of God'. It is also closely connected with a belief in free will.

6. The media have an ambiguous position in respect of any liability for the consequences of what they do, for reasons that have been discussed. To make the media liable for unintended and unpredictable effects would open the way for an unlimited 'chilling' effect on publication that could be regarded as equally or more pernicious than the harm thought to be caused and no better than the censorship that has been rejected. Despite this, there are certain specific circumstances where the media can be made liable for harm caused.

7. It is found where the central activity is some form of public performance (artistic, speaking, writing, etc.). The main criterion is the approval of the audience and the account comes in the form of either attendance and attention or applause, or both. While all businesses are accountable to their customers and clients, it rarely has such a public character as in the case of the media. Given the various public responsibilities of the media, this type of accountability is close to that of democratic political accountability.

8. For instance European television broadcasting is routinely monitored for compliance with the Television Directive of the EU in respect of several aspects of content, including the amount of European production, advertising rules, etc.

9. A growing form of public review and criticism arises from the growth of media studies and communication research. Many more books and journals about the media are now being published. These help to inform public debate, but are only indirectly and in the long term influential and the media generally do not take much notice.

10. In the context of interpersonal interaction Scott and Lyman (1968) defined an 'account' as a 'linguistic device employed whenever an action is subject of evaluative enquiry... By an account we mean a statement made by a social actor to explain unanticipated or untoward behaviour.' Examples that apply to interpersonal relations include various types of excuse; justifications; concessions; and rebuttals.

11. The original idea was developed by Charles Cooley (1908) in respect of an 'imaginary interlocutor' and later developed by Bauer (1964) and Pool and Shulman (1959) to capture the fact that journalists (but also other authors) often think in terms of an audience they would like to address. Although the relationship of sender to receiver is an imagined one it carries some pressure to be consistent.

10

A Framework of Assessment

THE ACCOUNTABILITY PROCESS AND RELATIONSHIP

Accountability, as we have seen, involves a relationship between two or more parties. In the wider social context, there are customary and institutional sources of the definitions and guidelines for managing the relations that arise. The case of the mass media is no different in principle. The activities of press, television, radio, etc., do not have to be explained on a continuous basis. They come ready furnished with accounts of their origins, purposes, and uses both in the affairs of society and also in the everyday lives of individuals, where the media have familiar, even ritual, uses. These more or less taken for granted schemas for media performance and use are embedded in a framework of shared norms or rules, also largely taken for granted. We know on the whole what the media are supposed to be for and they in turn feel no need to spell the matter out.

Despite the fact that much is settled by the familiar definitions, routines, and understandings, according to type of medium and context, there is a continuous and routine process of accounting. There are also recurring occasions when accountability is specifically called for in order to respond to breaches of normality and to repair or redefine relations.[1] Within a shared framework of understandings and norms, media agents and extra-media claimants engage in a dialogue in which the media are asked to act or not act in a certain way by way of certain channels of communication and procedures for adjudication.

VARIABLE FEATURES

Accounting procedures range from individual personal complaints through judicial hearings, to the actions of government. Because of the tension between the right of freedom to publish and the requirements of the 'public interest' and of individual interests, the distinction between procedures designed for answerability, on the one hand, and those for liability, on the other, is especially relevant. In the former case account-ability takes the form of a more or less balanced and informal dialogue between agents and claimants. In the latter case, the rules for procedure are more formal and there is usually provision for some form of inde-pendent adjudication.

Cutting across this distinction there is also a variable of the publicness or visibility of procedures and of possible adjudication. A certain amount of accountability takes place in private exchanges either within the media organization/institution or between the organization and affected persons. Most feedback to the media is not public or visible and even audience ratings are often confidential in principle and for the internal use of media themselves. While internal accounting facilitates an ongoing orientation to audience and market, many issues and claims involving the public interest call for an open process.

Two other kinds of variation should be mentioned. One relates to the *time scale* of procedures. Daily (or more frequent) media give rise to claims on the same short time scale and may call for similarly fast response, without elaborate procedure. This category includes the in-stant response of audiences by phone or other means, the reactions of referents to the way they are treated, reviews, and continuous audience research (the ratings). In non-democratic and disorderly contexts, im-mediate response can involve physical threats or legal injunctions against further publication. Longer-term accountability processes are those that require the collection of evidence and independent adjudi-cation. They are also associated with claims that refer to endemic or structural failings of the media.

Another variable relates to the *currency* of accountability. All social relationships involve an element of exchange, sometimes only of mean-ing, but often much more, especially various services and/or emotional benefits. The possible benefits or services offered by the media are varied and also expressed in terms of different currencies. As far as audiences are concerned, benefits include goods such as information, pleasure and other emotional satisfactions, diversion, and cultural and social iden-tifications. Audiences as consumers pay for their media benefits with money or attention and withholding either is a form of sanction. But audiences can also give or withhold their loyalty, attachment, affection, and respect, all of which are valued by many of the sources and commu-nicators and can be translated into money or status.

For would-be communicators and sources, the media mainly offer the service or benefit of access to an audience in return for direct or indirect financial rewards (from clients and audiences). Some communicators can also confer status on the media and respect from society by performing public communication tasks. For another set of parties to the media process, the referents, the relationship is more incidental and the exchange aspect less clear, since reference in the media may not be sought or wanted. But two main benefits from the media may be involved in receiving publicity, one being fame in itself and the other recognition. Unsought publicity can have a negative or positive value for the recipient.

Most private media seek profit as a primary aim, but some commercial owners, as well as non-profit bodies that run private media, are less interested in financial than in social or moral profit. They may want to influence society, spread beliefs, or do some cultural or ethical good. In such cases, the public esteem, approval, and influence that the media can provoke (or fail to) is the most potent sanction and stimulus. Public ownership of the media gives rise to different situations, where, at the very least, there are mixed currencies, including political rewards, reflecting the diversity of communication purpose.

In principle, all the forms of currency or value that arise in the normal working of the mass media can be involved in accountability in the form of penalties or rewards. According to the above analysis, the main forms of currency, each potentially positive or negative, are:

- popularity;
- financial benefit;
- freedom of action;
- fame, celebrity;
- esteem and respect;
- loyalty, attachment, and identification;
- trust;
- political influence.

Claimants seeking an account from the mass media have, according to this analysis, a number of options for bringing pressure to bear and imposing some penalty after the event. In the nature of things, there is a continuing tradeoff for the media between the costs and benefits of yielding to claims. Different media pursue different ends. For instance, fame and popularity may be financially rewarding so as far to outweigh any possible loss of esteem caused by pursuing this goal. A reputation for truth may be more valued than any costs incurred through offending powerful interests. These are choices that may have to be made. In terms of this rather abstract analysis, the fact that there are different currencies extends the sensitivity and range of possibilities of accountability processes but does not necessarily increase effectiveness or enforceability.

ACCOUNTING PROCEDURES AND FORMS OF ACCOUNT

In general the accounting process that anticipates, accompanies, and follows publication is a matter of continually matching promises, obligations, and expectations on the one hand with evidence and claims about performance on the other. The term accountability can refer either to a condition or state (of being accountable), but usually to a process, in which several actors and actions are sequentially related. Pritchard (2001: 3) describes the process succinctly as one of 'naming, blaming and claiming'. A problem with the media has first to be named as such. Naming need not be public and does not necessary go any further for various reasons, including low expectations of the media. Pritchard comments: 'the important point is that there can be no demand for accountability unless someone first names a problem'. A second, distinct, step is blaming: the media are blamed for some harm or failing with reference to rules and expectations (including voluntary promises as well as external obligations). Claims are lodged with a view to some remedy, apology, or even compensation. A formal assessment takes place either internally to the media, where compliance is voluntary, or by way of some outside adjudicatory process where obligations are involved. An assessment (in the case of voluntary promises) or a judgement (in the case of obligations) is made in the form of a statement of account. This can be rendered in a variety of currencies, as described above, and take the form of a response (apology, explanation, etc.) or the payment of some kind of penalty.

A summary guide to this discussion is provided in Tables 10.1 and 10.2. The tables are organized vertically according to the main types of issue and horizontally according to the three stages in the typical sequence of the accounting process. The distinction between promise–assessment and claim–adjudication described above is incorporated in the tables. An example is given to illustrate each entry or position in the matrix.

INTERNAL LINES OF ACCOUNTABILITY

The term 'lines of accountability' refers to the notional internal and external channels that connect the various parties in the larger mass

TABLE 10.1. *Accounting process and form of account: the promise–assessment variant*

Type of issue	Promises	Assessments	Outcome
Content and service	Licence application	Licence review	Renewal or cancellation
Quality/values	Code of ethics	Ombudsman/ professional Court	Dismissal, apology, or improvement promise
Effects social or cultural harm	General social responsibility	Research/public inquiry	Publication of evidence Public debate

TABLE 10.2. *Accounting process and form of account: claim–adjudication variant*

Type of issue	Claim	Adjudication	Outcome
Content and service	Failure to keep promise	Licence review	Judgment and loss or retention of licence
Quality/values	Breach of law	Prosecution and court procedure	Judgment: acquittal or sentence
Effects harm to individuals	Allegation (e.g. libel/ copyright breach)	Court procedure	Judgment: dismissal or penalty

communication process. Large-scale media organizations have their own internal and usually hierarchical lines of control that determine in a more or less formal way who is responsible for performing what task and thus who should answer to whom. This is the principal mechanism by which a media organization anticipates and deals with complaints and claims in a way that is least problematic for itself. It has less relevance to the claims made from or on behalf of the society or public interest, but it serves to identify who in the media should be addressed and at what level the responsibility for alleged failings might be located.

Internal lines of accountability are of interest on four main points. One has to do with what has been referred to earlier as unilateral forms of accountability (see Fig. 9.3). These relate to the personal responsibility for publication taken by an original source or author (and the personal freedom to do so) in those circumstances where the media are playing a channel or distributive role. Secondly, there is the case of personal or moral responsibility that can apply to any media employee (journalist, producer, etc.) that may or may not be recognized in the internal system of accountability. The question that arises is whether or not there is scope for such freedom of conscience and if not how it is provided for. Thirdly, there is the related matter of (professional) codes of ethics and practice that have their origin and scope outside the boundaries, and thus the control, of any one given media organization (see Chapter 5). These can be more or less integrated into an internal control system and also help to deal with issues of freedom and conscience. Finally there are complications that arise where media organizations and institutions operate self-regulatory procedures involving independent and external elements of deliberation and adjudication. The line between internal and external lines of accountability is a somewhat arbitrary one and one has to look also at points of interconnection.

Paradoxically the more the mass media heed demands to be more socially responsible, the more likely they are to strengthen internal control, to limit freedom, and to behave in a conformist way. The more they police themselves, motivated by the prospect of more trouble-free commercial operations and good public relations, the less likely they are to take risks or deviate from mainstream values and beliefs. The more insulated they also are from various forms of intervention or regulation on behalf of the 'public interest'.

EXTERNAL ACCOUNTABILITY

Figure 10.1 provides a sketch of external lines of accountability, as they might appear from the perspective of the media looking outward towards an operating environment in which its main points of contact are located. The latter are also sources of claims on the media and they exert pressure for varied kinds of accountability. In so far as each linkage implies some legitimate claim, the impression is given that the media are as much at the receiving end of social power as they are exercising it. Although there is no way of calculating the resulting balance of power, it is correct to suppose that the power of the media is limited by these outside constraints and demands. The extent to which claims are legitimate depends in part on the acknowledgement of responsibilities on the part of the media. In general, responsibility (and thus also accountability) is owed to the following: those who have been made certain

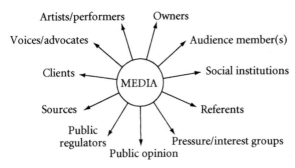

FIG. 10.1. External lines of accountability for publication

promises (albeit implicit); those with whom there are contractual ties; those with rights and interests that are affected by the actions of the media; owners of the media; those to whom there are legal responsibilities (as in the case of media regulators); and society or the public interest in general, although with much less certainty. In respect of power, any formal organization tends to behave in a more accountable way to those who have power to influence them in return (Brummer, 1991).

Although Fig. 10.1 seems to show the media as dependent on many outside agencies and partners, the pulls and pressures encountered do not all work in the same direction and may be mutually inconsistent. As a result, there is no accumulation of external pressure, but rather a confused and sometimes unequal struggle in which the media may hold the balance of power or effectively have a free hand to choose which of their partners to favour. It follows that it is not easy to generalize about the relative strength of different accountability claims, although most direct influence is likely to come from those on whom the media depend most directly for their continued operation, this varying according to the nature of the medium and media system. The most active links are likely to be with sources, owners, clients (especially advertisers), and audiences.

MEDIA–SOURCE LINKAGES

These often constitute a highly active channel directed towards the media, where voices seek access to the public, in a wide variety of forms, ranging from artistic products to self-chosen information. The media are answerable in principle to those to whom they give, or from whom they withhold, access, using the power that freedom of publication and ownership of publication property gives them. In practice, decisions about access will mainly be based on media self-interest (some source material is differentially profitable to transmit) and on the relative bargaining power as between source and medium. There is a well-documented tendency, for instance, for news media to give differentially most news attention to government and other official sources. This reflects the value of such certified information as a commodity, the real power governments possess, as well as the semi-legitimate claims to public attention of political figures and institutions.

OWNER–MEDIA LINKAGES

The links with owners may be seen as an aspect of internal accountability but have also to be considered in their external aspect, given the formal claims of many media to editorial and artistic independence. Owners of the media may identify with the outlook and ideology of the business class and may have a responsibility to weigh the financial interests of their own shareholders against publication considerations. Media owners may also be sought out by political and other actors as a means of securing access to channels or exerting some control over the media. McManus (1994) reports a good deal of disagreement in the literature on who has most influence on news, as between consumers, sources, advertisers, and owners. In line with Altschull's (1984) dictum that 'he who pays the piper calls the tune', McManus himself concludes that 'the primary role in shaping news is played by major investors and owners'. These are the ultimate bosses to whom the media are answerable (see also Bertrand, 2000).

These remarks mainly apply to privately owned commercial mass media. Other forms of ownership include the media that serve some political, religious, or other ideological interest and also public ownership as such. In the latter instance, in principle the public is the owner although in practice the government of the day usually exerts its powers on behalf of the public. Whatever the precise arrangements, this cannot be considered merely as an internal line of accountability. The society can legitimately set public communication goals and can in principle require conformity and answerability for performance by way of its rights of ownership.

CLIENT–MEDIA LINKAGES

The main clients of the media, aside from audiences, are advertisers or similar beneficiaries of publicity (suppliers of information, sponsors, etc.) who also have a strong, but selective, self-interest in the perform-ance of the media. Their accountability claims are limited but powerful where they do operate. The scope of their concern with how media perform is mainly limited to the matter of gaining public attention. Advertisers like to represent their own self-interest as identical with that of an audience in getting the content they most like. Viewed like this, the interests of all three parties seem to be mutually reinforcing. However, advertiser biases inevitably intervene in selection. It is also unrealistic to treat advertisers as independent of media owners. Aside from this, they are an important supplier of content, and sometimes an intrinsic part of the media rather than an outside agency.

Advertisers and other clients have the financial power to influence media publication decisions, ranging from editorial and presentation strategy to details of content. They also have interests of their own that are not identical with those of society, or audience, or media. The combination of the two makes them a very significant actor in the wider connections between the media and society. Other actors, espe-cially various pressure and interest groups, also sometimes try to direct the power of advertising towards achieving their own ends, which enmeshes advertising with public opinion and other social forces.

THE AUDIENCE–MEDIA LINKAGE

The audience plays the most complex as well as the most important part of all the external partners to media activities. By most definitions, aside from the various claims to be able to speak and express freely or impart information, the satisfaction of an audience is the main goal of all communication media. These exist not to provide channels of self-expression but to attract and keep audiences by meeting their needs for information, entertainment, and culture in its many forms. The strongest sanction that the media can face or fear is the collective judgement of an audience that can choose either not to pay money or not to pay attention. In this respect the power of control of the audience is great (albeit circuitous and diffuse) and has become more so as media forms and volume of output multiply. The media have to please their audiences and, taken as a whole, the media audience is also the public.

There are also a number of limitations to the power of the audience as an effective partner in the terms being discussed. It is, first of all, an abstraction rather than an actor as such (see Ang, 1991). It is a construc-tion based on the tastes and actions of numerous unrelated individuals.

As such, the perspective of the audience is open to a variety of interpretations by others. The audience as such cannot speak directly to the media or act for itself and from the perspective of media organizations and would-be communicators it is also hard to know. The data of audience or market research, based on what seem like small samples, are useful to management but not much use to actual communicators. In practice a more useful and personified view of the audience has to be constructed. In doing so, numerous transformations occur and the audience becomes more a reflection of the aspirations and intentions of the communicator and the media than a guiding or constraining voice.

Many of the contested issues about the purpose and effects of the mass media that have been discussed cannot be settled by reference to audience research and certainly not by the simple measurement of ratings.

OTHER LINKAGES

Beyond these most immediate links to the world outside the media there are a number of secondary connections, as shown in Fig. 10.1. Most of these belong to the category of those affected by the media's publications. This category includes three main entries. One is that of regulators on behalf of the public interest that have the task of applying legal requirements, varying a good deal from one medium to another and from society to society. Conditions may apply to any of the following: structure and ownership; technical standards; licensing conditions of electronic media; defence and security matters or emergency situations; elections; and some aspects of content (advertising, etc.).

The second entry, referents, concerns individuals that are directly affected by publication and have a claim on the grounds of rights (reputation, property, etc.). Logically in the same position are groups such as identifiable minorities (e.g. ethnic groups). Thirdly, there are organizations (e.g. firms) and social institutions (health, education, politics, the justice system) that rely on the media for their own activities and claim a certain kind of service for which they hold the media accountable. These may also have bargaining power as suppliers of information.

The last main entry in Fig. 10.1 identifies public opinion separately as an entity with which the media have to engage, despite the fact that it is not easy to identify or locate and that it works through other lines of communication, especially audiences. To some extent, public opinion also stands in for society in general. Nevertheless (as we have seen in Chapter 6), there are often quite well-formed attitudes towards what the media do on specific matters and in their general standards of conduct.

FRAMES OF ACCOUNTABILITY

This review of the diverse and overlapping lines of accountability indicates a complex, seemingly confused, field of activity, patterns of interaction, and also principles according to which problematic issues are assessed and approached. The intention of this and subsequent chapters is to expose the structures of thinking and action that underlie media accounting procedures. In order to do so it is necessary to introduce a further concept: that of 'frame of accountability' which refers to a distinctive constellation of the main elements that are involved in an accounting situation or procedure.

There are alternative logics, discourses, and modes of proceeding that are of varying appropriateness for the accountability situations that have been introduced. Different issues require the application of different frames and some frames offer more effective solutions than others to different problems. In practice, the single factor that is most helpful in distinguishing between various frames of accountability is the mechanism or form of procedure that is indicated, since responsibilities and principles can be formulated in innumerable ways and adapted to different situations. The frames are essentially theoretical constructions that provide the terms of discourse and logic appropriate for a meaningful discussion of disputed issues. A definition of the concept can be offered in the following terms:

a media accountability frame is a frame of reference within which expectations concerning conduct and responsibility arise and claims are expressed. It also indicates or governs the ways in which such claims should be handled.

To this extent, it has a normative dimension. Any given frame is characterized by typical issues, a given logic and discourse, appropriate procedures, and forms of account.

Dennis, Gillmor, and Glasser (1989) first identified certain models of accountability and their work has been followed in outline, although with changes, partly as a result of widening the scope of attention beyond the United States, and partly because of new media developments since that time. They named four main forms of media accountability in the following terms: the *market-place* model; the *self-regulatory* model; the *fiduciary* model; and the *legal* model. The distinctions involved are theoretical as well as procedural.

The first refers to all aspects of the media market and the central idea that virtually all claims against the media of a general or public kind in respect of responsibilities to society, whether accepted or only attributed, can be tested by way of the responses of the audience in the media market-place. According to the traditional theory of the 'free market-place of ideas', truth and goodness will be recognized and error and infamy will be rejected, albeit in a rough and ready way, by the normal processes of a competitive media market.

The self-regulatory model refers especially to the development and influence of codes of professional ethics, press councils, and journalistic courts that help to police conduct, raise standards, and offer some symbolic redress to critics or those offended by the media. The fiduciary model describes the system introduced to deal with the regulation of broadcasting in the United States, from the 1930s onwards. This was largely the domain of the Federal Communications Commission, which also established criteria of a 'public interest' in certain basic communication provision that should take precedence over market considerations. Finally, the legal model refers to the relatively small area of law that could (in the United States, under First Amendment principles) be invoked to proceed with a claim against publication (after the event).

In the classification adopted here and described in summary terms below, the same essential ideas have been retained although the categories have been adapted somewhat and their contents regrouped. Other classifications are possible, of course.[2] There are still four main frames that can be summarized as follows.

THE LEGAL–REGULATORY FRAME

This includes not only the territory of individual claims against the media on such grounds as defamation and violation of property rights but also a wide range of regulation that covers broadcasting, cable, and the conditions for operation of various new electronic media. Covered also are processes that might arise from claims on grounds of human rights. Laws and equivalent provisions governing media structures, especially in relation to concentration and ownership, are also included. Compared to the Dennis *et al.* legal model, this differs in including much of what they classify as fiduciary (having to do with the operation of the media as a public trust). This extension is necessary to cover electronic media provision (especially broadcasting and cable) that is private in ownership and operation but subject to public regulation with varying degrees of intrusion.

This frame typically establishes the basic principles and ground rules for the operation of media institutions and establishes the rights and duties of individuals in relation to the media. In modern liberal and law-based societies, the law guarantees rights of free publication and also sets limits to freedom for purposes of protecting the rights of others and taking care of some aspects of the general good of society. The main accountability issues handled within this frame include intellectual property rights; freedom of expression; ownership and monopoly questions (matters of structure); claims of harm to individuals, groups, organizations, the state, and society; and the essential needs of the judicial and political systems. This includes questions of state security and the integrity and independence of the judicial system. With reference to broadcasting and cable, regulation (sometimes law) is directed also at securing various public service benefits, especially those relating to the public sphere.

The main form of discourse and underlying logic of procedure is legal–rational and administrative in character. Procedures are laid down and formal in character. The forms of accounts are normally written texts which specify promises, obligations, standards, and relevant principles. Adjudications come with arguments and justifications for decisions that are favourable or unfavourable to claimant or defendant. These different elements that make up this frame are generally united by the fact that provisions are binding and the liability mode of accountability is involved.

THE MARKET FRAME

Within this, communication is viewed as a service and the operation of the media is a private commercial business in an open and competitive market in which the rights and responsibilities that go with ownership of the means of communication property are regulated by market mechanisms. Laws of supply and demand secure an approximate balance between the needs and interests of the media industry and those of the wider society. In principle, the market works in an open and self-correcting way. Free market principles support freedom to publish and to receive whatever content one chooses. The free market can support publication of minority publications, as long as some demand exists, but it also has tendencies towards concentration that work in the opposite direction.

The main issues handled within this framework, aside from property and freedom issues that also arise here, have to do with the quality of service provided (from the point of view of the consumer) and questions of value and pricing. They also relate to management and technology, with an emphasis on efficiency and innovation, since both appeal to consumers and improve competitiveness. The issue of choice for consumers and diversity in the wider sense is often handled within a market framework, since market theory holds that free markets encourage new providers and thus alternatives.

The market system appears to work without conscious overall direction or control (it reflects the proverbial unseen hand) and without normative principles, beyond that of freedom. Even so, norms do play a part in some aspects of media market activity, largely because media content is in many respects a normative product, embodying various cultural and other norms and values. The audience and also the general public have attitudes towards the media based on a variety of evaluative principles and make judgements about media quality. Such attitudes may influence audience behaviour and thus relative success in the market-place.

Publication decisions are made on the basis of awareness of public beliefs and expectations of an affective kind. It is in the interest of the media as organizations to be sensitive to the political and ideological context in which they offer a viewpoint, and interrelations between the media and politics are commonplace. The media market is more likely to be influenced by politics and other ideological concerns than are many other market sectors and more likely to be limited in some ways by law and regulation with a normative basis, as already indicated.

THE PUBLIC RESPONSIBILITY FRAME

This is more easy to identify according to ideas of the public interest and of media obligations to society than according to any specific mechanism or form of procedure. The term 'fiduciary', as used by Dennis *et al.* (1989) helps to explain an important aspect of it, since it is based on the idea of the media as ultimately operating on behalf of the public and held in trust by owners and managers. The idea of a trustee model of public broadcasting is also advanced by Hoffmann-Riem (1996: 340), and Feintuck (1999: 211) offers the similar concept of stewardship to apply to the case of media operated for the benefit of others, rather than owners.

The theory of social responsibility of the media provides a rationale for this frame. The general idea is that the media ought to serve public purposes and be socially responsible. This finds support from within the media that voluntarily choose an active participatory role in society and wish to have influence and contribute to the public good. Outside the media there are many individuals and groups, constituent of civil society and operating in the public sphere (including politicians and governments), that support the same principle and may claim access to the media in order to participate in democratic processes. These ideas have been shown to appeal to the general public. Responsibilities attributed to the media in this connection are generally voluntary or assigned in a non-binding way.

The issues that arise within this frame relate primarily to the public sphere, concerning cultural and informational quality from the point of view of society, both in a positive way (need for provision) and negatively (avoidance of harm to society and its members).

The appropriate forms of discourse are predominantly normative and prescriptive, embodying ideas of public purpose and altruism. The means of accountability and for achieving improvement are as diverse as the issues, ranging from informal public pressure to some forms of law and regulation. The central process of accountability and redress is exercised through public pressure, criticism, and debate, with appropriate responses by the media. Public opinion plays an important part in giving voice to criticism, proposing standards, and even providing a form of court. A special category is occupied by public service broadcasting which is regulated and monitored by external bodies specifically to ensure that public duties are adequately fulfilled.

PROFESSIONAL RESPONSIBILITY

We can distinguish a fourth frame, that of professional responsibility, that has some elements of the self-regulatory model and is not far in its normative content from the wider ranging public and social responsibility version. The criteria of conduct and performance are often similar, but there are divergent features. Professional accountability is not only concerned with desirable objectives and service to others, but also with protecting the freedom, and raising the status, of the members of the profession. The source of a willingness to accept responsibilities and submit to accounting is the sense of self-respect and personal conscientiousness of the media professionals themselves (whether journalists, advertisers, writers, or film-makers). They claim the autonomy to set their own standards and police their own failings.

Mechanisms and procedures may be similar to those of public regulation or industry self-regulation in some respects (codes, complaints procedures) and the issues dealt with are often similar. However, the motives for participation are different. Professionalism is concerned with positively advancing quality and not just avoiding offence or harm. Educational activities, rewards, and prizes are an integral part of the accounting process in the professional frame. Processes are typically entirely voluntary and internally managed, unlike many types of self-regulation that are designed to control the media from the outside.

COMPARISON AND EVALUATION

The main features of these four frames of accountability are summarized for comparison in Table 10.3. This may give an impression that all problems arising out of publication can be taken care of by appropriate procedures. It might also seem from the range of diversity mechanisms that there is little scope for media freedom or deviation from conventional norms. The impression is misleading on both counts. Firstly, all four frames are limited in their scope of application and effectiveness as a means of control (by design as much as by default for reasons of protecting freedom) and they may compete with each other or even work against each other. The market, for instance, will often reward what regulation and social responsibility try to inhibit. Professionalism seeks to limit the scope of law and regulation. Secondly, accountability mechanisms do not only work to restrict the media, but also help to shield them from external restraint or unreasonable controls. They can protect their own rights and interests by co-operating in voluntary procedures for handling complaints. Even so, the frames of accountability are all weak when it comes to promoting better performance in the 'public interest' rather than inhibiting particular actions which run counter to the reigning normative consensus.

It is evident that different frames are more suitable for different purposes and circumstances. It is also clear that particular issues can arise and be dealt with within the scope and terms of more than one

TABLE 10.3. *Four accountability frames compared*

	Legal/ regulatory	Financial/ market	Public and social responsibility	Professional responsibility
Main issues	Structure Harm Property Freedom	Product quality Efficiency Innovation Choice/diversity	Performance quality Public good/harm Public service	Content quality Autonomy Conduct
Main principles/ values	Order Justice Causal Responsibility	Freedom Profitability Volume/scale Choice	Various specific criteria: Diversity Equity Solidarity	Craft/art Ethics Task- related criteria
Logic/ discourse	Administrative Consequential Contractual	Calculative Commercial Populist	Normative Performative Theoretical	Philosophical Contractual Technical
Procedures	Formal Evidential Adjudicatory	Market forces	Public criticism and debate Inquiry and review Self-regulatory mechanisms	Voluntary Internal Self- managed
Instruments and forms of account	Texts Content classification Judgements	Audience ratings Balance sheets Sales	Codes of practice Evidence Proposals Public opinion Publicity	Codes of ethics Rewards Education Hearings
Currency of account	Material Penalties	Money Fame/popularity	Esteem	Praise or blame Explanation Apology

frame. It is easy to envisage circumstances, for instance, in which some particularly egregious conduct by a medium could be condemned by law, public opinion, the audience, and by professional judgement. Less likely, but possible, are claims that find no hearing in any of these frames of accountability. The circumstances in which this could occur would most likely involve some new or emerging issues and some new medium of publication for which no ground rules yet exist. This could apply to some uses of the Internet. Although in a given case there is only limited freedom to choose between frames for the handling of a claim, in the larger scheme of things there are choices of direction for policy or for the media themselves. With this in mind, the subsequent chapters are concerned with a more detailed assessment of the alternatives presented here. In doing so a number of questions are posed and some criteria of evaluation are outlined.

The most salient questions are as follows:

- What are the relative strengths and weaknesses of the alternative means available for advancing and protecting the public interest in communication?
- Which elements in these frames offer the best means of coping with changes in the media that are now occurring, especially the rise of the Internet?
- How do the existing media compare in terms of the application of these frames?
- How do the alternative frames perform in respect of the recurring issues of accountability as outlined in Chapter 5.?

There are a number of criteria to be applied, but they can be grouped under four main headings.

PRACTICALITY AND EFFECTIVENESS

How practical and feasible is it to implement the means of accountability indicated by the given frame? How effective are they likely to be in achieving intended objectives and how flexible in operation?

RANGE OF ISSUES AND VALUES

Which kind of issues are best dealt with and which principles and values are likely to be upheld or served? The question of public versus private good arises in this connection.

IN WHOSE INTEREST?

In whose interest are the measures likely to operate, considering the various parties to an accountability process? This criterion should take account of potentially undesirable side effects.

FREEDOM OF PUBLICATION

How well is freedom of publication safeguarded or advanced by the chosen mode of accountability? Here attention is directed at the choice

between an answerability and a liability mode of proceeding and also at
the degree of transparency and publicness of the process. In general
more public and open processes serve freedom better than internal ones.

NOTES

1. The possibilities are numerous, but fall into three main classes. Firstly, there is the
   case of some change of the rules, structure, or activities of the media themselves
   (for instance the arrival of a new medium, or a new entry into the spectrum of
   provision). Secondly, there is the case of some alleged breach or inconsistency
   between expectation and performance (involving a complaint against, or criticism
   of, the media). Thirdly, there is the case where societal circumstances change in a
   way not provided for in the existing institutional self-account (for instance in a
   war or crisis requiring new rules).
2. Laurence Lessig (1999) proposes a different fourfold classification for application
   to the regulation of the Internet. He speaks of four main types of constraint or
   modality: law; social norms; the market; and architecture. All play a part in the
   regulatory process. The new element is the fourth, referring to the characteristics
   of the system and especially to *code* or software mechanisms for steering and
   managing the system. Architecture has some affinity with the structural regulation
   of the traditional media and comes into the typical differentiation between
   sectors of the media (see Ch. 5). A missing element in Lessig's scheme is professional self-regulation. Otherwise, there are similarities between this and the
   scheme adopted.

PART V

Ways and Means of Accountability

11

The Media Market

The image of a market-place in idealized form is often invoked to exemplify the benefits of free expression and exchange between senders and receivers. It also offers a justification for treating the market as the primary means of accountability. The famous phrase 'market-place of ideas' is usually attributed to Judge Oliver Wendell Holmes in a 1919 US Supreme Court judgment.[1] According to Schmidt (1976) it 'remains the dominant imagery in the rhetoric of free expression'. The underlying thought is not particularly original, since it has weightier precedents in John Milton and John Stuart Mill and it is not even clear that the judge meant to add any new dimension by using an economic analogy.

The benefits claimed to flow from the free trade in ideas have also been much in dispute, especially the claim that it will in some way secure the emergence of truth (see Napoli, 2001: 100; Schauer, 1986; Barendt, 1998; Baker, 1998). More to the point, perhaps, is the argument that it leads to diversity of viewpoints and the exposure of antagonisms (Baker, 1978). For libertarians, the connection with the market-place is a source of support for protection against government intervention. However, for critics of the market, its tendency is to subordinate media decision-making to the interests of investors, sponsors, and advertisers (McManus, 1994: 85). Davis (1999) refers to the 'bizarre reinterpretation of libertarian notions at the end of the nineteenth century' that transposed 'the conception of media as public forum for ideas...into media as a marketplace of ideas'.

The market-place idea conjures up an image of the centre of a prosperous small town where many producers and sellers compete with each other to offer their wares, varying in type, quality, and price. The citizen-customers choose according to need, interest, personal taste, and depth of pocket. The presumption is that open display, competition, and the chance to sample and discuss, complain and talk back to suppliers will provide the necessary impetus to improving variety, quality, and value. The interest of suppliers/sellers lies almost entirely in pleasing their customers, responding and adapting to their needs. New products will come quickly to market and inferior, low value goods will disappear.

The great advantage of an ideal market is that the producer has to answer directly to the consumer in the most natural and efficient form of accountability. This is what Merrill (1989) means by describing the market as a 'court of first resort'.[2] His version of the market model of accountability assumes a market that is free from outside control, diversified, competitive, and relying primarily on audience support, whence the essential component of accountability. Within the audience are included the many pressure groups and special interests that should look out for potentially harmful effects. Beyond that, the principle of *caveat emptor* should also operate to ensure a watchful and critical audience, always checking and comparing for quality and value. According to liberal economic theory, the market should improve quality, drive down prices, and encourage diversity. Intervention is unnecessary and only leads to market distortion and inefficiency. The market is assumed to have a self-regulatory capacity when left to itself and a natural tendency to operate in the interest of all parties to an exchange, including the society as a whole.

The working of the markets in general have often been criticized and the limits of actual markets are well known. They include tendencies towards concentration and the combination of suppliers to limit competition. Many commentators have also remarked on the fact that the media market delivers not only power but also the freedom of the press into the hands of wealthy individuals or corporations. It is also the case that customers are not equal, their relative power depending on their disposable income, which determines their real access to diversity and quality.[3] These aspects of markets do not fit very well with the idealized notion of a free market-place of ideas, where truth will emerge triumphant and falsehood be exposed. As Schauer (1986: 777) points out, the market-place idea, of its essence, gives no special prominence to political or public matters. Nor does it necessarily lead to overall quality. In material markets, many customers have to make do with shoddy goods. A market-place as described does not seem to correspond with a forum where all can participate on an equal basis and enjoy the same chance of hearing and being heard. Perhaps, as Tuman (1999: 163) suggests, the Internet does allow a genuine free market in ideas to be established.

The part played by the market in respect of accountability does not, however, really depend on the theoretical value of the market-place idea or on the balance of arguments between pro- and anti-marketeers.[4] It stems from the reality that communications and the media are now predominantly, if not primarily, run as business organizations. As a result, most of the relations between agents of publication and their various partners (as set out in Fig. 10.1) are conducted according to the rules of one or other market. The most direct contacts and exchanges between media 'communicators' and audiences are effectively producer–consumer relations that are governed by market logic (McManus, 1994). We need to differentiate between at least four main levels or spheres of market activity and different levels of media operation: the market relations of production and distribution; relations with sources; relations with advertisers; and relations with audiences. For the most part, these contexts have their location within national societies and national markets, but some remarks about the global context of contemporary mass media are in order.

PRESSURE AND CONSTRAINT IN THE GLOBAL MEDIA MARKET

The media market now comprises a global system, divided by territorial, cultural, and other divisions, but also dominated in terms of financial muscle by a few large media firms with extensive transnational interests crossing a range of different media from book publishing to telecommunication services. Large firms buy and sell smaller firms, rights in products, authors, and performers. In these transactions, issues of accountability as such (to the public or society) for content, conduct, or performance play little or no part. There is little effective countervailing power to financial decisions that may have public consequences, beyond the limited amount of national protectionism still permitted in international trade and the rather permeable barriers of culture and language. At best, there may be locally owned media firms operated by local people and with some competence to take publication decisions in the light of prevailing conditions and expectations. Even so, it is hard to deny the proposition that the global market limits the autonomy of its various satellite units and less freedom probably means less responsibility and less accountability.

It is not simply the remoteness and autism of the global market system that limits the scope of accountability. The logic of the system requires that publication be subject to iron laws of profitability and as a practical matter locally owned media have to sell the products of the global firm and largely follow its management practices. In general, transnational ownership works against responsiveness to society and to the audience conceived in any other way than as large consumer markets. There is a large physical and cultural distance between production decision-making and ultimate audiences. Reactions and effects simply do not weigh heavily in the larger scheme of things, unless they have an economic impact.

A consequence of the ramifications of global media operations that weighs on the debit side of accountability is the competitive effect on domestic media operating in countries that are not integral to the global system (in practice mainly developing, small, or poor countries). These all have to operate in a climate determined by the global firms, their scope limited by the advantages of scale and the market dominance of international operators. The same criteria of maximum profitability have to be applied, and non-commercial publication decisions required in order to fulfil wider public responsibilities are under continuous pressure. Some socially responsible activities are supported by audience demands or by political and institutional pressures, but the climate is typically unfavourable to altruistic conduct. This affects not only the rights of audiences but also of those seeking access to the media.

THE PRODUCTION AND DISTRIBUTION MARKET AT NATIONAL LEVEL: IMPLICATIONS FOR ACCOUNTABILITY

In contrast to the global market, many national media are integrated into the political and social life in which they play a key part. Historically, book and newspaper publishing and, later, broadcasting developed with close, even if sometimes antagonistic, relations with national political, economic, and social agencies. This does not ensure that any particular 'public interest' is well served in every case, but it does mean that the idea of serving a relevant public (or national) interest is a familiar and accepted one. Our concern is with how market logic affects accountability. Internal lines of control and management in a media firm or conglomerate always have a contractual character, with goods or services being furnished according to agreed specifications concerning type and quality and at an agreed price, or one in which money is advanced to others in return for expectations of profit, based on promised activities.

This applies, first of all, to the relation between owners or investors and their media companies, then between companies and their own management, and then between management and their employees or service providers (writers, performers, designers, etc.). The various roles are all linked in terms of a cash nexus, which involves agreed minimum responsibilities and binding mutual obligations. The freedom of such market relations refers only to the freedom to bargain based on whatever factors of value are possessed, especially capital or relevant skills. The accountability involved is internal to the firm and the media institution, but has wider implications.

We can interpret the typical situation of market-driven media locked into a larger nexus of market relations as having certain consequences for accountability. Firstly, internal control, directed at protecting the interests of the firm, will be strong and hierarchical. Management is likely to accept responsibility for keeping promises of service and quality and also for obeying any laws and regulations that apply. The reigning norms of business responsibility and ethics are likely to be adhered to (which may include some service to the community and society). The responsibilities attaching to particular roles and occupational tasks are likely to be upheld (meaning support for skill and professionalism as well as technical standards). In effect, these remarks relate to three of the five types of responsibility summarized in Fig. 9.1.

As far as accountability goes (Fig. 9.2), the main features of the internal market as described promote financial accounting and a flow of information. The market system has a differential effect on the accountability relations discussed earlier (see Fig. 10.1). It strengthens the position of owners and management on the one hand (relative to creative personnel—the actual 'communicators') as well as that of the external agencies and clients that pay for access.

The type and degree of media concentration in a media system can make a significant difference to these conclusions. It is less likely that media firms within the same ownership will criticize each other (see Turow, 1994), thus weakening one of the means of public accountability, the surveillance of media performance by other media. Concentrated media power has other indirect consequences for accountability.[5] The costs of entry into the media market business are high and further accelerate trends towards concentration. The model of the media firm as an independent publisher is being superseded by that of a distributor whose main asset is its 'delivery' platforms (channels, satellites, cable systems, etc.). The increasing reliance on expensive reception hardware in the home increases the pressure to supply high value content, especially sports and entertainment, regardless of other considerations.

A key question that arises under conditions of big and fully commercial media firms is whether they are really able and willing not only to act independently of governments and perform a watchdog role, as suggested above, but also to respond constructively to criticism of their own performance. Pressures from government affecting economic activities are one potential threat, for instance where they affect supplies such as newsprint, levels of taxation, or burdensome regulations. Problems arise not only under undemocratic conditions (see Waisbord, 2000), but also where government decisions about future developments within their sphere of competence (especially telecommunications and electronic media) change conditions of competition or affect other interests of a particular media conglomerate.

MARKET ACCOUNTABILITY TO SOURCES

A market-based system inevitably has consequences for access to media channels (for outsiders) and for the type of content selected. In one way or another access has to be paid for, whether directly as by advertisers and clients or by way of returns in the audience market or by some other form of subsidy or bargain. There is a limit to the amount and kind of access to the media that is openly and directly paid for, the relevant conventions varying from one situation to another. Content is not generally admitted where it trespasses on the editorial autonomy and neutrality of an organization or disturbs its established profile. Even so, there are other currencies, especially having to do with power and influence, that have an ultimate value although they are not readily accountable in financial terms. This has a distorting effect on the market and reduces transparency.

Certain kinds of content and types of information are often poorly represented in mainstream media output because they do not fit established conventions of audience appeal. In effect, there is a continuing, systematic, and predictable selection process controlling the volume and internal balance of information about and representation of the world. This aspect of media conduct is quite different from censorship, since selection is an editorial prerogative. It is not usually directed for or against any particular cause or point of view although overall it does systematically favour some sources and views of the world over others.

There is a more active form of bias arising not from exclusion, but from the differential favour given to sources that provide free news or other content of interest to the media. A rather high proportion of news, depending on the publication, comes in some pre-packaged form from self-interested and well-funded organizations, commercial, governmental, non-governmental, and private.[6] Such sources provide ready-made news stories or documentary content that has advocacy aims. They are able to supply the right communication product at the right time to minimize the cost and maximize the convenience of the media. The suppliers of news typically operate in the public domain (and include public as well as private agencies) and may legitimately claim to have something of interest to say to the public.

Nevertheless, despite the normal resistance of news media to publishing propaganda, the best organized and resourced sources are more likely to gain access than weak or marginal interests and groups (Gans, 1979). It is arguable that the organizational self-interest of the media leads to routine inequality in the accountability relation with sources (in general, access-seekers). News media are willingly accountable to their valued suppliers of news, who are also likely to have more power in the territory covered by media, whether national, regional, or local. Any voices seeking access that are faint or poorly resourced are an inevitable disadvantage in a market system.

THE ADVERTISING AND PUBLICITY MARKET

The relationship of distribution media with their commercial clients, especially advertisers, is usually regarded by advocates of the free market-place of ideas as a beneficial force for constraining the media to serve their audiences and their society at the same time. Market forces oblige the media to balance the interests of audiences, advertisers, and the general good. In many developed media markets, revenue from advertisers is the largest single source of income for the main mass media, with the United States leading in this respect (Bogart, 1995: 71). In these circumstances, the media are as much accountable to advertisers as to their audience, and the former are much more likely to exact a more immediate and precise reckoning for the quality of service provided (as measured by audience reach and satisfaction).

The notional 'contract' between media and advertiser is for the delivery of a certain degree of audience attention to the message of the advertiser/client, with specification of audience type, in return for income. The promise has to be made good in a demonstrable way after the event (by agreed research procedures) and on a continuous basis. This puts a premium on this link in the network of accountability relations, with media distributors beholden to advertisers. It also draws attention to another actor in the whole process, the advertising agency. Advertising agencies are often very large international media firms exercising much power by their decisions to purchase media space, and it is they who primarily control the route of accountability from publication back to the original parties that pay for attention or access to the relevant public.

Free market-place theory blesses the link between the media and advertising on the grounds that financial support from advertising (without strings attached) increases media independence and also that satisfied audiences correspond largely with satisfied advertisers.[7] However, as Bogart (1995) describes the situation, advertisers often want rather more for their money than just audience attention and their claims have distorting effects on media performance and structure. Advertisers want supportive environments for their messages in terms of mood, style, and consumer-friendliness. They also want (as far as possible) freedom from criticism in the media of the activities of firms that do advertise, even if they have no formal claim in this respect. From time to time they threaten to remove their advertising and even intervene to suppress content (Bogart, 1995: 95–8).

There are also regular sources of pressure on news media, especially where editorial content is linked to areas of consumption such as fashion, travel, or motoring. Such content is often selected and presented so as to attract and support advertising, giving it a differential chance of attention than other topics. The more competitive the media market, with more choices for advertisers, the stronger is the pressure to adapt the content to the advertising that produces the income. The degree of such pressure on the media varies according to the relative share of advertising or related revenue in the overall balance.[8] There is a continuous risk that accountability to advertisers will take precedence over accountability to the public or society, especially as advertiser interests are clearer and come with a price attached. Whether or not this is problematic depends on the extent to which advertising and the interests of the public are divergent.

Pressure is experienced not only from commercial advertisers but also from governmental and other sources of advertising. In the Latin American situation described by Waisbord (2000) government has often been the largest single source of advertising and it has been used as a weapon to discipline the press without open censorship. In general, public advertising is normally a significant factor.[9] The more dominant any advertising source is in a particular media market (e.g. a local area), the more potential for constraint exists. The logic of advertising rewards media concentration, accentuating some of the market pressures discussed above.[10]

In respect to the criterion of diversity, market competition does offer permanent incentives for innovation, change and choice of media, and media content. On the other hand, the logic of competition for audiences promotes not only innovation but also a tendency to compete for the same mass audience by offering much the same popular content. The choice often facing the audience is an abundance of very similar content from similar or related producers. Mass media distribution tends to develop the characteristics of a natural monopoly, despite the seemingly open highway of the new electronic media. Although market theory supports access for new entrants into media businesses and technological developments have proved a potent force for opening market opportunities, there are well known barriers to entry. This indirectly affects accountability by cementing the market dominance of existing media firms. The more monopolistic the media, the less real alternative and thus the less effective are various claims or complaints against the media.

RELATIONS WITH THE AUDIENCE AS A MEANS OF ACCOUNTABILITY

It is in the *audience* market that the free market of ideas thesis should find most confirmation. Producers and distributors are connected to individual consumers who pay for and expect high standards of content and service. Consumers are also citizens whose opinions and needs for information and guidance lead media to serve the democratic process and wider public interest. The audience market is typically competitive and the media are motivated to succeed, as measured by profits and high ratings. It is, however, necessary to do more than just try to please the audience. Audiences also have to be actively recruited and held, tastes and preferences cultivated, and close and positive relations with the audience encouraged by the many means available. Aside from providing good quality content (of its type), these means include publicity, prizes, encouraging fandom, participative formats and events, flattery, and whatever might induce affection and loyalty. Such efforts are not inconsistent with accountability, but they have an ambiguous and potentially manipulative character that diminishes their integrity and value as 'answerability'.

In so far as audiences adopt the role of consumer and view their media as convenient suppliers of information and entertainment, their relationship with the media is much the same as that applying in other consumer markets. The more that the media for their part behave as commercial suppliers of certain services, rewarded either by direct payments, subscription, or advertising, a standard commercial relationship exists: one that is calculative and utilitarian rather than altruistic or normative.

The audience-as-consumer role overlaps inevitably with roles as citizens, parents, and members of various groups, thus injecting some normative content into the orientation to the media. Audiences develop channel-specific loyalties that exist independently of any particular moment of consumption or specific content. Such loyalties entail relations of accountability that exert pressure on the media to respond, especially since the loyalties concerned are commercially valuable, equivalent to goodwill and positive brand image in other business contexts. The more that the media are positively chosen on grounds of personal ideals and commitments, the less significant is the market character of the relationship.

In considering the contribution of the market to accountability it is useful to separate the communication role of the media from the distribution role, the former pertaining to original sourcing and performance, the latter to mediators (media firms, supply systems, channels). The distinctions are interrelated in Fig. 11.1. The figure incorporates the idea that it is possible for the same content or same media provider to attract differently motivated customers.

Each cell represents different possible types of accountability relations within the overall media–audience market. Where personal commitment applies, the accountability of source or performer to an audience is a self-chosen obligation based either on the wish to keep the respect and

AUDIENCE ORIENTATION

MEDIA ROLE	*Normative*	*Calculative*
Author, Performer Source (content)	COMMITMENT	FANDOM
Channel, Supplier	LOYALTY	CONSUMERISM

Fig. 11.1. Four types of media–audience relations

attachment of audience followers or maintain the line of communication. Where loyalty to the channel is involved, the media have a strong self-interest in being responsive to the wishes of audiences and in being consistent in raising and meeting expectations. In the case of fandom the communicator or performer values esteem and adulation and is motivated to do what is necessary to maintain it, although there is no normative or affective tie on the side of the media. Where consumerism describes the relationship, accountability is based on purely utilitarian, short-term, and practical considerations on both sides.

This analysis presumes that most media are indeed mixed in their self-definition and in their relations with an audience. It also reflects the fact that there are clear variations in types of media within most media systems. These types include, especially, public broadcasting with varying degrees of commercialism, but with ultimately non-profit goals; many small-scale non-profit media serving a variety of goals; some private media with non-profit goals; and the very mixed and unclassifiable sphere of Internet communication. Even within the category of large-scale commercial media there are distinctions to be made between media belonging to large chains and corporate groups and those that are independent; and between those with political or media-professional goals and those only interested in profit. In addition, the factor of localism can also have a large effect on the degree and kind of accountability relations with audiences.

THE MEDIA MARKET AS A MEANS OF ACCOUNTABILITY: AN ASSESSMENT

Four main areas of performance of accountability frames were identified and summarized at the close of Chapter 10. Here we look at the logic and working of the market in terms of these criteria, bearing in mind that actual markets cannot always live up to the unrealistic promise of theory and that markets can fail. There are, of course, innumerable deviations from any average. First of all, we ask how far the main features of market-driven media, especially the pursuit of profit, open competition, and care for consumers, tend to promote (or hold back) the working of effective accountability in the different senses that have been outlined.

CRITERION 1. PRACTICALITY AND EFFECTIVENESS

There is no doubt that the market does generally work very well in many respects in holding media suppliers to account by their customers. No special procedures are required or arrangements made, simply the freedom to operate. Each type of market develops the form most suitable to its needs and conditions in a natural way. Markets adapt continuously and flexibly to new conditions by their own logic. Markets can deal well with certain kinds of potential communication failure. For instance, in respect of information, where there is usually a clear test of reliability (one version of truth), the competitive market does tend to promote quality.

Media markets also seem to be good at initiating and speeding up innovations in forms and kinds of information services. This reflects responsiveness not only to audiences but also to other agencies that are involved, including manufacturers of distribution and reception equipment and also authors, artists, and performers. The judgements of the market are generally more enforceable than are legal regulations because compliance is often not only voluntary but is even embraced as a solution by the media themselves. They also avoid the unwanted side effects of legislation. Nevertheless the conditions for the optimal working of markets are not always present. Three obstacles in particular tend to arise: lack of openness to new entrants; limits on competitiveness amongst suppliers; and lack of structural diversity (many and different suppliers).

There are undoubtedly unwanted side effects to market relationships, most of which have been mentioned in general terms. Ultimately they come down to the lack of economic equality of consumers, the potential for market failure in its own terms, and the lack of any direct reference to ethical or normative considerations within the logic of the market-place. Since market relations are not in the first place designed as an account-ability mechanism, this weakness is hardly surprising. For critics of commercialization and commodification, the market is itself the problem and cannot by definition be an effective remedy. Any potential for truth, integrity, or creativity is subordinated to the maximization of the profit to the supplier in the communication market-place. The market has little tolerance for any other process of accountability, unless it happens to promote commercial success. It is possible that good ethics and good public relations do just that, although other forms of accountability tend to interfere with business.

CRITERION 2. RANGE OF ISSUES AND VALUES

Effectiveness can really only be judged in terms of goals and there is little doubt that the market works better on some issues than on others. The main recurrent issues of media accountability were summarized at the start of Chapter 5 under the following headings: social order; individual rights; cultural quality; preventing offence; preventing harm; property rights; providing public benefits; resource allocation; economic regulation; and international obligations. It is probable that market accountability is most effective in relation to social order, preventing harm or offence and protecting the property rights of individuals, but it is also effective on economic issues that arise at the level of media structure. The market makes the media most directly accountable to any source of income, especially audiences and advertisers, but they may become indirectly accountable to sources of power and authority, including, but not only, governments, where their influence can be translated into financial rewards or penalties.

Despite frequent criticism of the media for sensationalism and related failings, mainstream commercial media most of the time promote stability, social order, conformity, consensus, and conventional values. This is what majority audiences most of the time seem also to prefer. The same media are embedded in a network of social influence that requires them in some measure to respond to criticism on issues of harm or offence. It is in their interests to counter accusations of being anti-social that might well lead to restraints.

There are marginal sectors within the whole media system that do cater for content tastes that offend the wider public and may cause harm. As long as these activities remain within the law, the market offers no redress to those who complain. In practice, there is not one media market, but many, based on differences of taste and interest, with different participants. Essentially the market only supports accountability to or between those who are directly related to each other in the same market. To be heard as a claimant you have to be a participant. This is one way of interpreting the deafness of the market to complaints about very violent or pornographic content. Its consumers are not complaining.

The market has not generally been highly rated for encouraging *social* responsibility, especially where it is a question of the larger social and cultural responsibilities attributed to the media (as outlined in Chapter 3). The forms of the media or content that are most likely to help meet these responsibilities are not generally the most profitable ones. The market as such cannot be expected to perform any abstract public good or even to avoid harm beyond what might threaten profit. Although consumers and clients expect the media to meet some societal responsibilities and it can be profitable for them to do so, for instance in respect of political communication, there is no necessary correlation between making profit and doing good.

It is quite possible for the media to limit their wider responsibilities to the public and society simply to the matter of avoiding harm or bad publicity, without incurring any sanction within the terms of the market (or even the unwritten 'contract' they make with society). This limitation of the market is accentuated in underdeveloped countries where commercial media (television especially) use cheap, virtually dumped, imported entertainment to fill channels financed by advertising, with no reference to cultural or development needs.

Under some conditions, free market media show progressive tendencies, especially where they are free to act. A prosperous press has more possibility to be politically independent than an economically weak press, although the same rule may not apply to particular media outlets. A strong press has more chance to stand up to undemocratic actions or repressive government. Innovation encouraged by market opportunities has the potential for opening up new channels of political communications.

Market-driven media are not readily available as channels of access for governments or other political interest groups. Money to pay for access and campaigning has a distorting effect on the political arena, giving advantages to wealthy contenders for office or their supporters. The media market operates selectively and in a number of ways to reinforce social cohesion. Where media markets coincide, as they often do, with the boundaries of social organization, with, for instance, communities, cities, regions, and language or ethnic groups, the media are generally facilitative and supportive of the predominant forms of interconnection and identity. However, communities with little economic muscle or potential are not served or simply swallowed up in larger units. Market-based media tend also to reflect and even maintain a degree of social and cultural diversity, although differential support goes to groupings that have more social or purchasing power.

Reference has been made to issues on which the market is unlikely to provide an effective remedy for complaints. These mainly relate to numerous and diverse matters falling under the heading of commercialism as such and also cultural quality. Complaints and claims often relate to advertising, which has been criticized on the grounds of its excessive amount; misleading character; lack of taste; harmful effects on health or safety; denigration or stereotyping of some group; unwanted effects on other content; and various cultural and normative deficits; as well as damage to the integrity of artistic works. On some of these matters, the audience as a body of consumers can exert some influence towards moderation or reform, especially where there is clear evidence of public offence or a well-organized consumer revolt. A clear audience demand can also promote some forms of cultural quality, but the market has a bias towards low cost and high popularity. On more general issues of distant harm or offence there is little accountability to the audience (or society), since accountability to advertisers, as the direct source of income, takes precedence.

The media market has a double-edged tendency in relation to social equality. It does generally provide a widely shared common basis of information and culture, but it also widens gaps and opens up new gaps between the better and less well informed. Media technology innovations are initially adopted by the better-off and content is made and priced for them. This is currently apparent in the diffusion pattern of the Internet, globally as well as nationally. A new kind of social stratification between information rich and poor emerges, with new media effectively less, or not at all, accountable to the poor who are not in their customer base.

The internationalization of media markets is very uneven in its extent and effects, but the commercially driven global media have some potential for serving organizations and institutions of international co-operation and eventually global society itself. They could create a wider basis of shared knowledge, awareness, and respect. However, market forces are insufficient in themselves and often run counter to the goal of a more just international social order. Most media markets are still strongly rooted in nation states and their spheres of influence.

There is little or no effective accountability of the media outside the boundaries of the nation state, although the goal of exporting media content and the exposure of content in transnational markets acts as a check against racist, xenophobic, and aggressive content.

In a number of respects, the market provides incentives for promoting professionalism, especially in respect of the skill and the dependable quality of media products (informational and cultural). The same applies to management and to probity in financial affairs. Well-running markets have to maintain the confidence of investors, clients, and suppliers. Not all features that are typical of professionalism are rewarded by, or rewarding for, market operation. For instance, the autonomy, personal responsibility, and altruism of the professional is not easy to reconcile with the way firms operate.

Professional ethics may be regarded as good for business up to a point but where conflicts arise, their influence is subordinated to commercial considerations. The checks and balances that the market can apply are rarely sensitive to ethical concerns, until an extreme point of egregiousness is reached. Most of the ethical dilemmas that face journalists in relation to such matters as privacy or sensationalism cannot be resolved by reference to the market. Where they are, the market is quite likely to reward unethical conduct.[11] Under conditions of extreme commercialism, the most conventional and consensual values may be supported, but otherwise few positive ethical or moral constraints are exercised.

CRITERION 3. *CUI BONO?*

The question of in whose interest the media market operates, who benefits *most* from market-based accountability, is not difficult to answer, even if market-place theory holds that there is a mutual balance of advantage for all participants. In practice those who own or control the media take the initiative and control decisions. The profit motive requires that the system works to their advantage and this affects the outcome of all claims and complaints. Under normal free market conditions the interests of advertisers or clients may also be put ahead of those of the audience or public, where they are the primary source of income. According to market logic, the media are more likely to hold themselves accountable either to large audiences or to wealthy minority audiences. Sometimes political power comes into the equation, since governments have ways of exerting influence by inducements or threats or where an alleged national interest is at stake.

CRITERION 4. FREEDOM

The foremost advantage of market arrangements from the present perspective, despite the limitations alluded to, is that the market does depend fundamentally on the principle of freedom of communication: to express, publish, distribute, buy, attend to, react, and is in turn likely to promote freedom. There is a close connection between freedom, responsibility, and accountability, in the sense that freedom is a condition of genuine responsibility. Calling the media to account requires a freedom to act and the most valuable response to claim or blame is one that is freely made. In situations where the media are threatened by the state, power in the market can secure independence from pressure and should work to public advantage. Where they are threatened by excessive competition or where audiences are denied choice (their share of market power) by monopoly, the market itself should provide its own remedy.

Media operating under free market conditions are by definition independent, especially from government. Economic freedom to own and operate the means of publication is also a necessary condition for uncensored expression on any scale and is a bulwark against state control. In practice, as we have seen, markets bring with them their own (non-governmental) forms of dependency, limiting the accountability value of market forces. They have to serve interests other than those of their audience, even if the audience theoretically and in the last instance has the deciding vote. In practice the last instance is not usually reached.

One of the competing masters of what the media do is the complex of advertising interests, including agencies and clients. Responsibilities to these and to audiences do not necessarily correspond. However, the audience cannot register any demand or complaint in respect of what they are not offered. The formal independence of commercial media from government does not ensure complete independence. There are many favours they can do each other, without actual corruption or formal misuse of the freedom which the media have to dispose of their valuable property rights.

The free market makes it possible and sometimes rewarding to exercise the watchdog and critical function and to campaign against abuses by authority. There is a potential bias towards freedom in the relative blindness of the market towards content, despite earlier remarks about the market encouraging conformity and its lack of special protection for politics or ideas. This bias opens niches for freedom of expression and for conscience. The result is an inconsistent and patchy performance by commercial media.

The market erects it own particular barriers to freedom, even if not the same as those of government censorship or repression. It limits access to communicate, either because of the high barriers to entry into the media market (the cost of establishing a medium) or because of the price of access to existing channels. Large media can use their power in the market to compete on unequal terms (e.g. ruinous competition) by cutting prices. Mainstream commercial media can often operate profitably within narrow social and political constraints, even in undemocratic societies. This means that on purely economic grounds they can tolerate a degree of repression. Their tendency towards political and social neutrality, adopted in the pursuit of large audiences, goes well with social and political quiescence. Radical opposition or any questioning of the social order in whatever format does not seem to be especially popular with audiences or advertisers, except under temporary and unusual circumstances (e.g. in a national crisis).

The distinction between liability and answerability outlined in Chapter 9 does not really apply to the working of the market, although, in some respects, market mechanisms do reflect some features of the answerability mode of dealing with problems. There is no external compulsion, no penalty on any party and there is a certain kind of dialogue that takes place between suppliers and audience and other market participants. There is, at a minimum, the feedback of audience ratings. It is, however, quite an indirect form of exchange and it is limited to a narrow range of issues. On the whole, those who are dominant in a market do not feel any need to explain, justify, or apologise for anything and the more monopolistic the less so.

Markets are necessarily *open* in the way they operate, even if there may be obscurity about ownership and interconnections between media firms. There is typically no hidden agenda (covert propaganda or conscious ideology), even if the overt goal of maximizing profit may entail practices that are open to criticism and have unintended side effects on media performance. Transparency is, however, quite limited where most relevant information is privately held by the market suppliers (for instance about costs, audience ratings, and other market conditions). Neither the audience nor anyone else has any right to require disclosure and where private media respond to claims or complaints they do so at their own discretion, without having to disclose procedures or have independent adjudication.

IN CONCLUSION

Despite the wide currency and high status of the idea of a free market-place of ideas, the media market does not emerge as a fully effective instrument of accountability, beyond its own operational needs. Libertarian advocates of the free market do not generally set much store by accountability, which they see mainly in terms of restraints on freedom, however well intentioned. Even advocates of free market media see a place for a 'court of second resort', should the market fail (Merrill, 1989). Those whose main concern is increasing the effective responsibility of the mass media look either to the regulation of market media from outside or effective self-control inside (Christians, 1989). The predominant discourse on the topic of accountability portrays accountability and market forces as usually in tension, despite their evident compatibility on some points. To some extent this perception reflects the fact that the market cannot be expected to serve as a check on itself, where the alleged failings (e.g. those stemming from concentration or extreme forms of commercialization) are themselves largely caused by market forces.

It is also generally true that the market can really only be expected to look after the interests of those who directly and significantly participate in the market, whether as producers, suppliers, or consumers. Any estimation of how well the market does or can perform as an accountability mechanism depends very much on a broader assessment of the positive and negative consequences of media market forces.

NOTES

1. Holmes argued that 'the ultimate good desired is better reached by free trade in ideas...the best test of truth is the power of thought to get itself accepted in the competition of the market' (quoted in Napoli, 2001: 25).
2. In Merriu's view 'the market may not work perfectly in ensuring accountability but it, indeed, brings the public into the ultimate process of accountability through a kind of economic (or "public") determinism that goes a considerable distance in injecting audience values and preferences into the content decisions of our media' (1989: 11).
3. Christian Bay (1977: 31) puts it like this: 'Equality in any marketplace perishes quickly. Each victory tends to strengthen one competitor and weaken others; growing trends towards lopsidedness and unfair advantage are inescapable and monopoly or oligopoly is the normal end state...for ideas as well as commodities.'
4. There is also some disagreement about whether the market-place image should be taken literally or only as an analogy. Napoli quotes Owen (1975) in this respect as

follows 'I want to take the "marketplace" notion quite literally. There is a market in which information and entertainment, intellectual "goods" are bought and sold.'

5. Concentrated media have more access to larger audiences and thus more potential for influence on public opinion. This has mixed implications for accountability. Such media gain in power as social actors in relation to governments, but may also be courted by governments. Their economic independence makes it harder (and not always wise) for governments to remind them of their social responsibilities.

6. Schultz (1998: 56) found that about half of the articles in major Australian newspapers began as press releases. Other studies have shown similar results (e.g. Baerns, 1987).

7. The standard history of the US press dates its independence from party politics to the time in the early nineteenth century when it began to acquire enough income of its own from sales and advertising.

8. Income for commercial radio and television has in the past overwhelmingly come from advertising. The growth of cable and satellite distribution has opened the way for subscription income, but it is still a subsidiary factor even where well developed, as in the UK. There are large variations in the proportion of income that is derived by newspapers from advertising. In the United States typically more than 80 per cent, in European more like 60 per cent on average (see Gustafsson and Weibull, 1997). Both in Europe and the United States, there are now many free newspapers that depend entirely on advertising income.

9. There are other interesting sources apart from government. For instance, McChesney (2000b: 10) finds that in the year 2000, approximately 10 per cent of the total advertising revenue for the average TV station comes from political campaign advertising.

10. The so-called 'spiral of circulation' theory holds that the higher the extent of coverage of a given area by a given media, the greater the impulse towards concentration.

11. In television, film, and music, the same situation typically arises. More sensational content (sex, violence, scandal, etc.) is often popular and the media are only punished by advertisers or audience where they transgress the boundaries of taste quite severely or are viewed as harmful to child audiences.

12

Media Law and Regulation

BEYOND THE MARKET

The pure and undiluted theory of freedom of the press has little place for any mechanism of accountability beyond what is strictly necessary to prevent abuses of freedom of publication. If accountability is needed, advocates of media freedom suggest that the market, in as perfect a form as can be expected, is the only acceptable, or least worst, device for gaining compliance from the media with the needs of society. However, the performance of the market as an instrument of accountability is uneven and uncertain and has some systematic defects. Those not willing to put their whole faith in the libertarian purity of negative freedom (absence of restraint), as well as many supporters of free market media, have to look outside the market to achieve results, especially to law and regulation. The purpose of this chapter is to weigh up the potential of law and regulation for achieving a range of accountability goals in an acceptable way.

At issue is what can properly be done by, or in the name of, society to supplement the media market as a means of accountability or to correct its distortions. Law and regulation affecting the media predate the modern era and have at best a mixed record as an instrument of reform in relation to media, leaving aside the situation in past and present repressive regimes. Early press regulation sought to limit, not promote, the social role of the press (by punishing, censoring, licensing, monopolizing, or taxing).[1] In addition, law has been concerned with protecting the private interests of those who own the means of publication or who might be adversely affected by publicity. There are more positive achievements in relation to broadcasting but, in the light of this legacy, there is some reason for caution in looking to legal remedies for the failings of the media marketplace.

If we leave to one side the large question of harm to other individuals and to society, an alternative point of departure is provided by 'positive' theories of press freedom, according to which freedom of publication should contribute to other benefits. Much of the political theory discussed earlier (Chapter 3), especially that relating to the role of media in a democracy and ideas concerning the Fourth Estate, belong under this heading. Similar arguments underpin theories of media social responsibility, such as emerged from the American Commission on Freedom of the Press (Hutchins, 1947) which envisaged circumstances where some intervention by government might be necessary to correct the failings of the press and generally advanced a positive notion of press freedom.[2] The democratic theory of the press that gained ground (mainly in western Europe) in the decades following the Second World War went further. It provided a theoretical basis for legislation to subsidize the press and to regulate ownership in the interest of greater diversity, fairness of access, and higher standards of journalism.

The contemporary idea of a public sphere (see Chapter 3) emphasizes the necessity for a democratic society to have a wide range of means of communication independent of state and other powerful interests (Curran, 1996). Without this, active and informed citizenship is hardly possible. The idea of citizenship is itself an important concept for justifying and guiding media regulation (Keane, 1991; Feintuck, 1999). According to Feintuck (1999: 207–8), 'The public interest in the furtherance of citizenship, via universal access to a diverse range of media products, demands and justifies much more than structural regulation.' The same author proposes the concept of 'stewardship' as a suitable one to describe the terms under which the media should be operated in a democratic society.[3] The basis for the public regulation of electronic media in the United States is, or was, that broadcasters should act as 'trustees of the public interest' (see Barrow, 1968; Bazelon, 1982; Napoli, 2001). Stewardship in the wider contest would require media owners to meet the needs of society as indicated by regulators, without abolishing property rights.

Despite the divergent traditions concerning the relation of media publication to society, it is clear that a normative basis does exist for certain kinds of intervention designed to secure objectives judged important to society. Law and regulation are relevant to three main kinds of issue. Foremost is the protection of individual and property rights and the prevention of harm to the state and social order. Secondly, there is a necessity to protect freedom of publication and to promote diversity of ownership and access. Thirdly, there is the broad matter of securing the fulfilment of social, political, and cultural goals as decided within each society and which cannot simply be left to the vagaries of the market. While the first two kinds of goal clearly fall within the scope of law, it is less easy to see how regulation can secure the third set of goals outlined, without impinging on freedom. Aside from this, we are in a territory where there is often no legally responsible or accountable agent, but rather the media in general. In addition, although law and regulation provide numerous possibilities for an actual accounting to take place (for fulfilling the law), it is not part of the task of law in a free society to provide in any comprehensive way for the media to be called to account for their free acts of publication.

SCOPE AND RANGE OF LAW AND REGULATION AS A FRAME OF ACCOUNTABILITY

It is often far from clear what objectives are being pursued by what legal or regulatory means and therefore hard to evaluate actual or potential success or failure. We are here concerned with all formal rules, obligations, and conditions directly affecting publication. In general, law refers to specific legislative acts that become permanent instruments of adjudication and control, while regulations, albeit carrying ultimate legal obligations, are usually more temporary and detailed, less binding and principled, and often not directly administered by a government or enforced by way of the justice system. Account has also to be taken of various forms of media self-regulation for which there is some basis in statutory provision, even when, in the words of Feintuck (1999), 'there is no courtroom in sight'. Wall (2000) uses the concept of 'shadow law' to refer to forms of resolution that promote maintenance of order. He describes it as the 'space between social action and statute, where the law shapes action but does not determine it absolutely'. For the most part it operates to enforce social norms.

The general shape of law and regulation as they apply to media have been briefly described in Chapter 5. The relevant corpus includes measures not specific to the media that can also affect their operation indirectly. According to Feintuck (1999), there are four main 'law jobs'. The first of these is to play a part in the resolution of disputes, especially in either providing certain procedures for handling claims based on media responsibilities or directing disputes to other channels. In most legal adjudications an account is requested from the defendant and a judgment arising is itself a form of account.

Secondly, the law engages in 'preventive channeling' and in the case of the media this refers to the many ways in which the normal processes of media working are facilitated by rules and guidelines that indicate rights and duties as well as norms and standards of practice. The rendering of accounts is also part of this process. Thirdly, there is the 'constitution of groups', which is mainly the indication of lines of authority and accountability and questions of power and legitimacy. Fourthly, there is 'goal orientation', meaning the setting out of fundamental purposes and principles, starting perhaps with the objective of free expression and the 'right to communicate' and continuing through a range of larger public benefits that should be served by way of the media system. Under this heading may also be found the specific criteria and desiderata of media performance.

FREEDOM OF THE PRESS AND THE LAW

The issue of freedom is a special case, since freedom is both threatened and also advanced and protected by law. Freedom of the press becomes an accountability issue itself where it is threatened from various external sources, especially government, big business, or powerful interest groups. In these circumstances the press itself makes a claim for protection or remedy. But the press is also sometimes accused of misusing its power and is in turn a target for claims. In both cases legal remedies may be available, but only where there is democracy and rule of law and clearly established rights and conditions of press freedom. Law affecting newspapers is in fact centrally concerned with establishing the fact of press freedom, in an acceptable balance with the rights of others and the needs of society. Press law makes it clear that the press is not above the law and not completely free.

Typically, a framework of law and regulation is built around a guaranteed space within which the press and other media can enjoy rights to free expression. The boundaries around this space are restrictive but, without them, the degree of freedom within the space would be both smaller and less certain. Law can only create the conditions for free publication, without being able to ensure how or even if it might be used. Law can, however, extend the freedom of the press by enlarging the opportunities for communication by promoting access and the diversity of the media system. Much regulation of broadcasting can also be dealt with under this heading.

THE SCOPE OF MEDIA LAW: PROTECTING
ESSENTIAL INTERESTS OF STATE AND SOCIETY

There are a number of disputed frontier areas of the space referred to where claims are made by or against the press and where some legal restrictions apply, albeit varying from country to country. The main topics of dispute are dealt with in turn, beginning with that of national security and defence. Everywhere there is some limitation on press freedom to publish on matters where military and official secrets are involved and this is not considered in principle a violation of press rights, since citizens are also bound by the same or similar laws. Strong protection of the press in reporting on such matters is found, for instance, in the United States, Austria, and Sweden, while the publication of secret defence information can be regarded as criminal in France, the UK, and Canada, without any public interest defence being allowed (Article 19, 1993). There is a permanent state of conflict in most societies over the boundaries of what is legitimately kept secret on grounds of security, a war often waged by informal means of pressure, threat, and bargaining rather than through the courts, except in exemplary cases.

Similar rules spill over to affect the press during crises or declared states of emergency, or where severe disorder or terrorism is involved. These are occasions when the role of a free press as informant of the public and critic of authority may be of especial importance, since authorities have a tendency to overreach their powers. The legal forms enshrining the rights of states are not usually permanently embedded in constitutions or statutes, but are expressed in emergency regulations or the actions of authorities to suppress information, limit reporting, take over, or close down certain media. Emergency laws may also be passed that include clauses limiting what can be published, for instance statements or appearances by those identified as enemies of the state, information useful to the enemy, or likely to weaken morale. The real limits to freedom that can be set by law and regulation are usually only discovered during or after an actual crisis.[4]

In more routine matters of social conflict (for instance racial discrimination, hate speech, causing offence), the law is a rather blunt and ineffective instrument for enforcing official norms and conventions. Much the same applies to the cultural and social harm that is often rather vaguely attributed to the mass media. Most harm arises either from publication practices that cannot be forbidden or punished as a category (e.g. biased reporting; propaganda; violent drama; stereotypes and misrepresentation of reality; private censorship), or which are not intended (or cannot be foreseen) to cause harm.

Law and regulation also frequently seek to protect the integrity of the judicial system and the rights of individuals involved in court proceedings, despite general recognition of the important role of the press in ensuring open justice. Practice varies a good deal from one country to another, but courts always have powers to control the publication of matters relating to ongoing cases, even though, in practice, they are often not very effective.[5] In all societies the media are limited by the criminal law and in various ways forbidden to publish matter that promotes crime or assists criminals, beyond what might be defended on public interest grounds, especially a 'right to know'.

The essential working of the political system is sometimes protected by law, which can both enhance and limit media freedom. An example of the former is the greater latitude usually allowed the media to criticize public figures, candidates for election, office-holders, etc.[6] As far as the press is concerned, direct restrictions are minimal and in some countries (the United States certainly) non-existent. Even so, there is normally a body of electoral law that has some consequences for the media everywhere. Rules about how much candidates can spend on campaign advertising ultimately affect the press. In some cases there are rules about the timing of political advertising in relation to elections and about the publication of opinion poll results.[7]

A related issue is that of freedom of information, which is necessary to enable the press to collect as well as to publish information. There may be legislation that recognizes the claim of the press to have privileged access to information, because of their social role, but there is no general dispensation from rules concerning confidentiality and privacy. The rights of journalists, where they exist, to conceal the identity of sources, vary a great deal, especially according to whether criminal or civil cases are involved. In the United States, many states have 'shield laws' that protect journalists from demands to reveal sources.

Control of content is sometimes regarded as a frontier that should not be crossed by the law, although, as pointed out in Chapter 8, there are a good many exceptions, especially with reference to pornography or obscenity or where criminal acts are involved. But other subjects can be taboo, including drugs, racial minorities, religion, or offence to high office, or to military or national symbols. The definition of pornography and obscenity generally presents problems (see Chapter 7 n. 10), although the tendency is to emphasize the potential harm caused to its consumers or others. In practice, laws relating to obscenity and pornography have not been much applied to the newspaper press, but are reserved for specialist pornographic magazines (Article 19, 1993: 284). In countries where obscenity laws do exist (as in the UK), they are not easy to apply in a punitive way (except where children are involved) and mainly serve to signal where boundaries exist and as an expression of public opinion. In this and in other respects much law, in accordance with one of the 'law jobs' mentioned by Feintuck (1999), is to provide a public statement of standards and a warning, rather than to serve as an effective instrument of control or accountability.

THE PROTECTION OF INDIVIDUAL RIGHTS AND INTERESTS

A central feature of most press law deals with the alleged consequences of defamation, based on complaints by individuals. In doing so, the law that guarantees freedom to publish also protects the rights of those affected by publication. Protection of reputation against damaging effects is sometimes at constitutional level (as in the United States, Germany, and Sweden), sometimes in specific laws about libel and slander. Internationally, legal systems vary a good deal in the degree of severity of judgments and standards of proof required. There is a general recognition that under some circumstances causing offence to public officials may be necessary in the public interest (especially where it concerns public figures). There is also a good deal of variation of legal practice in relation to a defence on grounds of truth, to the issue of intention behind publication, and to the relative strength of claims based either on matters of fact or of opinion. Complaints of defamation made by powerful political or economic agencies are likely to be less favourably treated in law.[8] A new range of issues has been opened up by the Internet (Akdeniz and Rogers, 2000).[9]

Claims against the press on the grounds of violation of the privacy of the individual are somewhat related to defamation, since a certain kind of non-tangible harm is involved. Rights to privacy receive general protection in some countries (as in Germany and the Netherlands), while elsewhere certain features of privacy are protected against intrusion by the press. For instance, undue intrusion, the unauthorized use of photographs, and the exposure of private life in a degrading way can be actionable. Otherwise, there is recourse to self-regulatory bodies. A legal right of reply or correction of misrepresentation exists in many civil law countries, although it is cumbersome to invoke and not always very satisfactory in outcome.

Increasingly, legal protection is demanded from harm or offence caused by publication to various vulnerable groups and minorities. This might be viewed as an offence of collective defamation where this in recognised. The European Convention on Human Rights, administered by the European Court and also incorporated into law in many European countries, forbids any expression of hatred and incitement to violence on racial or religious grounds. Some countries have similar laws although not directed specifically at the media. The same principles have been widely incorporated in European broadcasting law and regulation, so that any problematic cases that arise are mainly confined to the newspaper press. The press is also typically free to report factually on the utterance of prohibited speech and, to some degree, free to publish letters expressing opinions that might be racist or derogatory.

REGULATION ON BEHALF OF GREATER FREEDOM: ACCESS AND DIVERSITY

Some strands of normative theory lead in the direction of governmental support for various types of media access, which in turn advances the goal of diversity. In one sense, one can view this area as one where government, on behalf of society, holds a media system or sector to account for its democratic potential and shortcomings, but without intervening with reference to any specific publication. In keeping with the social theory that attaches particular weight to the role of the press in democracy, most support has been given to the political and generally informational press, especially the traditional daily newspaper. Given that anti-concentration measures are generally regarded as legitimate instruments for regulating otherwise free markets, the way is open in principle for applying such measures even to the newspaper press although not without regard for possible negative consequences.

Measures have sometimes (as in France) taken the form of limits to the proportion of overall circulation that it is permissible for any one publisher to control. In practice it is less easy to implement limits of this kind or to prevent mergers and takeovers, and any measure that upsets the balance of press ownership is likely to be politically sensitive. There is an aversion to any action that can be interpreted as directly interfering in editorial content. Most regulation operates at the margin to prevent changes of ownership or cross-ownership that increase media industry concentration, usually applying the same kind of standard as with other branches of industry.

Where entirely new kinds of media effectively appear, as has happened with cable and satellite distribution, plus the Internet and other tele-communication-based media, there is regulatory scope for implementing principles of diversity of ownership and type. As Monroe Price (1995: 245) concludes: 'If the state has a legitimate stake in the machinery of democracy...then there is a public interest in establishing the infrastructure of communication,...It should not be a violation of constitutional or human rights principles for a government to establish an infrastructure that advances democratic process and helps to achieve an idealized public sphere'. The granting of operating licences with conditions of performance attached is the main instrument of future accountability that does not in itself breach ideas of freedom of communication.

There are several examples in Europe of media legislation designed to encourage new launches of print media, by economic means, especially with the aim of supporting minority voices. Economic support is also given in some cases to publications to prevent their loss to the spectrum of media voices. Subsidy provisions have been enacted to promote or maintain diversity (as in France, Austria, Norway, Sweden, and the Netherlands) although their impact has been fairly limited (Smith, 1977, Humphreys, 1996; Murschetz 1998). Most countries still provide some general indirect support for the press by way of tax concessions or transport, and postal and communication subsidies.

The ownership of the press (leaving aside the concentration issue) is sometimes regarded as a proper matter for regulation, without prejudice to its essential freedom and as part of the process of accountability. The notion of being a competent person is built into the general concept of personal responsibility (see Chapter 9). In the case of organizations, an adapted version of this idea is called for and is mainly provided by the concept of a legal person. The principle of transparency also applies. A media firm has a legal identity and address, a person or office with ultimate responsibility to whom questions or claims can be addressed.[10] A legal and regulatory framework for the media as businesses or public corporations always exists. Sometimes there are specific requirements that apply to the media, in recognition of their public role and potential influence.

There may be rules about the nationality of the owner, for a variety of reasons economic, political, or cultural. Where decisions about ownership are involved (e.g. in monopoly or cross-ownership issues) the general character of the proposed directorate can be assessed (e.g. by a television licensing authority). Commercial firms are subject to various rules about publishing accounts and informing shareholders and others of business activities and connections. Public media organizations are required to be totally open in virtually all respects. It seems likely that on these matters law and regulation are indispensable, even if they imply some limitation on access. However, conditions can arise where rules of the kind described are used to control the media and restrict dissent. Even under the conditions of freedom and democracy there is a place for media that exist either underground or at the margins, where enforced registration and institutionalization are inconsistent with their liberty. Such media do not submit to others' ideas of responsibility and are not really accountable (Downing, 2000).

PUBLIC SERVICE BROADCASTING AS A SYSTEM OF ACCOUNTABILITY

The legal position of broadcasting is both different from that of the press and also varies according to each national situation. The tighter legal control of broadcasting has a basis in its natural monopoly characteristics and its limited access possibilities, but it also stems from considerations of social power and effect. Public broadcasting systems in particular are protected from market forces and allotted certain public tasks. Private or commercial broadcasting (and cable) services may also have some public obligations as a condition of their operating licence. The existing broadcasting systems (especially the national public channels) have generally been protected by obligations on cable and satellite to carry them ('must carry' rules). Sometimes public service conditions relating to access for various local or other voices are also imposed.

Both public and private broadcasting in democracies can expect to have a basic freedom from advance censorship and from unreasonable punishment for what they publish. For the most part they are subject to the same principles as govern limits to any publication (especially the rights of others) although law and regulations that limit broadcast freedom are much more effective than any that apply to the printed press. Broadcasting (especially where it is public) is still the most accountable mass medium in virtually all respects, obliged to explain itself and having little escape from the many regulations to which it is subject. Hence the reason for characterizing it by its high degree of accountability.

The public service variant in particular has an exceptional status in relation to law and regulation. It is the only medium to which public law gives a set of clear positive tasks in society and has the means of enforcement. Although monopoly status (once common in Europe) has been withdrawn, it still has much financial security and often various ties with the political system. Arguments for retaining a (diminished) public sector, especially in Europe (East and West), have been found in the contribution it makes to system diversity, and in meeting needs neglected by the private media market. Governments and the political e¨lite generally still have an interest in keeping a sector of the media that is at least partially within their sphere of influence. But there is also growing opposition, on grounds of interference with the market and of unfairness to competitors

The original goal of public broadcasting was to provide the whole population (universal service obligation) with basic services of good quality information, entertainment, and educational or cultural content, quality being defined according to local needs.[11] Perhaps equally important, was, and as remains, service to the political system (in the interests of both politicians and citizens) by providing fair and guaranteed access to alternative views, without taking sides. It is also designed to serve the communication needs of minorities as well as the majority, in terms of access, suitable representation, and relevant content. The basis for minority identity is variable, but includes language, ethnicity, gender, age, and various disabilities.

Public ownership and control is intended to safeguard essential provision from the uncertainties and pressures of the market and also to allow the public to exert a directive influence, primarily by way of the democratic political process. In principle, this means that public broadcasting is the only medium with clearly stated 'public interest' goals and furnished with the necessary means of effective accountability to a range of outside interested parties (Atkinson and Raboy, 1997). Public service broadcasting does involve limits on freedom to editorialize or to advocate on many controversial topics, but at the same time it widens access and creates a protected public space for diverse voices and otherwise unprofitable content. In practice, there is no reason to think that a fully commercial system, as in the United States, is any more inclined to controversy or advocacy or even diversity. The contrary is just as likely to be true, because of audience market constraints. The constitution and regulation of public broadcasting tries to balance as much editorial independence as possible with responsiveness to the public interest in various forms.

With variations from place to place, the regulations and laws governing public broadcasting provide a range of different mechanisms by which the broadcasters have to give an account of themselves. These include:

- the obligation to provide annual or other reports;
- the requirement to answer to a statutory supervisory body which in a number of countries acts as an intermediary between government and media (Robillard, 1995);
- a variety of mechanisms for responding to complaints from the audience or others;
- parliamentary control by way of questions and inquiries, leading potentially to government action;
- subjection to periodic public inquiry relating to performance, policy guidance, and financing;
- the involvement of various advisory and consultatory bodies and forums representing the audience and various interests in society;
- in some countries political parties play a more direct role in the system and have certain agreed spheres of influence; and
- actions taken to enforce broadcasting law and regulation by way of the courts.

INTERNATIONAL OBLIGATIONS

Despite the relatively high level of national media autonomy there are real and probably growing constraints on the freedom to make national media policy. There is an international system for agreeing on the allocation of spectrum and satellite orbits. Precedents for such international agreements go back a long way to the arrangements for shipping and postal services, and later to telegraph and wireless telephony. Such agreements are in the mutual self-interest of all participating nations. Another notable exception to national sovereignty is the European Television Directive (1989/1994) which establishes agreed common rules, affecting content and other matters, as a condition for the cross-border transmission of television within the European Union. A similar, non-binding set of rules has been agreed by member states of the larger Council of Europe. These arrangements are accompanied by the monitoring of compliance, reporting, and national governmental willingness to implement rules.

There is a distinct accountability deficit in relation to international mass communication which stems from the lack of any forum, jurisdiction, or set of rules that applies across frontiers, apart from the exceptions mentioned. Foreign media content often does not meet local cultural and informational standards and its originators are not directly accountable in any way to foreign audiences or the importing society in general. Where foreign content is distributed by national media, rules of accountability can be applied, but restrictions are often difficult to enforce and may also be challenged on grounds of freedom to communicate.[12] More and more cross-border delivery can also take place by technical means that are not limited or subject to any content rules.

The single largest issue that now arises under this heading relates to the Internet and its regulatory future. Problems of control stem from the largely unplanned technological development in a regulatory vacuum that lack's national locatedness, making it hard to determine jurisdiction (see Reed, 2000). Despite its growing significance nationally and internationally and potential relevance to the public interest, so far there is little in the way of dedicated law or regulation and, as noted already, great uncertainty. On most points of dispute the Internet as a means of publication now falls within existing law and national jurisdiction (Gringras, 1997; Lessig, 1999). Nevertheless, the Internet does have an international system of governance (see Chapter 5) and efforts are being made to extend the scope of public forms of supervisory action, if only at the level of general principles (see Charlesworth, 2000; Hamelink, 2000).

ASSESSING LAW AND REGULATION AS A MEANS OF ACCOUNTABILITY

Law and regulation, viewed as a means of accountability, can be judged according to some of the same broad criteria as were deployed in evaluating the media market frame of accountability. However, unlike the market, the law is itself a primary means of accountability and has to be judged according to its objectives and achievements, as well as its basic characteristics as a mechanism or system of accountability. We can begin with this second point, adapting the criteria accordingly. In the assessments that follow, no general distinction will be made between different types of media, despite their different legal and regulatory status, especially as between the printed press and broadcasting. The situation of broadcasting has just been outlined and exceptions to generalizations will be noted where necessary.

CRITERION 1. PRACTICALITY AND EFFECTIVENESS

Although it is always possible to write laws and regulations requiring certain standards of conduct and content and in some circumstances possible to get political (and public opinion) support for enactment, the path is not an easy one to follow. Any attempt to apply legal obligations on the media touches on very sensitive constitutional issues of state interference as well as affecting many economic interests. This applies especially to established media and to the press in particular. Where new media opportunities are being opened up, especially in relation to electronic media, the need for regulation is likely to be accepted and it is possible to impose obligations and conditions. Otherwise, the further the distance regulation is from content and publication (thus in matters of structure, technicalities, and infrastructure) and the less immediate the effects on current actors, the better the chance of enacting law.

Once enacted, law cannot easily be adapted to changed circumstances. Existing law comes to be regarded in the light of some inherited good by its beneficiaries and removing or changing it may be as difficult as enacting it in the first place. The example of press subsidies supports this view (see Murschetz, 1998). The survival of public broadcasting, leaving its merits aside, owes something at least to the difficulty of changing an established institution, with many vested interests. In general the law cannot move as fast as the media can in the changing environment, which means it is usually pursuing a disappearing train.

The degree of effectiveness in achieving intended outcomes depends very much on the objective in question, on the circumstances, and on whether the media themselves have some interest in the outcomes. The case of the Internet illustrates the practical difficulty of enforcing any law on a medium without a clear organizational and ownership structure, or jurisdiction. For law to operate an accountable person or organization has to be identified. This is difficult in the case of the Internet. But it is also difficult where complaints are levelled at the the media or the press in general, since the institution cannot be charged or brought to court. This arises, for instance, on such matters as the invasion of privacy, the pursuit of public figures, or political imbalance.

Even so, the simple fact of enforceability is probably itself the principal benefit of law, where it can be applied. It can deliver some redress and act as an advance warning. The threat of enforceable rules can lead to more effective self-regulation than would otherwise be achieved. It has the potential to make the media accountable for their own self-regulatory procedures. It also makes agencies of government accountable for misuse of power in relation to the media. Since the media are increasingly owned by powerful corporations, nothing short of legal liability may be effective. The process of formulation and enactment is an occasion for inquiry and debate about issues and should lead to clarity of thinking. The legal process is educative for the society and is in itself a part of the accountability process. Even when not directly effective, law does serve to express and give substance to the idea of a public interest and can put pressure on the media to reform their ways in order to avoid intervention.

The primary disadvantage is a mirror image of the main advantage. Because of its enforceable character, law necessarily limits freedom and cannot readily be applied. There are prima facie grounds for being suspicious of all interventions of law in publication, hence the appeal of the US First Amendment, despite its other limitations. The real effectiveness of law may also be much less than its promise on paper. It is certainly risky to read the texts of regulations as if they describe actual practice or what could be achieved in a predictable way. Legal enforcement may have to be considered as an instrument of last resort since, in the absence of voluntary compliance, the very fact of resistance undermines its influence.

There are always unpredictable consequences of laws and regulations, especially where those affected seek to avoid some of the intended consequences. Some side effects are predictable. Broadcast media regulation that was designed to achieve balance and fairness on controversial issues has been accused of having a chilling effect on the coverage of very sensitive social or political issues. The media tend to avoid making trouble for themselves, except where controversy is going to sell newspapers. It can also make for blandness and a lack of criticism. Sensitive news topics may be avoided because of possible libel actions and the potential expense of pursuing investigations. Legal support for press diversity has been suspected of increasing government influence on the press. However, it is not easy to separate out the effects of law and regulation from other pressures tending in the same direction.

CRITERION 2. RANGE OF ISSUES AND VALUES

Law and regulation work best in gaining accountability in matters of individual rights, especially where property is involved and where liability for specific forms of harm to an individual is at issue. Where the clear and essential interests of the state or society are involved, especially in relation to public order, crime, defence, and security issues, law and regulation can be applied to secure compliance. Where harm to society is alleged to occur more indirectly through the mass media effects, law proves a weak means of accountability after the event. The difficulty of proving effect, and the lack of identifiable victims and claimants, are obstacles to effectiveness. In such matters, law and regulation are mainly suited to establishing conditions in advance by way of licensing and where possible (as with many audiovisual media) monitoring the supply and imposing some forms of censorship on potentially harmful content.

As we have seen, it is not easy for law to impose positive social obligations on the press that have direct implications for content, since this is generally inconsistent with freedom of publication. However, broadcasting, especially where it is under public control, can be used for such purposes and certain general public service goals can be included as licence conditions. In international matters, law and regulation play some part in relation to the operation of the communication system and infrastructure, but have little influence in relation to content. In general there are few firm media rules or regulations that cross frontiers and little accountability for the consequences of the media beyond their borders (paradoxically, the Internet is beginning to change this situation). There is no agreed jurisdiction and no court in which disputes can be heard or settled.

In general, there is little hope that law can make a free press behave 'better', however egregious its conduct. When the press does exercise its right to irresponsibility, especially in a collective way, there is little that can be done by making or applying rules.

CRITERION 3. *CUI BONO*?

Law and regulation are necessarily instituted by government and political actors and reflect their interests and perspectives somewhat more than the interests of the media, or of other interested parties. The presumption is that the public ultimately benefits most from law and regulation, but there is unlikely to be a single (or even majority) public interest on many issues. Apart from this, in practice, despite the even-handedness of the law, it is much more readily available to those who can afford lawyers. This applies obviously to wealthy complainants in cases of alleged defamation, violation of privacy or copyright claims, making the media more circumspect in their supposed role as watchdog. When the media themselves are wealthy and are fighting for a cause against powerful interests, this can be considered a benefit. But it is usually a deficit where they, in turn, are facing the complaints of injured individuals or using their muscle on their own behalf. The media can also afford to defend themselves at attempts by law to improve their performance or make them more accountable.

CRITERION 4. FREEDOM

This is the central issue, since the main objections to the application of law and regulation to accountability is the threat they pose to freedom. Despite this, it is arguable that much indirect support for freedom is given, in ways described, especially through promoting access and diversity. This is especially true of well-functioning public broadcasting that creates and reserves communication space for voices that might not otherwise be heard and equalizes chances in the media market-place. Legal procedures are also characterized by their public and, in principle, democratic character and this applies to relevant processes of bringing the media to account. It is clearly a beneficial feature, along with enforce-ability and it serves the secondary purpose of publicizing and amplifying the circulation of norms and standards applicable to the media. On the other hand, public processes of formal adjudication are cumbersome and time consuming and this may limit their practicality, beyond the symbolic function mentioned. Much technical regulation does not take place in public, is not debated, and may be effectively concealed from view.

Under this heading we can also refer to the distinction made earlier (Chapter 9) between a liability and an answerability mode of account-ability. While legal processes ultimately involve liability and leave no

uncertainty about which mode is involved, they also require accounts to
be given in the form of explanations and justifications, thus contributing
to answerability in some respects. Law also sometimes prompts relevant
actors to adopt the answerability form in order to avoid liability. Finally,
law and regulation does not have much to offer in the way of support for
internal media freedom.

IN CONCLUSION

It is clear from this account that law and regulation still have an
important part to play in respect of the accountability of all media,
despite current deregulatory trends and the increasing convergence of
the media. There are still impulses to strengthen as well as weaken
regulation in response to some incident or crisis that alarms the public
or politicians. Although there is some force in the argument that law is
mainly called upon when the free market of ideas fails in some respect,
there are also some areas where the market is not likely to work well as a
court of first resort. The law provides an independent line of accountability that involves the polity and, indirectly, public opinion. The
special case of public broadcasting offers a model of regulation that
relies on prescription rather than proscription and establishes strong ties
of reciprocality between audiences and communicators.

NOTES

1. Early laws in England, for instance De Scandalis Magnatum, 1275, penalized 'false
   talk' about the king. This was the origin of the offence of seditious libel (Foerstal,
   1998: 2). In 1798, the US Congress passed a Sedition Act, not withstanding the First
   Amendment, that penalized false or malicious writing against Congress or President (Price, 1995: 159).
2. Siebert et al. (1956) supported a form of positive liberty—'freedom for', not
   'freedom from'. They wrote: 'Social responsibility theory holds that the government must not merely allow freedom; it must actively promote it...When
   necessary, therefore, the government should act to protect the freedom of its
   citizens' (95). The authors were mainly thinking of threats from monopoly
   ownership and commercialization. The form of intervention was not specified,
   but public ownership was not ruled out.
3. Feintuck compares the task of regulating the media to that of managing any other
   important public asset, such as national parks. He remarks: 'the media are at least
   as important to democracy and citizenship as conservation of wild and open
   spaces and maintenance of access to them' (212).

4. See, for instance, accounts by Foerstal (1998); Smith (1999); Knightley (1991). At the time of writing the UK is being accused of breaching law and convention by publishing sensational accounts of arrests of alleged terrorits which make fair trial later impossible.

5. Some systems (e.g. in France and the UK) prohibit publication of information about the substance of jury deliberations following a verdict.

6. Politics could hardly be conducted without the freedom to attack individuals and wrongdoing in business calls for publicity. Most legislative bodies allow privilege for criticism of public figures. In the United States a famous Supreme Court judgment (*New York Times* v. *Sullivan*, 1964) extended the protection for press criticism of public officials by making it necessary for the plaintiff to prove 'actual malice' on the part of the critic, rather than requiring the critic to prove the facts of any criticism.

7. France is exceptional in forbidding paid political advertising in print and broadcast media for three weeks before an election.

8. In Sweden, for example, companies, organizations, and government authorities have no right to initiate libel actions.

9. Although in principle defamation via the Internet can be treated under existing national laws and jurisdictions, there are a number of difficulties. These concern, first, the meaning of 'publication', since there are several new types of publication (e.g. e-mails, discussion-group postings, bulletin boards, electronic journals, WWW pages). Then, there are problems in determining the place of publication and locating the jurisdiction. Not least problematic is the sheer volume of defamation that must flow through the Internet, even if much is inconsequential. Finally, the status and liability of Internet service providers is still uncertain in law.

10. In some countries, press law requires newspapers to have a registered address and responsible editor (as in France and Russia).

11. The criterion of quality includes reference to the national or regional origins traditions and cultural values plus the national point of view or interest. It implies a support for professionalism, but also aesthetic, moral, and religious values where these matter (see Blumler and Hoffmann-Riem, 1992a).

12. An effort was initiated in the 1970s in the international community to apply some form of accountability (if not control) in relation to the international flow of mass communication. The aim was to remedy the international 'imbalance' (mainly from north to south and west to east) and deal with 'cultural imperialism' and international propaganda. A Unesco 'Media Resolution' in 1978 and a plan for a 'New World Information and Communication Order' were key elements, as well as a commission (McBride *et al.*, 1980) to survey the issues and suggest remedies. The outcomes of these various efforts have largely been nugatory (see Golding and Harris, 1997; Hamelink, 1998; Vincent *et al.*, 1999).

13

Alternatives to Law and the Market

THE BASIS FOR GENERAL PUBLIC ACCOUNTABILITY

In the framework of analysis described in Chapter 10, besides law and the market, two frames of accountability were proposed, one encompassing various forms of external public pressure, the other originating within the media institution itself. The main driving force of the first can be seen as public opinion, in the second case a mixture of professionalism and the wish to protect media independence. Both lend support to alternative and supplementary means of accountability besides the discipline of the market or the interventions of law and regulation. However, the reality is less simple and it is hard to disentangle either the pure essence of pressure from public opinion or that of professional idealism. The media also operate under the watchful gaze of state, government, and many other powerful institutional interests.

Some key features of media institutions (especially their public presence, mutual competitiveness, and occasionally critical or adversarial stance) also lead the media towards self-evaluation (even criticism), active self-presentation, and improvement. These internal impulses are an essential element in the system by which the media are held informally to public account for failures and achievements and according to which they can make some claim to hold others to account. The key to social accountability lies in the effective harnessing together of different lines of influence and pressure, including those of creativity, professionalism, and civic engagement. The media are also an object of continual evaluation by the public not only as an audience but also as a body of citizens. There are, consequently, numerous informal channels by which the media are made aware of expectations, satisfactions, and dissatisfactions from the society.

Much publication takes place within frameworks where review and criticism are institutionalized in various ways, depending on the sphere of publication (professional, general public, mass entertainment, etc.). As a result, not only the media, but individual works, authors, performances, and performers are also evaluated continuously and, to a large extent, openly (thus in the media themselves). At the mass entertainment end of the spectrum, it is often hard to distinguish review and comment from marketing and publicity, but there is still a notional form of accountability involved and even celebrities revealing themselves in media interviews for publicity purposes are engaged in a form of self-explanation.

The forms of accountability described in this chapter are not simply supplementary informal means of control dealing with issues which law and formal regulation cannot deal with. Nor are they just devices to make the workings of the market more respectable or acceptable. There may be an element of both, but their character involves different means of restraint and they have somewhat different theoretical underpinnings. All the forms of accountability indicated here lack binding force, and are correspondingly more flexible and adaptable. They also involve informational exchange and dialogue, so that they fit the answerability model rather than that of liability. They are also more collectivist than individualist in character.

The forces that give the strength of public opinion to accountability processes are not necessarily benign in respect of promoting the publication values outlined in Chapter 4. Creativity and truth are not always popular and majority values are not necessarily valuable. We are speaking of populism or whatever gives weight to the majority view of what is acceptable or not in a society and legitimizes the right of the majority to decide what should, or should not, be expressed in public. On some media issues, the general public expresses itself strongly and even intolerantly, and the voice of the people is listened to by popular media, as it is by populist politicians.

The idea that the media should be responsive to the voice of society as expressed directly by the members of society is also rooted in notions of community and localism (and thus nationalism in a global age), which allocate a role to some kinds of public communication for expressing and maintaining identity and looking after the essential interests of a set of constituents. Rather similar ideas apply to social groups based on other identities, such as a minority language or ethnicity, as well as to radical and opposition movements. Here accountability is very direct and exercised by the audiences of particular media, and the special publics for whom they exist, and to whom they have to respond. In the case of public journalism (see Chapter 3) there is an impulse for the media to respond to public expectations and needs from a mixture of professionalism and (local) public service.[1] Media professionalism has its own theoretical foundations which include a value placed on meeting public needs for information (or right to know), but this may not predominate.

Overlapping with professional forms of accountability are various types of media self-regulation. These are diverse and sometimes help to reinforce professionalism, but sometimes exist as alternatives or even as challenges, because they are not fully voluntary (see Bertrand, 2000). They can be instituted by the industry to look after its own interests or manage its external relations. Or they can be put in place after pressure from government as a means of avoiding direct control. In general, they are based on an acceptance by the media that they have to answer for the power they deploy.

Two main alternative mechanisms of accountability need to be considered here. Firstly, there are pressures directly or indirectly from the public (rather then the government) in various forms, both as public opinion as expressed in surveys and also as organized campaigns by special interests, lobbies, and civil society organizations that seek to mobilize public pressure for some claim against the media. Secondly, there are matters of professionalism and self-regulation, putting together two different things, but still ones that have a common origin in the perspectives and interests of media personnel (as distinct from original communicators or voices).

CONSTRAINT FROM ABOVE

There is yet another kind of accountability process from society that occupies the grey area between control and accountability, identified as external and informal forms of governance in Chapter 5 (Fig. 5.2). Most centrally, it is related to the political process, although it has some administrative aspects. Governments and political parties have the mandate or goal of representing the public interest in governing the media system. Despite freedom of the press and a pronounced deregulatory trend in media policy, much remains within the scope of political influence. The condition or future development of the media is rarely a pressing political issue, although it occasionally surfaces as one. Even so, there are departments of government concerned with communications, media culture, and related matters and there are ongoing processes of debate and policy-making about what should be done, especially at a time of rapid innovation and increased economic and social significance of communications.

Governments in many countries are still deeply involved in exploring and advancing scenarios for the future structure and governance of the media. There is an unabated concern about the media on the part of the public. In any case, law and regulation (or even deregulation) are only the tip of a more or less permanent iceberg of the ideas, debates, and proposals that are formulated by governments, ministries, political parties, and numerous interested participants. Much of the content of exchanges between government, the media, and lobbyists enters into the public domain by way of the mass media themselves and this provides, albeit incidentally, an important element of public accountability. There is a general acceptance that governments should have some view on behalf of the public interest about the media and this assumption facilitates wider public debate.

A form of symbolic intervention in the media that is linked to policy-making resides in the power of public authority to institute inquiries into the structure and conduct of the media (see Chapter 5).[2] These inquiries had no formal power but they collected evidence, expert advice, opinions, and information about the working or influence of the media and they published influential reports. Aside from considering policy moves, they tended to deal with a familiar range of issues, especially competition and diversity, informational and cultural quality of the media, and potential harm to the young (and indirectly society). Many other initiatives designed to improve and invigilate the social responsibility of the media are taken by foundations and research centres, often supported by public funding or the media industry.

Although the era of this form of wide-ranging public inquiry sponsored by governments into media standards seems now to be behind us, society has not surrendered its potential to activate or express public opinion on the key issues of media operation. Often the outcome of political and governmental pressures on the media of the kind described has been pressure to introduce some form of self-regulation, as an alternative to legal restraint.[3] The media themselves often provide the indispensable element of publicity in these different processes of social accountability. Without it, there could be no debate or public opinion.

As a means of public accountability, this type of activity cannot really be evaluated in general terms, since it is not really institutionalized and depends on local circumstances. Nevertheless, it remains important because of its typically democratic and open character. Debate is promoted and publicity given to issues of concern about the media and the agenda for public action can be influenced. Historical experience suggests that efforts to mobilize significant pressure for public accountability have rarely had much direct effect, although they have influenced policy choices. Public inquiries are usually outgunned by the media and other vested interests, are too politically sensitive, or do not mobilize enough popular support for reform.

ACCOUNTABILITY AS RESPONSE TO PUBLIC OPINION

The network, or rather patchwork, of means of accountability linking media and public is fissured by one main line of division that distinguishes the public as audience from the public as body of citizens. Rather different criteria as well as mechanisms are involved. For the most part, audience needs are dealt with by the market, although not always satisfactorily, as we have seen. Here we are mainly concerned with public response to the media that differs from the media market mechanism in two main respects. First, the criteria of satisfaction or assessment are not simply those of individual consumer likes and dislikes, but relate to the various social roles they occupy and to larger issues. Secondly, the initiative in the relationship derives from the public itself, or at least from outside.

THE (NON-MARKET) INFLUENCE OF THE AUDIENCE

In respect of wider public and citizen concerns, Mitchell and Blumler suggest (1994: 237) the following defining criteria for a system that is responsive to the needs and interests of the television audience. Provision should be widely available and diverse enough to give meaningful choice. 'Civic communication' (thus relating to the public sphere) should cover important events, be accurate and fair, and provide a forum for debate. It should be independent from extraneous influences, be sensitive to social and cultural values, and offer some means for redress of complaints and full relevant information. As well as research there should be forums for society–broadcasting interchange, with representation of the interests and concerns of viewers. We could add that there is also a need for media that provide advocacy and contribute to opinion-forming. This ideal blueprint is unlikely to be matched by the reality, even in the case of broadcasting, and its application would result in the press being even more limited, but it provides a useful tool for assessment.

Public pressure that is specifically concerned with standards of media performance, from an audience perspective, is mainly directed at television. This stems largely from the same features that make television a target for greater regulation, namely its popularity, reach, reputed impact, and fear of harm. Mitchell and Blumler (1994) refer to 'mainstream' broadcast consumer organizations plus specialist consumer/ viewer and listener organizations in a number of countries, often with an ideological, educational, or moral project. Sometimes they are designed as part of the public service broadcasting structure.[4] Not unimportant is the movement to encourage media education at school level and later. The early history of the cinema was also marked by attempts by religious or other groups to impose voluntary self-censorship in order to conform with dominant or majority views of good taste and decency.

Not all media are massive and remote from their audiences. Local and community media and many specialist forms of public communication (minority, professional, and confessional) can be effectively monitored if not directly controlled by their self-selected audiences, whose needs and interests come before profits or other goals. Public television and radio in the United States have always been financially supported by, and quite responsive to, many voluntary associations and public bodies as well as to individual viewer/donors (Krattenmaker and Powe, 1994). Where specific minorities are served by specific media, these are usually close in contact and spirit with their audiences. This is either their *raison d'etre* or a necessary condition for success. Accountability to an audience is high in such cases because of the mutuality between the two sides of the communication. The Internet has some potential for creating similar conditions (virtual communities), without the physical closeness but having some prospects for extended accountability.

Individuals can and do express wishes and reactions and relay them back to the media, independently of their appointed or self-appointed representatives and guardians. All media receive a certain amount of spontaneous feedback from their audiences by way of letters, phone calls, and other means and sometimes this form of response is strongly encouraged.[5] Mitchell and Blumler (1994) found that relatively few people ever respond directly and such response can never be regarded as typical. Often it is highly skewed or the result of some organized campaign.[6] The increasing use of the Web and e-mail, with more media sources of all kinds being accompanied by a website or e-mail address, has facilitated and stimulated comment and interaction. For opinion-forming journalism in particular it seems to have opened up a genuine possibility of knowing more about the audience they are addressing.

There are obstacles on the side of the media in the way of attaining these desirable types of accountability relation with their own public. The main relevant message from research into media organizations has been to emphasize their autism in the face of their audience and wider society, paradoxical though this seems for a communicative institution (Burns, 1977). It stems from several sources: one, the valued autonomy of the communicator role; secondly the requirements of routine production and media logic; thirdly, the salience of the profit motive, to which public responsiveness adds little, beyond what is needed for marketing; fourthly, the intrinsic difficulty of making any meaningful contact with a mass audience or public. We could also add that there is limited evidence that the mass audience is itself very active is making use of opportunities for response and interaction with its sources of information and entertainment.

PRESSURE FROM THE PUBLIC AS CITIZENS

The streams of influence directed from society to the media, either in response to what they do, or to claim some preferable treatment (leaving official pressures aside) vary widely in their claim to represent the public legitimately. Much depends on the precise source and purpose. From time to time, public opinion surveys produce evidence concerning the general reputation of the media (see Chapter 6) and their performance on particular matters (such as elections). The sporadic and unsystematic nature of this form of feedback (to society and media) makes it an uncertain means of accountability, but it should not be dismissed. It is a reminder that public processes of accounting go on all the time in daily conversations about the media experience that most people engage in. These conversations tend to feed into public opinion and the direction of flow is reversed when survey results are given publicity by the media.

More sharply focused expressions of opinion come from various pressure and lobby groups that aim specifically to influence media content on behalf of some group or cause (see Montgomery, 1989). These use a variety of methods of organized protest, in addition to expressing a selective version of public opinion. They generally share the aim of naming and shaming a medium or source, and giving it bad publicity rather than winning by persuasion or argument. The target can be the distribution medium itself (cinema or television channel), the performers, or the originators of particular content or the owners and shareholders of a particular media firm. Many efforts of this kind are not primarily concerned with either reproving or improving the media at all, but have other political, social, or cultural goals. Even so, the total effect is to provide a reality check and a certain kind of feedback about the social forces in play.

There is a particular variant of such media pressure groups that looks out for the interests of political parties and causes. Many political party organizations keep a close watch on how their candidates and causes are portrayed and how much access they receive in television and radio, with particular reference to alleged bias and unfairness in selection or to expose unacknowledged ideological and propaganda tendencies. The activities of such groups are usually enhanced at times of election or crisis, where public opinion becomes an important element in politics. This applies also to international crises.[7] Much of this kind of public accounting involves the systematic monitoring of content, from the point of view of some interest or political/ideological or principled standpoint (Griffin and Nordenstreng, 1999). It has its origins in the critical media theory of the 1960s and 1970s and especially the application to the case of the international flow of communication.[8]

Media monitoring now embraces a wide range of causes beyond the party political or the objection to violent or sensational content and has become more international in scope. These causes relate, for instance, to the subordinate position of women in news representations (Gallagher, 1999), race and ethnicity (Downing and Husband, 1999), news coverage of human rights (Ovsiovitch, 1999), the interests of children (Carlsson and von Feilitzen, 1998), and alleged media bias (e.g. Lichter and Rothman, 1986). The typical method is some form of systematic content analysis and the aim is often to demonstrate that the media are in some way unfair, biased, distorting the truth, failing to inform, or potentially harmful. Monitoring is both a source of reliable evidence in advocacy and criticism and also a form of publicity. The same procedures can of course be used as a defence against charges of bias on the part of the media (see e.g. Westerstahl, 1983).

Usually, the media are interested in themselves and criticism of the media is a staple and probably increasing topic for public consumption, even if it does not produce any change. Some of the critical media reporting is now carried out in a formal way by media correspondents, with the media having become a journalistic specialism in their own right. There continue to be traditional forms of reviewing other media's publications by way of film, television, radio, etc. Media-related subjects are a major topic for columnists and features in soft-news areas. While much of the material is free publicity rather than critical exposure, it contributes to the wider discourse about media that is a feature of contemporary public cultural life. It also contributes to a more media-literate public opinion.

A substantial tradition of media research has been directed at the evaluation of media performance, according to numerous criteria (see e. g. Lemert, 1989; McQuail, 1992; Ishikawa, 1996). Athough mainly located in the academy, it has links with government, media critics, profession-als, and the industry itself, aiming to improve in some respects. The essential feature is the effort to ground criticism on reliable evidence, guided by evaluative concepts, but using empirical social scientific methods. These include content analysis, audience surveys, and obser-vational studies. Lambeth (1992: 174) suggests that if journalism is to evolve into a more responsible social practice, then media performance assessment 'must become an art embedded in the doing of journalism itself'. Critical research designed to influence the media in the public interest is not confined to journalism. A great deal of effort has been made on behalf of special sectors of the public, especially children. The focus is primarily on potential harm from violence and pornography (see e.g. Carlsson and von Feilitzen, 1998), but also on the need to provide positive content.

THE MEDIA'S OWN EFFORTS TO BE MORE ACCOUNTABLE TO THEIR AUDIENCE AND THE PUBLIC

Lines of accountability go from the media as well as towards them and are to some extent within their control, whether motives are altruistic or self-interested. Most media make some efforts not only to cultivate their audiences and encourage their loyalty but also to discover their interests and needs. For large-scale media this is an essential task, mostly carried out by market research and continuous measurement (ratings). But other possibilities exist that can be counted as instruments of account-ability. One is by way of audience research that is not only directed at measurement of size (ratings) but seeks also to measure the quality of response and obtain evaluations of performance. Such research has normally always been carried out by public service broadcasting as part of their mission to serve the audience in various ways and not just make profits. Systematic attempts have been made to develop ratings of programmes on one or more dimension of quality (Leggat, 1991). The resulting 'quality scores' are always open to interpretation but have some potential for assessing audience satisfaction with specific content.

The value of research as a means of accountability depends on the integrity of purpose with which it is carried out. Any potential for applying results is often limited by the resistance of media professionals to any form of assessment which does not conform to their own criteria of quality. The statistics provided by ratings fail to provide meaningful feedback and indeed cannot really do so. They are tools primarily meant for management. Alternative qualitative methods involving depth interviews or focus groups probably communicate more to interested professionals.[9]

Studies of the attitudes of mass communicators to their audience have often shown that journalists, editors, producers, etc., tend to deploy an image or selective perception of their preferred or actual audience, which provides some orientation, in the absence of direct contact or reliable information (McQuail, 1997). The resulting image may not be favourable or accurate but it helps to support a mental process of anticipatory accountability to a chosen group. Just as often, studies of communicators reported on a tendency for media people to look for a response to their work and guidance amongst family, friends, and even casual personal contacts. If nothing else, it confirms a wish to have some real interlocutors in the absence of a physical audience.

Other devices that are increasingly deployed by the electronic media for getting a response from actual audiences and the public as a whole involve varying degrees and kinds of audience participation. Formats are chosen in which the public is actively involved in ongoing media experience, either in a surrogate way by way of studio audiences or by being encouraged to phone in. Talk shows, discussions, and debates with an audience present on screen are popular forms of participant television. The increasingly interactive potential of digital or on-line television allows extensions of these formats, with more active participation from the absent audience in the form of voting or comment. The extent to which these developments really contribute to greater public accountability depends on the purpose behind them. The predominant aim is to involve the audience and keep its attention and loyalty rather than engage in a dialogue.

PRESSURE FROM THE PUBLIC AS ACCOUNTABILITY: AN EVALUATION

The actual contribution of these various forms of media–public inter-action is extremely variable and uncertain, depending on the medium, the context, and the means of response under review. Nevertheless some general evaluative conclusions are in order, referring once more to the same criteria as before.

CRITERION 1. PRACTICALITY AND EFFECTIVENESS

Aside from favourable situations, for instance where the media have a local or committed following, it is not easy to set up or institutionalize any continuous form of public feedback that genuinely represents the audience or public view on matters beyond what the ratings deal with anyway. Audiences are not typically highly involved, critical, or strongly motivated to talk back on any scale to their media and, aside from public broadcasting bodies with obligations in this direction, big media are not usually very interested in encouraging audience response, beyond their own needs of management. These remarks have implications for effec-tiveness, since this depends on the media being willing to listen, which depends in turn on the volume and weight behind the expression of public wishes. There are some matters on which public opinion does express strong feelings and the media do occasionally bow to majority or influential representation. They do so usually because it is in their own self-interest (Montgomery, 1989). Pressure from a medium's own loyal audience also carries weight. Effective public pressure is likely to involve a good deal of organization, motivation, and also expense. Some of the conditions of a participant and active civil society have already to exist for direct accountability to work.

CRITERION 2. RANGE OF ISSUES

Perennial issues of morality, taste, and harmful effects, falling standards plus issues of alleged political bias are most likely to stimulate vocal public expression of opinion, and most easy to harness by pressure groups seeking redress. Media treatment of minorities, by neglect or negative portrayal, can also be exposed by some of the means outlined, although redress or even response is much more uncertain.

CRITERION 3. CUI BONO?

While the public is the ostensible beneficiary of the pressure of public opinion, in fact most pressure is likely to come from well-organized sectional interests and lobbies. For this reason public accountability as described here has a downside on two main points. One, a general chilling effect, can occur in relation to controversy, innovation, and creativity, as the media are warned off sensitive topics or minority concerns. Secondly, some causes are likely to be pressed more strongly and effectively than others because of better organization and financial backing. Such efforts are vulnerable to being co-opted by special interests, leading to a neglect of socially and economically weaker causes. In other words, the market and political power intrude and cannot be excluded.

CRITERION 4. FREEDOM

There is no necessary threat to freedom from the activities described on behalf of audiences and various interests affected by publication, provided forms of pressure remain verbal and restrained. As long as a media system is diverse and extensive, there is no concentration of power behind complaints or demands from the public. On the other hand, public pressure is no guarantee of freedom and public opinion is not a very faithful friend of freedom (as evidenced in Chapter 6). There can be a potentially hostile and intolerant environment, open to mobilization by powerful interests, that inhibits the media from originality or nonconformity and closes down access, especially under conditions of conflict or crisis. De Tocqueville warned of the 'tyranny of the majority' in writing about the American press in the early nineteenth century (Schleifer, 1994). The media can be both a victim and an instrument of popular tyranny in this sense, which casts some doubt on the efficacy of public pressure as a means of accountability. In principle, however, the central processes involved are dialogic and in accord with the model of answerability, rather than that of liability, even where accusations of harmful effect are made. The general effect is to provide feedback and potential guidance to media channels or sources. The precise forms of exchange vary a good deal, some manipulative on the part of media, but others empowering in some degree for receivers.

MEDIA PROFESSIONALISM AND SELF-REGULATION

In Chapter 6 various perspectives on media responsibilities were outlined including those of owners, journalists, producers, and the many different occupational groups within the media complex. The concept of professionalism has embedded within it the idea of self-regulation by its members. This involves the determination of appropriate standards by practitioners and the effective 'policing' of activities to maintain the standards. Few of the many trades and skills deployed on a large scale in media work can lay claim to the term professional, except in the minimum sense of having some trained skill and being paid for the work. In the single case of journalism, where the idea of a profession has at least taken root, a good deal of uncertainty still persists. It is unclear what exactly the core skill of the profession is. Moreover, most journalists are subordinate to management and their work is governed more by market criteria than professionalism.

True professionalism requires sufficient freedom in the exercise of skill to be able to make and follow judgements about what is right as well as what is effective and appropriate. Few media professionals exercise this kind of freedom. Even so, the claim to professionalism on the part of journalists has, at least, encouraged the formulation of codes of ethics and practice. It has created some space within organizations for making ethical choices, since media organizations are also under pressure to conform to ideas of proper conduct. Professionalism also supports the idea that responsibility, accountability, and freedom are interrelated, rather than in conflict.[10]

Professional autonomy finds expression in the search for internal media freedom, including the right to take exception on grounds of conscience to certain editorial policies (see Chapter 5). In some cases a board of independent directors has some supervision over such matters. In their study of European broadcasting, Blumler and Hoffmann-Riem (1992*b*: 222) make some suggestions for improved public accountability, including a strengthening of the autonomy and role of media professionals. This could involve, *inter alia*, rights to information about decisions, more professional organizations, rights to veto appointments, and rights to refuse to carry out decisions on professional grounds.

Despite much agonizing over the inadequate professionalization of the media, especially journalism, it is arguable that too much weight has been given to meeting tests of professionalism derived from traditional areas of practice.[11] Some of these tests (for instance for altruism or vocationalism) can only be met by formal definitions and institutional arrangements and may mean little in everyday practice. There is no reason to think that in respect of the central element of work skills (even if these are hard to define and may not seem of vital importance to any given client), media practitioners are especially different from other occupations. Journalism is arguably concerned with the central value of truth (defined as verisimilitude) and as such has something in common with other information professionals, including librarians, scientists, and other information workers (Airiksonen, 2001). Distinction in performance is avidly pursued and where achieved it is marked in much the same ways as elsewhere: by the accolades of experts; the respect of colleagues; and the satisfaction of employers and audiences.

All this means that media professionals are very sensitive and responsive to meaningful evidence of success or failure and motivated to adjust their behaviour accordingly. However, the fact remains that these responses are not institutionalized and there may be competing and even irreconcilable goals that are supposed not to exist in other professions, especially between satisfying an employer, or an audience, or colleagues, or self-aggrandizement.

PRESS SELF-REGULATION

This can be defined as the voluntary agreement to live up to certain formally stated standards plus the adjudication of external complaints by an appropriate body with some independence and credibility (the main instruments and contents of codes of practice are described in Chapters 5 and 6). It overlaps with, but is not the same as, professional self-control. It has been remarked (by Nordenstreng, 2000: 78) that 'while media professionals speak warmly about responsibility, they remain lukewarm about accountability'. In practice, the first without the second is rather empty of meaning and media have gone some way towards meeting the accountability demand by various forms of self-regulation which do not seriously impair their freedom to publish what and how they like. Several motives play a part in self-regulation. One reflects an element of idealistic public purpose that has helped to define the press institution since its earliest days.

Secondly, voluntary accountability is a form of protection against compulsory accountability and in some cases has been urged by governments as the only alternative to stricter law or regulation. The promulgation of ethical guidelines is also good for the image of the press and contributes to better public relations in the society or community. Fourthly, accountability when expressed in the form of an agreed written code can be of use in handling some difficult issues, resolving conflicts, and maintaining internal discipline. Finally, a voluntary code with a complaints mechanism provides an alternative to court procedures, which can be costly for newspapers as well as for complainants (Dennis, 1995).

Many of the issues for self-regulation relate to immediate and practical challenges and dilemmas that arise on a daily basis. The central task of the journalist is defined nearly everywhere in terms of the speedy transmission of reliable (that is, objective) information about current events (see Chapter 6). Beyond that there are varying views about how far journalism should play an active investigative or political role. The most widely occurring ethical dilemmas relate firstly to the methods for collecting information, which involves questions of confidentiality, eavesdropping, deception, and privacy, and secondly to the issue of responsibility for (secondary) consequences of publication. Here 'consequences' is to be understood more as the effect of publicity and media attention on individuals in the news, rather than the effects of the media on events or on the main topic or person in the news.

The press does not usually accept responsibility for alleged and unproven harmful consequences, possibly to avoid compromising their position in legal actions alleging harm (see Chapter 7). There are quite large differences between countries in their journalistic cultures (see Weaver, 1998) as well as between individuals on both points and there can scarcely be said to be a professional consensus. This reflects the very different kind of media that are to be found, ranging from gossip and scandal papers to the prestige national newspaper or political newspaper.

The relative willingness of the press in many countries to endorse written codes of ethics testifies to the acceptability and convenience of the practice, which has been gradually extending since the early twentieth century. Codes are often no more than minimal standards of practice that do not cause much inconvenience or that state general ideals. The existence of high-minded codes does not guarantee deep commitment, never mind enforcement.

The implementation of the many different codes of ethics is carried out (or not) by a variety of means and with varying effectiveness from country to country (Pritchard, 2000). In the case of the press the main instrument is often some form of Press Council representing the industry as well as the general public and other outside interests.[12] According to Nordenstreng (2000), drawing on the same research as Laitila (1995) of thirty-five European countries with professional code of ethics, twenty-four had a press council or similar 'court of honour' for journalism. To qualify, such bodies have to be independent of the state or the judicial system and to involve co-operation between publishers and journalists.

In addition to such councils there may also be a press ombudsman following the original Swedish model and particular newspapers may have their own ombudsmen for complaints (as in Canada, the UK, and the United States, see Pritchard, 1991). The United States has largely resisted the press council institution, mainly due to the opposition of publishers and the fear of restraint on the press, although some state press (news) councils exist.[13] In general, the United States is least likely to offer or tolerate any form of self-regulation by the press that is in any way influenced by government or public pressure. On the other hand, it may have a more developed and respected code of professional journalistic ethics than is found in other countries.[14]

The main task of press councils is to hear and adjudicate on complaints made against the press by members of the public or other organizations, with reference to the agreed code of principles. Most complaints tend to relate to news reporting. Press councils have a twofold mandate of protecting the public and also journalists and the press, especially against the state or other powerful interests. In most cases where complaints are made by individuals, the only remedy available is publication of the judgement and the publication (by agreement) of some apology or correction. Although judgements are not legally enforceable, this form of accountability is modelled quite closely on the legal model and usually requires some claim of individual harm. Complaints often relate to matters that might be covered by law, offering an alternative way of getting some redress, especially in a symbolic form. In practice many alleged failings in the quality of press performance are not subject to any adjudication at all.

Besides codes, councils, and complaints procedures, there are numerous other informal and scattered elements that promote professionalism and accountability of journalism in the wider sense. The United States again is rich in examples, in line with an early advantage in promoting journalism education. Foundations and research centres, often located at universities and funded by publishers, provide support for journalism education and for professional initiatives by way of training, awards, conferences, and study leaves. Obligations to society and the local community are often supported. Initiatives of this kind advance the self-interest of the media industry as well as the public good and the interests of individuals.

Another weapon in the journalistic accountability armoury is the publication of professional reviews, both academic and practical. As with press councils, there is considerable uncertainty about how much the potential for self-examination and criticism provided by reviews is actually achieved.[15] With respect to newspaper journalism in particular, the movement known as either 'civic' or 'public' journalism has a place in this analysis (see Chapter 3). The ideals of public journalism do involve a genuine element of voluntary accountability, following the answerability mode on the part of a media sector that has generally rejected externally imposed accountability forms.

There is a potential for the press and the media generally to operate as a means of self-accountability by paying critical attention to their own performance (in practice this means the performance of other media organs). Dorman (1991: 198) concludes after reviewing self-regulation that instead of a formal watchdog 'the best way to keep the press accountable is precisely the manner in which the press keeps government accountable, namely to hold its actions up to public attention'. He recognizes the disinclination of the press to do this at all systematically or actively. Incentives for professional self-improvement are not confined to journalism. There is a well-developed system of prizes and awards for different media branches, nationally and internationally, that promotes and publicizes excellence, as judged by professional experts. This is a case of accountability by reward rather than penalty.

BROADCAST AND OTHER SELF-REGULATION

Broadcast self-regulation (in relation to content standards) is hard to distinguish from external regulation. It is pervasive and often involuntary, since it is usually required by operating conditions and often supervised by independent agencies appointed by government. Self-restraint is expected on matters of public concern, which mainly revolve around violence, sex, crime, bad language, and perceived abuses. There is widespread reference to detailed production codes on these matters. Broadcast journalists have to deal with much the same ethical and professional dilemmas as print journalists and they are also much more likely to be called rather quickly and authoritatively to account by governments, audiences, and interested parties for perceived transgressions.

Aside from the usual matters of taste and decency the internal rules are more likely to include requirements about fairness and objectivity than the press is faced with. In the United States, a quite different history (see Hoffmann-Riem, 1996) led to genuine internal self-regulation playing a much more prominent role. Before deregulation, most broadcast stations subscribed to a voluntary code of conduct formulated and administered by the National Association of Broadcasters (NAB). Subsequently, the voluntary codes were formally abandoned on the grounds of their conflict with freedom (of trade and expression). They had consistently been criticized for both lack of effectiveness and excessive interference.

Self-regulation of various branches of the media (including film, video, and music) has been growing steadily as the media have expanded. Often supervisory regimes are public–private partnerships, serving mutual interests. The Internet is very largely self-regulating, in the absence of much dedicated legal control. Its international governing bodies (see Chapter 5) are essentially private bodies, serving the interests of users and taking account of the 'public interest'. At national level, most supervision is in the hands of associations of service providers (see Hamelink, 2000). There are two unusual features of Internet self-regulation. One is the fact that users, as subscribers to the services, undertake contractually not to engage in a long list of forbidden practices and can be expelled for delinquency at the ISP's discretion (see Drucker and Gumpert, 1999). The contract also allows the ISP to monitor use of the service. In principle this makes the user of the medium accountable (to the ISP) for their own conduct. Secondly, there is informal self-regulation by cyber communities themselves. The effectiveness of both forms of self-regulation is questionable.

REVIEW AND CRITICISM

In professional publication, review and criticism are more or less institutionalized activities involving several stages: submission to editorial judgement; review by experts; and openness to published replies from colleagues or clients. In the case of general publication, for instance novels, non-fiction, plays, films, TV productions, performances, etc., reviews are normally published, typically in media which act as vehicles of accountability for their own activity. There is a wide variety of genres of review available ranging from specialized publications to highly personalized interviews with authors, performers, etc., where reviews are rarely critical or easy to distinguish from self-publicity.

Despite the great range of possibilities there are some underlying principles involved in public review and criticism even if they are honoured more in the breach than the observance. One is that of the independence of the reviewer from whatever or whoever is being reviewed. Another is the representation by the reviewer of a particular constituency, whether of experts, or fans, or audience, or some other constituency or interest. Thirdly, there is a principle of fairness, balance, or lack of bias. Fourthly, there is that question of truth. All in all, reviewers are governed by much the same code of principles as authors. While there are divergent estimates of the influence or value of reviewing, there is little doubt that it matters to authors and not only for reasons of self-advancement. Nor is there doubt that, however selectively and perversely, it has a way of connecting producers of published work with their public in a significant and indispensable way that has a potential for accountability different from that of either law of market.

PROFESSIONALISM AND SELF-REGULATION: AN EVALUATION

Although linked here, professionalism and self-regulation diverge in their underlying logic and spirit. Self-regulation is associated with management and, however indirectly, external pressure, while professionalism, despite institutionalization, has its home base in personal autonomy, conscience, and altruism. Both approaches to accountability do, however, share a respect for the freedom to publish without restraint, albeit differently framed.

CRITERION 1. PRACTICALITY AND EFFECTIVENESS

Professionalism cannot be constructed or invented for an occupation, although conditions for its growth can be promoted. Experience suggests that the dominant climate of media systems and organizations is fundamentally unfavourable to professionalization where it challenges commercial or political logic, which it ultimately does. On the other hand self-regulation is quite a feasible project that does not require large legal or political projects or cost money. It can benefit media firms, but it requires the voluntary surrender of some degree of owner and managerial prerogative autonomy that commercial media enterprises do not typically welcome.

In respect of press councils Dorman (1991: 177) points out that there is little recognition of the group or collective rights of complainants. His criticism goes deeper, since he points out that such bodies are set up to adjudicate on whether the press has played by the rules, but they are 'not in a position to entertain seriously the charge that the rules themselves are suspect'. Press councils have been widely accused of being slow, inefficient, and self-serving of the press itself (see Clift, 1981; Curran and Seaton, 1997; Campbell, 1999; Pritchard, 2000).

Voluntarism has drawbacks and the most common complaint is that these forms of accountability are ineffective, because they are not enforceable (Bertrand, 2000). Evidence suggests that actual complainants are rarely satisfied with self-regulatory procedures and outcomes, where they exist (Pritchard, 2000). We cannot be confident that organized professionalism as such has actually made much difference to the quality of media performance, although there is no way of proving this either way. The likelihood is that there is simply too little of either professionalism or self-regulation to have made (or be making) much difference. Pritchard's general conclusion about media self-regulation is gloomy. He writes (2000: 191) 'Various mechanisms of media self-regulation can seem to be an appealing compromise between the heavy hand of government and the anarchy of market forces, but ethics codes, media criticism and news councils often fail to live up to the claims made by their supporters'. Bertrand (2000: 146) offers another basic reason for the weakness of self-regulation, which is that 'major decisions are taken at the top, not by the rank and file...The important responsibilities are not in the hands of journalists. It is media firms that are responsible for the serious transgressions of ethics.'

CRITERION 2. RANGE OF ISSUES

Despite the loftiness of the principles espoused in professional codes, most effects tend to focus on a very narrow range of issues, involving individual complaints handled in a semi-judicial way. These issues include accuracy, truthfulness, harm to reputation, privacy, honesty, and probity of conduct. Specific failings are picked up, while broad failures or gaps in meeting claims for social responsibility are not dealt with. Remedies that result are correspondingly specific and short term. It is simplistic to suppose that most ethical questions about press performance can simply be dealt with by reference to a code, however necessary this may be.

CRITERION 3. CUI BONO?

The question of who really benefits is an intriguing one in this case and the answer is at best ambivalent. It is no secret that self-regulation is intended to support the media and the media organization and media professionals can benefit in various ways (more prestige, security, and rewards). It is less clear that the more ostensible beneficiaries—society at large, consumers, potential victims of media harm—do gain, except in some rather nebulous way. There is as much chance that ethicality and good intentions are selective, malleable, and serve as a smokescreen behind which media organizations are free to cater for what the media market (including the audience) rewards (e.g. gossip, sensation, scandal, excitement). Not all the accountability mechanisms are fully independent of the media, which are ultimately in control and do not give away what they do not want to. The main (undesirable) side effect is the potential for self-regulation being appropriated as a means of self-defence or alibi rather than response, making genuine dialogue more rather than less difficult.

CRITERION 4. FREEDOM

The views of commentators on these forms of accountability in respect of freedom are likely to be mixed. True libertarians dislike all forms of constraint, especially where they involve firm commitments to listen to outside demands and procedures for hearing complaints. Those committed to social responsibility generally welcome these kinds of arrangements for reconciling accountability with a reasonable degree of freedom. The intention behind such devices has generally been to enhance the autonomy and thus the freedom of action of professionals. However, the division of opinion is not just a matter of ideology. It separates media proprietors from their professional employees. There is a largely hidden battle going on within the walls of the media and these accountability forms are part of the field of combat. Despite the impossibility of settling this matter objectively, there is no reason to believe that the freedom of the press is anywhere seriously threatened by the very limited types of professional self-regulation that are established. However, what might be threatened is the right of management to take various commercial decisions.

The criterion of transparency is normally met in the case of self-regulation by the publication of relevant codes of principle and by known procedures with some degree of openness. Professional self-control does not, however, guarantee openness. Underlying professionalism and self-regulation there are clear notions supportive of voluntary answerability, more so than in the case of self-regulation. Professionalism in fact implies the acceptance of an element of liability by the individual communicator. It reinforces the notion of responsibility to conscience and to an ethical code. However, in journalism it is sometimes invoked alongside the freedom of the press as a reason for refusing to explain or apologise, on the grounds of professional autonomy. The assessment here is mixed but both these means (professionalism and self-regulation) reflect a broad understanding of accountability that includes promise-making and moral responsibility as well as a commitment to the central occupational role.

IN CONCLUSION

The territory covered by this chapter is very disparate. Relevant issues of concern about publication arise at different levels and have to be dealt with according to the means appropriate. Thomass (2000) has suggested a model of six different levels at which ethical questions of journalism can be formulated and answers sought. Much the same model applies to broadcasting and advertising and is useful for present purposes. At the most general level, fundamental issues are discussed, for instance the relation between the principle of freedom and the need for social accountability. At the level of society, the political culture and the given political and social background influence how principles will be translated into practice.

The next level is that of the media system where media politics differentiates rights and obligations according to technology and other factors. Within a media sector there is further differentiation of potential responsibilities and reasonable expectations, for instance as between broadcast and cable television or an élite and a popular press. At the professional level, issues are discussed and settled between colleagues according to the principles of the branch of the profession. Finally at the individual level a journalist or other mass communicator has to act in specific cases according to conscience and circumstance as well as to the organizational and professional rules.

Different considerations and sources and degrees of pressure apply at different stages and different means of accountability will also be called for.

NOTES

1. Schudson (1999: 122) concludes that public journalism 'does not offer any direct accountability, however, of the news institution to the public'. It 'exhorts journalists to put citizens first even to share setting the news agenda with individuals and groups in the community—but always authority about what to write stays with the professionals'. Public journalism is related to what Schudson calls the 'trustee model of journalism' (as opposed to the 'market model' or the 'advocacy model').

2. In the United States, government-inspired inquiry into the media as such was ruled out, but high-level semi-official inquiries were launched into the causes of certain social problems. These include the Surgeon General's report (1972) into the causes of crime and violence and the Kerner Commission Report (1968) into the causes of urban riots. The UK had a series of Royal Commissions on the Press between 1947 and 1977, as well as a series of commissions of inquiry into broadcasting developments. The most notable equivalent in North America was the Canadian Royal Commission on Newspapers (Canada, 1981).

3. In the UK, for instance, the post-war General Council of the Press and its successor (after 1992), the Press Complaints Committee, were established following critical public inquiries and strong pressure to take some voluntary action, especially on complaints about inaccurate reporting and violation of privacy. Such bodies often have a semi-public character because of the nature of the issues involved.

4. In an exceptional anomaly, the Dutch broadcasting system still maintains the principle that most television and radio programming is provided by voluntary associations of members who are also audiences and can choose to support a particular ideology, style, or profile of broadcasting. Members have rights to decide on policy and the amount of broadcasting time allocated is still notionally related to the number of members each organization has (Brants, 2003).

5. Examples of response levels are quoted by Mitchell and Blumler (1994: 219). The numbers are quite high, but not very significant in relation to the size of actual audiences. The same authors say that most feedback concerns the content or timing of programmes and there is some doubt as to its actual effect on content decisions.

6. Even so, on a day-to-day basis, note is usually taken of unusual increases in the level and kind of feedback from the mass audience. When a medium is criticized for some particular lapse, the number of messages of support or criticism are usually cited in the defence.

7. A prominent example of a critical media watchdog, not confined to television in its attention, is the (by origin US, but now international) organization Media Watch which has a long record of exposing media news subordination to governmental and business pressure. Several right-wing organizations have also devoted themselves to uncovering liberal or left-wing bias in the news (Foerstal, 1998).

8. Probably the longest running and best known media monitoring project is that started in 1973 by George Gerbner and colleagues to chart the incidence, character, and consequences of violence in US mainstream television. The project is now embedded within a larger organization the Cultural Environment Movement (CEM) that seeks to 'build a coalition of independent organizations committed to joint action in developing mechanisms of greater public participation in cultural decision making' (Gerbner *et al.*, 1999: 238).

9. Such methods are also used to pre-test television programmes, but used in this way by media organizations they scarcely count as accountability, even if there is a dialogue.

10. Although it has some ideological and mythical aspects and may be overlaid by commercial motivations, a distinct vision of the social purpose of the press survives. It is the basis for claims to wider respect and respectability in society and to some privileges that the press itself would be reluctant to relinquish (see Klaidman, 1994). It is also important to the claim of journalism to be considered a profession.

11. Lambeth (1998) names six characteristics of a profession: it is a full-time occupation; it is a 'calling'; it has a formal organization and entry standards; it must serve society and have a code of ethics; it requires specialized knowledge and training; it needs to be autonomous. In his view, by these criteria, journalism is not a profession.

12. The model for many was the former British General Council of the Press (now replaced by the Press Complaints Commission), although it was long preceded by similar bodies in several Scandinavian countries.

13. Bertrand (2000) reported that in 1999 there were thirty newspaper ombudsmen in the United States and three state councils.

14. As noted in Chapter 12, statutory right of reply is observed in some countries in cases of criticism or alleged inaccuracy on the part of the press.

15. A study of the *St Louis Journalism Review* by Bunton (2000) concluded that it 'does not provide meaningful professional self-regulation'. Walker (2000) described a situation of near total disinterest on the part of practising journalists in the journalism reviews published in the UK.

PART VI

Drawing Conclusions

14
Lessons from Accountability Theory

THE MEDIA HAVE RESPONSIBILITIES TO SOCIETY

Fundamental principles of media freedom in western society hold that the media, whether as firm, production organization, or individual communicator, can disclaim any general or particular obligation not laid down in law (mostly certain prohibitions on possible harm, plus public service regulations). At the same time, in the final resort, they can be (if not forced to comply) threatened and cajoled or supplemented and even supplanted by other media that will be more obliging to society. In practice the final resort is not usually reached, although there are plenty of examples around the world, usually not ones to be followed, where it has been.

The limits set to media rights to behave irresponsibly stem from the fact that the media are both an indispensable societal resource for government and other essential institutions and also a power in their own right, or regarded as such, which comes to much the same thing. The distinction between responsibility and accountability is important here, since the former is a chosen or attributed standard of behaviour while the latter, in this context, usually implies some external pressure to comply (Hindman, 1997: 150). In other words, responsibility of the media is voluntary, accountability is not. In fact, this is true according to only one version of the meaning of accountability as we have seen in Chapter 9.[1]

This strong view of the ultimate responsibilities of the media is, however, just as unhelpful as an entry point into a discussion of accountability as the reverse, libertarian, position that denounces the notion of responsibility as a cloak for government control and an attack on private property and personal liberty. Most publication activities of the media are not carried out to 'serve society', but in order to satisfy many communicative and expressive purposes and to meet the needs of their individual consumers, who view them in a similar light, with little or no thought to society. Besides this, the purposes of organized publication are also to provide employment and profit. The flow of communication is, in one sense, a manifestation of society in action, rather than an activity directed at society. The media are not outside, but part of society. This perspective captures more of the reality of what is going on than the responsibility to society formulation.

In practice, disputes turn not on the idea of having responsibilities as such but on the degree and kind of obligation that might be involved. Potentially deep conflicts of interest are involved, since the mass media have to serve several different masters at the same time: the public in various manifestations; political power; and the market. The proper role of the media is thus perceived according to different and divergent expectations. Saying this does not make it easier in practice to reconcile the various pressures that stem from conflicts of role and expectation. The media cannot, for instance, easily serve the political system and at the same time hold government accountable to the public for its failings. The media cannot be devoted wholly to profit as well as to meeting the needs of minorities or even of the democratic system.

Despite these and other tensions, and without repeating what has been written in earlier chapters about the nature of media responsibilities, we can summarize the essence in terms of several principles of rights and responsibilities that both satisfy essential requirements of society and also command wide acceptance by the mainstream media institution. These are as follows:

- As much freedom to communicate as possible should be available to as many as possible, including a public right to receive information. The media enjoy the benefit of this freedom and should help to extend it to others.
- The use of this freedom brings with it a responsibility to adhere to truth, in the widest sense, including informativeness, openness, integrity, honesty, and reliability.
- The media have solidaristic obligations as collective participants in social life. This includes expressing and supporting the needs and interests of component groups in the society as well as meeting the essential informational, social, and cultural needs of society.
- The media can legitimately be held to account for the use they make of their power of publication.

- Public communication by the media is subject to the ethical and normative requirements of society as appropriate to place, time, context, and content. The general public and groups within it have rights to be listened to on these matters.
- The human rights, especially as codified, of all those affected by communication should be respected. This has an international range of application.
- A range of private rights, ranging from privacy to property, should be recognized and respected in public communication.

MEDIA FREEDOM AND UNFREEDOM

The media in their organized forms do not possess precisely the same right to free expression that any citizen of a free society can claim (freedom of speech). In some respects they have less freedom, although they have more opportunity to exercise the right of public expression. They may also have a number of rights or privileges in order to enable them to fulfil their roles, especially in matters of access to sources of information and greater protection against claims of harm done by critical speech. Individuals have no right to speak through the media (unless they own them) and when they do have access, their freedom of expression is limited because it is usually subject to editorial or other control.

The relative unfreedom of the media (compared to that of the individual) has four main sources. One is the additional communicative power acquired by the capacity to amplify the message (greater reach and more attention) and the status they can acquire as credible sources. Where this power is exercised there are likely to be actual or supposed consequences (it may not matter which) for which they may be held to account. Secondly, even though there is freedom of expression for all, there is not an equal degree of freedom of publication for all types of published content. There is a bias in favour of politics, religion, science, and art and against some forms of entertainment, advertising, and socially or culturally disapproved forms. Thirdly, media freedom is restricted by the facts of ownership and the primacy given to non-communicative purposes (especially profit) by those who do own and control the media. Fourthly, the general public, supposedly the ultimate beneficiary of the freedom of the media (and in a way its ultimate guarantor), does not support it as strongly as theory proposes or as the media themselves usually claim. They seem to rank it below other values (especially security and order, decency, and even fairness).

The variations in degrees of freedom as between persons and the media and also between different kinds of media and different contents are governed by a certain logic, although no firm lines can be drawn. The smaller in scale the medium in question (limited audience, short reach, quiet voice—in effect, the more powerless), the more freedom it is likely to enjoy in practice (and by this rule an individual with no means of amplification is most free). The more media content has no aim or potential either to offend authority or to cause public harm or offence, the more freedom there is in practice. In a sense, the less a publication is likely to have effects or to make any difference, the more freedom is available. Other things being equal, there is an inverse correlation between degree of freedom and amount of influence, although efforts to protect the freedoms that matter (for instance of belief and political opinion) run counter to this correlation.

Freedom of expression means different things. One meaning is the libertarian one of there being no limits, no prohibitions or taboos, nor obligations either. Another meaning is being able to use the media actively and with impunity to question and oppose dominant groups and ideologies for a shared social purpose. A third meaning is having the real possibility of access to the means of communication in public. A fourth, more individual, meaning is the freedom to express a personal belief or a view of the truth openly and honestly without constraint or impediment. A fifth meaning is the commercial one of freedom to trade in media goods in the open market without restrictions on competition or other conditions. These different meanings have often been confused in the arguments for and against freedom for the media and have varying implications for accountability.

In the extreme case, there is no immunity or impunity from the consequences of the act of publication, and to that extent there can be no complete freedom from accountability.[2] Since classical times, brave or foolhardy individuals have spoken out against their own or public enemies or against an existing power or authority, whether or not legitimate. They have accepted the possibility of violent reprisal and often suffered the penalty (Nerone, 1994). There continue to be many heroic journalists as well as other writers in this number, although this extent of devotion to freedom is usually reckoned as beyond the call of media duty. Where conditions threatening to publication apply there is effectively no freedom to be enjoyed.

COMMUNICATION THEORY AND ACCOUNTABILITY FOR PUBLICATION

According to general theory, for communication to occur there has to be some mutual orientation of one person to another and usually some interaction between interlocutors as well. There is some dispute about whether or not completely solipsistic expression counts as communication. But there is little disagreement that for intentional influence to occur some attention and willingness on the part of a receiver is required. We might say the messenger can knock, but the door has to be opened from the inside. Despite the differences noted in mass communication, this general principle also applies. Mass media 'door-knocking' is not usually very selective, but there is a good deal of 'inviting in', where audiences search out what they want (most clearly perhaps in relation to the Internet and similar consultation media). In any case, it is important to take account of a significant core of co-orientation within the larger volume of allocutory flows (those that follow a one-way direct address pattern, Bordewijk and van Kaam, 1986). A simple conclusion to be drawn is that responsibility for the consequences of media publication is shared between senders and receivers although not necessarily equally.

Some versions of the meaning of accountability have roots in ideas about interpersonal communication, implying that ideal speech communication acts require interlocutors to be accountable to each in a more or less balanced way (Semin and Mansfield, 1983; Shotter, 1984; Giddens, 1984; Day and Klein, 1987). Successful or meaningful dialogue is only possible where participants can and do mutually relate to each other. This situation cannot really obtain to any great extent in mass media communication which is, in principle, open and unbounded. In short the 'mediated communication' typical of the mass media (Thompson, 1995) has intrinsically less chance of being 'accountable' in the way described and the communication experience is to that extent less ideal and/or fulfilling. Even so, mediated communication diverges from the ideal in widely varying degrees and at its best it can have significant elements of genuine mutual participation.

In line with communication theory, we can propose a concept of communicative responsibility as something that arises where a communication event or situation involves joint participation and is interactive. This would apply where communication involves response, feedback, or mutuality that are fairly normal ingredients, even if much diluted by practicality in mass communication. The central point of the concept is to underline the fact that responsibility is to some extent shared by both parties to communication—receivers as well as senders. In mass communication, the audience shares some of the responsibility for content and effects, in so far as its choices stimulate supply and its reactions determine effects.

ON BEING PUBLISHED

Publication has been defined (see Chapter 1) in a way that distinguishes it from non-public processes of personal communication. It will generally be regarded by the publicist (author) as qualitatively different (although the designation of an act as public is not entirely in the hands of the author). It certainly involves crossing a border that cannot be recrossed (publication cannot be undone). It usually implies a degree of completion and decisiveness that makes it different from private reflections, provisional ideas, drafts, etc. It produces a new kind of text, one that will circulate independently of the author and have a life of its own. It often involves making a statement or declaration, which can be expected to provoke a reaction. If it receives attention, it can also be expected to have some short- or long-term effects.

An essential aspect of being published is that it involves the identification of the author, or another origin. Without this, a communication is neither fully public (because an important aspect is concealed) nor is accountability possible, except by holding a gatekeeper (publisher) liable, which is only variably justifiable or possible. Even so, there is no possibility at all for answerability, only for liability. This has a particular relevance to the Internet, where much about sources is not known or revealed, where there may not be an accountable gatekeeper at all, and where in certain contexts (e.g. some newsrooms, chat groups, and other virtual communities) there is a common practice of concealing identity or even seeking to deceive. The technology facilitates this more than in any other medium.

Publication by way of the mass media is generally associated with professionalism, according to several criteria. These relate to the application of special knowledge and skills and also involve an economic element. Although there are some shared features in all kinds of media publication, there are also significant differences between types of authors, types of texts, and types of media (in socio-technical terms) that lead to quite large differences in the meaning of publication. Most of this book has been written as if acts of publication are more or less of the same kind as compared with private forms of expression. It is hard to discuss the mass media in general without making this assumption, although it is arguable that the difference between a small-scale media publication and a global publishing event is much greater than that between a privately circulated letter and one published in a newspaper.

On the other hand, there is something enduring about the fundamentals of media publication between the early print age and now. The entry into print and being put on sale in the sixteenth century does not seem so very different conceptually from what it does today. Then as now an author receives satisfaction, possible rewards, esteem, and possible criticism or worse, plus the elements mentioned above. Nevertheless, much has changed and been added. The massive, industrialized production and distribution processes of modern media firms have little in common, except conceptually, with the early days of printing.[3]

There is also much variation according to the amount and kind of power that can be attributed to publication. Large-scale institutionalized mass media, usually nation based, have a special kind of potential for influence stemming from the authority they have acquired, and their capacity to reach and capture the attention of a large audience with known and shared views and interests. In a diverse media system there should also be less-established media whose voices challenge this dominance and offer alternative definitions and values. Individuals, too, can speak out by various means.

The kinds of power are as important as their amount and in fact it is meaningless to speak of degree of power without qualification as to type. For instance, moral influence, the provocation of emotional or critical response, informing giving pleasure, and directing attention are examples of different effects that reflect aspects of the power of media, communication, or publication. Despite this, ideas about power have been overly dominated by notions of scale and ubiquity, with too little qualitative evaluation and attention to other conditions of influence.

The point of these remarks is to underline the possibility and necessity of differentiating more clearly within the range of forms of publication that are now available, especially as the Internet opens up what are in practice new possibilities for individual and non-mass media publication. This point is taken up below (see Chapter 15), but it must be obvious that different types of publication are likely to carry very different degrees and kinds of responsibility and accountability, just as they involve very different kinds of communicative power. The model (or stereotype) of publication as a massive intervention in public consciousness by an essentially purposeless media business organization believed to have large-scale effects on knowledge, behaviour, and attitudes is a very unreliable guide to what is going on.

There are alternative possibilities for differentiating between forms of publication depending on whether we choose technology, or scale, or regulatory regime, or content, or some institutional feature as providing the main criterion. A simple, hybrid, possibility that captures many of the distinctions that have had to be made at different points during this book would be a three- or fourfold classification as follows: firstly, the press, mainly newspapers and magazines in their primarily political and social role; secondly the mass media, mainly audiovisual, entertainment oriented, and mass cultural in character; thirdly, true individual authorship, mainly by way of literary, scientific, or scholarly writing, but also in other media; finally the Internet, an as yet undetermined and mixed form of publication. This typification breaks down on close examination, yet it retains a rule of thumb guide for initial orientation to many of the issues that arise in accountability.

THE SACRED VERSUS PROFANE DIMENSION

There is another dimension (fissure might be a better word) affecting media publication that deserves attention. This is the division between the sacred and the profane aspects of the media, which goes back to the earliest days of printing. It relates to the purposes of authors in the widest sense, the content, the motives of the audience, and the attitudes of social guardians from the days of the Greek censor to the present-day custodians of values and conscience, for instance those seeking to classify Internet content according to its suitability for children (Price, 1998). This dimension underlies the varying protection of free expression, distinguishes commercial from ideal motives, and may also vitiate journalistic aspirations to professionalism. In terms of the typology introduced above, the press is about equally sacred and profane, the mass media more profane than not, and books and authored works more sacred.

On the whole, service to the public or the society belongs to the sacerdotal range of motives and role definitions. This implicitly links the profane with the more libertarian view of the media and with the market perspective. Most public claims against media attribute a sacerdotal role that media themselves find it difficult to live up to, but sometimes convenient to accept when their profane, but more profitable, pursuits provoke unease. In a rough and ready way, through no obvious design, the mass media are more likely to be held accountable by law and regulation more for their profane than their sacred activities, on the dual ground that the former deserve less protection of their freedom and might cause harm. Paradoxically, market-based media are thus most protected in their freedoms where they have least economic interest and least inclination to be irresponsible.

ON RESPONSIBILITY

Our exploration of the responsibility concept detached it from a close identification with theories of social responsibility or with the straw man that libertarians and marketers like to knock around. It has several other distinct forms that are relevant and can be chosen independently of each other. For instance, a medium or journalist could be motivated to meet higher standards of provision by any of the following: a commitment to professional standards; a sense of citizenship and public duty; a concern for the effects of publication on others; or personal conscience and/or beliefs. Each of these involves responsibility of varying kinds, but ultimately with a similar outcome. The choice of commitment made by an individual or organization is an essential aspect of the freedom of the press. The same is true of the choice *not* to accept responsibility in any of the senses (even if that has ultimate limits).

What is more difficult to conceive is the freedom of action by competent (responsible) persons that occurs without reference to either type of choice (to be responsible in a certain way or reject some attributed duty), as if in complete ignorance. To disregard or deny a particular responsibility is a free action. To act without recognizing any dimension of responsibility at all is a reckless act which cannot be accounted for, but which is also without much meaning and has little place in the ideas of freedom embodied in theory.

Secondly, it is important to distinguish between responsibilities that are positive and those that are negative, in the sense of identifying goals to be pursued as against conduct or consequences that are to be avoided. From a theoretical point of view the type of responsibility involved in the two modalities (positive or negative) is different, with consequences for accountability. The means of securing compliance with prohibitions are different from those that promote the pursuit of a positive goal, certainly also in terms of relative effectiveness. It is question of carrots or sticks, both of which may have the same effect but perhaps not on the same recipient or under the same conditions. The distinction between positive and negative goals should not be confused with the distinction between a positive or negative attitude towards the idea of being responsible, or with the question of the internal versus external origination of responsibility. The media can be self-motivated to do good *and* to avoid harm. External compulsion may also be required to achieve either or both kinds of objective. However, 'doing good' (in media terms, higher quality, more diversity, less sensationalism, etc.) is less easy to achieve by external pressure than by self-motivation.

Professional responsibility figures in publication at several points and in relation to different tasks. The most frequent reference is to journalistic professionalism, especially as manifested in the observance of ethical norms and rules of conduct in relation to sources, to those reported on, and to possible media effects. There seems to be some agreement that journalism is not a profession in the sense of being a calling, involving an inviolable trust or altruistic end. Nor is it really autonomous. It even seems unlikely that it can ever be a profession in this sense since it cannot be closed to non-members. Moreover some of the tasks it is expected to fulfil, such as entertaining audiences, do not rank high in the canon of established professions. They may also run counter to more worthy goals (such as taking trouble and risks to publish the truth and to inform society). Despite these limitations affecting the occupation as a whole, there is no reason to withhold the attributes and consequences of professional status from all individuals and branches of media activity.[4]

The distinction between responsibility and accountability has been emphasized at various points, and is discussed further below. An important aspect of the difference is the more voluntary and self-directed character of the former. Responsibilities are typically accepted, not imposed by force, although they can be contracted and attributed. In contrast, accountability has a more external character, although it can also be voluntary. The more voluntary it is, the more it is compatible with freedom and even coterminous with responsibility. The two concepts are complementary, the one an extension of the other. We could also say that responsibility precedes publication while accountability follows. Although both are related in some way to the condition of freedom, they are conceptually independent of freedom as well as of each other.

CAUSAL RESPONSIBILITY

The question of effects arising from the mass media is central to the whole debate about accountability and thus needs some separate attention. A conclusion reached in this book is that it is doubtful if it makes much sense to apply a model that links particular publication acts in a causal way with particular effects—specific events. Nevertheless, this has been the most commonly chosen model for framing issues of causal responsibility. It has a clear logic and it makes it possible to proceed in a quasi-judicial way to assess the possible liability of the media. In fact it lies at the basis of notions of liability in English and Roman law. It reflects a way of thinking that classifies certain types or acts of publication as intrinsically in error, dangerous to faith or morals, or tending to harmful consequences, even if not necessarily evil in intention. It is the way in which forbidden printed works or lewd performances were traditionally dealt with. It also fits the typical research paradigm of media effect analysis. However, it is not very suitable in a secular age for handling diffuse categories of media content that are distributed routinely through the media, with uncertain or debatable meanings and tendencies and even more uncertain connections with audiences. It is equally unsuited for handling issues where potential harm is generalized and collective, more omission than commission.

The distinction made in communication theory between a transmission and a ritual model is helpful in these matters (see Carey, 1975; Calvert, 1997). A ritual model emphasizes the expressive aspect of communication. Communication provides, and is itself a part of, a social and cultural environment in which consciousness is formed by individuals and groups and which in turn permits or inhibits certain ways of thinking and behaviour, for instance in matters of alleged hate speech in relation to groups, based on race, gender, or other features. The linear model looks for specific emotional or behavioural effects on individuals, which may not be easy to find. The ritual model emphasizes the climate of attitudes and ideas that may be created by negative communication, one that has extensive, intangible, but unhappy consequences for recipients or third parties, in terms of feelings of self-esteem, identity, security, or well-being. This way of conceptualizing media effects does not eliminate responsibility, but shifts it more from the causal to the moral variety, reversing a historical tendency towards scientism and legalism (Dhavan and Davies, 1978). Nor does it necessarily remove a challenge to freedom of speech but shifts the mechanism of constraint, if there is any, from law to moral and public pressure.

For many issues of media accountability, leaving questions of property and individual injury aside, it is more appropriate to think in terms of larger and collective consequences. These cannot be tackled on the basis of punishing the individual errors and failings of authors or the isolated decisions of editors. Problems stem more often from the institutionalized patterns of content and conduct that are often deeply rooted in the market circumstances of mass media. This may imply that they cannot be cured (neither by regulation nor external corrective measures), but it does open the way to the correct identification and acknowledgement of failings, and the possible awakening of social responsibility.

ON ACCOUNTABILITY

Although an element of accountability is present in all communication, because it is ideally relational and interactive, we are mainly concerned here with consciously accepted or purposeful forms of accountability appropriate to mass mediated communication. There are a number of alternative purposes and the appropriate mechanism or means of accountability will differ accordingly. The main purposes of accountability (or justifications for requiring it) are as follows:

- To improve the quality of the product or service.
- To promote trust on the part of the receiver or audience.
- To ensure the performance of some wider public duty.
- To prevent some harm to an individual or society (by warning of liability).
- For reasons of control by authorities, or by the media industry.
- To protect the interests of the communicator (whether organizationally or professionally).

These different aims call for different means. Law and regulation, for instance, may be required to limit certain kinds of harm, but will not usually contribute to the creation of trust and loyalty in relations between the media and their audience. For this, either professional self-regulation or an established fiduciary framework may be required. The market is probably good at promoting certain kinds of product quality (especially if popularity is the criterion) but not good at providing an incentive to performing various public duties. A number of other such connections and disconnections can be instanced and are indicated in a provisional way in Table 14.1.

Table 14.1. *The relationship between accountability purpose and means*

	MEANS			
Purpose	Market	Law	Public opinion	Professional and self-regulation
Quality	x			x
Trust				x
Public duty			x	x
Prevent harm to society	x		x	
Prevent harm to individuals		x		x
Control	x	x	x	
Protect communicator				x

Almost any of the means of accountability referred to make some contribution to the objective of control, although accountability is clearly not the *same* as control. It does not necessarily diminish the freedom of a communicator and can enlarge it. At issue are two conceptually distinct phenomena. Control involves the use of power to achieve some desired outcome or behaviour on the part of another (or place limits on action). Accountability has primarily to do with securing from an actor an explanation or justification of actions. Unlike control, it takes place after the event. Clearly the anticipation of accountability does potentially inhibit action and can be designed as a method of control, but the anticipation of consequences is intrinsic to rational, let alone responsible, action.

The proposition advanced above that accountability is an intrinsic element in human communication also depends on accountability being reconcilable with freedom. There are several possible versions of what counts as ideal communication and it is impossible to find one that covers the entire range of private and public expression, purposeful or utilitarian as well as emotional or artistic.[5] Even so, there are some characteristics widely accepted as desirable. These include integrity, good faith, rationality, sincerity, honesty, and respect for others (including the audience). Accountability is supportive of these and similar communication virtues. Ideally, the 'dialogue of accountability' should exhibit the same attributes.

The good communicator of the ideal model of public communication wants to be accountable not in order to be good but to achieve purposes. Most mass media publication cannot be considered as ideal in intention or execution in this full sense, although none of the characteristics mentioned is impossible or unknown in mass communication, especially where individual authorship is involved. The principle of freedom of communication permits a person to choose their own ideal, or none at all. Even so, freedom of expression, when it is idealized, usually turns out to include a number of qualities that imply being accountable to others. These include an awareness of consequences, honesty of purpose, and an interest in challenge, response, and debate.

ACCOUNTABILITY TO WHOM?

Where the communicator is a mass medium there are several parties involved, several lines of accountability, and thus no single partner to an exchange. As we have seen accountability is required not just by the audience, but by quite differently placed agents. It becomes a process that accompanies and surrounds the communicative exchange rather than being an intrinsic part of it. In its internal form of management it is built into the process of publication. In this supervisory form (whether internal or external) it does have more of the character of control. But this depends on the perspective adopted. Where accountability mechanisms are put in place by some action on behalf of the public as audience they may be regarded as representing an audience that cannot easily act or speak for itself.

Different partners/participants to the publication process have different means of accountability at their disposal, involving different kinds of carrots or sticks (money, esteem, penalties, blame, etc.). To some extent communicators have a choice of what or whose accountability to face, depending on their choice of primary partner. This is one important aspect of the freedom of publication. Rather than being a choice of more or less (or no) accountability it is a choice of what kind of accountability. The option of not choosing to be accountable at all is not really available, since others will have views on this. Non-accountability cannot be achieved simply by claiming it (unlike the case of responsibility).

The multiplicity of lines of accountability makes it important to distinguish between the different media roles, or in some similar way. The key question is 'who is accountable to whom?'. The 'whom' includes owners, professional colleagues, different types of audience, social institutions, referents, pressure groups, advertisers, regulators, public opinion, and even includes potential voices seeking access to the channels (see Fig. 10.2). This is a disparate lot, unlikely to be served by the same procedures, governed by the same norms, or involved in the same kind of accountability. Nor are the various potential ties of accountability likely to be compatible with each other.

The different roles mentioned in Chapter 7 are those of author (any original source) for whom the media serve as publisher; an advocate for whom the media are a gatekeeper; an informant (the news conduit); an entertainer, for whom the media are a stage; and a publicist for whom the media are a billboard or podium. The number of different combinations of types of linkages is rather high, although the fundamental structure set out in Fig. 5.1 still holds of the media being linked reciprocally to state or government, the market, and the public, all three in different manifestations. The potential for conflicts and discontinuities in any claimed or acknowledged accountability relationship is clearly quite large.

WHAT FORM OF ACCOUNTABILITY?

These considerations are linked to the differences of type of accountability, each with a distinct meaning (see Table 9.2). We can nevertheless simplify the picture (there are different ways of doing so) by proposing there be two main variants of meaning. One of these is essentially the basic notion of giving an account, unilaterally (voluntarily and openly) or bilaterally (in response to a request or claim), which covers the activities of explaining, justifying, informing, confessing, and apologizing. The other is trilateral and involves some external or independent adjudication of claims according to different criteria. These are, especially, financial; qualitative; and liability for effect. This criterion tends to separate the form of procedure, the type of issue, and the types of role that are linked together in the accountability relationship, as just summarized.

The last step is to make the distinction introduced in Chapter 9 and applied as a criterion in evaluating different frames and mechanisms of accountability, that between answerability and liability. On the whole this corresponds to, and underlies, the twofold distinction made in the preceding paragraph, but the correspondence is not complete. It is quite possible, and according to the argument of this book, often desirable, to adopt the anwerability mode of procedure even where adjudication is involved. This can be widely applied even where causal responsibility is alleged, as in complaints by individuals who claim to have been harmed by the media or where the media are blamed for some wider social evil or failure of public responsibility. However, there are some issues and lines of accountability and some particular cases that are unlikely to be dealt with without some punitive elements. The most likely circumstances are those involving serious security matters, the rules of business (where money and contracts are involved), contempt of the justice system, and clear evidence of malice.

Where market relationships are involved we can recall the sacred–profane dimension mentioned earlier in this chapter. On the whole, the service that the media give to their owners and shareholders and to their various business clients, especially advertisers but also those who buy access for other reasons, belong to the profane end of the spectrum. Certain services to audiences might also be thought of in this way, when services and products of a certain quality are promised. On the whole these cannot be effectively dealt with by words alone, but require financial compensation governed by legal rules.

THE INTERNET AGAIN

In respect of the Internet, there are a number of reasons why this discussion does not easily apply. One is simply the diversity of communication situations supported by the Internet. Sometimes familiar mass media roles are replicated. But there are also new situations, especially where interactivity is involved and where exchanges, although accessible to all, are not meant for all. A certain (unknown) amount of Internet-based communication does not seek a large or undifferentiated audience, but is designed for like-minded circles of people linked by some value, topic of interest or activity, or just for solidarity. In such contexts, what people send may be semi-private.

Branscomb (1995) has underlined in particular the conflict between the principle of anonymity which the Internet protects and that of accountability (which she defines as an acceptance of responsibility for one's actions). As she points out anonymity makes it possible to escape responsibility: 'a right of absolute anonymity may foreclose accountability, whereas full accountability of users may mean the prohibition of anonymity'. Anonymity cannot be forbidden, but the more it is practised the less the Internet can expect legal protection for its freedoms and its solutions for its ethical problems. Somewhat similar arguments can be applied to what is probably the more important question of encryption.

THE RELATIONSHIP BETWEEN RESPONSIBILITY AND ACCOUNTABILITY

Pains have been taken from the start to distinguish these concepts, even though they overlap in meaning and are interchangeable in some uses. An essential aspect of the difference is that *being responsible* differs from *bearing responsibility*. The former is voluntary and accepted before the event, while the latter is akin to accountability, which follows the event and may not be voluntary. Even so, there are essential connections between the two concepts, starting with the point that all accountability presumes or alleges some prior responsibility on the part of the recipient of a claim. There is no legitimate accountability without the justifiable presumption of responsibility in one or other of its meanings. The term 'legitimacy' is used here quite loosely, since in the present context it often has a subjective basis. If one honestly feels offended or hurt or even dissatisfied by some content, it is clearly quite legitimate to complain, despite this being an objection to an act of free speech. Here legitimacy means appropriate and understandable. In a legal action for libel involving a heavy claim for damages or where a government regulator comes down hard on a mass medium, legitimacy has the meaning of lawfulness (it might not be justifiable or appropriate on other grounds). We are talking essentially of proceedings following the liability model.

On many communication issues there are no rules determining what is or is not legitimate, even in the examples cited. A case also depends on the position of the claim recipient (or media) apropos of responsibility. A newspaper that claims the right to transgress norms relating to privacy or confidentiality (even if ostensibly on public interest grounds) or an author or journalist standing on the right of individual conscience can still be faced with legitimate claims for harm. Two legitimacies can clash fundamentally, even if the law can settle a case one way or the other. Accountability procedures are likely to run more smoothly where such conflicts are not involved, as they are often not. In fact one of the keys to achieving effective accountability, especially in its more discursive and positive forms, is a measure of agreement about what the nature and limits of media responsibility actually are. Full agreement will not be reached because of different outlooks that cannot be reconciled, or because of the ultimate right of the media to be irresponsible.

IN CONCLUSION

A number of more general implications can be derived from these reflections on theory. One is that there is no unique path to better media, by strengthening formal processes of accountability. This is not only because of the number of alternative goals and criteria, but also because of the lack of agreement on what is desirable and the frequent complicity of the audience in the origins of the problem. Audiences' views (or just public opinion) on what is good have often been shown to diverge from their own behaviour. It is very common to find double standards sincerely adhered to. Secondly, it can hardly be claimed that there is a general deficit of accountability in the contemporary media scene, even if there may be a lack of effective means of gaining redress from many of the complaints against the media. The reasons for this have to be sought more widely, for instance in the demands that are placed on the media by their audiences and others. Not least amongst the causes is the development of a so-called 'blame society' in which not only causes but responsible agents have to be found and made to pay for whatever goes wrong in institutional conduct. Solutions have to be sought beyond instituting more rigorous regimes of regulation and procedures of assessment.

NOTES

1. Hindman (1997) bases her view of limited freedom on the actions and statements of the US Supreme Court over a period of time in relation to the First Amendment. She writes: 'each time they determined whether to require the media to be responsible, they ran directly into a conflict over how both to protect media freedom . . . and acknowledged the media as only one of many institutions operating in society, institutions that cannot have complete freedom if society is to function. . . . The media necessarily must have limits on their behavior . . . no institution . . . can do whatever it wants' (149).
2. A Latin tag, designed to remind us that we will be ultimately called to account for our life's doings and failures, reads *ratio cuique reddenda* (everyone must render account).
3. It is worth noting that the very volume of contemporary publication compared to earlier times has the effect of reducing relative impact. Under conditions of

scarcity (as under strict censorship or information deprivation) all new texts and information receive enhanced attention.

4. Max Weber, writing in 1918, acknowledged the professionalism of journalists as follows: 'Not everybody realizes that a really good journalistic accomplishment requires at least as much "genius" as any scholarly accomplishment, especially because of the necessity of producing at once and "on order", and because of the necessity of being effective, to be sure, under quite different conditions of publication. It is almost never acknowledged that the sense of responsibility of every honourable journalist is, on the average, not a bit lower than that of a scholar' (Weber, 1948: 96.)

5. J. H. Habermas's *The Theory of Communicative Action* (1984) has often been cited as providing a concept of an 'ideal speech situation', based on principles of rationality. In a summary comment, Slevin (2000: 188) refers to Habermas's thesis 'that when one person communicates something to another, that person makes a series of claims'. These include claims of intelligibility, truth, sincerity, and justification to communicate. Important features of an ideal speech situation according to Habermas are mutual understanding, lack of constraint, and equality of participation in the dialogue.

15
Policy Implications

The issue of accountability for publication can be posed in a number of ways. This much at least should be clear from the amount of attention already paid in this book to the various meanings and uses of the term. Although preference has been given to a particular meaning—one that underlines the self-generated responsibility (also of various kinds) that goes with the authorship of all public communication—there are uses and contexts, where external demands for accountability arise, whatever an author or publisher chooses to think. The choice that has been made, to begin the search for meaning with the situation of an archetypal author, provides insight into the essential character of publication and even into the role of a media organization, when it acts in a quasi-authorial role or as a key gatekeeper for publication.

In practice, however, we cannot equate the acts a media organization with those of an author. The distinction has become confused by the fact that modern authors (in the widest sense) need the media to achieve their aim of public communication. Rights to free expression also apply more or less equally to individuals and to publication organizations. Nevertheless, while media organizations have most capacity to publish, they are not, in reality, as free to do so (because of many obligations and pressures) as individuals. They also, de facto, have a different range of responsibilities to others, however acquired. The short conclusion of these remarks is that a shift from personal to media accountability inevitably takes us away from the realm of communication theory and into a nexus of interaction where political and economic forces play an enhanced role, and where other dimensions and meanings of accountability are involved.

There is a case to be made for the view that contemporary mass media have so little in common with the ideal case of authored publication that an entirely different analysis of accountability is required. At the heart of the argument is the fact that mass media industries are not even centrally either in the business of publication or of communication, except possibly in the bastardized forms of publicity of all kinds, marketing, advertising, and propaganda. Apart from this they are leisure industries, selling cheap time-filling entertainment and connecting together a set of non-worktime activities such as shopping, travel, vacations, sport, clubbing, cooking, gardening, and much more. It is now a long time since Phillip Elliot (1972) came to the rather depressing conclusion (for would-be communicators) that mass communication is not really communication at all, merely spectatorship.

This position suggests two important conclusions for present purposes. One is that the ideal of free communication by the mass media is close to being mythical. Another is that if this is what mass media are really about, then there is a very weak claim to the freedom of expression claimed by our ancestors and that it now really comes down to market freedom. There is also no reason why the activities of media industries should not be extensively regulated on grounds of health, safety, ethics, culture, and other public policy criteria. In which case the effort made here to reconcile freedom and accountability is largely superfluous. However, the situation is not necessarily one of either/or and since significant public expression in our time is obliged to take place by way of the mass media, whatever else they are doing most of the time, we cannot simply abandon the media to their fate, or ourselves to our fate at the hands of the media.

In practice there are two main directions in which we may be taken by the considerations outlined, both of which have wide-ranging implications for the central issue of how the media might account for themselves or be held to account for their acts of publication. One of these takes us directly into the territory of control and regulation, despite the effort made here to distinguish between control and accountability. Mass media are subject to intense and varied efforts at control at the hands of powerful outside agencies with interests in publicity, ranging from governments to influential lobbies. Coupled with this are the pressures from public opinion, not very concerned with the niceties of free expression, that also typically views the media as a potential danger to be controlled. It is not surprising that the language of responsibility and accountability is viewed by the media with some suspicion. For those media that have not yet given up on the aspiration to question, innovate, and report the truth, calls for more accountability are little more than softer forms of control, but control none the less.

Secondly, there is the option of treating the media as the means rather than the object of accountability in society. There is no doubt that the mass media in an open society can operate as an important instrument for holding powerful institutions, both public and private, to account to the people. This role is probably the most important of the tasks for society that the press has actually volunteered to carry out and the principal reason for constitutional guarantees of freedom. The democratic system and justice system are supposed to be adequate to the same end, but few doubt that in fact the media do play an indispensable part in informing and mobilizing public opinion (or certainly ought to be doing so).

Even the institutions (of politics and law) that are supposed to protect society from its endemic tendencies to corruption, inefficiency, and collective deviance cannot now operate without the help of the mass media. From this perspective media accountability has much wider consequences and ramifications. It is positioned diametrically opposite to the equation of accountability with control. In this context, the publication virtues described at the outset (see Chapter 4), as well as the various professional norms that have been developed for journalism, have a very practical character. Telling the truth, courage, reliability, etc., are the ingredients that make the very large media task of extracting some accountability from our particular lords of the universe at all possible, where it is so. Moreover, there is extra reason for wondering how far any responsible public or private power can be entrusted to perform a self-checking role.

REDEFINING THE CRISIS

With these considerations in mind, we still need to turn to the question of what can be done to facilitate the attainment of desirable forms of media responsiveness to their society. Formal accountability of the media directly to society by law or regulation is quite marginal in democracies and is likely to remain so, limited to establishing and policing a frontier of acceptability, according to agreed basic principles and dealing with technical and economic issues. There is no need for a programmatic solution to any supposed new crisis of accountability. Nevertheless there are new and recurring accountability problems and there are numerous actions or omissions on the part of government that have a bearing on the conduct of the media. As we have seen, the relation between government and the media is only one part of a much wider spectrum of media accounting to other parties (audiences, clients, pressure groups, etc.). Given the restricted role of government in matters to do with publication, it is the rest of the spectrum that matters most.

The core issue concerns the promotion of responsibility on the part of the media in the sense of being willing to meet relevant public needs and avoid harm and a willingness to answer openly for actions and omissions. There is still an extensive branch of public policy that bears directly or indirectly on achieving this, primarily through the encouragement of conditions (of the media system and environment) that are conducive to this goal. The media also promote their own notions of public responsibility, which do not necessarily correspond to those of public policy. Nevertheless, many of the potential benefits from publication that are postulated by press theory have been voluntarily chosen by the media and this will continue to be the case. There is no need to contemplate a regime of enforcement of public duty even if this stood any chance of success.

Despite an outpouring of alarm and criticism from diverse quarters about the failings of contemporary mass media, on social, cultural, and political grounds (see Chapter 1),[1] the evidence for any general and new state of true *crisis* is not convincing. There may not be a *new* crisis, but there are endemic problems and large changes under way in the media and society, all of which raise issues of accountability in the three main senses just outlined: the matter of personal responsibility; the urge to control media more stringently; and the doubts surfacing about the adequacy of the media in holding powerful forces in society to account or in helping the political system to achieve that. The changes are related to four main media trends that have become familiar, especially globalization; commercialization; increased scale and abundance of media; and increasing concentration or conglomeration. The problems for accountability arising from these trends, assessed according to the principles advanced in this book, can be expressed in terms of the following propositions.

- An ever more narrowly defined core of the media industry is increasing its power to control the gates of publication. Their essentially commercial assessment of gains and risks governs publication. No accountability can be claimed from owners and top decision-makers, since typically no rules are broken. There is absence of responsibility rather than irresponsibility.
- Commercial and media organizational logic combine to promote patterns of omission and misrepresentation that work to the

disadvantage of access for oppositional, minority, or deviant expression and have other disinformational effects.

- Global concentration has increased the impersonality of media publication and the remoteness of the media and their sources from actual societies and communities as well as individual consumers, making it less likely or possible that they can adequately serve them, except as aggregates of consumers. Nor are global media expected to serve any wider public good either in the national society or internationally.

- Media culture is increasingly dominated by the adulation of success in quantitative and market terms, threatening the integrity of minority media cultural forms. The spectre of the 'tyranny of the majority' is again raised.

- More strongly, we might say that increasingly conscienceless media have become willing to victimize individuals for profit, in respect of their privacy, reputation, or innocence. The price of self-regulation or even self-restraint on grounds of ethics and human decency is higher than many media are prepared to pay.

- Larger media organizations are more and more integrated in the structure of business and political power and less able to serve as neutral or independent agencies capable of fulfilling the social accountability task, except in superficial ways when it becomes profitable to do so.

- Private accountability of the media to shareholders replaces public accountability, whether to audiences, government, or society at large. For the most part only individual and demonstrable harm provide for the most part a basis for actionable claims against the media. Larger issues of long-term and moral responsibility cannot be handled.

- The diminishing journalistic core of major media inhibits the development of the press as a self-regulating and professional institution, voluntarily accountable for traditional democratic benefits.

- Internal media freedom within large media organizations becomes harder to achieve and the scope for personal conscience or even professional autonomy that much less.

- Ubiquitous and unchallenged free market theory trumps any civic or government inspired attempts to preserve a public space and a non-profit presence.

- The dominant conditions of the media market environment in which the new media, especially the Internet, are being introduced work against their great potential in terms of access, alternative voices, and participatory communication.
- The Internet becomes an object of regulation but with little capacity for self-regulation or autonomous responsibility.
- Self-regulation of the Internet has limited scope in circumstances where authorship is obscure and media gatekeepers are complex multiple carriers rather than publishers in the traditional sense with a known face and a public presence. The concept of responsible publication is less and less applicable to the world of modern media, which constitutes an amorphous, shifting, kaleidoscopic environment of large-scale production and transmission.

This bill of grievances is discouragingly long and offers little hope that the media will become more responsible or accountable either by their own volition or through outside pressure. To a large extent, the signalled failings and deficits stem from enduring circumstances that are largely and literally beyond control, although not thereby out of control.

LIGHT AS WELL AS DARKNESS

There are, even so, some mitigating features of the general situation. Threats to freedom as a result of state intervention have probably diminished, partly because control has been increasingly relinquished to market forces, and partly because the capacity of the media to exert political power has increased relative to the state, even if the main beneficiaries are large media firms. It is more difficult for nation states to limit the media that operate on a global scale. There have certainly been opportunities for new entrants into the media market as the system has expanded, even if barriers to entry as a mass medium remain much as before. The public as audience probably has more choice and more ways of enjoying different media cultural lifestyles.

It cannot be said that the old order of governance has actually passed away, despite liberalization and supposed convergence. Deregulation has meant a withdrawal from direct intervention and greater coherence of rules but it has not meant less regulation, if only because the industrial, financial, and technological foundations of media operation cannot be left to themselves or to chance. Although names are still named, there is less reason for concern about individual media tycoons or magnates using their power arbitrarily for personal ends or ideological crusades. At the fringes of centres of concentrated media power there are many new opportunities for small-scale, local, and quite free publication that can develop unpredictably into significant social or cultural influences, and not all will be incorporated into the dominant media culture.

It can be accounted a benefit as well as a frustration of accountability that the media system is less fixed and monolithic but continually adapting, shifting, and expanding in new directions in ways that defy full and effective control on the part of political and economic élites. This is not the loss of control feared by conservative traditionalists, but it does reflect the limited governability of the media (for various reasons) that guarantees some degree of political freedom, although not of any particular public benefit. It also suggests that the media are also ultimately non-accountable except to technological and market forces that have no given direction or end point.

POLICY PARADIGMS LOST AND REGAINED

If the basic conditions of media operation are not particularly reassuring, the current state and direction of public policy for the media in many countries is not very promising either. Quite a lot has changed and continues to change since the foundations for media governance, as described in Chapter 5, were laid down. Although the claims on the media to fulfil social responsibilities have enduring theoretical foundations and are supported by the dynamics of civil society, some elements are obsolescent. We cannot confidently appeal to ideas that were largely consensual fifty or even twenty-five years ago. This also applies in some degree to the freedom claim. In the post Second World War decades, there developed something like a philosophy of communication welfare in a number of countries that cast broadcasting as a socially responsible medium with cultural and educational goals and governments as the referee more generally over the media system to ensure a minimum degree of fairness, diversity, and public service (a trustee or fiduciary model).

However, it is widely accepted that this old order has passed or is passing, not overthrown in the name of liberty but deprived of its rationale and most of its means of influence by changes of technology and the new imperative of expanding and innovating in communication technology, with commercial entrepreneurship as the engine of change (van Cuilenburg and McQuail, 2003). The dominant aspiration now is to kick-start a communication technology revolution and an information society. At the very least it is expected to provide the foundation for new forms of industry and commerce and an abundance of new services to consumers. At the same time, there is a belief (despite lack of evidence) that the shortages and barriers that gave power and privilege to a few and kept the majority informationally and culturally impoverished are gradually being eliminated.

The ideas of communication welfare and reform are not obsolete, nor the values on which they are based, but the original means for achieving them (especially by direct public provision, subsidy, or content regulation) are no longer viable. There is no longer a wide presumption that it is the task of some authority to ensure that the public will be elevated, educated, and informed or that the democratic process is well served. A society of ever abundant information and opportunities for intercommunication, it is argued, should not need subsidies or controls to provide what is necessary, leaving aside the problem of motivating people to use the opportunities enlarged by public policy. It is also argued that the very scale of the explosion of media and information flow already unleashed by new technologies, deregulatory polices, and the activities of new media entrepreneurs has made the idea of containing, correcting, or directing this flood by acts of policy largely unrealistic.

Public broadcasting in quite a few countries still represents the best chance for ensuring that democratically defined cultural and informational needs can be met and principles of equality honoured in reality. This sector of the media has been portrayed by its (usually self-interested) opponents as increasingly anomalous, if not obsolescent, as judged by the dominant logics of commercial operation and liberal political creeds. It is also subject to strong pressure to adapt by imitation to its competitive environment. Nevertheless, it has been around for three-quarters of a century and where well established it is a long time in dying (see Siune and Hulten, 1998). The most recent assessments are that it has even stopped expiring. In fact it has a good many friends as well as enemies. Whatever the reasons for this, it does offer a mass media service that is transparently accountable to the public and has the unusual benefit of making the mass media accountable for certain things to governments.

In a landscape of commercially free media it offers an alternative point of reference to the otherwise all-powerful market, without itself threatening freedom. It creates a space in which non-commercial relations can be established between sources, communicators, and audiences and it enlarges the scope for access to channels that are not determined by financial criteria. It also provides the possibility for editorial decision-making independent of the interests of any proprietor or body of shareholders, but maintaining professional standards. In a world dominated by remote, sometimes foreign, media owners it is an increasingly valuable national or regional asset that would be impossible to recreate if allowed to disappear, just as it is impossible to introduce where it is not already established.

These remarks relate to one side of the central question of accountability—the scope for ensuring that the media do fulfil reasonable expectations of public service, a scope that has clearly diminished. The other aspect of the question concerns the prevention of harm. In this, there has been less change as far as the legitimate goals of public action are concerned. While thresholds of what is acceptable have shifted (for instance in relation to sexual matters), a widespread expectation remains that law and regulation should protect the public from transgressions of the new normative frontier. Some new standards have also been introduced, along with social and cultural change. There is more concern with human rights and the rights of minorities, not to mention matters of health, environment, and animal rights, on which there are strong feelings about what is represented on the mass media. There is a move to match globalization of the media with some institutional means of protecting human rights (see Raboy, 2000). There are also potentially new kinds of perceived harm, such as those from video game addiction, violent pop music, and new means by which old harm can be done (corruption through the World Wide Web).

Traditional motives for the public control of publication (in order to protect morality and order) are probably stronger now than the impulses to ensure that the media positively do some good. Most contemporary approaches to accountability still emanate from the same dominant political culture and mindset, limited by conceptions of purpose and procedure. They still follow a way of thinking that involves identifying an agent of potentially harmful publication who can be held to account for certain effects or consequences and if necessary punished after due testing of cases according to procedures of a quasi-scientific or judicial kind. Little account is taken of the increased scale and complexity of mass media publication, nor of newer issues of ethical or moral harm and offence that cannot be individualized nor measured in a way that meets conventional standards of proof. The same applies to questions with an international reference, where other countries may be harmed or affected by the media in another country. There have been changes in general policy approaches, for instance a shift from external to self-regulation and co-regulation, and there is relatively less effort to control content directly. There is also greater reliance on economic incentives and market forces to gain compliance with the public interest as defined by government and ruling élites.

SCOPE FOR ALTERNATIVE FORMS OF ACCOUNTABILITY

If the enduring core of public accountability efforts has remained focused on the idea of causal responsibility (for harm, rather than good), the question arises as to how other types of responsibility and accountability can be encouraged. The most relevant and viable alternatives involve either enhanced professionalism and self-regulation or more scope for guidance by conscience and the acceptance of moral responsibility, desirable things that in their nature are not to be imposed and not to be regulated for. They belong to the fuller expression of the role of communicator. They also encompass positive goals rather then just avoiding harm. They may not be legislated for, but they can be given encouragement by policy, for instance by support for education and training, research, the flow of information, the growth of professionalism, and efforts to enlarge internal freedom.

Moreover, policy can be indirectly supportive of the development of the alternative, more desirable forms of accountability procedures, by way of structural interventions designed to foster and protect diversity and access. The conditions in which accountability is likely to develop naturally are ones in which there is a diversity of independent media outlets, considerable opportunities for access to media gates and platforms, a certain amount of internal media freedom as well as freedom at the point of publication for would-be communicators, and an absence of intense commercial pressure. As remarked earlier, modern conditions of concentrated global media conglomerates are not conducive to personal responsibility for communication or adequate accountability beyond compliance with the letter of whatever law applies. These conditions cannot be changed at will, but some limits can be set to concentration in a given sector (they already exist in many countries) and there are ways of encouraging new entrants and competition (Trappel and Meier, 1998).

To judge from experience, whatever is done is likely to be quite modest in its effectiveness, more suited to preserving some elements of the status quo than bringing fundamental change. Apart for public broadcasting, it is unlikely that the various interventions in line with communication welfare policy or other actions on behalf of social responsibility have made much difference for good (as hoped) or for ill (as charged by libertarian critics). They mainly work at the boundaries of the system, setting, as it were, the rules of the game. They are much less influential than either the working of the market or the more direct pressure from public opinion and other interested parties not linked to governments. Although this is a fairly pessimistic assessment of what can really be done by society directly through policy, law, and regulation, it does mean that some values can be protected and a potential scope for action reserved for circumstances where public opinion gives its support. Basic publication values that have their own well-springs in the spontaneous needs and aspirations of communicators and audiences are also an enduring resource.

Truth is still an indispensable quality in all the significant information processes of society, whether it is defined in terms of trust in sources, reliability, and accuracy of information or as integrity and honesty of purpose in the realm of ideas, art, and culture. Communication processes are not driven mainly or exclusively by the media, with their evident limitations, but by politics, business, science, education, and innumerable personal needs. In turn, truth is as much dependent on the confidence (trust) of those who receive and use communication as it is on the freedom (and independence) of those who produce and transmit information (authors). The indispensable link between the claim to truth and integrity and its acknowledgement in the form of trust is a willingness, even a strong wish, to account for and substantiate truth claims. It is only in the much attenuated and mediated communication linkages that are typical of the mass media that there is any doubt about this.

ANOTHER LOOK AT MEDIA GOVERNANCE

The media landscape, as described in Chapter 5, is still largely divided up for purposes of regulation into three main domains: print; broadcasting; and common carriers, that now include the Internet, despite its differences from traditional point to point media. This division was largely circumstantial in origin, varying according to the distribution technology. There is still a certain administrative logic to the arrangements despite media convergence and new anomalies (such as cable) and the fact that freedom of publication is not confined to print media. Governments still have a say in how public communication is conducted and how the technology for communication is operated (and sometimes even owned). Governments also set and police certain boundaries of what is acceptable in publication. The nature of these limits and the reasons for regulation are transparent enough,[2] and the division of the media spectrum according to technology also assists procedures that identify accountable entities and keep track of the specific locations and moments where publication occurs.

The regulatory system of accountability is still largely guided by ideas associated with the old order: the larger in scale and wider in reach the media, the more they are oriented to entertainment, and the more constraint is acceptable as well as deemed necessary. Television broadcasting is still most under control everywhere, while the mainstream newspaper press is safely in the hands of long established institutions with close informal links to political and economic power. The Internet is taking a growing share of the spectrum of media use, without yet being incorporated into the system. This is not because it is beyond the scope of regulation, but it is not yet worth the trouble of attempting general and effective control.

At the margins of the mainstream media system there are many outlets for publication that, in practice, escape regulatory attention.[3] They are usually small in terms of direct reach and amplitude. They are not very commercial and neither interest nor threaten the market (except where copyright is breached). They are often ephemeral and non-professional. Such media are not allocated public responsibilities (even if their value to the public sphere is acknowledged) and they are not usually called to account by any of the usual mechanisms, except by their own small audiences. The status as publication of this rich assortment of media forms is often uncertain, sometimes even to the originators, with widely varying motives for venturing into the public domain. Such small-scale, but extensive, publication is already governed in principle by forms of accountability that conform to the answerability mode, with communicative motives based on opinion, belief, or art that invite a response from someone out there. None of this is especially new as a phenomenon,[4] although it has grown vastly in scale.

It is clear from the variable imposition of accountability in the form of regulation that control is selectively directed. It is mainly applied where the media concerned are presumed to exercise some power or where they impinge on the interests of power holders. It is the potential *effect*, not any principle, that leads to liability claims. It is a reminder of how much the liability form of accountability has always been driven by considerations of power. No proposal for change has a chance unless it grapples with this issue. Absence of strict accountability does not matter to authorities if the publications concerned are thought to be of no consequence because the reach of the message is too restricted.[5]

As noted in the previous chapter, the nature of publication has been changing, along with it the notion of an author and publisher. In so far as this goes, much debate about freedom and accountability, including much of this book, is based on a model that is becoming obsolete. Essentially this model represents publication as following a sequential path marked by a few gates or decision points, the most decisive of which turns a private act or idea into a public one, with ramifying consequences. The essence of freedom of publication in this model is concentrated at the threshold between private and public and this was the threshold policed by early forms of censorship and control. There are many differences between the current and late medieval circumstances of publication, but a key one is the replacement of publication by *amplification* as the process that matters most from the point of view of both power and public opinion.

Amplification is not only a matter of reach and volume and the focusing of wide attention on a message. It also involves a dimension of impact, invasiveness, and presumed influence on those reached. It could be said that absolute freedom to publish is not as such the issue any more, rather it is to publish and disseminate beyond an acceptable limit in terms of potential effect. Systems of control are thus more usefully directed at the disseminator rather than the author, although not as in the early days of punishing and licensing printers, but by confining suspect messages to minority channels. For the most part, the market achieves this result, although public control of broadcasting has often worked effectively to the same end.

These remarks have two main implications for accountability. First of all, they underline the view that the industrialized processing and distribution of media content is hardly the same as free expression, with an inalienable right to protection (as noted above). Those who are in the business of mass distribution may be more legitimately limited and regulated and thus called to account in strict terms (as to some extent they still are). Secondly, if so much space in large-scale and amplified media channels is occupied by a narrow range of content, the potential for impact is indeed greater. There are probable consequences that flow from systematic patterns of selection and omission, bias and distortion (intended or not). There is a strong case for treating this in a different light from the individual acts of publication introduced earlier as a basic model. If the contemporary mass communication outlined is indeed so different, then different applications of concepts of freedom, responsibility, and accountability are called for. Different rules should apply, despite the difficulty of any formulation. A central problem is that there is typically no responsible agent to be identified and thus no one to call to account.

Current regulatory arrangements have for long been criticized for their failure to adapt to the laws of convergence that derive from the increasing overlap in technologies, forms, and content between the different media. With the end of spectrum scarcity, there is no longer an obvious reason, for instance, for denying to broadcasting the freedoms that are enjoyed by newspaper or Internet-based journalism (leaving aside the argument just advanced). On the other hand, for reasons partly explained above, complete freedom of publication will never in practice be available to powerful media.

Instead of abandoning the fundamentals of the technology-based regulatory regime, the most likely development and one already occurring is for the development of horizontal forms of regulation or other means of accountability that can apply different norms of good practice or codes of ethics to different types of communication (genres, forms, functions) on different media delivery systems. The principle for discrimination between content types already exists in different interpretations of the right to free publication for different types of content (see Chapter 8). There are already cross-sector convergences in accountability in a variety of forms that apply to advertising; political communication; some entertainment; news and information; film and video; opinion and advocacy. Certain legal restrictions relating to publication (e.g. libel and copyright) apply across all forms of media publicity, even if not all legal freedoms are enjoyed equally. As Goldberg *et al.* (1998: 300) argue, there may be 'justification for regulating *part* of the media while leaving other parts free in order to achieve true pluralism'. There is no reason why this process of differentiation should not be extended to apply to some positive goals of communication and the development of softer forms of accountability.

CONTROL OF THE INTERNET

The Internet, even in its present underdeveloped form, has a claim to be considered a new mass medium on the basis of its open and wide availability, even if its diffusion is limited by material circumstances (Morris and Ogan, 1996). It also offers a range of functions similar to other mass media, providing services of news, entertainment, advertising, and information to all. It is also different from previous media in certain respects. According to Castells (2001: 200) it is a 'communication medium with its own logic and its own language'. In his view 'The kind of communication that thrives on the Internet is that related to free expression in all its forms. . . . It is open source, free posting, decentralized broadcasting, serendipitous interaction, purpose-oriented communication, and share creation that find their expression on the Internet'.

Important to the character of the medium is that it is not in the traditional allocutive media mode, but suited primarily to consultation and interaction (Bordewijk and van Kaam, 1986). Amongst other consequences, this shifts the balance of responsibility from senders to individual users, with considerable implications for accountability principle and practice. If the Internet is used as a medium of public address, it is remarkable in having immediately a potential audience of hundreds of millions around the world. The reality of course is different.

We can add that a good deal of its use is personal or private in intention or to an uncertain degree a matter of publication. It also differs from other mass media in being much more international in organization and structure and being scarcely subject to the main forms of national governance and accountability outlined in this book. There are few direct or medium specific laws or regulations for the Internet, even if it is not exempt from general laws affecting publication where jurisdiction can be established. It is hardly possible to perceive any clear market structure or any control from audiences or advertisers, because the system is so diverse, undeveloped, and fragmented. Public opinion and other kinds of pressure are not well organized to focus on the Internet as an institution, only as a technology and a rather loosely identified set of services.

Even so, on certain issues, such as child pornography and violence, there is some effective public pressure, although no clear object on which it can be applied. As a result, a number of countries, including the United States, Germany, Canada, and Australia, have introduced laws on specific aspects of Internet content, such as pornography, crime, or racism. The EU has also agreed a Convention on these aspects of Internet use. Often these efforts lead to pressures on service providers and other gatekeepers to self-censor and deny access. The effect of threats of defamation suits is additional to this. Self-regulation, except in this undesirable form, is difficult to achieve and professionalism is only marginally developed on the Net (see Drucker and Gumpert, 1999).

The story of the origin of the Internet has often been told (see Naughton, 1999; Castells, 2001; Abbate, 1999) and all agree that it began in almost total freedom as to purpose and with a culture of freedom that is still strongly rooted and supportive of its loose form of international ownership and control. It belonged initially to its users and it was not required to be accountable to any outside regulator or authority even if originally funded by the US Defense Department. Since the emergence of the World Wide Web in 1990, the Internet has been the object of a gold rush in pursuit of immense potential profits and its development and uses have been extensively commercialized, without eliminating many of its libertarian features, including anti-social and criminal applications. At this point in the story it is now widely agreed that further development will require more clear regulation and the subjection of activities to various forms of accountability.

It is no longer possible to maintain, as once supposed, that the Internet of its nature is simply not regulable. As Lessig (1999) notes: 'The architecture of cyberspace makes regulating behaviour difficult, because those whose behavior you're trying to control could be located in any place... on the Net.' He goes on to argue, however, that it is no longer impossible to regulate the Net, now that the commercial imperative has arrived to be able to identify and authenticate users of the Net and also to create secure spaces and channels for purposes of commercial transactions. The future immense prizes of e-commerce are dependent on a degree of control and predictability that are foreign to the original culture of the Internet as a loose network of networks connecting innumerable unidentified points.

The key to control, according to Lessig, lies not in regulating individual behaviour on the Net, but in regulating the architecture of the Net. He distinguishes between four 'modalities of constraint' that make up a general system of social regulation. Three of these are familiar as more or less equivalent to the frames of accountability described earlier. They are 'market', 'law', and the social 'norms' (i.e. pressure of public opinion). The additional factor is 'architecture', the physical arrangements of (in this case) a medium. Traditional media have a form of 'architecture' that render them more or less easy to control. Broadcasting and cable are the simplest to control since they depend on a limited transmission facility. The architecture of the Internet was originally designed to maximize its ability to operate in adverse circumstances and to escape control.

Nevertheless, it too has potential weaknesses. In particular, Lessig foresees the development of cheap and effective forms of hardware and software (what he calls 'code') that will enable authorities to identify and certify all users (by their apparatus). The motives will be primarily commercial, since the selling of services and financial transactions require security. Surveillance can also take cognizance of all users for purposes of police or security services. Encryption can be controlled and ultimate privacy can be abolished. Gradually the means will develop for filtering content according to various criteria as a means of regulation. Chalaby (2000: 27) argues that the means to curb freedom of speech have not disappeared, but have become more flexible and less visible: 'It is not flames that now suppress information, but invisible and anonymous digital codes'.

Once the means exist, the servers that provide facilities can be required or pressured into restrictions. Agreements can be made amongst different jurisdictions to exchange restrictions on various locally unwanted uses of the Net. According to Castells (2001: 178), the overall tendency is towards 'a curtailment of privacy of communication on the Internet—to shift the Internet from being a space of freedom to becoming a glass house'. He concurs with Lessig in saying that 'the new Internet architecture, the new code, becomes the fundamental tool of control, making it possible to exercise regulation and policing by traditional forms of state power' (179).

None of this is science fiction. It has become clear that the peculiar architecture of the Net that (largely unintentionally) protected it from law and regulation is gradually being adapted to enable quite extensive invasion of the privacy of communication. The economic motives are strong, since e-commerce requires user confidence and security. The governmental urge to support law and order is growing, especially with the start in 2001 of the war on terrorism, following on growing evidence of Internet-related fraud and crime. Normative pressure for effective limits on antisocial and criminal uses of the Net is growing on the part of general publics.

ACCOUNTABILITY OF THE INTERNET?

All this is very relevant to the issue of accountability, although not the whole story. It means, first of all, that the means of enforcing any rules about what is or is not permitted to be carried over the Web are becoming available and that misuses of the Web, including spreading viruses, hate messages, defamation, fraud, and crime, are open to sanction. It suggests that server managements and service providers may find themselves more effectively liable for some alleged harm and thus obliged to be accountable. One might also conclude that there is a danger of this new medium losing its position as the ideal free medium (as Lessig thinks it is in principle) and, in the absence of any specific protection, becoming less free in some respects than the established mass media. In most other respects there are still large deficits in respect of the means of both control and accountability and even the aspiration to be accountable.

Typically, in the discussion of Internet regulation, control and accountability are inextricably intertwined, not least because of the starting assumption that the Internet is neither controlled nor accountable. Verhulst (2002: 438), drawing on European-level discussions of Internet regulation, outlines four approaches to accountability, including codes of conduct for content and service providers, rating and filtering systems, response and complaint systems, and raising user awareness of their powers to filter and block content. In general, there are large problems with applying the concept of self-regulation to the Internet, starting with the uncertain identity of the 'self'. There are simply too many and too diverse entities involved for any common approach or shared code of conduct to be feasible. As Verhulst points out, there is no single 'industry' and the whole complex is still young and developing. Effective self-regulation would seem to require conditions that are contrary to the essential character of the Internet as described above. There is no doubt that rating, filtering, and zoning systems can be developed and applied (see Price, 1998), but they are not very precise, objective, or culture-free and in they end they require a gatekeeper at the user end for them to be effective. This is not necessarily a deficiency since it does connect with the fact that the Internet medium, more than mass communication, places the onus of responsibility on the user not the sender.

It is arguable that the notion of accountability is as alien to the Web/ Internet in the capacity of publisher as is (or was) the idea of regulation. It is an open network, without purpose of its own, existing only to facilitate communication by others. Looked at in this way, the Internet should not have to account for the actions of its users (providers and receivers) any more than the telephone network has to. This was the original reason for placing it along with common-carrier media for most purposes of regulation. Those who (inter-)communicate by way of the Web may choose to be accountable, or not, to their interlocutors.

Often, though not always, the sociability and sense of belonging of various networks and virtual communities give rise to a spontaneous interpersonal form of accountability, although the nature of the Web also supports inauthentic and intrinsically non-accountable participation. In so far as uses are private and personal this is also a private and voluntary matter. Nevertheless, there are gateways (portals) and gatekeepers on the Internet (e.g. ISPs and search engines) and they are of growing significance. The more that communications are directed at a public and are thus consciously designed as publications, the same considerations apply as to the other forms of publications already discussed, from medieval manuscript lectures to cinema films. The principle of horizontality discussed above comes into play.

The fact is that certain uses of the Internet are becoming more like other publication types. This applies to advertising, offers of services for sale, and supplies of news and data, music, video, and entertainment. These have an identified source and have to earn the trust of their intended or actual audiences. They need to show they are authentic and also accountable, if they are to be of any use and have their intended effects. There has to be an equivalent degree and type of professionalism and contractual behaviour that is found in the real (non-cyberspace) world. Hamelink (2000) describes a number of professional codes of conduct for computer professionals, but they are very limited and have little reference to any publication role. So far, it does not seem that the Internet has produced any satisfactory virtual alternative. Such professionalism as is found is largely borrowed from other fields, such as journalism, advertising, and commerce.

THE INTERNET AND PUBLIC COMMUNICATION

The Internet is becoming more like other media in other ways, especially in terms of global ownership and control. It is misleading to say that no one owns the Internet. As Hamelink (2000: 141) points out: 'Even if no-one can own the Internet, it remains possible that some industrial players own all the technical means that are required to access and use the Net.' If there is a threat to free speech on the Internet it is posed by those who own the infrastructure and provide and distribute content. It is not even hard to say who these are. Hamelink identifies a concentration of key players made up of manufacturers of PCs; sellers of operating systems; producers of browsers; telecom operators; Internet service providers (ISPs); and search engines and other content providers. He concludes (2000: 153): 'If the current trend continues, governance of and access to cyberspace will be in the hands of a few gate-keepers ... controlled by a small group of mega-market leaders.'

Patelis (2000) contrasts the anti-statist and libertarian ideology of 'Internetphiliacs' with the reality of a system in which portals such as ISPs actually control the flow of content by structuring and customizing it, in the name of eliminating chaos, but with their own interests in mind. The outcome is to direct attention and to aggregate traffic in much the same way as in traditional media. She concludes that the proper functioning of democracy now requires some public accountability of the new mediators, or even a public service sector that would be directly accountable to society, with its own portals and search engines.

If the public good, in the terms outlined earlier, especially with regard to various services to the public sphere and the democratic process, is to be advanced by way of the great potential of the Internet, it means that existing political actors have to enter the arena of cyberspace or create new public places which are widely recognized as non-manipulative, trustworthy, and valuable spaces for debate, finding information, and expressing opinion. The idea of a 'public commons' in cyberspace, somewhat equivalent to the public spaces offered by public service broadcasting, may need to be developed (Blumler and Gurevitch, 1995). Ann Branscomb (1995) calls for some cyberspace to be declared a 'public forum' where messages can circulate freely. This would facilitate the granting of First Amendment (or similar) protection to Internet speech. Just as important as establishing a more public presence in the Internet are measures to advance, protect, and guarantee rights of free expression that are at least equal to those enjoyed by other media. The anarchic freedom of the early Internet is simply not adequate and is in any case being whittled away. Bardoel (2002) advocates an extension of traditional European press policy to apply in adapted form to the Internet, in order to promote public communication. This means creating adequate conditions for an independent journalism on the Internet. Instead of supporting a media sector, policy should support journalistic functions, regardless of the platform.

The alternative in Branscomb's view is the transformation of a major element of the public sphere into an uninhabited market-place of ideas. Sunstein (1995) argues that such a move would be consistent with what he describes as the 'Madisonian' tradition of deliberative democracy. He writes that courts of law should be concerned to harness these technologies for democratic ends—including the aspiration to politicial deliberation, citizenship, political equality, and even a certain kind of virtue. Individual harm, meanwhile, can be combated by existing legal means, even if hampered by the 'delocation' or anonymity of offenders (1804).

As far as potential social harm is concerned, there is no easy way of resolving problems posed by lawless and unethical uses of the Internet, except by the application of measures that diminish essential freedoms and privacy unreasonably (the glass-house or panopticon effect). On the other hand, the nature of these threats may be exaggerated by authorities that have no counterbalancing interest in the loss of freedom and privacy. It is possible that ongoing developments will lead to more and more identifiable and voluntarily socially responsible actors in gate-keeping positions and certainly to more corporate control. It is also possible that the Internet will never become fully institutionalized and will retain elements of liberty and lawlessness, but all far short of early hopes and fears.

FREEDOM AND ACCOUNTABILITY: LAST WORDS

It was noted at the start of this chapter that freedom is itself an important goal of public policy for the media, and one that the media heartily support. However, the freedom pursued by governments should include not only freedom for the media, but also for citizens and various bodies seeking to use the media (i.e. access), the wider goal of freedom of communication in fact. It is not usually very easy to reconcile these two requirements, since giving more freedom to the media as organizations allows them to decline responsibility, while making accountability more compulsory devalues it. The relationship with accountability is thus a complex one. Freedom is one of the conditions of adequate account-ability (both to governmental authority and to citizens), especially when this is understood as open and responsive dialogue and integrity, not just compliance with the minimum requirements of law and regula-tion, or under duress. As Klaidman (1994: 106) points out, for the press to be accountable also goes beyond professional self-regulation. It is 'to be answerable to someone or some group to whom accountability is owed ... It requires explanations and justifications of why controversial stories were reported as they were'. In his view this form of voluntary answerability enhances media credibility rather than promoting control by outsiders.

The main focus of public policy should thus be on establishing the conditions that make voluntary and effective accountability more likely. These conditions generally include both the diversity and extensiveness of the media system, enabling access to many on widely differing terms and encouraging quality of performance through competition. Diversity of accountability is also beneficial for freedom, meaning both multiple lines of accountability and avoiding concentrations of power over a range of media in the hands of a single office or regulator. The first occurs naturally and the second has occurred de facto because of the several different media and different regimes.

The freedom of the mass media in publication matters is often held back by fears concerning media effects. This leads to calls for them to be more strictly accountable for the harm they cause. As we have seen, many such fears are exaggerated or misplaced (since the causes generally lie elsewhere) and they also impose an undue burden on the media to satisfy a limited section of, vocal, opinion. Such opinion may be well founded in value terms and has a claim to be heard, but not primarily on the basis of the causal responsibility of the media. The media may indeed have a moral responsibility if they take unknown risks for purposes of profit.

Trying to solve these problems by compulsory and restrictive regula-tion often leads to unwanted side effects and it denies to the audience part of its freedom to choose. There is no escape from this particular source of constraint, but the need for the media to take risks should also be recognized. In general these matters are best dealt with by open debate and inquiry. We do need not more, but better, accountability. It is better to reward positive performance than punish failures. The pursuit of effective control is illusory, since it too is based on a notion of measurability (more control = less harmful effects) that cannot be validated. Effectiveness of accountability in the sense of compliance with regulation is not the main issue, since it may have no other effects.

The pursuit of freedom in communication should take account not only of the restrictive effects of law and regulation. Attention should also be given to other forms of accountability that may have restrictive results. These include the internal control exercised by media firms (private censorship), the tyranny of the ratings, and the pressures of advertising. All have an undoubted effect on limiting freedom by making certain publication options more costly or less profitable. In many respects they have a more enduring and pervasive influence than any regulation, although the effects are generally invisible compared to the occasional intrusion of law.

The internal freedom of the media guarantees to various communicator roles a degree of personal freedom of conscience in respect of what might be the policy of a medium (editorially). There is not a great deal that any public policy can do about this, beyond giving it general support. Both of the other tendencies are built into commercial systems, but they should be considered when decisions are taken about public broadcasting and any rules for advertising that exist. They also form part of the argument in favour of diversity of ownership, although competition in itself does not lessen such pressures and may even increase them.

Although this has been a study of liberal and democratic systems, it is salutary to recall that there are other systems and abnormal occasions when accountability takes other unacceptable forms, ranging from bribes to death sentences. In these circumstances, accountability has an illegitimate character and is diametrically opposed to freedom. In the climate of fear created by international terrorism and the reaction to it, there is also a real danger that even in democracies what is abnormal becomes normal. The freedom of publication that is a necessary condition for the forms of accountability advocated here is permanently vulnerable and in need of active defence and continuing advocacy.

NOTES

1. The sources of criticism are disparate and include remnants of the old left (once the new left) who have never accepted defeat at the hands of the new right; long-

standing critics of rampant commercialism, such as Bogart (1995); traditional moralists who see loss of control and a media flood of sensation, crime, violence, pornography, and worse; liberal democrats who fear the loss of rational, balanced, and adequate political information and fair opportunities for advocacy; and professional journalists, whose standards are no longer as respected in an entertainment-driven world.

2. These are firstly, to protect the interests of the state; secondly, to protect private rights and interests; and thirdly, to secure the orderly development of communication technology, presumably for the common good.

3. The main categories of such media are all kinds of small and irregular print publications, various forms of artistic displays, plays and other stage performances, music and song composition and performance, much photography and film, public speaking, poetry reading, pirate radio, and much more. The telephone and mail are also media for more than private communication. To this has been added possibilities for desktop publishing by computer and all the riches of Web-based communication that emanate from individuals, groups, and informal communication networks.

4. The general pattern described, leaving the technology aside, goes back at least to the late Middle Ages. Artists, authors, religious reformers, and performers unconnected with official communication channels of the Church, court, or state sought their own means of reaching an audience. Popular entertainments, stories, and plays circulated in oral form. Early newspapers circulated in the form of handwritten letters.

5. While this is true of liberal societies at ease with themselves (even if it has been called 'repressive tolerance'), it does not apply under conditions of crisis or of national paranoia (as in the deep cold war or the war on terrorism). It has never applied in total or dictatorial societies.

Bibliography

ABBATE, J. (1999), *Inventing the Internet* (Cambridge, Mass.: MIT Press).

ABRAMS, M. E., and HAWKINS, J. E. (1984), 'Legislators' perceptions of newspaper functions', *Newspaper Research Journal*, 5, 4: 51–7.

ADORNO, T., and HORKHEIMER, M. (1972), 'The culture industry: enlightenment as mass deception', in *The Dialectic of the Enlightenment* (New York: Herder and Herder).

AIRIKSONEN, T. (2001), 'Professional ethics', in R. T. Chadwick (ed.), *The Concise Encyclopedia of Ethics in Politics and the Media* (San Diego: Academic Press), 263–73.

AKDENIZ, Y., and ROGERS, H. (2000), 'Defamation on the Internet', in Y. AKDENIZ, C. WALKER, and D. WALL (eds.) (2000), *The Internet, Law and Society* (London: Longman), 294–396.

AKDENIZ, Y., WALKER, C., and WALL, D. (eds.) (2000), *The Internet, Law and Society* (London: Longman).

ALTHAUS, S. L., and TEWKESBURY, D. (2000), 'Patterns of Internet and news media use', *Political Communication*, 17, 1: 21–46.

ALTSCHULL, H. J. (1984), *Agents of Power: The Role of the Media in Human Affairs* (New York: Longman).

ANDERSON and LEIGH, F. A. (1992), 'How newspaper editors and broadcast news directors view media ethics', *Newspaper Research Journal*, Winter/Spring, 112–21.

ANDSAGER, J. C., and MILLER, M. M. (1994), 'Willingness of journalists to support freedom of expression', *Newspaper Research Journal*, 15, 1: 102–14.

ANG, I. (1991), *Desperately Seeking the Audience* (London: Routledge).

ARTICLE 19 (1993), *Press Law and Practice: A Comparative Study of Press Freedom in European and Other Democracies* (London: Article 19).

ATHERTON, I. (1999), ' "The Itch grown a Disease": Manuscript transmission of news in the seventeenth century', in J. Raymond (ed.), *News, Newspapers and Society in Early Modern Britain* (London: Frank Cass), 39–65.

ATKINSON, D., and RABOY, M. (eds.) (1997), *Public Service Broadcasting: The Challenges of the 21st Century* (Paris: Unesco).

AXFORD, B., and HUGGINS, R. (eds.) (2001), *New Media and Politics* (London: Sage).

BAERNS, B. (1987), 'Journalism versus public relations in the Federal Republic of Germany', in D. L. Paletz (ed.), *Political Communication Research* (Norwood, NJ: Ablex), 88–107.

BAKER, C. E. (1978), 'Scope of the First Amendment freedom of speech', *UCLA Law Review*, 25, 5: 964–1040.

BAKER, C. E. (1989), *Human Liberty and Freedom of Speech* (New York: Oxford University Press).

—— (1994), *Advertising and a Democratic Press* (Princeton: Princeton University Press).

—— (1998), 'The media that citizens need', *University of Pennsylvania Law Review*, 147: 317–407.

—— (2001), 'Implications of rival visions of electoral campaigns', in W. L. Bennett and R. Entman (eds.), *Mediated Politics* (Cambridge: Cambridge University Press), 342–61.

BARAN, S. A. (2001), 'The guises of dissemination in early 17th century England', in B. Dooley and S. Baran (eds.), *The Politics of Information in Early Modern Europe* (London: Routledge).

BARBROOK, R. (1995), *Media Freedom: The Contradictions of Communications in the Age of Modernity* (London and Boulder, Colo.: Pluto Press).

BARDOEL, J. H. L. (2002), 'The Internet, journalism and public communication policies', *Gazette*, 64, 5: 501–11.

BARENDT, E. (1985), *Freedom of Speech* (Oxford: Clarendon Press).

—— (1993), *Broadcasting Law: A Comparative Study* (Oxford: Clarendon Press).

—— (1998), 'The First Amendment and the media', in I. Loveland (ed.), *Importing the First Amendment* (Oxford: Hart Publishing), 29–51.

—— (2000), *Privacy* (Aldershot: Ashgate).

BARROW, R. A. (1968), 'The equal opportunities and fairness doctrines in broadcasting: Pillars in the forum of democracy', *Cincinatti Law Review*, 37 (3): 447–557.

BAUER, R. A. (1964), 'The communicator and the audience', in L. A. Dexter and D. M. White (eds.), *People, Society and Mass Communication* (New York: Free Press), 125–39.

BAY, C. (1977), 'Access to political knowledge as a human right', in I. Galnoor (ed.), *Government Secrecy in Democracies* (New York: Harper).

BAZELON, D. L. (1982), 'The First Amendment and the new media', in D. L. and W. L. Rivers (eds.), *Free But Regulated: Conflicting Traditions in Media Law*, (Ames, Ia.: Iowa State University Press), 52–63.

BECKER, L., *et al.* (1978), 'Public support for the press', *Journalism Quarterly*, 55: 421–30.

BELSEY, A., and CHADWICK, R. (eds.) (1992), *Issues in Journalism and the Media* (London: Routledge).

BENNETT, W. L., and ENTMAN, R. (eds.) (2001), *Mediated Politics* (Cambridge: Cambridge University Press).

BERELSON, B. (1952), *Content Analysis in Communication Research* (Glencoe, Ill.: Free Press).

BERGEN, S. A., LAFKY, S. A., and WEAVER, D. (2000), 'Local news source opinions of their newspapers', *Newspaper Research Journal*, 21, 3: 14–26.

BERLIN, I. (1958/1969), 'Two concepts of liberty', in *Four Essays on Liberty* (New York: Oxford University Press), 118–72.

BERTRAND, J. C. (2000), *Media Aaccountability Systems* (Brunswick, NJ: Transaction Books).

BETTIG, R. V. (1997), 'The enclosure of Cyberspace', *Critical Studies in Mass Communication*, 14: 138–57.

BIEGEL, S. (2001), *Beyond our Control? Confronting the Limits of our Legal System in the Age of Cyberspace* (Cambridge, Mass.: MIT Press).

BLANCHARD, M. A. (1977), 'The Hutchins Commission, the Press and the Responsibility Concept', *Journalism Momographs, 49*.

BLATZ, C. V. (1972), 'Accountability and answerability', *Journal for the Theory of Social Behavior*, 6, 2: 253–9.

BLASI, V. (1977), 'The checking value in First Amendment theory', *American Bar Foundation Research Journal*, 521.

BLIZEK, W. (1971), 'The social concept of accountability', *Southern Journal of Philosophy*, 7: 107–11.

BLUMER, H. (1939), 'The mass, the public and public opinion', in A. M. Lee (ed.), *New Outline of the Principles of Sociology* (New York: Barnes and Noble).

BLUMLER, J. G. (ed.) (1992), *Television and the Public Interest* (London: Sage).

—— (1997), 'Wrestling with the public interest in organized communication', in K. Brants, J. Hermes, and L. van Zoonen (eds.), *The Media in Question* (London: Sage), 51–63.

—— and HOFFMANN-RIEM, W. (1992), 'New roles of public service broadcasting', in Blumler, 1992, 202–17

—— and —— (1992), 'Toward renewed public accountability in broadcasting', in Blumler, 1992, 218–28.

BLUMLER, J. G., and GUREVITCH, M. (eds.) (1995), *The Crisis of Public Communication* (London: Routledge).

BLUMLER, J. G., and KAVANAGH, D. (1999), 'The third age of political communication: influences and features', *Political Communication*, 16, 3: 209–30.

BOGART, L. (1995), *Commercial Culture: The Media System and the Public Interest* (New York: Oxford University Press).

BOLLINGER, L. C. (1991), *Images of a Free Press* (Chicago: University of Chicago Press).

BORDEWIJK, J. L., and VAN KAAM, B. (1986), 'Towards a new classification of tele-information services', *Intermedia*, 14, 1: 16–21.

BOYLE, K. (1988), *Information Freedom and Censorship* (London: Article 19 Report).

BRACKEN, H. M. (1994), *Freedom of Speech: Words are not Deeds* (New York: Praeger).

BRAMAN, S. (1988), 'Public expectations of media standards in codes of ethics', *Journalism Quarterly*, 65: 71–7.

BRANSCOMB, A. W. (1995), 'Anonymity, autonomy and accountability: Challenges to the First Amendment in Cyberspace', *Yale Law Journal*, 104, 7: 1639–79.

BRANTS, K. (2003), 'The Netherlands', in M. Kelly, G. Mazzoleni, and D. McQuail (eds.), *The Media in Europe* (London: Sage).

BREED, W. (1995), 'Social control in the newsroom: A functional analysis', *Social Forces*, 33: 326–55.

BRIGGS, A., and BURKE, P. (2002), *A Social History of the Media: From Gutenberg to the Internet* (Oxford: Polity).

BRODASSON, T. (1994), 'The sacred side of professional journalism', *European Journal of Communication*, 9, 3: 227–48.

BROMLEY, M., and STEPHENSON, H. (1998), *Sex, Lies and Democracy: The Press and the Public* (New York: Longman).

BRUMMER, J. (1991), *Corporate Responsibility: An Interdisciplinary Analysis* (Westport, Conn.: Greenwood Press).

BRYANT, J., and ZILLMANN, D. (eds.) (1994), *Media Effects* (Hillsdale, NJ: Laurence Erlbaum).

BUNTON, K. (2000), 'Media criticism as professional self-regulation', in D. Pritchard (ed.), *Holding the Media Accountable* (Bloomingdale Ind.: Indiana University Press), 68–89.

BURNS, T. (1977), *The BBC: Public Institution and Private World* (London: Macmillan).

BUTTRY, R. (1993), *Social Accountability in Communication* (Thousand Oaks, Calif.: Sage).

CALHOUN, C. (ed.) (1992), *Habermas and the Public Sphere* (London: MIT Press).

CALVERT, C. (1997), 'Free speech and its harms: A communication theory perspective', *Journal of Communication*, 47, 1: 4–19.

CAMPBELL, A. (1999), 'Self-regulation and the media', *Federal Communications Law Review*, 1: 711–72.

CANADA (1981), *Report of the Royal Commission on Newspapers* (Ottawa: Ministry of Supply and Services).

CANTOR, M. (1971), *The Hollywood Television Producer* (New York: Basic Books).

CAPELLA, J., and JAMIESON, K. H. (1997), *The Spiral of Cynicism* (New York: Oxford University Press).

CAREY, J. (1975), 'A cultural approach to communication', *Communication*, 2: 1–22.

—— (1989), *Communication and Culture* (Boston, Mass.: Unwin Hyman).

CARLSSON, U., and VON FEILITZEN, C. (eds.) (1998), *Children, Media and Violence* (Goteborg: University of Goteborg).

CASTELLS, M. (1996), *The Information Age*, i. *The Rise of the Network Society* (Oxford: Blackwell).

—— (2001), *The Internet Galaxy* (Oxford: Oxford University Press).

CATE, F. H. (1997), *Privacy in the Information Age* (Washington: Brookings).

CHADWICK, R. T. (ed.) (2001), *The Concise Encyclopedia of Ethics in Politics and the Media* (San Diego: Academic Press).

CHALABY, J. K. (2000), 'New media, new freedoms, new threats', *Gazette*, 62, 1: 19–30.

CHARLESWORTH, A. (2000), 'The governance of the Internet in Europe', in Y. Akdeniz, C. Walker, and D. Wall (eds.), *The Internet, Law and Society* (London: Longman), 47–78.

CHRISTIANS, C. (1989), 'Self-Regulation: A critical role for codes of ethics', in E. E. Dennis, D. M. Gillmor, and T. L. Glasser (eds.), *Media Freedom and Accountability* (Westport, Conn.: Greenwood Press), 35–54.

—— (1993), *Good News: Social Ethics and the Press* (New York: Oxford University Press).

CLARK, T. N. (ed.) (1969), *On Communication and Social Control: Collected Essays of Gabriel Tarde* (Chicago: University of Chicago Press).

CLIFT, D. (1981), 'Press councils and ombudsmen', in *The Journalists*, vol. ii of the research studies of the Royal Commission on Newspapers (Ottowa: Minister of Supply and Services).

COHEN, B. (1963), *The Press and Foreign Policy* (Princeton: Princeton University Press).

COMSTOCK, G., CHAFFEE, S., KATZMAN, N., McCOMBS, M., and ROBERTS, D. (eds.) (1978), *Television and Human Behavior* (New York: Columbia University Press).

COOLEY, C. H. (1908), *Human Nature and the Social Order* (New York: Charles Scribner & Sons).

CRAUFORD-SMITH, R. (1997), *Broadcasting Law and Fundamental Rights* (Oxford: Clarendon Press).

CUILENBURG, J. J. VAN, and McQUAIL, D. (2003), 'Media policy paradigm shifts: in search of a new communications policy paradigm', *European Journal of Communication*, 18, 2, forthcoming.

CURRAN, J. (1996), 'Mass media and democracy revisited', in J. Curran and M. Gurevitch (eds.), *Mass Media and Society*, 2nd edn. (London: Edward Arnold), 81–119.

CURRAN, J., and SEATON, J. (eds.) (1997), *Power Without Responsibility: The Press and Broadcasting in Britain* (London: Routledge).

DAHLBERG, L. (2001), 'The Internet and democratic discourse', *Information, Communication and Society (ICS)*, 4, 4: 615–33.

DAHLGREN, P. (1995), *Television and the Public Sphere* (London: Sage).

DANCE, F. E. X. (1970), 'The concept of communication', *Journal of Communication*, 20: 201–10.

DAVIS, D. K. (1999), 'Media as public arena', in R. C. Vincent, K. Nordenstreng, and M. Traber (eds.), *Towards Equity in Global Communication* (Creskill, NJ: Hampton Press), 155–68.

DAY, P., and KLEIN, R. (1987), *Accountabilities* (London and New York: Tavistock).

DAYAN, D., and KATZ, E. (1992), *Media Events* (Cambridge, Mass.: Harvard University Press).

DEARING, J. W., and ROGERS, E. M. (1996), *Agenda Setting* (Thousand Oaks, Calif.: Sage).

DEE, J. L. (1987), 'Media accountability for real-life violence: a case of negligence or free speech', *Journal of Communication*, 38, 1: 106–32.

DEFLEUR, M. L., and BALL-ROKEACH, S. (1989), *Theories of Mass Communication*, 2nd edn. (New York: Longman).

DEMAC, D. (1988), *Liberty Denied: The Current Rise of Censorship in America* (New York: PEN America Center).

DENNIS, E. E. (1991), *The Media at War* (New York: Gannett Foundation).

—— (1995), 'Internal examination: Self-regulation and the American media', *Cardozo Arts and Entertainment Law Journal*, 13, 3: 697–703.

—— GILLMOR, D., and GLASSER, T. L. (eds.) (1989), *Media Freedom and Accountability* (New York: Greenwood Press).

DHAVAN, R., and DAVIES, C. (1978), *Censorship and Obscenity* (London: Martin Robertson).

DIJK, J. G. VAN (1999), *The Network Society* (London: Sage).

DIJK, J. A. VAN, and HACKER, K. (eds.) (2000), *Digital Democracy* (London: Sage).

DONSBACH, W. (1983), 'Journalists' conception of their role', *Gazette*, 32,1: 19–36.

DOOLEY, B., and BARAN, S. (eds.) (2001), *The Politics of Information in Early Modern Europe* (London: Rouutledge), 41–56.

DORMAN, C. (1991), 'Free to be responsible: the accountability of the print media', in F. Fletcher (ed.), *Reporting the Campaign: Election Coverage in Canada*, Royal Commission on Electoral Reform, vol. xxii (Toronto and Oxford: Dundurn Press), 147–88.

DOWNIE, R. (1964), 'Social roles and moral responsibility', *Philosophy*, Jan: 29–36.

DOWNING, J. D. H. (2000), *Radical Media: Rebellious Communication and Social Movements* (Thousand Oaks, Calif.: Sage).

—— and HUSBAND, C. (1999), 'Media, ethnicity and the construction of difference', in M. Griffin and K. Nordenstreng (eds.), *International Media Monitoring* (Creskill, NJ: Hampton Press), 277–306.

DRECHSEL, R. (1992), 'Media ethics and media law: The transformation of moral obligation into legal principle', *Notre Dame Journal of Law, Ethics and Public Policy*, 6: 5–32.

DRUCKER, S., and GUMPERT, G. (eds.) (1999), *Real Law @ Virtual Space* (Creskill, NJ: Hampton Press).

DWORKIN, R. (1985), *A Matter of Principle* (Cambridge, Mass.: Harvard University Press).

EASTON, S. (2001), 'Pornography', in R. T. Chadwick (ed.), *The Concise Encyclopedia of Ethics in Politics and the Media* (San Diego: Academic Press), 241–50.

EDWARDS, L. (ed.) (1997), *Law and the Internet: Regulating Cyberspace* (Oxford: Hart Publishing).

EINSIEDEL, E. (1988), The British, Canadian and US pornography commissions and their use of social research', *Journal of Communication,* 38, 2: 108–21.

EISENSTEIN, E. (1978), *The Printing Press as an Agent of Change,* 2 vols. (New York: Cambridge University Press).

ELLIOTT, D. (1986), *Responsible Journalism* (Beverly Hills, Calif.: Sage).

ELLIOTT, P. (1972), 'Mass communication—A contradiction in terms?', in McQuail (ed.), *Sociology of Mass Communication,* 237–58 (Harmondsworth: Penguin).

EMERSON, T. I. (1970), *The System of Free Expression* (New York: Random House).

ENGWALL, L. (1978), *Newspapers as Organisations* (Farnborough: Saxon House).

ENTMAN, R. (1989), *Democracy Without Citizens: Mass Media and the Decay of American Politics* (New York: Oxford University Press).

ENZENSBERGER, H. M. (1970), 'Constituents of a theory of the media', *New Left Review,* 64: 13–36.

ETTEMA, J., and GLASSER, T. (1987), 'Public accountability or PR?' Newspaper ombudsmen define their role', *Journalism Quarterly,* 64, 1: 3–12.

—— and —— (1998), *Custodians of Conscience: Investigative Journalism and Public Virtue* (New York: Columbia University Press).

EUROBAROMETER (1999), No. 51 (Brussels: European Commission).

EUROPEAN JOURNAL of COMMUNICATION, 15, 3 (September 2000).

EVERS, H. (2000), 'Codes of ethics', in B. Pattyn (ed.), *Media Ethics* (Leuven: Peeters), 265–92.

FALLOWS, J. (1996), *Breaking the News: How the Media Undermine American Democracy* (New York: Pantheon).

FEBVRE, L., and MARTIN, H. J. (1984), *The Coming of the Book* (London: Verso).

FEDERMAN, J. (1998), 'Media rating systems: A comparative analysis', in M. E. Price (ed.), *The TV-chip Debate* (Mahwah, NJ: LEA), 92–132.

FEINBERG, J. (1987), *Harm to Others* (New York: Oxford University Press).

FEINTUCK, M. (1999), *Media Regulation, Public Interest and the Law* (Edinburgh: Edinburgh University Press).

FISS, O. (1991), 'Why the state?', *Harvard Law Review,* 781.

—— (1997), *The Irony of Free Speech* (Cambridge, Mass.: Harvard University Press).

FITZSIMON, M., and McGILL, L. T. (1995), 'The citizen as media critic', *Media Studies Journal,* Spring: 91–102.

FJAESTAD, B., and HOLMLOV, P. G. (1976), 'The journalist's' view', *Journal of Communication*, 28, 2: 108–114.

FOERSTAL, H. N. (1998), *Banned in the Media: A Reference Guide to Censorship in Press, Picture, Broadcasting and the Internet* (Westport, Conn.: Greenwood Press).

FRANKEL, E., MILLER, F. D., and PAUL, J. (eds.) (1999), *Responsibility* (Cambridge: Cambridge University Press).

GALLAGHER, M. (1999), 'The global media monitoring project: Women's networking for research and action', in M. Griffin and K. Nordenstreng (eds.), *International Media Monitoring* (Creskill, NJ: Hampton Press), 199–218.

GALTUNG, J. (1999), 'State, capital and the civil society: The problem of communication', in R. Vincent, K. Nordenstreng, and M. Traber (eds.), *Towards Equity in Global Communication: McBride Update* (Cresskill, NJ: Hampton Press), 3–21.

GANS, H. J. (1979), *Deciding What's News* (New York: Vintage Books).

GARRY, P. (1994), *Scrambling for Protection: The New Media and the First Amendment* (Westport, Conn.: Greenwood Press).

GAZIANO, C., and McGRATH, K. (1986), 'Measuring the concept of credibility', *Journalism Quarterly*, 63: 451–62.

—— and —— (1987), 'Newspaper credibility and relationships of journalists to communities', *Journalism Quarterly*, 64, 2: 237–64.

GERBNER, G., GROSS, L., MORGAN, M., and SIGNORIELLI, N. (1984), 'The political correlates of TV viewing', *Public Opinion Quarterly*, 48: 283–300.

—— MORGAN, M., and SIGNORIELLI, N. (1999), 'Profiling television violence', in M. Griffin and K. Nordenstreng (eds.), *International Media Monitoring* (Creskill, NJ: Hampton Press), 335–66.

GIDDENS, A. (1984), *The Constitution of Society* (Cambridge: Polity Press).

GIEBER, W., and JOHNSON, W. (1960), 'The City Hall beat: A study of reporters and source roles', *Journalism Quarterly*, 38: 289–97.

GILLMOR, D. (1989), 'The terrible burden of free and accountable media', in E. E. Dennis *et al.*, *Media Freedom and Accountability* (New York: Greenwood Press), 1–10.

GLASSER, T. L. (1986), 'Press responsibility and First Amendment values', in D. Elliott (ed.), *Responsible Journalism* (Beverly Hills, Calif.: Sage).

—— (ed.) (1998), *The Idea of Public Journalism* (New York: Guilford Press).

—— and CRAFT, J. (1998), 'Public journalism and the search for democratic ideals', in T. Liebes and J. Curran (eds.), *Media, Ritual and Identity* (London: Routledge).

GLEASON, T. W. (1994), *The Watchdog Concept* (Ames, Ia.: Iowa State University Press).

GOLDBERG, D., PROSSER, T., and VERHULST, S. (1998), *Regulating the Changing Media: A Comparative Study* (Oxford: Clarendon Press).

GOLDING, P., and HARRIS, P. (eds.) (1997), *Beyond Cultural Imperialism* (London: Sage).

GOLDING, P., and SNIPPENPERG, L. VAN (1995), 'Government communications and the media', in *Beliefs in Government*, 30 (London: Oxford University Press).

GOULDNER, A. (1976), *The Dialectic of Ideology and Technology* (London: Macmillan).

GRABER, D. (1986), 'Press freedom and the general welfare', *Political Science Quarterly*, 101, 2: 257–75.

GRABER, M. (1991), *Transforming Free Speech* (Berkeley: University of California Press).

GRAMSCI, A. (1971), *Selections from the Prison Notebooks* (London: Lawrence and Wishart).

GREENBERG, R. S. (1999), 'Free speech on the Internet: Controversy and control', in L. J. Pourciau (ed.), *Ethics and Electronic Information in the Twenty First Century* (Westfayette, Ind.: Purdue University Press), 93–126.

GRIFFIN, M., and NORDENSTRENG, K. (eds.) (1999), *International Media Monitoring* (Creskill, NJ: Hampton Press).

GRINGRAS, C. (1997), *The Laws of the Internet* (London: Butterworth).

GUNTER, B. (1994), 'The question of media violence', in J. Bryant and D. Zillmann (eds.), *Media Effects* (Hillsdale, NJ: Lawrence Erlbaum), 163–212.

—— and WINSTONE, B. (1993), *Public Attitudes to Television* (Hillsdale, NJ: Laurence Erlbaum).

GUSTAFSSON, K. E., and WEIBULL, L. (1997), 'European newspaper readership: structure and developments', *Communications: The European Journal of Communication Research*, 22, 3: 249–73.

HABERMAS, J. (1962/1989), *The Structural Transformation of the Public Sphere* (Cambridge, Mass.: MIT Press).

—— (1984), *The Theory of Communicative Action* (London: Heinemann).

HACKETT, R. (1984), 'Decline of a paradigm: Bias and objectivity in news media studies', *Critical Studies in Mass Communication*, 1: 229–59.

HAIMAN, F.S. (1991), 'Minorities against the First Amendment', *Communication Monographs*, 60, 1: 98–105.

HALASZ, A. (1997), *The Marketplace of Print: Pamphlets and the Public Sphere in Early Modern England* (Cambridge: Cambridge University Press).

HALL, J. (2000), 'Serving the public interest', *Media Studies Journal*, Fall: 68–75.

HALL, S. (1977), 'Culture, the media and the ideological effect', in J. Curran *et al.* (eds.), *Mass Communication and Society* (London: Edward Arnold), 315–48.

HALLIN, D. (1996), *Keeping America on Top of the World* (New York: Routledge).

HALLIN, D., and MANCINI, P. (1984), 'Political and representational forms in US and Italian TV news', *Theory and Society*, 13, 4: 829–50.

HAMELINK, C. (1994), *Global Communication* (London: Sage).

—— (2000), *The Ethics of Cyberspace* (London: Sage).

HARDT, H. (1979), *Social Theories of the Press: Early German and American Perspectives* (Beverly Hills, Calif.: Sage).

—— (1991), *Critical Communication Studies* (London: Routledge).

HARRIS, R. J. (1994), 'The impact of sexually explicit media', in J. Bryant and D. Zillmann (eds.), *Media Effects* (Hillsdale, NJ: Lawrence Erlbaum), 247–72.

HAYDON, G. (1978), 'On being Responsible', *Philosophical Quarterly*, 28: 46–51.

HEINS, M. (2000), 'Blaming the Media', *Media Studies Journal*, Fall: 14–23.

HELD, D. (1989), *Models of Democracy* (Stanford Calif.: Stanford University Press).

HELD, V. (1970), *The Public Interest and Individual Interests* (New York: Basic Books).

HELLINGA, L., and TRIBE, J. B. (eds.) (1998), *The Cambridge History of the Book in Britain* (Cambridge: Cambridge University Press).

HENTOFF, N. (2000), 'The diminishing first amendment', *Media Studies Journal*, Fall: 76–81

HERMAN, E., and CHOMSKY, N. (1988), *Manufacturing Consent: The Political Economy of Mass Media* (New York: Pantheon).

HINDMAN, E. B. (1992), 'First Amendment theories and press responsibility', *Journalism Quarterly*, 69: 48–62.

—— (1997), *Rights vs. Responsibilities: The Supreme Court and the Media* (Westport, Conn.: Greenwood Press).

HOCKING, W. E. (1947), *Freedom of the Press: A Framework of Principle* (Chicago: University of Chicago Press).

HODGES, L. W. (1986), 'Defining press responsibility: A functional approach', in D. Elliott (ed.), *Responsible Journalism* (Beverly Hills, Calif.: Sage), 13–31.

HOFFMANN-RIEM, W. (1992), 'Defending vulnerable values', in J. G. Blumler (ed.), *Television and the Public Interest* (London: Sage), 173–201.

—— (1996), *Regulating Media* (New York: Guilford).

HOLMES, S. (1990), 'Liberal constraints on private power? Reflections on the origins and rationale of access regulation', in J. Lichtenberg (ed.), *Democracy and the Mass Media* (Cambridge: Cambridge University Press), 21–65.

HOLSTI, O. (1969), *Content Analysis for the Social Sciences and Humanities* (Reading, Mass.: Addison Wesley).

HOVLAND, C. I., LUMSDAINE, A. A., and SHEFFIELD, F. D. (1951), *Experiments in Mass Communication* (Princeteon: Princeton University Press).

HUMPHREYS, P. (1996), *Mass Media and Media Policy in Western Europe* (Manchester: Manchester University Press).

HUTCHINS, R. (1947), *A Free and Responsible Press: Report of the Commission on Freedom of the Press* (Chicago: Chicago University Press).

IMMERWAHR, J., and DOBLE, J. (1982), 'Public attitudes towards freedom of the press', *Public Opinion Quarterly*, 46, 2: 177–94.

INGBER, S. (1984), 'The marketplace of ideas: A legitimising myth', *Duke Law Journal*, 1.

INGRAM, P. S. (2000), *Censorship and Free Speech* (Aldershot: Ashgate).

INNIS, H. (1951), *The Bias of Communication* (Toronto: Toronto University Press).

ISHIKAWA, S. (ed.) (1996), *Quality Assessment of Television* (Luton: Luton University Press).

ISHIKAWA, S., and MURAMATSU, Y. (1991), 'Quality assessment of broadcast programming', *Studies of Broadcasting*, 27: 207–20.

IYENGAR, S. (ed.) (1997), *Do the Media Govern?* (Thousand Oaks, Calif: Sage).

JANOWITZ, M. (1952), *The Community Press in an Urban Setting* (New York: Free Press).

—— (1975), 'Professional models in journalism: The gatekeeper and advocate', *Journalism Quarterly*, 54, 4: 618–26.

JANSEN, S. C. (1988), *Censorship: The Knot that Binds Power and Knowledge* (New York: Oxford University Press).

JOHNS, A. (1998), *The Nature of the Book* (Chicago: Chicago University Press).

JOHNSON, T. J., and KAYE, B. K. (1998), 'Cruising is believing: Comparing Internet and traditional sources on media credibility measures', *Journalism and Mass Communication Quarterly*, 75, 2: 325–40.

JOHNSTONE, J. W. L., SLAVSKI, E. J., and BOWMAN, W. W. (1976), *The News People* (Urbana, Ill.: University of Urbana Press).

JONES, S. G. (1997), *Virtual Culture: Identity and Communication in Cybersociety* (London: Sage).

KATZ, E. (1980), 'Publicity and pluralistic ignorance: notes on the "spiral of silence"', in H. Baier and H. M. Kepplinger (eds.), *Public Opinion and Social Change: For Elisabeth Noelle-Neumann* (Wiesbaden: Westdeutscher Verlag), 28–38.

KAUFER, D. S., and CARLEY, K. M. (1994), *Communication at a Distance* (Hillsdale, NJ: Laurence Erlbaum).

KEANE, J. (1991), *The Media and Democracy* (Oxford: Polity Press).

KEPPLINGER, H. M., and KOECHER, R. (1990), 'Professionalism in the media world', *European Journal of Communication*, 5, 2/3: 285–311.

KERNER COMMISSION (1968), *National Commission on the Causes and Prevention of Violence* (Washington: GPO).

KIM, J.-Y. (1999), 'First Amendment rights on the Internet: A snowball's chance in hell', in L. J. Pourciau (ed.), *Ethics and Electronic Information in the Twenty First Century* (Westfayette, Ind.: Purdue University Press), 76–92.

KLAIDMAN, S. (1994), 'The roles and responsibilities of the American press', in P. S. Cook (ed.), *Liberty of Expression* (Washington: Wilson Center Press), 91–107.

KLAPPER, J. (1960), *The Effects of Mass Communication* (New York: Free Press).

KLEINSTEUBER, H. (1997), 'Federal Republic of Germany', in Euromedia Research Group, *The Media in Western Europe* (London: Sage), 75–97.

KNIGHTLEY, P. (1991), *The First Enemy* (London: Pan).

KÖCHER, R. (1986), 'Role definitions of British and German journalists', *European Journal of Communication*, 1, 1: 43–64.

KRATTENMAKER, T. G., and POWE, L. A. (1994), *Regulating Broadcasting Programming* (Cambridge, Mass.: MIT Press).

——— and ——— (1995), 'Converging First Amendment principles for converging mass media', *Yale Law Journal*, 104, 7: 1719–41.

LAHAV, P. (ed.) (1985), *Press Law in Modern Democracies: A Comparative Study* (London: Longman).

LAITILA, T. (1995), 'Journalistic codes of ethics in Europe', *European Journal of Communication*, 10, 4: 513–26.

LAMBETH, E. B. (1992), 'The news media and democracy', *Media Studies Journal*, Fall: 161–75.

——— (1992/1998), *Committed Journalism: An Ethic for the Profession* (Bloomingdale, Ind.: Indiana University Press).

LANGFORD, D. (1999), 'Beyond human control: Some ethical implications of today's Internet', in L. J. Pourciau (ed.), *Ethics and Electronic Information in the Twenty First Century* (Westfayette, Ind.: Purdue University Press), 65–75.

——— (2000), *Internet Ethics* (London: Macmillan).

LASSWELL, H. (1948), 'The structure and function of communication in society', in L. Bryson (ed.), *The Communication of Ideas* (New York: Harper), 32–51.

LEES, T., RALPH, S., and LANGHAM BROWN, J. (2000), *Is Regulation an Option in a Digital Universe?* (Luton: University of Luton Press).

LEGGATT, T. (1991), 'Identifying the undefinable', *Studies of Broadcasting*, 27: 113–32.

LEMERT, J. B. (1989), *Criticizing the Media* (Newbury Park, Calif.: Sage).

LERNER, D. (1958), *The Passing of Traditional Society* (New York: Free Press).

LESSIG, L. (1999), *Code and Other Laws of Cyberspace* (New York: Basic Books).

LEVY, F. (1999), 'The decorum of news', in J. Raymond (ed.), *News, Newspapers and Society in Early Modern Britain* (London: Frank Cass), 12–38.

LICHTENBERG, J. (ed.) (1990a), *Democracy and the Mass Media* (Cambridge: Cambridge University Press).

——— (1990b), 'Foundations and limits of freedom of the press', in J. Lichtenberg (ed.), *Democracy and the Mass Media* (Cambridge: Cambridge University Press), 102–35.

LICHTER, S. R., and ROTHMAN, S. (1986), *The Media Elite: America's New Power Brokers* (Bethesda, Md.: Adler and Adler).

LIND, R. A. (1999), 'Viewer response to ethical issues in TV news', *Journalism Monographs*, 142.

LIPPMANN, W. (1922), *Public Opinion* (New York: Harcourt Brace).

LOVELAND, I. (1998), *Importing the First Amendment* (Oxford: Hart Publishing).

LOWENTHAL, L. (1961), *Literature, Popular Culture and Society* (Englewood Cliffs, NJ: Prentice-Hall).

LUCAS, J. (1993), *Responsibility* (Oxford: Clarendon Press).

LUHMANN, N. (2000), *The Reality of the Mass Media* (Cambridge: Polity Press).

MCBRIDE, S., *et al.* (ed.) (1980), *Many Voices, One World* (Paris: Unesco; London: Kogan Page).

MCCHESNEY, R. W. (2000*a*), *Rich Media, Poor Democracy: Communication Politics in Dubious Times* (New York: The New Press).

——(2000*b*), 'Campaign spending and the first amendment', *Media Studies Journal,* Fall: 8–13.

MCGUIGAN (1992), *Cultural Populism* (London: Routledge).

MCGUIRE, W. (1973), 'Persuasion, resistance and attitude change', in I. De sola Pool *et al.*, *Handbook of Communication* (Chicago: Rand McNally), 216–52.

——(1986), 'The myth of mass media impacts: salvagings and savings', in G. Comstock (ed.), *Public Communication and Behavior,* vol. 1 (Orlando, Fla.: Academic Press), 173–257.

MACINTYRE, J. S. (1981), *After Virtue: A Study in Moral Theory* (Notre Dame, Ind.: Notre Dame University Press).

——(1987), 'Repositioning a landmark: The Hutchins Commission and freedom of the press', *Critical Studies in Mass Communication,* 4: 136–60.

MCLUHAN, M. (1962), *The Gutenberg Galaxy* (Toronto: Toronto University Press).

MCMANUS, J. H. (1994), *Market-drive Journalism: Let the Citizen Beware* (Thousand Oaks, Calif.: Sage).

MCMASTERS, P. K. (2000), 'Unease with excess', *Media Studies Journal,* Fall: 108–12.

MCQUAIL, D. (1983), *Mass Communication Theory: An Introduction* (London: Sage).

——(1992), *Media Performance: Mass Communication in the Public Interest* (London: Sage).

——(1997), *Audience Analysis* (London: Sage).

——(2000), *Mass Communication Theory* (London: Sage).

—— and WINDAHL, S. (1993), *Communication Models* (London: Longman).

MARCUSE, H. (1964), *One-Dimensional Man* (London: Routledge Kegan Paul).

MARSDEN, C. T. (2000), *Regulating the Global Information Society* (London: Routledge).

MEALE, C. M., and BOFFEY, J. (1998), 'Gentlewomen's reading', in L. Hellinga and J. B. Tribe (eds.), *The Cambridge History of the Book in Britain* (Cambridge: Cambridge University Press), 526–40.

MENDELSOHN, H. (1966), *Mass Entertainment* (New Haven: College and University Press).

MERRILL, J. C. (1989), 'The market place—A court of first resort', in E. E. Dennis, D. M. Gillmor, and T. L. Glasser (eds.), *Media Freedom and Accountability* (Westport, Conn.: Greenwood Press), 35–54.

MEYER, P. (1987), *Ethical Journalism* (New York: Longman).

MEYER, T. (2002), *Mediated Politics* (Cambridge: Polity Press).

MILL, J. S. (1869/1986), *On Liberty* (Harmondsworth: Penguin).

MILLS, C. W. (1956), *The Power Elite* (New York: Oxford University Press).

MILTON, J. (1644/1969), *For the Liberty of Unlicensed Printing: Areopagitica* (Paris: Aubier-Flammarion).

MINNIS, A. (1984), *Medieval Theory of Authorship* (London: Scolar Press).

MITCHELL, J., and BLUMLER, J. G. (eds.) (1994), *Television and the Viewer Interest* (London: John Libbey).

MONTGOMERY, K. (1989), *Target: Prime-Time* (New York: Oxford University Press).

MORRIS, M., and OGAN, C. (1996), 'The Internet as mass medium', *Journal of Communication*, 46, 1: 39–50.

MORRISON, D., and TUMBER, H. (1988), *Journalists at War* (London: Sage).

MURDOCK, G., and GOLDING, P. (1977), 'Capitalism, communication and class relations', in J. Curran *et al.* (eds.), *Mass Communication and Society* (London: Edward Arnold), 12–43.

MURPHY, D. (1976), *The Silent Watchdog* (London: Constable).

MURSCHETZ, P. (1998), 'State support for the daily press in Europe: A critical appraisal', *European Journal of Communication*, 13, 3: 291–314.

NAPOLI, P. M. (2001), *Foundations of Communications Policy: Principles and Process in the Regulation of Electronic Media* (Creskill, NJ: Hampton Press).

NAUGHTON, J. (1999), *A Brief History of the Future* (London: Wiedenfeld and Nicholson).

NERONE, J. (1994), *Violence Against the Press* (New York: Oxford University Press).

—— (ed.) (1995), *Last Rights: Revisiting Four Theories of the Press* (Urbana, Ill.: University of Illinois Press).

NOELLE-NEUMANN, E. (1984), *The Spiral of Silence* (Chicago: University of Chicago Press).

NORDENSTRENG, K. E. (1984), *The Mass Media Declaration of Unesco* (Norwood, NJ: Ablex).

—— (1997), 'Beyond the four theories of the press', in J. Servaes and N. Lie (eds.), *Media and Politics in Transition* (Leuven: Acco), 97–110.

—— (2000), 'The structural context of media ethics: How media are regulated in democratic society', in B. Pattyn (ed.), *Media Ethics* (Leuven: Peeters), 69–86.

—— and TOPUZ, H. (eds.) (1989), *Journalist: Status, Rights and Responsibilities* (Prague: IOJ).

NORRIS, P. (2000), *A Virtuous Circle* (Cambridge: Cambridge University Press).

OLEDZKI, J. (1998), 'Polish journalists: Professionals or not?', in D. H. Weaver (ed.), *The Global Journalist* (Creskill, NJ: Hampton Press), 277–98.

OLEN, J. (1988), *Ethics in Journalism* (Englewood Cliffs, NJ: Prentice-Hall).

OVSIOVITCH, J. S. (1999), 'News coverage of human rights', in M. Griffin and K. Nordenstreng (eds.), *International Media Monitoring* (Creskill, NJ: Hampton Press), 243–62.

OWEN, B. M. (1975), *Economics and Freedom of Expresssion: Media Structure and the First Amendment* (Cambridge, Mass.: Ballinger).

PALETZ, D. (1988), 'Pornography, politics and the press: The US Attorney General's Commission on Pornography', *Journal of Communication*, 38, 2: 122–37.

——and ENTMAN, R. (eds.) (1981), *Media, Power, Politics* (New York: Free Press).

PARK, R. (1923/1967), 'The natural history of the newspaper', in R. H. Turner (ed.), *On Social Control and Collective Behavior* (Chicago: University of Chicago Press), 97–113.

PARSONS, T. (1967), *Sociological Theory and Modern Society* (Glenoce, Ill.: Free Press).

PATELIS, K. (2000), 'Beyond Internetophilia: Regulation, public service media and the Internet', in T. Lees, S. Ralph, and J. Langham Brown (eds.), *Is Regulation an Option in a Digital Universe?* (Luton: University of Luton Press), 283–92.

PATTERSON, T. (1993), 'Fourth branch or fourth rate: The press's failure to live up to the founders' expectations', *Political Communication*, 10: 8–16.

——(1998), 'Political roles of the journalist', in D. Graber, D. McQuail, and P. Norris (eds.), *The Politics of News: News of Politics* (Washington: CQ Press), 17–33.

PERSE, E. M. (2001), *Media Effects and Society* (Hillsdale, NJ: Laurence Erlbaum).

PETERSON, T. (1956), 'The social responsibility theory', in F. Siebert, T. Peterson, and W. Schramm, *Four Theories of the Press* (Urbana, Ill.: University of Illinois Press), 73–104.

PICARD, R. (1985), *The Press and the Decline of Democracy* (Westport, Conn.: Greenwood Press).

——(1988), *The Ravens of Odin: The Press in the Nordic Countries* (Ames, Ia.: Iowa State University Press).

PLAISANCE, P. L. (2000), 'The concept of media accountability reconsidered', *Journal of Mass Media Ethics*, 15, 4: 257–68.

POOL, I. DE SOLA (1983), *Technologies of Freedom* (Cambridge, Mass.: Harvard University Press).

——and SHULMAN, I. (1959), 'Newsmen's fantasies, audiences and newswriting', *Public Opinion Quarterly*, 23, 2: 145–58.

PORTER, V. (1995), 'The new European order for public service broadcasting', in E. M. Barendt (ed.), *The Yearbook of Media Entertainment Law* (Oxford: Clarendon Press), 81–100.

POURCIAU, L. J. (ed.) (1999), *Ethics and Electronic Information in the Twenty First Century* (Westfayette, Ind.: Purdue University Press).

POWE, L. (1991), *The Fourth Estate and the Constitution* (Berkeley: University of California Press).

President's Commission (1970), *Report of the Commission on Obscenity and Pornography* (Washington: US Government Printing Office).

Press Complaints Commission (1999), *Code of Practice* (London: PCC).

PRICE, M. E. (1995), *Television, the Public Sphere, and National Identity* (Oxford: Oxford University Press).

—— (ed.) (1998), *The TV-chip Debate* (Mahwah, NJ: LEA).

PRITCHARD, D. (1991), 'The role of press councils in a system of media account-ability: The case of Quebec', *Canadian Journal of Communication*, 16, 2: 73–93.

—— (ed.) (2000), *Holding the Media Accountable* (Bloomingdale, Ind.: University of Indiana Press).

PROSSER, T. (2000), 'International lessons on law and regulation', in T. Lees, S. Ralph, and J. Langham Brown (eds.), *Is Regulation an Option in a Digital Universe?* (Luton: University of Luton Press), 99–104.

RABOY, M. (2000), 'Global communication policy and human rights', in R. G. Noll and M. E. Price (eds.), *A Communications Cornucopia: Markle Foundation Essays on Communication Policy* (Washington: Brookings Institute Press), 218–42.

RAYMOND, J. (ed.) (1999), *News, Newspapers and Society in Early Modern Britain* (London: Frank Cass).

REED, A. (2000), 'Jurisdiction and choice of law in a borderless electronic environment', in Y. Akdeniz, C. Walker, and D. Wall (eds.), *The Internet, Law and Society* (London: Longman), 79–105.

Reporters sans Frontieres (1995), *Report Freedom of Press Throughout the World* (London: John Libbey).

RIVERS, W. L., and NYHAN, M. J. (1973), *Aspen Notebooks on Government and the Media* (New York: Praeger).

ROBERTS, D. E. (1998), 'Media content labelling systems', in M. E. Price (ed.), *The TV-chip Debate* (Mahwah, NJ: LEA), 157–77.

ROBILLARD, S. (1995), *Television in Europe: Regulatory Bodies* (London: John Libbey).

ROBINSON, J., and LEVY, M. (1986), *The Main Source* (Beverly Hlls, Calif.: Sage).

ROGERS, E. M. (1962), *The Diffusion of Innovations* (Glencoe, Ill.: Free Press).

RORTY, R. (1989), *Contingency, Irony and Solidarity* (New York: Cambridge University Press).

ROSEN, J. (1993), 'Beyond objectivity', *Niemann Reports*, 47: 48–53.

ROSENGREN, K. E. (2000), *Communication: An Introduction* (London: Sage).

Royal Commission on the Press (1949), *Report*. Cmd. 7700 (London: HMSO).

Royal Commission on the Press, 1974–7 (1977*a*), *Report*, Cmnd. 6810 (London: HMSO).

Royal Commission on the Press, 1974–7 (1977b), *Attitudes to the Press*, Research report no. 3, Cmnd. 6810–3 (London: HMSO).

RUGGLES, M. (1994), *The Audience Reflected in the Medium of Law: Political Economy of Speech Rights* (Norwood, NJ: Ablex).

RYAN, M. (2001), 'Journalistic ethics, objectivity, existential journalism, standpoint epistemology and public journalism', *Journal of Mass Media Ethics*, 16, 1: 3–22.

SANDEL, M. J. (1982), *Free Speech and the Limits of Justice* (Cambridge: Cambridge University Press).

SANFORD, B. W. (1999), *Don't Shoot the Messenger: How Our Growing Hatred of Media Threatens Free Speech* (New York: Free Press).

—— (2000), 'News gathering and the new economy', *Media Studies Journal*, Fall: 52–7.

SCANLON, T. M. (1990), 'Content regulation reconsidered', in J. Lichtenberg (ed.), *Democracy and Mass Media* (Cambridge: Cambridge University Press).

SCHAUER, F. (1982), *Free Speech: A Philosophical Inquiry* (Cambridge, Mass.: Harvard University Press).

—— (1986), 'The role of the people in First Amendment Theory', *California Law Review*, 74: 761–88.

SCHILLER, H. (1969), *Mass Media and American Empire* (New York: Augustus M. Kelly).

SCHLEIFER, J. T. (1994), 'Tocqueville as an observer', in P. S. Cook (ed.), *Liberty of Expression* (Washington: Wilson Center Press).

SCHMID, A., and GRAAF, J. DE (1982), *Violence as Communication* (Beverly Hills, Calif.: Sage).

SCHMIDT, B. C. (1976), *Freedom of the Press versus Public Access* (New York: Praeger).

SCHROEDER, T. (2001), 'The origins of the German press', in B. Dooley and S. Baran (eds.), *The Politics of Information in Early Modern Europe* (London: Routledge), 123–50.

SCHUDSON, M. (1998), 'The public journalism movement and its problems', in D. Graber, D. McQuail, and P. Norris (eds.), *The Politics of News: News of Politics* (Washington: CQ Press), 132–49.

—— (1999), 'What public journalism knows about journalism but does not know about "Public"', in T. L. Glasser (ed.), *The Idea of Public Journalism* (New York: Guilford Press), 118–35.

SCHULTZ, J. (1998), *Reviving the Fourth Estate* (Cambridge: Cambridge University Press).

SCHWARTZ, B. (1992), *Freedom of the Press* (New York: Facts on File).

SCHWEIGER, W. (2000), 'Media credibility—Experience or image?', *European Journal of Communication*, 15, 1: 37–60.

SCOTT, M. B., and LYMAN, S. (1968), 'Accounts', *American Sociological Review*, 33: 46–62.

SELDES, G. (1938), *Lords of the Press* (New York: Julian Messner).

SEMIN, G. R., and MANSWELD, A. S. R. (1983), *The Accountability of Conduct: A Social-Psychological Approach* (London: Academic Press).

SEYMOUR-URE, C. (1974), *The Political Impact of Mass Media* (London: Constable).

SHELTON, P., and GUNARATNE, S. A. (1998), 'Old wine in new bottles: Public journalism, development journalism and social responsibility', in M. E. Roloff and G. D. Paulson (eds.), *Communication Yearbook* 21 (Thousand Oaks: Sage), 277–321.

SHOEMAKER, P. (1991), *Gatekeeping* (Thousand Oaks, Calif.: Sage).

SHOTTER, J. (1984), *Social Accountability and Selfhood* (Oxford: Blackwood).

SIEBERT, F. R., PETERSON, T., and SCHRAMM, W. (1956), *Four Theories of the Press* (Urbana, Ill.: University of Illinois Press).

SINGLETARY, M. W. (1982), 'Commentary: Are journalists "professionals"?' *Newspaper Research Journal*, 3: 75–78.

SIUNE, K., and HULTEN, O. (1998), 'Does public broadcasting have a future?', in D. McQuail and K. Siune (eds.), *Media Policy* (London: Sage), 22–37.

SKINNER, B. F. (1959), *Verbal Behavior* (London: Methuen).

SKOGERBO, E. (1997), 'The press subsidy system in Norway', *European Journal of Communication*, 12, 1: 99–118.

SLEVIN, J. (2000), *The Internet and Society* (Cambridge: Polity Press).

SMILEY, M. (1992), *Moral Responsibility and the Boundaries of Community: Power and Accountability from a Pragmatic Point of View* (Chicago: University of Chicago Press).

SMITH, A. (1977), 'Subsidies and the press in Europe', *Political and Economic Planning* 43 (London: PEP).

SMITH, A. (1989), 'The public interest', *Intermedia*, 17, 2: 10–24.

SMITH, J. (1999), *War and Press Freedom* (New York: Oxford University Press).

SMOLLA, R. (1992), *Free Speech in a Open Society* (New York: Knopf).

SNODDY, R. (1992), *The Good, the Bad and the Unacceptable* (London: Faber).

SOLOSKI, J. (1989), 'News reporting and professionalism', *Media, Culture and Society*, 11: 207–28.

STEWART, D. W., and WARD, S. (1994), 'Media effects on advertising', in J. Bryant and D. Zillmann (eds.), *Media Effects* (Hillsdale, NJ: Laurence Erlbaum), 315–63.

SUNSTEIN, C. (1993), *Democracy and the Problem of Free Speech* (New York: Free Press).

—— (1995), 'The First Amendment in Cyberspace', *Yale Law Journal*, 104, 7: 1757–1804.

Surgeon General's Scientific Advisory Committee on Television and Social Behavior (1972), *Television and Growing Up: The Impact of Televised Violence* (Washington: US Government Printing Office).

SUTTER, G. (2000), 'Nothing new under the sun: Old fears and new media', *International Journal of Law and Information Technology*, 8, 3: 338–78.

SVENNEVIG, M., and TOWLER, B. (2000), 'Regulating the future; the users views', in T. Lees, S. Ralph, and J. Langham Brown (eds.), *Is Regulation an Option in a Digital Universe?* (Luton: University of Luton Press).

SWANSON, D., and MANCINI, P. (eds.) (1996), *Politics, Media and Modern Democracy* (Westport, Conn.: Praeger).

TAYLOR, C. (1989), *Sources of the Self: The Making of the Modern Identity* (Cambridge, Mass.: Harvard University Press).

THOMASS, B. (2000), 'Journalism ethics', in B. Pattyn (ed.), *Media Ethics* (Leuven: Peeters), 249–64.

THOMPSON, J. B. (1995), *The Media and Modernity* (Cambridge: Polity Press).

TRAPP, J. B. (1998), 'Literacy, books and readers', in L. Hellinga and J. B. Tribe (eds.), *The Cambridge History of the Book in Britain* (Cambridge, Cambridge University Press), 31–46.

TRAPPEL, J., and MEIER, W. (1998), 'Media concentration: Policy options', in D. McQuail and K. Siune (eds.), *Media Policy* (London: Sage), 191–205.

TRENAMAN, J. S. M. (1967), *Communication and Comprehension* (London: Hutchinson).

TUMAN, S. (1999), 'The old rules may not apply any more', in S. Drucker and G. Gumpert (eds.), *Real Law @ Virtual Space* (Creskill, NJ: Hampton Press), 151–65.

TUMBER, H. (1982), *Television and the Riots* (London: British Film Institute).

TUNSTALL, J. (1971), *Journalists at Work* (London: Constable).

TUROW, J. (1994), 'Hidden conflicts and journalistic norms: The case of self-coverage', *Journal of Communication*, 44, 2: 29–44.

US Attorney General's Commission on Pornography (1986), *Final Report* (Washington: Department of Justice GPO).

VAN ALSTYNE, W. W. (1984/1992), 'A graphic review of the free speech clause', in J. H. Garvey and F. Schauer (eds.), *The First Amendment Reader* (St Paul, Minn.: West Publishing Co), 161–72.

VERHULST, S. (2002), 'About scarcities and intermediaries: The regulatory paradigm shift of digital content reviewed', in L. Lievrouw and S. Livingstone (eds.), *Handbook of New Media* (Thousand Oaks, Calif.: Sage), 432–60.

VINCENT, R. C., NORDENSTRENG, K., and TRABER, M. (eds.) (1999), *Towards Equity in Global Communication* (Creskill, NJ: Hampton Press).

VOAKES, P. S. (2000), 'Rights, wrongs and responsibilities: Law and ethics in the newsroom', *Journal of Mass Media Ethics*, 15, 1: 29–42.

WAISBORD, S. (2000), *Watchdog Journalism in South America* (New York: Columbia).

WALKER, D. (2000), 'Newspaper power: A practitioner's account', in H. Tumber (ed.), *Media Power, Professionals and Policies* (London: Routledge), 2236–246.

WALL, D. (2000), 'Policing the Internet: Maintaining order and law on the cyberbeat', in Y. Akdeniz, C. Walker, and D. Wall (eds.), *The Internet, Law and Society* (London: Longman), 154–74.

WALZER, M. (1983), *Spheres of Justice: A Defense of Pluralism and Equality* (New York: Basic Books).

WARTELLA, E., OLIVAREZ, A., and JENNINGS, N. (1998), 'Children and television violence in the United States', in U. Carlsson and C. von Feilitzen (eds.), *Children and Media Violence on the Screen* (Göteborg: Nordicom), 447–59.

WEAVER, D. (ed.) (1998), *The Global Journalist* (Creskill, NJ: Hampton Press).

—— and WILHOIT, C. (1986), *The American Journalist* (Bloomingdale, Ind.: Indiana University Press).

—— and —— (1996), *The American Journalist in the 1990s* (Mahwah, NJ: LEA).

WEBER, M. (1948) 'Politics as a vocation', in H. Gerth and C. W. Mills (eds.), *Max Weber Essays* (London: Heinemann).

—— (1964), *Theory of Social and Economic Organization*, ed. T. Parsons (New York: Free Press).

WESTERSTAHL, J. (1983), 'Objective news reporting', *Communication Research*, 10, 3: 403–24.

WESTLEY, B., and MACLEAN, M. (1957), 'A conceptual model for communication research', *Journalism Quarterly*, 34: 31–8.

WHITNEY, C. (1986), *The Media and the People* (New York: Gannett Center for Media Studies).

WILSON, W. C. (1975), 'Belief in freedom of speech and the press', *Journal of Social Issues*, 69–76.

WRIGHT, C. R. (1960), 'Functional analysis and mass communication', *Public Opinion Quarterly*, 24: 606–20.

WU, W., WEAVER, D., and JOHNSON, O. V. (1998), 'Professional roles of Russian and U.S. journalists: A comparative study', *Journalism and Mass Communication Quarterly*, 75, 2: 534–48.

WUESTE, D. E. (ed.) (1994), *Professional Ethics and Social Responsibility* (Lanham, Md.: Rownan and Littlefield).

WYATT, R. O. (1991), *Free Expression and the American Public: A Survey* (Washington: ASNE).

Index